ROUTLEDGE
STUDENT STATUTES

Public Law and Human Rights Statutes

'Focused content, layout and price – Routledge competes and wins in relation to all of these factors' – Craig Lind, University of Sussex, UK

'The best value and best format books on the market' – Ed Bates, Southampton University, UK

Routledge Student Statutes present all the legislation students need in one easy-to-use volume. Developed in response to feedback from lecturers and students, this book offers a fully up-to-date, comprehensive, and clearly presented collection of legislation – ideal for LLB and GDL course and exam use.

Routledge Student Statutes are:

- **Exam Friendly:** un-annotated and conforming to exam regulations
- **Tailored to fit your course:** 80% of lecturers we surveyed agree that *Routledge Student Statutes* match their course and cover the relevant legislation
- **Trustworthy:** *Routledge Student Statutes* are compiled by subject experts, updated annually and have been developed to meet student needs through extensive market research
- **Easy to use:** a clear text design, comprehensive table of contents, multiple indexes and highlighted amendments to the law make these books the more student-friendly Statutes on the market
- **Competitively Priced:** *Routledge Student Statutes* offer content and usability rated as good or better than our major competitor, but at a more competitive price
- **Supported by a Companion Website:** presenting scenario questions for interpreting Statutes, annotated web links, and multiple-choice questions, these resources are designed to help students to be confident and prepared.

Philip Jones is Senior Lecturer in Law at the University of the West of England.

Praise for Routledge Student Statutes

'The best value and best format books on the market' – Ed Bates, University of Southampton, UK

'Focused content, layout and price – Routledge competes and wins in relation to all of these factors' – Craig Lind, University of Sussex, UK

'comprehensive and reliable' – Andromachi Georgosouli, University of Leicester, UK

'user friendly and sensibly laid out' – John Stanton, Kingston University, UK

'An exciting and valuable selection of the key legislative material' – David Radlett, University of Kent, UK

'I prefer the layout of the Routledge statute book to other statute books that I have seen' – Nicola Haralambous, University of Hertfordshire, UK

'Well-presented and has thorough content [. . .] clearly a good competitor' – Brian Coggon, University of Lincoln, UK

'. . . given the addition of the useful web resource and the easy to read section headings, I would be more inclined to recommend this book than other statute texts' – Emma Warner-Reed, Leeds Metropolitan University, UK

'excellent and relevant' – Sarwan Singh, City University London, UK

'I personally prefer the Routledge series as it is better laid out and more accessible' – Jonathan Doak, University of Nottingham, UK

'*Routledge Student Statutes* are practical and carefully designed for the needs of the students' – Stelios Andreadakis, Oxford Brookes University, UK

'an excellent statute text' – Fang Ma, University of Hertfordshire, UK

'Other statute books are not as attractive in look or feel, not as easy to navigate, more expensive and amendments are less clear' – Jason Lowther, University of Plymouth, UK

'Gives good coverage and certainly includes all elements addressed on our current syllabus. I personally think this statute is more clearly set out than other statute books and is more user friendly for it' – Samantha Pegg, Nottingham Trent University, UK

'This statute book is a student friendly material. Index features as well as the overall content make this book a valuable contribution to student reading lists' – Orkun Akseli, Newcastle University, UK

'A very welcome publication' – Simon Barnett, University of Hertfordshire, UK

'I am sticking with *Routledge Student Statutes*' – Francis Tansinda, Manchester Metropolitan University, UK

ROUTLEDGE
STUDENT STATUTES

Public Law and Human Rights Statutes

PHILIP JONES
Senior Lecturer in Law at the University of the West of England

Routledge
Taylor & Francis Group

LONDON AND NEW YORK

First published 2014
by Routledge
2 Park Square, Milton Park, Abingdon, Oxon OX14 4RN

Simultaneously published in the USA and Canada
by Routledge
711 Third Avenue, New York, NY 10017

Routledge is an imprint of the Taylor & Francis Group, an informa business

British Library Cataloguing in Publication Data
A catalogue record for this book is available from the British Library

Library of Congress Cataloging in Publication Data
A catalog record for this book has been requested

Parliamentary material is reproduced with the permission
of the Controller of HMSO on behalf of Parliament.

ISBN: 978–0–415–63390–1 (pbk)

Typeset in Sabon
by RefineCatch Limited, Bungay, Suffolk

Contents

Acknowledgements

The publishers and editor thank the following organisations for their permission to reproduce the materials listed:

Council of Europe (Convention for the Protection of Human Rights and Fundamental Freedoms 1950, as amended by Protocol No. 11; Protocol to the Convention for the Protection of Human Rights and Fundamental Freedoms; Protocol No. 13 to the Convention for the Protection of Human Rights and Fundamental Freedoms, concerning the abolition of the death penalty).

The United Nations Department of Public Information (Universal Declaration of Human Rights 1948; International Covenant on Civil and Political Rights 1966; International Covenant on Economic, Social and Cultural Rights 1966).

European Parliament (European Union Charter of Fundamental Rights 2000).

Please note: Only European Union legislation printed in the paper edition of the *Official Journal of the European Union* is deemed authentic.

Guide to the Companion Website

www.routledge.com/cw/statutes

Visit the Companion Website for *Routledge Student Statutes* in order to:

- Understand how to use a statute book in tutorials and exams;

- Learn how to interpret statutes and other legislation to maximum effect;

- Gain essential practice in statute interpretation prior to your exams, through unique problem-based scenarios;

- Test your understanding of statutes through a set of Multiple Choice Questions for revision or to check your own progress;

- Understand how the law is developing with updates, additional information and links to useful websites.

Alphabetical Index

Chronological Index

Statutes and Statutory Instruments of the United Kingdom

MAGNA CARTA 1297
(c. 29)

THE GREAT CHARTER OF THE LIBERTIES OF ENGLAND, AND OF THE LIBERTIES OF THE FOREST; CONFIRMED BY KING EDWARD, IN THE TWENTY-FIFTH YEAR OF HIS REIGN

EDWARD by the Grace of God King of England, Lord of Ireland, and Duke of Guyan, [. . .]

We have seen the Great Charter of the Lord Henry sometimes King of England, our Father, of the Liberties of England in these words:

HENRY by the Grace of God King of England, Lord of Ireland, Duke of Normandy and Guyan, and Earl of Anjou, to all Archbishops, Bishops, Abbots, Priors, Earls, Barons, Sheriffs, Provosts, Officers, and to all Bailiffs, and other our faithful Subjects, which shall see this present Charter, Greeting: Know Ye, that We, unto the honour of Almighty God, and for the salvation of the souls of our Progenitors and Successors [Kings of England,] to the advancement of Holy Church and amendment of our Realm, of our meer and free will, have given and granted to all Archbishops, Bishops, Abbots, Priors, Earls, Barons, and to all [Freemen] of this our Realm, these Liberties following, to be kept in our Kingdom of England for ever.

I CONFIRMATION OF LIBERTIES

FIRST, We have granted to God, and by this our present Charter have confirmed, for Us and our Heirs for ever, that the Church of England shall be free, and shall have all her whole Rights and Liberties inviolable. We have granted also, and given to all the Freemen of our Realm, for Us and our Heirs for ever, these Liberties under-written, to have and to hold to them and their Heirs, of Us and our Heirs for ever.

[. . .]

XXIX IMPRISONMENT, &C. CONTRARY TO LAW. ADMINISTRATION OF JUSTICE

NO Freeman shall be taken or imprisoned, or be disseised of his Freehold, or Liberties, or free Customs, or be outlawed, or exiled, or any other wise destroyed; nor will We not pass upon him, nor [condemn him] but by lawful judgment of his Peers, or by the Law of the Land. We will sell to no man, we will not deny or defer to any man either Justice or Right.

[. . .]

BILL OF RIGHTS 1688
(c. 2)

An Act declareing the Rights and Liberties of the Subject and Setleing the Succession of the Crowne.

Whereas the Lords Spirituall and Temporall and Comons assembled at Westminster lawfully fully and freely representing all the Estates of the People of this Realme did upon the thirteenth day of February in the yeare of our Lord one thousand six hundred eighty eight present unto their Majesties then called and known by the Names and Stile of William and Mary Prince and Princesse of Orange being present in their proper Persons a certaine Declaration in Writeing made by the said Lords and Comons in the Words following viz

The Heads of Declaration of Lords and Commons, recited
Whereas the late King James the Second by the Assistance of diverse evill Councellors Judges and Ministers imployed by him did endeavour to subvert and extirpate the Protestant Religion and the Lawes and Liberties of this Kingdome.

Dispensing and Suspending Power
By Assumeing and Exerciseing a Power of Dispensing with and Suspending of Lawes and the Execution of Lawes without Consent of Parlyament.

Committing Prelates
By Committing and Prosecuting diverse Worthy Prelates for humbly Petitioning to be excused from Concurring to the said Assumed Power.

Ecclesiastical Commission
By issueing and causeing to be executed a Commission under the Great Seale for Erecting a Court called The Court of Commissioners for Ecclesiasticall Causes.

Levying Money
By Levying Money for and to the Use of the Crowne by pretence of Prerogative for other time and in other manner then the same was granted by Parlyament.

Standing Army
By raising and keeping a Standing Army within this Kingdome in time of Peace without Consent of Parlyament and Quartering Soldiers contrary to Law.

Disarming Protestants, &c.
By causing severall good Subjects being Protestants to be disarmed at the same time when Papists were both Armed and Imployed contrary to Law.

Violating Elections
By Violating the Freedome of Election of Members to serve in Parlyament.

Illegal Prosecutions
By Prosecutions in the Court of Kings Bench for Matters and Causes cognizable onely in Parlyament and by diverse other Arbitrary and Illegall Courses.

Juries
And whereas of late yeares Partiall Corrupt and Unqualifyed Persons have beene returned and served on Juryes in Tryalls and particularly diverse Jurors in Tryalls for High Treason which were not Freeholders,

Excessive Bail

And excessive Baile hath beene required of Persons committed in Criminall Cases to elude the Benefitt of the Lawes made for the Liberty of the Subjects.

Fines

And excessive Fines have beene imposed.

Punishments

And illegall and cruell Punishments inflicted.

Grants of Fines, &c. before Conviction, &c.

And severall Grants and Promises made of Fines and Forfeitures before any Conviction or Judgement against the Persons upon whome the same were to be levyed.

All which are utterly directly contrary to the knowne Lawes and Statutes and Freedome of this Realme.

Recital that the late King James II. had abdicated the Government, and that the Throne was vacant, and that the Prince of Orange had written Letters to the Lords and Commons for the choosing Representatives in Parliament

And whereas the said late King James the Second haveing Abdicated the Government and the Throne being thereby Vacant His [Hignesse] the Prince of Orange (whome it hath pleased Almighty God to make the glorious Instrument of Delivering this Kingdome from Popery and Arbitrary Power) did (by the Advice of the Lords Spirituall and Temporall and diverse principall Persons of the Commons) cause Letters to be written to the Lords Spirituall and Temporall being Protestants and other Letters to the severall Countyes Cityes Universities Burroughs and Cinque Ports for the Choosing of such Persons to represent them as were of right to be sent to Parlyament to meete and sitt at Westminster upon the two and twentyeth day of January in this Yeare one thousand six hundred eighty and eight in order to such an Establishment as that their Religion Lawes and Liberties might not againe be in danger of being Subverted, Upon which Letters Elections haveing beene accordingly made.

The Subject's Rights

And thereupon the said Lords Spirituall and Temporall and Commons pursuant to their respective Letters and Elections being now assembled in a full and free Representative of this Nation takeing into their most serious Consideration the best meanes for attaining the Ends aforesaid Doe in the first place (as their Auncestors in like Case have usually done) for the Vindicating and Asserting their auntient Rights and Liberties, Declare

Dispensing Power

That the pretended Power of Suspending of Laws or the Execution of Laws by Regall Authority without Consent of Parlyament is illegall.

Late Dispensing Power

That the pretended Power of Dispensing with Laws or the Execution of Laws by Regall Authoritie as it hath beene assumed and exercised of late is illegall.

Ecclesiastical Courts illegal

That the Commission for erecting the late Court of Commissioners for Ecclesiasticall Causes and all other Commissions and Courts of like nature are Illegall and Pernicious.

Levying Money

That levying Money for or to the Use of the Crowne by pretence of Prerogative without Grant of Parlyament for longer time or in other manner then the same is or shall be granted is Illegall.

Right to Petition
That it is the Right of the Subjects to petition the King and all Commitments and Prosecutions for such Petitioning are Illegall.

Standing Army
That the raising or keeping a standing Army within the Kingdome in time of Peace unlesse it be with Consent of Parlyament is against Law.

Subjects' Arms
That the Subjects which are Protestants may have Arms for their Defence suitable to their Conditions and as allowed by Law.

Freedom of Election
That Election of Members of Parlyament ought to be free.

Freedom of Speech
That the Freedome of Speech and Debates or Proceedings in Parlyament ought not to be impeached or questioned in any Court or Place out of Parlyament.

Excessive Bail
That excessive Baile ought not to be required nor excessive Fines imposed nor cruell and unusuall Punishments inflicted.

Juries
That Jurors ought to be duely impannelled and returned [. . .]

Grants of Forfeitures
That all Grants and Promises of Fines and Forfeitures of particular persons before Conviction are illegall and void.

Frequent Parliaments
And that for Redresse of all Grievances and for the amending strengthening and preserveing of the Lawes Parlyaments ought to be held frequently.

The said Rights claimed. Tender of the Crown. Regal Power exercised. Limitation of the Crown
And they doe Claime Demand and Insist upon all and singular the Premises as their undoubted Rights and Liberties and that noe Declarations Judgements Doeings or Proceedings to the Prejudice of the People in any of the said Premisses ought in any wise to be drawne hereafter into Consequence or Example. To which Demand of their Rights they are particularly encouraged by the Declaration of this Highnesse the Prince of Orange as being the onely meanes for obtaining a full Redresse and Remedy therein. Haveing therefore an intire Confidence That his said Highnesse the Prince of Orange will perfect the Deliverance soe farr advanced by him and will still preserve them from the Violation of their Rights which they have here asserted and from all other Attempts upon their Religion Rights and Liberties. The said Lords Spirituall and Temporall and Commons assembled at Westminster doe Resolve That William and Mary Prince and Princesse of Orange be and be declared King and Queene of England France and Ireland and the Dominions thereunto belonging to hold the Crowne and Royall Dignity of the said Kingdomes and Dominions to them the said Prince and Princesse dureing their Lives and the Life of the Survivour of them And that the sole and full Exercise of the Regall Power be onely in and executed by the said Prince of Orange in the Names of the said Prince and Princesse dureing their joynt Lives And after their Deceases the said Crowne and Royall Dignitie of the said Kingdoms and Dominions to be to the Heires of the Body of the said Princesse And for default

of such Issue to the Princesse Anne of Denmarke and the Heires of her Body And for default of such Issue to the Heires of the Body of the said Prince of Orange. And the Lords Spirituall and Temporall and Commons doe pray the said Prince and Princesse to accept the same accordingly.

New Oaths of Allegiance, &c.
And that the Oathes hereafter mentioned be taken by all Persons of whome the Oathes of Allegiance and Supremacy might be required by Law instead of them And that the said Oathes of Allegiance and Supremacy be abrogated.

Allegiance
I A B doe sincerely promise and sweare That I will be faithfull and beare true Allegiance to their Majestyes King William and Queene Mary Soe helpe me God.

Supremacy
I A B doe sweare That I doe from my Heart Abhorr, Detest and Abjure as Impious and Hereticall this damnable Doctrine and Position That Princes Excommunicated or Deprived by the Pope or any Authority of the See of Rome may be deposed or murdered by their Subjects or any other whatsoever. And I doe declare That noe Forreigne Prince Person Prelate, State or Potentate hath or ought to have any Jurisdiction Power Superiority Preeminence or Authoritie Ecclesiasticall or Spirituall within this Realme Soe helpe me God.

Acceptance of the Crown. The Two Houses to sit. Subjects' Liberties to be allowed, and Ministers hereafter to serve according to the same. William and Mary declared King and Queen. Limitation of the Crown. Papists debarred the Crown. Every King, &c. shall make the Declaration of 30 Car. II. If under 12 Years old, to be done after Attainment thereof.
King's and Queen's Assent
Upon which their said Majestyes did accept the Crowne and Royall Dignitie of the Kingdoms of England France and Ireland and the Dominions thereunto belonging according to the Resolution and Desire of the said Lords and Commons contained in the said Declaration. And thereupon their Majestyes were pleased That the said Lords Spirituall and Temporall and Commons being the two Houses of Parlyament should continue to sitt and with their Majesties Royall Concurrence make effectuall Provision for the Setlement of the Religion Lawes and Liberties of this Kingdome soe that the same for the future might not be in danger againe of being subverted, To which the said Lords Spirituall and Temporall and Commons did agree and proceede to act accordingly. Now in pursuance of the Premisses the said Lords Spirituall and Temporall and Commons in Parlyament assembled for the ratifying confirming and establishing the said Declaration and the Articles Clauses Matters and Things therein contained by the Force of a Law made in due Forme by Authority of Parlyament doe pray that it may be declared and enacted That all and singular the Rights and Liberties asserted and claimed in the said Declaration are the true auntient and indubitable Rights and Liberties of the People of this Kingdome and soe shall be esteemed allowed adjudged deemed and taken to be and that all and every the particulars aforesaid shall be firmly and strictly holden and observed as they are expressed in the said Declaration And all Officers and Ministers whatsoever shall serve their Majestyes and their Successors according to the same in all times to come. And the said Lords Spirituall and Temporall and Commons seriously considering how it hath pleased Almighty God in his marvellous Providence and mercifull Goodness to this Nation to provide and preserve their said Majestyes Royall Persons most happily to Raigne over us upon the Throne of their Auncestors for which they render unto him from the bottome of their Hearts their humblest Thanks and Praises doe truely firmely assuredly and in the Sincerity of their Hearts thinke and doe hereby recognize acknowledge and declare That King James the Second haveing abdicated the Government and their Majestyes haveing accepted the Crowne and Royall Dignity aforesaid Their said Majestyes did become were are and of right ought to be by the Lawes of this Realme our Soveraigne Liege Lord and Lady King and Queene of England France and

Ireland and the Dominions thereunto belonging in and to whose Princely Persons the Royall State Crowne and Dignity of the said Realmes with all Honours Stiles Titles Regalities Prerogatives Powers Jurisdictions and Authorities to the same belonging and appertaining are most fully rightfully and intirely invested and incorporated united and annexed And for preventing all Questions and Divisions in this Realme by reason of any pretended Titles to the Crowne and for preserveing a Certainty in the Succession thereof in and upon which the Unity Peace Tranquillity and Safety of this Nation doth under God wholly consist and depend The said Lords Spirituall and Temporall and Commons doe beseech their Majestyes That it may be enacted established and declared That the Crowne and Regall Government of the said Kingdoms and Dominions with all and singular the Premisses thereunto belonging and appertaining shall bee and continue to their said Majestyes and the Survivour of them dureing their Lives and the Life of the Survivour of them And that the entire perfect and full Exercise of the Regall Power and Government be onely in and executed by his Majestie in the Names of both their Majestyes dureing their joynt Lives And after their deceases the said Crowne and Premisses shall be and remaine to the Heires of the Body of her Majestie and for default of such Issue to her Royall Highnesse the Princess Anne of Denmarke and the Heires of her Body and for default of such Issue to the Heires of the Body of his said Majestie And thereunto the said Lords Spirituall and Temporall and Commons doe in the Name of all the People aforesaid most humbly and faithfully submitt themselves their Heires and Posterities for ever and doe faithfully promise That they will stand to maintaine and defend their said Majesties and alsoe the Limitation and Succession of the Crowne herein specified and contained to the utmost of their Powers with their Lives and Estates against all Persons whatsoever that shall attempt any thing to the contrary. And whereas it hath beene found by Experience that it is inconsistent with the Safety and Welfaire of this Protestant Kingdome to be governed by a Popish Prince or by any King or Queene marrying a Papist the said Lords Spirituall and Temporall and Commons doe further pray that it may be enacted That all and every person and persons that is are or shall be reconciled to or shall hold Communion with the See or Church of Rome or shall professe the Popish Religion or shall marry a Papist shall be excluded and be for ever uncapeable to inherit possesse or enjoy the Crowne and Government of this Realme and Ireland and the Dominions thereunto belonging or any part of the same or to have use or exercise any Regall Power Authoritie or Jurisdiction within the same [And in all and every such Case or Cases the People of these Realmes shall be and are hereby absolved of their Allegiance] And the said Crowne and Government shall from time to time descend to and be enjoyed by such person or persons being Protestants as should have inherited and enjoyed the same in case the said person or persons soe reconciled holding Communion or Professing or Marrying as aforesaid were naturally dead [And that every King and Queene of this Realme who at any time hereafter shall come to and succeede in the Imperiall Crowne of this Kingdome shall on the first day of the meeting of the first Parlyament next after his or her comeing to the Crowne sitting in his or her Throne in the House of Peeres in the presence of the Lords and Commons therein assembled or at his or her Coronation before such person or persons who shall administer the Coronation Oath to him or her at the time of his or her takeing the said Oath (which shall first happen) make subscribe and audibly repeate the Declaration mentioned in the Statute made in the thirtyeth yeare of the Raigne of King Charles the Second Entituled An Act for the more effectuall Preserveing the Kings Person and Government by disableing Papists from sitting in either House of Parlyament But if it shall happen that such King or Queene upon his or her Succession to the Crowne of this Realme shall be under the Age of twelve yeares then every such King or Queene shall make subscribe and audibly repeate the said Declaration at his or her Coronation or the first day of the meeting of the first Parlyament as aforesaid which shall first happen after such King or Queene shall have attained the said Age of twelve yeares.] All which Their Majestyes are contented and pleased shall be declared enacted and established by authoritie of this present Parliament and shall stand remaine and be the Law of this Realme for ever And the same are by their said Majesties by and with the advice and consent of the Lords Spirituall and Temporall and Commons in Parlyament assembled and by the authoritie of the same declared enacted and established accordingly.

II NON OBSTANTES MADE VOID

Noe Dispensation by Non obstante of or to any Statute or any part thereof shall be allowed but the same shall be held void and of noe effect Except a Dispensation be allowed of in such Statute [. . .]

ACT OF SETTLEMENT 1700
(c. 2)

An Act for the further Limitation of the Crown and better securing the Rights and Liberties of the Subject
[. . .]

I

Whereas in the First Year of the Reign of Your Majesty and of our late most gracious Sovereign Lady Queen Mary (of blessed Memory) An Act of Parliament was made intituled [An Act for declaring the Rights and Liberties of the Subject and for setling the Succession of the Crown] wherein it was (amongst other things) enacted established and declared That the Crown and Regall Government of the Kingdoms of England France and Ireland and the Dominions thereunto belonging should be and continue to Your Majestie and the said late Queen during the joynt Lives of Your Majesty and the said Queen and to the Survivor And that after the Decease of Your Majesty and of the said Queen the said Crown and Regall Government should be and remain to the Heirs of the Body of the said late Queen And for Default of such Issue to Her Royall Highness the Princess Ann of Denmark and the Heirs of Her Body And for Default of such Issue to the Heirs of the Body of Your Majesty And it was thereby further enacted That all and every Person and Persons that then were or afterwards should be reconciled to or shall hold Communion with the See or Church of Rome or should professe the Popish Religion or marry a Papist should be excluded and are by that Act made for ever [incapable] to inherit possess or enjoy the Crown and Government of this Realm and Ireland and the Dominions thereunto belonging or any part of the same or to have use or exercise any regall Power Authority or Jurisdiction within the same And in all and every such Case and Cases the People of these Realms shall be and are thereby absolved of their Allegiance And that the said Crown and Government shall from time to time descend to and be enjoyed by such Person or Persons being Protestants as should have inherited and enjoyed the same in case the said Person or Persons so reconciled holding Communion professing or marrying as aforesaid were naturally dead [. . .]

And it being absolutely necessary for the Safety Peace and Quiet of this [Realm] to obviate all Doubts and Contentions in the same by reason of any pretended Titles to the [Crown] and to maintain a Certainty in the Succession thereof to which Your Subjects may safely have Recourse for their Protection in case the Limitations in the said recited [Act] should determine Therefore for a further Provision of the Succession of the Crown in the Protestant Line We Your Majesties most dutifull and Loyall Subjects the Lords Spirituall and Temporall and Commons in this present Parliament assembled do beseech Your Majesty that it may be enacted [. . .]

[. . .]

That the most Excellent Princess Sophia Electress and Dutchess Dowager of Hannover Daughter of the most Excellent Princess Elizabeth late Queen of Bohemia Daughter of our late Sovereign Lord King James the First of happy Memory be and is hereby declared to be the next in Succession in the Protestant Line to the Imperiall Crown and Dignity of the [said] Realms of England France and Ireland with the Dominions and Territories thereunto belonging after His Majesty and the Princess Ann of Denmark and in Default of Issue of the said Princess Ann and of His Majesty respectively and that from and after the Deceases of His said Majesty our now Sovereign Lord and of Her Royall Highness the Princess Ann of Denmark and for Default of Issue of the said Princess Ann and of His Majesty respectively the Crown and Regall Government of the said Kingdoms of England France and Ireland and of the Dominions thereunto belonging with the Royall State and Dignity of the said Realms and all Honours Stiles Titles Regalities Prerogatives Powers Jurisdictions and Authorities to the same belonging and appertaining shall be remain and continue to the said most Excellent Princess Sophia and the Heirs of Her Body being Protestants And thereunto the said Lords Spirituall and Temporall and Commons shall and will in the Name of all the People of this Realm most humbly and faithfully submitt themselves their Heirs and Posterities and do faithfully promise That after the Deceases of His Majesty and Her Royall Highness and the failure of the Heirs of their respective Bodies to stand to maintain and defend the said Princess Sophia and the Heirs of Her Body being [Protestants] according to the Limitation and Succession of the Crown in this Act specified and contained to the utmost of their Powers with their Lives and Estates against all Persons whatsoever that shall attempt any thing to the contrary.

II THE PERSONS INHERITABLE BY THIS ACT, HOLDING COMMUNION WITH THE CHURCH OF ROME, INCAPACITATED AS BY THE FORMER ACT; TO TAKE THE OATH AT THEIR CORONATION, ACCORDING TO STAT. 1 W. & M. C. 6

Provided always and it is hereby enacted That all and every Person and Persons who shall or may take or inherit the said Crown by vertue of the Limitation of this present Act and is are or shall be reconciled to or shall hold Communion with the See or Church of Rome or shall profess the Popish Religion or shall marry a Papist shall be subject to such Incapacities as in such Case or Cases are by the said recited Act provided enacted and established And that every King and Queen of this Realm who shall come to and succeed in the Imperiall Crown of this Kingdom by vertue of this Act shall have the Coronation Oath administred to him her or them at their respective Coronations according to the Act of Parliament made in the First Year of the Reign of His Majesty and the said late Queen Mary [. . .]

III FURTHER PROVISIONS FOR SECURING THE RELIGION, LAWS, AND LIBERTIES OF THESE REALMS

[. . .] Be it enacted by the Kings most Excellent Majesty by and with the Advice and Consent of the Lords Spirituall and Temporall and Commons in Parliament assembled and by the Authority of the same

That whosoever shall hereafter come to the Possession of this Crown shall joyn in Communion with the Church of England as by Law established

That in case the Crown and Imperiall Dignity of this Realm shall hereafter come to any Person not being a Native of this Kingdom of England this Nation be not obliged to ingage in any Warr for the Defence of any Dominions or Territories which do not belong to the Crown of England without the Consent of Parliament [. . .]

[That after the said Limitation shall take Effect as aforesaid no Person born out of the Kingdoms of England Scotland or Ireland or the Dominions thereunto belonging (although he be [. . .] made a Denizen (except such as [are] born of English Parents) shall be capable to be of the Privy Councill or a Member of either House of Parliament or to enjoy any Office or Place of Trust either Civill or Military or to have any Grant of Lands Tenements or Hereditaments from the Crown to himself or to any other or others in Trust for him]

[. . .]

That no Pardon under the Great Seal of England be pleadable to an Impeachment by the Commons in Parliament.

IV THE LAWS AND STATUTES OF THE REALM CONFIRMED

[. . .] The said Lords Spirituall and Temporall and Commons do therefore further humbly pray That all the Laws and Statutes of this Realm for securing the established Religion and the Rights and Liberties of the People thereof and all other Laws and Statutes of the same now in Force may be ratified and confirmed And the same are by His Majesty by and with the Advice and Consent of the said Lords Spirituall and Temporall and Commons and by Authority of the same ratified and confirmed accordingly.

UNION WITH SCOTLAND ACT 1706
(c. 11)

An Act for an Union of the Two Kingdoms of England and Scotland

Most gracious Sovereign

[. . .]

Whereas Articles of Union were agreed on the Twenty Second day of July in the Fifth year of Your Majesties reign by the Co'mmissioners nominated on behalf of the Kingdom of England under Your Majesties Great Seal of England bearing date at Westminster the Tenth day of April then last past in pursuance of an Act of Parliament made in England in the Third year of Your Majesties reign and the Commissioners nominated on the behalf of the Kingdom of Scotland under Your Majesties Great Seal of Scotland bearing date the Twenty Seventh day of February in the Fourth year of Your Majesties Reign in pursuance of the Fourth Act of the Third Session of the present Parliament of Scotland to treat of and concerning an Union of the said Kingdoms

And Whereas an Act hath passed in the Parliament of Scotland at Edinburgh the Sixteenth day of January in the Fifth year of Your Majesties reign wherein 'tis mentioned that the Estates of Parliament considering the said Articles of Union of the two Kingdoms had agreed to and approved of the said Articles of Union with some Additions and Explanations And that Your Majesty with Advice and Consent of the Estates of Parliament for establishing the Protestant Religion and Presbyterian Church Government within the Kingdom of Scotland had passed in the same Session of Parliament an Act intituled Act for securing of the Protestant Religion and Presbyterian Church Government which by the Tenor thereof was appointed to be inserted in any Act ratifying the Treaty and expressly declared to be a fundamental and essential Condition of the said Treaty or Union in all times coming the Tenor of which Articles as ratified and approved of with Additions and Explanations by the said Act of Parliament of Scotland follows

ARTICLE I

The Kingdoms United; Ensigns Armorial
That the two Kingdoms of England and Scotland shall upon the First day of May which shall be in the year One thousand seven hundred and seven and for ever after be united into one Kingdom by the name of Great Britain [. . .]

[. . .]

ARTICLE III

Parliament
That the United Kingdom of Great Britain be represented by one and the same Parliament to be stiled The Parliament of Great Britain.

ARTICLE IIII

Trade and Navigation and other Rights
That all the Subjects of the United Kingdom of Great Britain shall from and after the Union
have full freedom and Intercourse of Trade and Navigation to and from any port or place
within the said United Kingdom and the Dominions and Plantations thereunto belonging [. . .]

[. . .]

ARTICLE VI

Regulations of Trade, Duties, &c
That all parts of the United Kingdom for ever from and after the Union shall have the same
Allowances Encouragements and Drawbacks and be under the same prohibitions restrictions
and regulations of Trade and liable to the same Customs and Duties on Import and Export
And that the Allowances Encouragements and Drawbacks prohibitions restrictions and
regulations of Trade and the Customs and Duties on Import and Export settled in England
when the Union commences shall from and after the Union take place throughout the whole
United Kingdom [. . .]

[. . .]

ARTICLE XXV

Laws inconsistent with the Articles, void
That all Laws and Statutes in either Kingdom so far as they are contrary to or inconsistent with
the Terms of these Articles or any of them shall from and after the Union cease and become void
and shall be so declared to be by the respective Parliaments of the said Kingdoms. As by the said
Articles of Union ratified and approved by the said Act of Parliament of Scotland relation
thereunto being had may appear

[. . .]

V CAP. 8 ANTE, AND THE SAID ACT OF PARLIAMENT OF SCOTLAND TO BE OBSERVED AS FUNDAMENTAL CONDITIONS OF THE SAID UNION; AND THE SAID ARTICLES AND ACTS OF PARLIAMENT TO CONTINUE THE UNION

And it is hereby further enacted by the Authority aforesaid That the said Act passed in this
present Session of Parliament intituled An Act for securing the Church of England as by Law
established and all and every the matters and things therein contained And also the said Act of
Parliament of Scotland intituled Act for securing the Protestant Religion and Presbyterian
Church Government with the Establishment in the said Act contained be and shall for ever be
held and adjudged to be and observed as Fundamental and Essential Conditions of the said
Union And shall in all times coming be taken to be and are hereby declared to be essential and
fundamental parts of the said Articles and Union And the said Articles of Union so as aforesaid
ratified approved and confirmed by Act of Parliament of Scotland and by this present Act And
the said Act passed in this present Session of Parliament intituled an Act for securing the Church
of England as by Law established And also the said Act passed in the Parliament of Scotland
intituled Act for securing the Protestant Religion and Presbyterian Church Government are
hereby enacted and ordained to be and continuein all times coming the complete and intire
Union of the two Kingdoms of England and Scotland

OFFICIAL SECRETS ACT 1911
(c. 28)

An Act to re-enact the Official Secrets Act 1889 with Amendments.

1 PENALTIES FOR SPYING

(1)   If any person for any purpose prejudicial to the safety or interests of the State—
   (a)   approaches, [inspects, passes over] or is in the neighbourhood of, or enters any prohibited place within the meaning of this Act; or
   (b)   makes any sketch, plan, model, or note which is calculated to be or might be or is intended to be directly or indirectly useful to an enemy; or
   (c)   obtains, [collects, records, or publishes,] or communicates to any other person [any secret official code word, or pass word, or] any sketch, plan, model, article, or note, or other document or information which is calculated to be or might be or is intended to be directly or indirectly useful to an enemy;
   he shall be guilty of felony [. . .]

(2)   On a prosecution under this section, it shall not be necessary to show that the accused person was guilty of any particular act tending to show a purpose prejudicial to the safety or interests of the State, and, notwithstanding that no such act is proved against him, he may be convicted if, from the circumstances of the case, or his conduct, or his known character as proved, it appears that his purpose was a purpose prejudicial to the safety or interests of the State; and if any sketch, plan, model, article, note, document, or information relating to or used in any prohibited place within the meaning of this Act, or anything in such a place [or any secret official code word or pass word], is made, obtained, [collected, recorded, published], or communicated by any person other than a person acting under lawful authority, it shall be deemed to have been made, obtained, [collected, recorded, published] or communicated for a purpose prejudicial to the safety or interests of the State unless the contrary is proved.

[. . .]

3 DEFINITION OF PROHIBITED PLACE

For the purposes of this Act, the expression "prohibited place" means—

[(a)   any work of defence, arsenal, naval or air force establishment or station, factory, dockyard, mine, minefield, camp, ship, or aircraft belonging to or occupied by or on behalf of His Majesty, or any telegraph, telephone, wireless or signal station, or office so belonging or occupied, and any place belonging to or occupied by or on behalf of His Majesty and used for the purpose of building, repairing, making, or storing any munitions of war, or any sketches, plans, models or documents relating thereto, or for the purpose of getting any metals, oil, or minerals of use in time of war];

(b)   any place not belonging to His Majesty where any [munitions of war], or any [sketches, models, plans] or documents relating thereto, are being made, repaired, [gotten,] or stored under contract with, or with any person on behalf of, His Majesty, or otherwise on behalf of His Majesty; and

(c)   any place belonging to [or used for the purposes of?] His Majesty which is for the time being declared [by order of a Secretary of State] to be a prohibited place for the purposes of this section on the ground that information with respect thereto, or damage thereto, would be useful to an enemy; and

(d)   any railway, road, way, or channel, or other means of communication by land or water (including any works or structures being part thereof or connected therewith), or any place used for gas, water, or electricity works or other works for purposes of a public character, or any place where any [munitions of war], or any [sketches, models, plans] or documents relating thereto, are being made, repaired, or stored otherwise than on behalf of His Majesty, which is for the time being declared [by order of a Secretary of State] to be a prohibited place for the purposes of this section, on the ground that information with respect thereto, or the destruction or obstruction thereof, or interference therewith, would be useful to an enemy.

[. . .]

9 SEARCH WARRANTS

(1)   If a justice of the peace is satisfied by information on oath that there is reasonable ground for suspecting that an offence under this Act has been or is about to be committed, he may grant a search warrant authorising any constable [named therein] to enter at any time any premises or place named in the warrant, if necessary, by force, and to search the premises or place and every person found therein, and to seize any sketch, plan, model, article, note, or document, or anything of a like nature or anything which is evidence of an offence under this Act having been or being about to be committed, which he may find on the premises or place or on any such person, and with regard to or in connexion with which he has reasonable ground for suspecting that an offence under this Act has been or is about to be committed.

(2)   Where it appears to a superintendent of police that the case is one of great emergency and that in the interest of the State immediate action is necessary, he may by a written order under his hand give to any constable the like authority as may be given by the warrant of a justice under this section.

PARLIAMENT ACT 1911
(c. 13)

An Act to make provision with respect to the powers of the House of Lords in relation to those of the House of Commons, and to limit the duration of Parliament.

[. . .]

Whereas it is expedient that provision should be made for regulating the relations between the two Houses of Parliament:

And whereas it is intended to substitute for the House of Lords as it at present exists a Second Chamber constituted on a popular instead of hereditary basis, but such substitution cannot be immediately brought into operation:

And whereas provision will require hereafter to be made by Parliament in a measure effecting such substitution for limiting and defining the powers of the new Second Chamber, but it is expedient to make such provision as in this Act appears for restricting the existing powers of the House of Lords:

1 POWERS OF HOUSE OF LORDS AS TO MONEY BILLS

(1)   If a Money Bill, having been passed by the House of Commons, and sent up to the House of Lords at least one month before the end of the session, is not passed by the House of

Lords without amendment within one month after it is so sent up to that House, the Bill shall, unless the House of Commons direct to the contrary, be presented to His Majesty and become an Act of Parliament on the Royal Assent being signified, notwithstanding that the House of Lords have not consented to the Bill.

(2)   A Money Bill means a Public Bill which in the opinion of the Speaker of the House of Commons contains only provisions dealing with all or any of the following subjects, namely, the imposition, repeal, remission, alteration, or regulation of taxation; the imposition for the payment of debt or other financial purposes of charges on the Consolidated Fund, [the National Loans Fund] or on money provided by Parliament, or the variation or repeal of any such charges; supply; the appropriation, receipt, custody, issue or audit of accounts of public money; the raising or guarantee of any loan or the repayment thereof; or subordinate matters incidental to those subjects or any of them. In this subsection the expressions "taxation", "public money", and "loan" respectively do not include any taxation, money, or loan raised by local authorities or bodies for local purposes.

(3)   There shall be endorsed on every Money Bill when it is sent up to the House of Lords and when it is presented to His Majesty for assent the certificate of the Speaker of the House of Commons signed by him that it is a Money Bill. Before giving his certificate the Speaker shall consult, if practicable, two members to be appointed from the Chairmen's Panel at the beginning of each Session by the Committee of Selection.

2   RESTRICTION OF THE POWERS OF THE HOUSE OF LORDS AS TO BILLS OTHER THAN MONEY BILLS

(1)   If any Public Bill (other than a Money Bill or a Bill containing any provision to extend the maximum duration of Parliament beyond five years) is passed by the House of Commons [in two successive sessions] (whether of the same Parliament or not), and, having been sent up to the House of Lords at least one month before the end of the session, is rejected by the House of Lords in each of those sessions, that Bill shall, on its rejection [for the second time] by the House of Lords, unless the House of Commons direct to the contrary, be presented to His Majesty and become an Act of Parliament on the Royal Assent being signified thereto, notwithstanding that the House of Lords have not consented to the Bill:

Provided that this provision shall not take effect unless [one year has elapsed] between the date of the second reading in the first of those sessions of the Bill in the House of Commons and the date on which it passes the House of Commons [in the second of these sessions.]

(2)   When a Bill is presented to His Majesty for assent in pursuance of the provisions of this section, there shall be endorsed on the Bill the certificate of the Speaker of the House of Commons signed by him that the provisions of this section have been duly complied with.

(3)   A Bill shall be deemed to be rejected by the House of Lords if it is not passed by the House of Lords either without amendment or with such amendments only as may be agreed to by both Houses.

(4)   A Bill shall be deemed to be the same Bill as a former Bill sent up to the House of Lords in the preceding session if, when it is sent up to the House of Lords, it is identical with the former Bill or contains only such alterations as are certified by the Speaker of the House of Commons to be necessary owing to the time which has elapsed since the date of the former Bill, or to represent any amendments which have been made by the House of Lords in the former Bill in the preceding session, and any amendments which are certified by the Speaker to have been made by the House of Lords [in the second session] and

agreed to by the House of Commons shall be inserted in the Bill as presented for Royal Assent in pursuance of this section:

Provided that the House of Commons may, if they think fit, on the passage of such a Bill through the House [in the second session,] suggest any further amendments without inserting the amendments in the Bill, and any such suggested amendments shall be considered by the House of Lords, and, if agreed to by that House, shall be treated as amendments made by the House of Lords and agreed to by the House of Commons; but the exercise of this power by the House of Commons shall not affect the operation of this section in the event of the Bill being rejected by the House of Lords.

[. . .]

[. . .]

As amended by the Parliament Act 1949, section 1; Fixed-Term Parliaments Act 2011, Schedule, paragraph 4

STATUTE OF WESTMINSTER 1931
(c. 4)

An Act to give effect to certain resolutions passed by Imperial Conferences held in the years 1926 and 1930.

Whereas the delegates of His Majesty's Governments in the United Kingdom, the Dominion of Canada, the Commonwealth of Australia, the Dominion of New Zealand, the Union of South Africa, the Irish Free State and Newfoundland, at Imperial Conferences holden at Westminster in the years of our Lord nineteen hundred and twenty-six and nineteen hundred and thirty did concur in making the declarations and resolutions set forth in the Reports of the said Conferences:

And whereas it is meet and proper to set out by way of preamble to this Act that, inasmuch as the Crown is the symbol of the free association of the members of the British Commonwealth of Nations, and as they are united by a common allegiance to the Crown, it would be in accord with the established constitutional position of all the members of the Commonwealth in relation to one another that any alteration in the law touching the Succession to the Throne or the Royal Style and Titles shall hereafter require the assent as well of the Parliaments of all the Dominions as of the Parliament of the United Kingdom:

And whereas it is in accord with the established constitutional position that no law hereafter made by the Parliament of the United Kingdom shall extend to any of the said Dominions as part of the law of that Dominion otherwise than at the request and with the consent of that Dominion:

And whereas it is necessary for the ratifying, confirming and establishing of certain of the said declarations and resolutions of the said Conferences that a law be made and enacted in due form by authority of the Parliament of the United Kingdom:

And whereas the Dominion of Canada, the Commonwealth of Australia, the Dominion of New Zealand, the Union of South Africa, the Irish Free State and Newfoundland have severally requested and consented to the submission of a measure to the Parliament of the United Kingdom for making such provision with regard to the matters aforesaid as is hereafter in this Act contained:

1 MEANING OF "DOMINION" IN THIS ACT

In this Act the expression "Dominion" means any of the following Dominions, that is to say, the Dominion of Canada, the Commonwealth of Australia, the Dominion of New Zealand, [. . .], the Irish Free State and Newfoundland.

2 VALIDITY OF LAWS MADE BY PARLIAMENT OF A DOMINION

[. . .]

(2) No law and no provision of any law made after the commencement of this Act by the Parliament of a Dominion shall be void or inoperative on the ground that it is repugnant to the law of England, or to the provisions of any existing or future Act of Parliament of the United Kingdom, or to any order, rule or regulation made under any such Act, and the powers of the Parliament of a Dominion shall include the power to repeal or amend any such Act, order, rule or regulation in so far as the same is part of the law of the Dominion.

3 POWER OF PARLIAMENT OF DOMINION TO LEGISLATE EXTRA-TERRITORIALLY

It is hereby declared and enacted that the Parliament of a Dominion has full power to make laws having extra-territorial operation.

4 PARLIAMENT OF UNITED KINGDOM NOT TO LEGISLATE FOR DOMINION EXCEPT BY CONSENT

No Act of Parliament of the United Kingdom passed after the commencement of this Act shall extend, or be deemed to extend, to a Dominion as part of the law of that Dominion, unless it is expressly declared in that Act that that Dominion has requested, and consented to, the enactment thereof.

[. . .]

PUBLIC ORDER ACT 1936
(c. 6)

An Act to prohibit the wearing of uniforms in connection with political objects and the maintenance by private persons of associations of military or similar character; and to make further provision for the preservation of public order on the occasion of public processions and meetings and in public places.

1 PROHIBITION OF UNIFORMS IN CONNECTION WITH POLITICAL OBJECTS

(1) Subject as hereinafter provided, any person who in any public place or at any public meeting wears uniform signifying his association with any political organisation or with the promotion of any political object shall be guilty of an offence:

Provided that, if the chief officer of police is satisfied that the wearing of any such uniform as aforesaid on any ceremonial, anniversary, or other special occasion will not be likely to involve risk of public disorder, he may, with the consent of a Secretary of State, by order permit the wearing of such uniform on that occasion either absolutely or subject to such conditions as may be specified in the order.

(2)   Where any person is charged before any court with an offence under this section, no further proceedings in respect thereof shall be taken against him without the consent of the Attorney-General [except such as are authorised by [section 6 of the Prosecution of Offences Act 1979]], so, however, that if that person is remanded in custody he shall, after the expiration of a period of eight days from the date on which he was so remanded, be entitled to be [released on bail] without sureties unless within that period the Attorney-General has consented to such further proceedings as aforesaid.

2 PROHIBITION OF QUASIMILITARY ORGANISATIONS

(1)   If the members or adherents of any association of persons, whether incorporated or not, are—
    (a)   organised or trained or equipped for the purpose of enabling them to be employed in usurping the functions of the police or of the armed forces of the Crown; or
    (b)   organised and trained or organised and equipped either for the purpose of enabling them to be employed for the use or display of physical force in promoting any political object, or in such manner as to arouse reasonable apprehension that they are organised and either trained or equipped for that purpose;
then any person who takes part in the control or management of the association, or in so organising or training as aforesaid any members or adherents thereof, shall be guilty of an offence under this section:

Provided that in any proceedings against a person charged with the offence of taking part in the control or management of such an association as aforesaid it shall be a defence to that charge to prove that he neither consented to nor connived at the organisation, training, or equipment of members or adherents of the association in contravention of the provisions of this section.

[...]

(5)   If a judge of the High Court is satisfied by information on oath that there is reasonable ground for suspecting that an offence under this section has been committed, and that evidence of the commission thereof is to be found at any premises or place specified in the information, he may, on an application made by an officer of police of a rank not lower than that of inspector, grant a search warrant authorising any such officer as aforesaid named in the warrant together with any other persons named in the warrant and any other officers of police to enter the premises or place at any time within one month from the date of the warrant, if necessary by force, and to search the premises or place and every person found therein, and to seize anything found on the premises or place or on any such person which the officer has reasonable ground for suspecting to be evidence of the commission of such an offence as aforesaid:

Provided that no woman shall, in pursuance of a warrant issued under this subsection, be searched except by a woman.

(6)   Nothing in this section shall be construed as prohibiting the employment of a reasonable number of persons as stewards to assist in the preservation of order at any public meeting held upon private premises, or the making of arrangements for that purpose or the instruction of the persons to be so employed in their lawful duties as such stewards, or their being furnished with badges or other distinguishing signs.

[...]

9 INTERPRETATION, &C

(1)   In this Act the following expressions have the meanings hereby respectively assigned to them, that is to say:—

[. . .]

"Meeting" means a meeting held for the purpose of the discussion of matters of public interest or for the purpose of the expression of views on such matters;

"Private premises" means premises to which the public have access (whether on payment or otherwise) only by permission of the owner, occupier, or lessee of the premises;

"Public meeting" includes any meeting in a public place and any meeting which the public or any section thereof are permitted to attend, whether on payment or otherwise;

[. . .]

STATUTORY INSTRUMENTS ACT 1946
(c. 36)

An Act to repeal the Rules Publication Act 1893, and to make further provision as to the instruments by which statutory powers to make orders, rules, regulations and other subordinate legislation are exercised.

1 DEFINITION OF "STATUTORY INSTRUMENT"

(1)   Where by this Act or any Act passed after the commencement of this Act power to make, confirm or approve orders, rules, regulations or other subordinate legislation is conferred on His Majesty in Council or on any Minister of the Crown then, if the power is expressed—
   (a)   in the case of a power conferred on His Majesty, to be exercisable by Order in Council;
   (b)   in the case of a power conferred on a Minister of the Crown, to be exercisable by statutory instrument,
   any document by which that power is exercised shall be known as a "statutory instrument" and the provisions of this Act shall apply thereto accordingly.

[. . .]

2 NUMBERING, PRINTING, PUBLICATION AND CITATION

(1)   Immediately after the making of any statutory instrument, it shall be sent to the King's printer of Acts of Parliament and numbered in accordance with regulations made under this Act, [. . .]

(2)   Any statutory instrument may, without prejudice to any other mode of citation, be cited by the number given to it in accordance with the provisions of this section, and the calendar year.

[. . .]

[. . .]

4 STATUTORY INSTRUMENTS WHICH ARE REQUIRED TO BE LAID BEFORE PARLIAMENT

(1)   Where by this Act or any Act passed after the commencement of this Act any statutory instrument is required to be laid before Parliament after being made, a copy of the

instrument shall be laid before each House of Parliament and, subject as hereinafter provided, shall be so laid before the instrument comes into operation:

Provided that if it is essential that any such instrument should come into operation before copies thereof can be so laid as aforesaid, the instrument may be made so as to come into operation before it has been so laid; and where any statutory instrument comes into operation before it is laid before Parliament, notification shall forthwith be sent [to the Speaker of the House of Commons and the Speaker of the House of Lords] drawing attention to the fact that copies of the instrument have yet to be laid before Parliament and explaining why such copies were not so laid before the instrument came into operation.

[. . .]

5 STATUTORY INSTRUMENTS WHICH ARE SUBJECT TO ANNULMENT BY RESOLUTION OF EITHER HOUSE OF PARLIAMENT

(1)   Where by this Act or any Act passed after the commencement of this Act, it is provided that any statutory instrument shall be subject to annulment in pursuance of resolution of either House of Parliament, the instrument shall be laid before Parliament after being made and the provisions of the last foregoing section shall apply thereto accordingly, and if either House within the period of forty days beginning with the day on which a copy thereof is laid before it, resolves that an Address be presented to His Majesty praying that the instrument be annulled, no further proceedings shall be taken thereunder after the date of the resolution, and His Majesty may by Order in Council revoke the instrument, so, however, that any such resolution and revocation shall be without prejudice to the validity of anything previously done under the instrument or to the making of a new statutory instrument.

[. . .]

CROWN PROCEEDINGS ACT 1947
(c. 44)

An Act to amend the law relating to the civil liabilities and rights of the Crown and to civil proceedings by and against the Crown, to amend the law relating to the civil liabilities of persons other than the Crown in certain cases involving the affairs or property of the Crown, and for purposes connected with the matters aforesaid.

Part I SUBSTANTIVE LAW

1 RIGHT TO SUE THE CROWN

Where any person has a claim against the Crown after the commencement of this Act, and, if this Act had not been passed, the claim might have been enforced, subject to the grant of His Majesty's fiat, by petition of right, or might have been enforced by a proceeding provided by any statutory provision repealed by this Act, then, subject to the provisions of this Act, the claim may be enforced as of right, and without the fiat of His Majesty, by proceedings taken against the Crown for that purpose in accordance with the provisions of this Act.

2 LIABILITY OF THE CROWN IN TORT

(1)   Subject to the provisions of this Act, the Crown shall be subject to all those liabilities in tort to which, if it were a private person of full age and capacity, it would be subject:—

    (a)   in respect of torts committed by its servants or agents;

    (b)   in respect of any breach of those duties which a person owes to his servants or agents at common law by reason of being their employer; and

    (c)   in respect of any breach of the duties attaching at common law to the ownership, occupation, possession or control of property:

Provided that no proceedings shall lie against the Crown by virtue of paragraph (a) of this subsection in respect of any act or omission of a servant or agent of the Crown unless the act or omission would apart from the provisions of this Act have given rise to a cause of action in tort against that servant or agent or his estate.

(2)   Where the Crown is bound by a statutory duty which is binding also upon persons other than the Crown and its officers, then, subject to the provisions of this Act, the Crown shall, in respect of a failure to comply with that duty, be subject to all those liabilities in tort (if any) to which it would be so subject if it were a private person of full age and capacity.

(3)   Where any functions are conferred or imposed upon an officer of the Crown as such either by any rule of the common law or by statute, and that officer commits a tort while performing or purporting to perform those functions, the liabilities of the Crown in respect of the tort shall be such as they would have been if those functions had been conferred or imposed solely by virtue of instructions lawfully given by the Crown.

(4)   Any enactment which negatives or limits the amount of the liability of any Government department [, part of the Scottish Administration] or officer of the Crown in respect of any tort committed by that department [, part] or officer shall, in the case of proceedings against the Crown under this section in respect of a tort committed by that department [, part] or officer, apply in relation to the Crown as it would have applied in relation to that department [, part] or officer if the proceedings against the Crown had been proceedings against that department [, part] or officer.

(5)   No proceedings shall lie against the Crown by virtue of this section in respect of anything done or omitted to be done by any person while discharging or purporting to discharge any responsibilities of a judicial nature vested in him, or any responsibilities which he has in connection with the execution of judicial process.

(6)   No proceedings shall lie against the Crown by virtue of this section in respect of any act, neglect or default of any officer of the Crown, unless that officer has been directly or indirectly appointed by the Crown and was at the material time paid in respect of his duties as an officer of the Crown wholly out of the Consolidated Fund of the United Kingdom, moneys provided by Parliament [the Scottish Consolidated Fund], [. . .] or any other Fund certified by the Treasury for the purposes of this subsection or was at the material time holding an office in respect of which the Treasury certify that the holder thereof would normally be so paid.

[. . .]

4 APPLICATION OF LAW AS TO INDEMNITY, CONTRIBUTION, JOINT AND SEVERAL TORTFEASORS, AND CONTRIBUTORY NEGLIGENCE

(1)   Where the Crown is subject to any liability by virtue of this Part of this Act, the law relating to indemnity and contribution shall be enforceable by or against the Crown in

respect of the liability to which it is so subject as if the Crown were a private person of full age and capacity.

[. . .]

11 SAVING IN RESPECT OF ACTS DONE UNDER PREROGATIVE AND STATUTORY POWERS

(1) Nothing in Part I of this Act shall extinguish or abridge any powers or authorities which, if this Act had not been passed, would have been exercisable by virtue of the prerogative of the Crown, or any powers or authorities conferred on the Crown by any statute, and, in particular, nothing in the said Part I shall extinguish or abridge any powers or authorities exercisable by the Crown, whether in time of peace or of war, for the purpose of the defence of the realm or of training, or maintaining the efficiency of, any of the armed forces of the Crown.

(2) Where in any proceedings under this Act it is material to determine whether anything was properly done or omitted to be done in the exercise of the prerogative of the Crown, [. . .] a Secretary of State may, if satisfied that the act or omission was necessary for any such purpose as is mentioned in the last preceding subsection, issue a certificate to the effect that the act or omission was necessary for that purpose; and the certificate shall, in those proceedings, be conclusive as to the matter so certified.

[. . .]

Part II JURISDICTION AND PROCEDURE

17 PARTIES TO PROCEEDINGS

(1) The [Minister for the Civil Service] shall publish a list specifying the several Government departments which are authorised departments for the purposes of this Act, and the name and address for service of the person who is, or is acting for the purposes of this Act as, the solicitor for each such department, and may from time to time amend or vary the said list.

Any document purporting to be a copy of a list published under this section and purporting to be printed under the superintendence or the authority of His Majesty's Stationery Office shall in any legal proceedings be received as evidence for the purpose of establishing what departments are authorised departments for the purposes of this Act, and what person is, or is acting for the purposes of this Act as, the solicitor for any such department.

(2) Civil proceedings by the Crown may be instituted either by an authorised Government department in its own name, whether that department was or was not at the commencement of this Act authorised to sue, or by the Attorney General.

(3) Civil proceedings against the Crown shall be instituted against the appropriate authorised Government department, or, if none of the authorised Government departments is appropriate or the person instituting the proceedings has any reasonable doubt whether any and if so which of those departments is appropriate, against the Attorney General.

[. . .]

21 NATURE OF RELIEF

(1) In any civil proceedings by or against the Crown the court shall, subject to the provisions of this Act, have power to make all such orders as it has power to make in proceedings between subjects, and otherwise to give such appropriate relief as the case may require: Provided that:—

(a) where in any proceedings against the Crown any such relief is sought as might in proceedings between subjects be granted by way of injunction or specific performance, the court shall not grant an injunction or make an order for specific performance, but may in lieu thereof make an order declaratory of the rights of the parties; and

(b) in any proceedings against the Crown for the recovery of land or other property the court shall not make an order for the recovery of the land or the delivery of the property, but may in lieu thereof make an order declaring that the plaintiff is entitled as against the Crown to the land or property or to the possession thereof.

(2) The court shall not in any civil proceedings grant any injunction or make any order against an officer of the Crown if the effect of granting the injunction or making the order would be to give any relief against the Crown which could not have been obtained in proceedings against the Crown.

[. . .]

LIFE PEERAGES ACT 1958
(c. 21)

An Act to make provision for the creation of life peerages carrying the right to sit and vote in the House of Lords.

[. . .]

1 POWER TO CREATE LIFE PEERAGES CARRYING RIGHT TO SIT IN THE HOUSE OF LORDS

(1) [. . .] Her Majesty shall have power by letters patent to confer on any person a peerage for life having the incidents specified in subsection (2) of this section.

(2) A peerage conferred under this section shall, during the life of the person on whom it is conferred, entitle him—

(a) to rank as a baron under such style as may be appointed by the letters patent; and

(b) subject to subsection (4) of this section, to receive writs of summons to attend the House of Lords and sit and vote therein accordingly,

and shall expire on his death.

(3) A life peerage may be conferred under this section on a woman.

[. . .]

PEERAGE ACT 1963
(c. 48)

An Act to authorise the disclaimer for life of certain hereditary peerages; to include among the peers qualified to sit in the House of Lords all peers in the peerage of Scotland and peeresses in their own right in the peerages of England, Scotland, Great Britain and the United Kingdom; to remove certain disqualifications of peers in the peerage of Ireland in relation to the House of Commons and elections thereto; and for purposes connected with the matters aforesaid.

[. . .]

Disclaimer of Peerage

1 DISCLAIMER OF CERTAIN HEREDITARY PEERAGES

(1)   Subject to the provisions of this section, any person who, after the commencement of this Act, succeeds to a peerage in the peerage of England, Scotland, Great Britain or the United Kingdom may, by an instrument of disclaimer delivered to the Lord Chancellor within the period prescribed by this Act, disclaim that peerage for his life.

[. . .]

3 EFFECTS OF DISCLAIMER

(1)   The disclaimer of a peerage by any person under this Act shall be irrevocable and shall operate, from the date on which the instrument of disclaimer is delivered,—
       (a) to divest that person (and, if he is married, his wife) of all right or interest to or in the peerage, and all titles, rights, offices, privileges and precedence attaching thereto; and
       (b) to relieve him of all obligations and disabilities [. . .] arising therefrom,
       but shall not accelerate the succession to that peerage nor affect its devolution on his death.

(2)   Where a peerage is disclaimed under this Act, no other hereditary peerage shall be conferred upon the person by whom it is disclaimed [. . .]

(3)   The disclaimer of a peerage under this Act shall not affect any right, interest or power (whether arising before or after the disclaimer) of the person by whom the peerage is disclaimed, or of any other person, to, in or over any estates or other property limited or settled to devolve with that peerage.

[. . .]

Parliamentary qualifications of Scottish Peers, Irish Peers and Peeresses in own right

4 SCOTTISH PEERAGES

The holder of a peerage in the peerage of Scotland shall have the same right to receive writs of summons to attend the House of Lords, and to sit and vote in that House, as the holder of a peerage in the peerage of the United Kingdom; and the enactments relating to the election of Scottish representative peers shall cease to have effect.

[. . .]

6 PEERESSES IN OWN RIGHT

A woman who is the holder of a hereditary peerage in the peerage of England, Scotland, Great Britain or the United Kingdom shall (whatever the terms of the letters patent or other instrument, if any, creating that peerage) have the same right to receive writs of summons to attend the House of Lords, and to sit and vote in that House, and shall be subject to the same disqualifications in respect of membership of the House of Commons and elections to that House, as a man holding that peerage.

[. . .]

OBSCENE PUBLICATIONS ACT 1959

An Act to amend the law relating to the publication of obscene matter; to provide for the protection of literature; and to strengthen the law concerning pornography.

[29th July 1959]

1   Test of obscenity.
   (1) For the purposes of this Act an article shall be deemed to be obscene if its effect or (where the article comprises two or more distinct items) the effect of any one of its items is, if taken as a whole, such as to tend to deprave and corrupt persons who are likely, having regard to all relevant circumstances, to read, see or hear the matter contained or embodied in it.
   (2) In this Act "article" means any description of article containing or embodying matter to be read or looked at or both, any sound record, and any film or other record of a picture or pictures.
   (3) For the purposes of this Act a person publishes an article who—
      (a) distributes, circulates, sells, lets on hire, gives, or lends it, or who offers it for sale or for letting on hire; or
      (b) in the case of an article containing or embodying matter to be looked at or a record, shows, plays or projects it or, where the matter is data stored electronically, transmits that data.
   (4) For the purposes of this Act a person also publishes an article to the extent that any matter recorded on it is included by him in a programme included in a programme service.
   (5) Where the inclusion of any matter in a programme so included would, if that matter were recorded matter, constitute the publication of an obscene article for the purposes of this Act by virtue of subsection (4) above, this Act shall have effect in relation to the inclusion of that matter in that programme as if it were recorded matter.
   (6) In this section "programme" and "programme service" have the same meaning as in the Broadcasting Act 1990.

2   Prohibition of publication of obscene matter.
   (1) Subject as hereinafter provided, any person who, whether for gain or not, publishes an obscene article or who has an obscene article for publication for gain (whether gain to himself or gain to another) shall be liable—
      (a) on summary conviction to a fine not exceeding [one hundred pounds] or to imprisonment for a term not exceeding [6 months];
      (b) on conviction on indictment to a fine or to imprisonment for a term not exceeding three years or both.
   (2)
   (3) A prosecution for an offence against this section shall not be commenced more than two years after the commission of the offence.

(3A)   Proceedings for an offence under this section shall not be instituted except by or with the consent of the Director of Public Prosecutions in any case where the article in question is a moving picture film of a width of not less than sixteen millimetres and the relevant publication or the only other publication which followed or could reasonably have been expected to follow from the relevant publication took place or (as the case may be) was to take place in the course of a film exhibition; and in this subsection "the relevant publication" means—

   (a)   in the case of any proceedings under this section for publishing an obscene article, the publication in respect of which the defendant would be charged if the proceedings were brought; and

   (b)   in the case of any proceedings under this section for having an obscene article for publication for gain, the publication which, if the proceedings were brought, the defendant would be alleged to have had in contemplation.

(4)   A person publishing an article shall not be preceeded against for an offence at common law consisting of the publication of any matter contained or embodied in the article where it is of the essence of the offence that the matter is obscene.

(4A)   Without prejudice to subsection (4) above, a person shall not be proceeded against for an offence at common law—

   (a)   in respect of a film exhibition or anything said or done in the course of a film exhibition, where it is of the essence of the common law offence that the exhibition or, as the case may be, what was said or done was obscene, indecent, offensive, disgusting or injurious to morality; or

   (b)   in respect of an agreement to give a film exhibition or to cause anything to be said or done in the course of such an exhibition where the common law offence consists of conspiring to corrupt public morals or to do any act contrary to public morals or decency.

(5)   A person shall not be convicted of an offence against this section if he proves that he had not examined the article in respect of which he is charged and had no reasonable cause to suspect that it was such that his publication of it would make him liable to be convicted of an offence against this section.

(6)   In any proceedings against a person under this section the question whether an article is obscene shall be determined without regard to any publication by another person unless it could reasonably have been expected that the publication by the other person would follow from publication by the person charged.

PARLIAMENTARY COMMISSIONER ACT 1967
(c. 13)

An Act to make provision for the appointment and functions of a Parliamentary Commissioner for the investigation of administrative action taken on behalf of the Crown, and for purposes connected therewith.

The Parliamentary Commissioner for Administration

1 APPOINTMENT AND TENURE OF OFFICE

(1)   For the purpose of conducting investigations in accordance with the following provisions of this Act there shall be appointed a Commissioner, to be known as the Parliamentary Commissioner for Administration.

(2)   Her Majesty may by Letters Patent from time to time appoint a person to be the Commissioner [. . .]

(2A) A person appointed to be the Commissioner shall hold office until the end of the period for which he is appointed.

(2B) That period must be not more than seven years.

(2C) Subsection (2A) is subject to subsections (3) and (3A).

(3) A person appointed to be the Commissioner may be—
 (a) relieved of office by Her Majesty at his own request, or
 (b) removed from office by Her Majesty, on the ground of misbehaviour, in consequence of Addresses from both Houses of Parliament.

[. . .]

3 ADMINISTRATIVE PROVISIONS

(1) The Commissioner may appoint such officers as he may determine with the approval of the Treasury as to numbers and conditions of service.

(1A) The Commissioner may appoint and pay a mediator or other appropriate person to assist him in the conduct of an investigation under this Act.

(2) Any function of the Commissioner under this Act may be performed by any officer of the Commissioner authorised for that purpose by the Commissioner [. . .]

[. . .]

Investigation by the Commissioner

4 DEPARTMENTS ETC. SUBJECT TO INVESTIGATION

(1) Subject to the provisions of this section and to the notes contained in Schedule 2 to this Act, this Act applies to the government departments, corporations and unincorporated bodies listed in that Schedule; and references in this Act to an authority to which this Act applies are references to any such corporation or body.

[. . .]

5 MATTERS SUBJECT TO INVESTIGATION

(1) Subject to the provisions of this section, the Commissioner may investigate any action taken by or on behalf of a government department or other authority to which this Act applies, being action taken in the exercise of administrative functions of that department or authority, in any case where—
 (a) a written complaint is duly made to a member of the House of Commons by a member of the public who claims to have sustained injustice in consequence of maladministration in connection with the action so taken; and
 (b) the complaint is referred to the Commissioner, with the consent of the person who made it, by a member of that House with a request to conduct an investigation thereon.
 [. . .]

(2) Except as hereinafter provided, the Commissioner shall not conduct an investigation under this Act in respect of any of the following matters, that is to say—
 (a) any action in respect of which the person aggrieved has or had a right of appeal, reference or review to or before a tribunal constituted by or under any enactment or by virtue of Her Majesty's prerogative;

(b) any action in respect of which the person aggrieved has or had a remedy by way of proceedings in any court of law:

Provided that the Commissioner may conduct an investigation notwithstanding that the person aggrieved has or had such a right or remedy if satisfied that in the particular circumstances it is not reasonable to expect him to resort or have resorted to it.

[. . .]

(3) Without prejudice to subsection (2) of this section, the Commissioner shall not conduct an [investigation under subsection (1) of this section] in respect of any such action or matter as is described in Schedule 3 to this Act.

[. . .]

(5) In determining whether to initiate, continue or discontinue an investigation under this Act, the Commissioner shall, subject to the foregoing provisions of this section, act in accordance with his own discretion; and any question whether a complaint is duly made under this Act shall be determined by the Commissioner.

[. . .]

[. . .]

6 PROVISIONS RELATING TO COMPLAINTS

(1) A complaint under this Act may be made by any individual, or by any body of persons whether incorporated or not, not being—
(a) a local authority or other authority or body constituted for purposes of the public service or of local government or for the purposes of carrying on under national ownership any industry or undertaking or part of an industry or undertaking;
[(b) any other authority or body within subsection (1A) below.

(1A) An authority or body is within this subsection if—
(a) its members are appointed by—
(i)   Her Majesty;
(ii) any Minister of the Crown;
(iii) any government department;
(iv) the Scottish Ministers;
(v)   the First Minister; or
(vi) the Lord Advocate, or
(b) its revenues consist wholly or mainly of—
(i)   money provided by Parliament; or
(ii) sums payable out of the Scottish Consolidated Fund (directly or indirectly).]

(2) Where the person by whom a complaint might have been made under the foregoing provisions of this Act has died or is for any reason unable to act for himself, the complaint may be made by his personal representative or by a member of his family or other individual suitable to represent him; but except as aforesaid a complaint shall not be entertained under this Act unless made by the person aggrieved himself.

(3) A complaint shall not be entertained under this Act unless it is made to a member of the House of Commons not later than twelve months from the day on which the person aggrieved first had notice of the matters alleged in the complaint; but the Commissioner may conduct an investigation pursuant to a complaint not made within that period if he considers that there are special circumstances which make it proper to do so.

(4)   [Except as provided in subsection (5) below] A complaint shall not be entertained under this Act unless the person aggrieved is resident in the United Kingdom (or, if he is dead, was so resident at the time of his death) or the complaint relates to action taken in relation to him while he was present in the United Kingdom or on an installation in a designated area within the meaning of the Continental Shelf Act 1964 or on a ship registered in the United Kingdom or an aircraft so registered, or in relation to rights or obligations which accrued or arose in the United Kingdom or on such an installation, ship or aircraft.

[. . .]

7 PROCEDURE IN RESPECT OF INVESTIGATIONS

(1)   Where the Commissioner proposes to conduct an investigation pursuant to a complaint under [section 5(1) of] this Act, he shall afford to the principal officer of the department or authority concerned, and to any other person who is alleged in the complaint to have taken or authorised the action complained of, an opportunity to comment on any allegations contained in the complaint.

[. . .]

(2)   Every [investigation under this Act] shall be conducted in private, but except as aforesaid the procedure for conducting an investigation shall be such as the Commissioner considers appropriate in the circumstances of the case; and without prejudice to the generality of the foregoing provision the Commissioner may obtain information from such persons and in such manner, and make such inquiries, as he thinks fit, and may determine whether any person may be represented, by counsel or solicitor or otherwise, in the investigation.

8 EVIDENCE

(1)   For the purposes of an investigation under [section 5(1) of] this Act the Commissioner may require any Minister, officer or member of the department or authority concerned or any other person who in his opinion is able to furnish information or produce documents relevant to the investigation to furnish any such information or produce any such document.

[. . .]

(2)   For the purposes of any [investigation under this Act] the Commissioner shall have the same powers as the Court in respect of the attendance and examination of witnesses (including the administration of oaths or affirmations and the examination of witnesses abroad) and in respect of the production of documents.

(3)   No obligation to maintain secrecy or other restriction upon the disclosure of information obtained by or furnished to persons in Her Majesty's service, whether imposed by any enactment or by any rule of law, shall apply to the disclosure of information for the purposes of an investigation under this Act; and the Crown shall not be entitled in relation to any such investigation to any such privilege in respect of the production of documents or the giving of evidence as is allowed by law in legal proceedings.

(4)   No person shall be required or authorised by virtue of this Act to furnish any information or answer any question relating to proceedings of the Cabinet or of any committee of the Cabinet or to produce so much of any document as relates to such proceedings; and for the purposes of this subsection a certificate issued by the Secretary of the Cabinet with the

approval of the Prime Minister and certifying that any information, question, document or part of a document so relates shall be conclusive.

[. . .]

10 REPORTS BY COMMISSIONER

(1)   In any case where the Commissioner conducts an investigation under this Act or decides not to conduct such an investigation, he shall send to the member of the House of Commons by whom the request for investigation was made (or if he is no longer a member of that House, to such member of that House as the Commissioner thinks appropriate) a report of the results of the investigation or, as the case may be, a statement of his reasons for not conducting an investigation.

(2)   In any case where the Commissioner conducts an investigation under [section 5(1) of] this Act, he shall also send a report of the results of the investigation to the principal officer of the department or authority concerned and to any other person who is alleged in the relevant complaint to have taken or authorised the action complained of.

[. . .]

(3)   If, after conducting an investigation under [section 5(1) of] this Act, it appears to the Commissioner that injustice has been caused to the person aggrieved in consequence of maladministration and that the injustice has not been, or will not be, remedied, he may, if he thinks fit, lay before each House of Parliament a special report upon the case.

[. . .]

(4)   The Commissioner shall annually lay before each House of Parliament a general report on the performance of his functions under this Act and may from time to time lay before each House of Parliament such other reports with respect to those functions as he thinks fit.

[. . .]

Supplemental

12 INTERPRETATION

(1)   In this Act the following expressions have the meanings hereby respectively assigned to them, that is to say—

"action" includes failure to act, and other expressions connoting action shall be construed accordingly;

"the Commissioner" means the Parliamentary Commissioner for Administration;

"the Court" means, in relation to England and Wales the High Court, in relation to Scotland the Court of Session, and in relation to Northern Ireland the High Court of Northern Ireland

[. . .]

SCHEDULES

[. . .]

SCHEDULE 3 MATTERS NOT SUBJECT TO INVESTIGATION

1   Action taken in matters certified by a Secretary of State or other Minister of the Crown to affect relations or dealings between the Government of the United Kingdom and any other Government or any international organisation of States or Governments.

2   (1) Action taken, in any country or territory outside the United Kingdom, by or on behalf of any officer representing or acting under the authority of Her Majesty in respect of the United Kingdom, or any other officer of the Government of the United Kingdom [other than,
     (a) action which is taken by an officer (not being an honorary consular officer) in the exercise of a consular function on behalf of the Government of the United Kingdom [. . .]

3   Action taken in connection with the administration of the government of any country or territory outside the United Kingdom which forms part of Her Majesty's dominions or in which Her Majesty has jurisdiction.

[. . .]

5   Action taken by or with the authority of the Secretary of State for the purposes of investigating crime or of protecting the security of the State, including action so taken with respect to passports.

[. . .]

[6A Action taken by any person appointed by the Lord Chancellor as a member of the administrative staff of any court or tribunal, so far as that action is taken at the direction, or on the authority (whether express or implied), of any person acting in a judicial capacity or in his capacity as a member of the tribunal.]

[6B (1) Action taken by any member of the administrative staff of a relevant tribunal, so far as that action is taken at the direction, or on the authority (whether express or implied), of any person acting in his capacity as a member of the tribunal.
     (2) In this paragraph, "relevant tribunal" has the meaning given by section 5(8) of this Act.]
[. . .]

7   Any exercise of the prerogative of mercy or of the power of a Secretary of State to make a reference in respect of any person to [. . .] the High Court of Justiciary or the [Court Martial Appeal Court].

[. . .]

9   Action taken in matters relating to contractual or other commercial transactions, whether within the United Kingdom or elsewhere, being transactions of a government department or authority to which this Act applies or of any such authority or body as is mentioned in paragraph (a) or (b) of subsection (1) of section 6 of this Act and not being transactions for or relating to—
     (a) the acquisition of land compulsorily or in circumstances in which it could be acquired compulsorily;
     (b) the disposal as surplus of land acquired compulsorily or in such circumstances as aforesaid.

10   [(1)] Action taken in respect of appointments or removals, pay, discipline, superannuation or other personnel matters, in relation to—
     (a) service in any of the armed forces of the Crown, including reserve and auxiliary and cadet forces;

(b) service in any office or employment under the Crown or under any authority [to which this Act applies]; or

(c) service in any office or employment, or under any contract for services, in respect of which power to take action, or to determine or approve the action to be taken, in such matters is vested in Her Majesty, any Minister of the Crown or any such authority as aforesaid.

[. . .]

11   The grant of honours, awards or privileges within the gift of the Crown, including the grant of Royal Charters.

[. . .]

EUROPEAN COMMUNITIES ACT 1972
(c. 68)

An Act to make provision in connection with the enlargement of the European Communities to include the United Kingdom, together with (for certain purposes) the Channel Islands, the Isle of Man and Gibaltar.

[. . .]

Part 1 GENERAL PROVISIONS

1 SHORT TITLE AND INTERPRETATION

(1)   This Act may be cited as the European Communities Act 1972.

(2)   In this Act [. . .]

"the EU" means the European Union, being the Union established by the Treaty on European Union signed at Maastricht on 7th February 1992 (as amended by any later Treaty),

"the Communities" means the European Economic Community, the European Coal and Steel Community and the European Atomic Energy Community;

"the Treaties" or "[the EU Treaties]" means, subject to subsection (3) below, the pre-accession treaties, that is to say, those described in Part I of Schedule 1 to this Act, taken with—

(a)   the treaty relating to the accession of the United Kingdom to the European Economic Community and to the European Atomic Energy Community, signed at Brussels on the 22nd January 1972; and

(b)   the decision, of the same date, of the Council of the European Communities relating to the accession of the United Kingdom to the European Coal and Steel Community; and
[. . .]

(j)   the following provisions of the Single European Act signed at Luxembourg and The Hague on 17th and 28th February 1986, namely Title II (amendment of the treaties establishing the Communities) and, so far as they relate to any of the Communities or any Community institution, the preamble and Titles I (common provisions) and IV (general and final provisions);[and]

(k)   Titles II, III and IV of the Treaty on European Union signed at Maastricht on 7th February 1992, together with the other provisions of the Treaty so far as they relate to those Titles, and the Protocols adopted at Maastricht on that date and annexed to the Treaty establishing the European Community with the exception of the Protocol on Social Policy on page 117 of Cm 1934;[and]

[. . .]

(o) the following provisions of the Treaty signed at Amsterdam on 2nd October 1997
amending the Treaty on European Union, the Treaties establishing the European
Communities and certain related Acts—

(i) Articles 2 to 9,

(ii) Article 12, and

(iii) the other provisions of the Treaty so far as they relate to those Articles,
and the Protocols adopted on that occasion other than the Protocol on Article J.7 of
the Treaty on European Union;[and]

(p) the following provisions of the Treaty signed at Nice on 26th February 2001
amending the Treaty on European Union, the Treaties establishing the European
Communities and certain related Acts—

(i) Articles 2 to 10, and

(ii) the other provisions of the Treaty so far as they relate to those Articles,
and the Protocol adopted on that occasion;

[. . .]

[(s) the Treaty of Lisbon Amending the Treaty on European Union and the Treaty
Establishing the European Community signed at Lisbon on 13th December 2007
(together with its Annex and protocol), excluding any provision that relates to, or in
so far as it relates to or could be applied in relation to, the Common Foreign and
Security Policy; and

(t) the Protocol amending the Protocol (No. 36) on transitional provisions annexed to
the Treaty on European Union, to the Treaty on the Functioning of the European
Union and to the Treaty establishing the European Atomic Energy Community, signed
at Brussels on 23 June 2010;

and any other treaty entered into by the EU(except in so far as it relates to, or could be
applied in relation to, the Common Foreign and Security Policy), with or without any of
the member States, or entered into, as a treaty ancillary to any of the Treaties, by the
United Kingdom;

and any expression defined in Schedule 1 to this Act has the meaning there given to it.

[. . .]

2 GENERAL IMPLEMENTATION OF TREATIES

(1) All such rights, powers, liabilities, obligations and restrictions from time to time created
or arising by or under the Treaties, and all such remedies and procedures from time to
time provided for by or under the Treaties, as in accordance with the Treaties are without
further enactment to be given legal effect or used in the United Kingdom shall be
recognised and available in law, and be enforced, allowed and followed accordingly; and
the expression "[enforceable EU right]" and similar expressions shall be read as referring
to one to which this subsection applies.

(2) Subject to Schedule 2 to this Act, at any time after its passing Her Majesty may by Order
in Council, and any designated Minister or department may [by order, rules, regulations
or scheme], make provision—

(a) for the purpose of implementing any [EU obligation] of the United Kingdom, or
enabling any such obligation to be implemented, or of enabling any rights enjoyed or
to be enjoyed by the United Kingdom under or by virtue of the Treaties to be
exercised; or

(b) for the purpose of dealing with matters arising out of or related to any such obligation
or rights or the coming into force, or the operation from time to time, of subsection (1)
above;

and in the exercise of any statutory power or duty, including any power to give directions or to legislate by means of orders, rules, regulations or other subordinate instrument, the person entrusted with the power or duty may have regard to the [objects of the EU] and to any such obligation or rights as aforesaid.

In this subsection "designated Minister or department" means such Minister of the Crown or government department as may from time to time be designated by Order in Council in relation to any matter or for any purpose, but subject to such restrictions or conditions (if any) as may be specified by the Order in Council.

[. . .]

(4)   The provision that may be made under subsection (2) above includes, subject to Schedule 2 to this Act, any such provision (of any such extent) as might be made by Act of Parliament, and any enactment passed or to be passed, other than one contained in this Part of this Act, shall be construed and have effect subject to the foregoing provisions of this section; but, except as may be provided by any Act passed after this Act, Schedule 2 shall have effect in connection with the powers conferred by this and the following sections of this Act to make Orders in Council [or orders, rules, regulations or schemes].

[. . .]

3 DECISIONS ON, AND PROOF OF, TREATIES AND [EU INSTRUMENTS] ETC.

(1)   For the purposes of all legal proceedings any question as to the meaning or effect of any of the Treaties, or as to the validity, meaning or effect of any [EU instrument], shall be treated as a question of law (and, if not referred to the European Court, be for determination as such in accordance with the principles laid down by and any relevant [decision of [the European Court]]).

(2)   Judicial notice shall be taken of the Treaties, of the Official Journal of the Communities and of any decision of, or expression of opinion by, [the European Court] on any such question as aforesaid; and the Official Journal shall be admissible as evidence of any instrument or other act thereby communicated of [the EU] or of any [EU institution].

[. . .]

As amended by the European Union Act 2011, section 15(2)

LOCAL GOVERNMENT ACT 1972
(c. 70)

An Act to make provision with respect to local government and the functions of local authorities in England and Wales; to amend Part II of the Transport Act 1968; to confer rights of appeal in respect of decisions relating to licences under the Home Counties (Music and Dancing) Licensing Act 1926; to make further provision with respect to magistrates' courts committees; to abolish certain inferior courts of record; and for connected purposes.

[. . .]

Part I **LOCAL GOVERNMENT AREAS AND AUTHORITIES IN ENGLAND**

New local government areas

1 NEW LOCAL GOVERNMENT AREAS IN ENGLAND

(1)   For the administration of local government on and after 1st April 1974 England (exclusive of Greater London and the Isles of Scilly) shall be divided into local government areas to be known as counties and in those counties there shall be local government areas to be known as districts.

(2)   The counties shall be the metropolitan counties named in Part I and the non-metropolitan countries named in Part II of Schedule 1 to this Act and shall comprise the areas respectively described (by reference to administrative areas existing immediately before the passing of this Act) in column 2 of each Part of that Schedule.

[. . .]

Principal councils

2 CONSTITUTION OF PRINCIPAL COUNCILS IN ENGLAND

(1)   For every non-metropolitan county there shall be a council consisting of a chairman and councillors and the council shall have all such functions as are vested in them by this Act or otherwise.

(2)   For every district there shall be a council consisting of a chairman and councillors and the council shall have all such functions as are vested in them by this Act or otherwise.

(2A) Where a council mentioned in subsection (1) or (2) above are operating executive arrangements which involve a mayor and cabinet executive , the council shall consist of an elected mayor, a chairman and councillors.

        [. . .]

(3)   Each council mentioned in subsection (1) or (2) above shall be a body corporate by the name "The County Council" or "The District Council", as the case may be, with the addition of the name of the particular county or district.

[. . .]

7 ELECTIONS OF COUNCILLORS

(1)   The ordinary elections of county councillors shall take place in 1973 and every fourth year thereafter, their term of office shall be four years and they shall retire together in every such fourth year on the fourth day after the ordinary day of election of county councillors, and in and after 1977 the newly elected councillors shall come into office on the day on which their predecessors retire.

        [. . .]

[. . .]

Parishes

9 PARISH MEETINGS AND COUNCILS

(1)   For every parish there shall be a parish meeting for the purpose of discussing parish affairs
and exercising any functions conferred on such meetings by any enactment and, subject to
the provisions of this Act or any instrument made thereunder, for every parish or group of
parishes having a parish council before 1st April 1974 there shall continue to be a parish
council.

[. . .]

[. . .]

13 CONSTITUTION OF PARISH MEETING, ETC.

(1)   The parish meeting of a parish shall consist of the local government electors for the parish.

(2)   Any act of a parish meeting may be signified by an instrument signed by the person
presiding and two other local government electors present at the meeting, or, if an
instrument under seal is required, by an instrument signed by those persons and sealed
with the seal of the parish council in the case of a parish having a separate parish council
or the parish trustees in any other case, if that council or those trustees have a seal, or, if
they do not, with the seals of those persons.

(3)   In a parish not having a separate parish council the chairman of the parish meeting and
the proper officer of the district council shall be a body corporate by the name of "the
Parish Trustees" with the addition of the name of the parish.

[. . .]

14 CONSTITUTION AND POWERS OF PARISH COUNCIL

(1)   A parish council shall consist of the chairman and parish councillors and shall have all
such functions as are vested in the council by this Act or otherwise.

(2)   The parish council shall be a body corporate by the name "The Parish Council" with the
addition of the name of the particular parish.

[. . .]

[Part VA ACCESS TO MEETINGS AND DOCUMENTS OF CERTAIN AUTHORITIES, COMMITTEES AND SUB-COMMITTEES]

100A ADMISSION TO MEETINGS OF PRINCIPAL COUNCILS

(1)   A meeting of a principal council shall be open to the public except to the extent that they
are excluded (whether during the whole or part of the proceedings) under subsection (2)
below or by resolution under subsection (4) below.

(2)   The public shall be excluded from a meeting of a principal council during an item of
business whenever it is likely, in view of the nature of the business to be transacted or the
nature of the proceedings, that, if members of the public were present during that item,
confidential information would be disclosed to them in breach of the obligation of
confidence; and nothing in this Part shall be taken to authorise or require the disclosure of
confidential information in breach of the obligation of confidence.

[. . .]

100B ACCESS TO AGENDA AND CONNECTED REPORTS

(1)   Copies of the agenda for a meeting of a principal council and, subject to subsection (2) below, copies of any report for the meeting shall be open to inspection by members of the public at the offices of the council in accordance with subsection (3) below.

(2)   If the proper officer thinks fit, there may be excluded from the copies of reports provided in pursuance of subsection (1) above the whole of any report which, or any part which, relates only to items during which, in his opinion, the meeting is likely not to be open to the public.

[. . .]

Part VI DISCHARGE OF FUNCTIONS

101 ARRANGEMENTS FOR DISCHARGE OF FUNCTIONS BY LOCAL AUTHORITIES

(1)   Subject to any express provision contained in this Act or any Act passed after this Act, a local authority may arrange for the discharge of any of their functions—
(a)   by a committee, a sub-committee or an officer of the authority; or
(b)   by any other local authority.

[. . .]

Part VII MISCELLANEOUS POWERS OF LOCAL AUTHORITIES

Subsidiary powers

111 SUBSIDIARY POWERS OF LOCAL AUTHORITIES

(1)   Without prejudice to any powers exercisable apart from this section but subject to the provisions of this Act and any other enactment passed before or after this Act, a local authority shall have power to do any thing (whether or not involving the expenditure, borrowing or lending of money or the acquisition or disposal of any property or rights) which is calculated to facilitate, or is conducive or incidental to, the discharge of any of their functions.

[. . .]

Part XI GENERAL PROVISIONS AS TO LOCAL AUTHORITIES

Legal proceedings

222 POWER OF LOCAL AUTHORITIES TO PROSECUTE OR DEFEND LEGAL PROCEEDINGS

(1)   Where a local authority consider it expedient for the promotion or protection of the interests of the inhabitants of their area—
(a)   they may prosecute or defend or appear in any legal proceedings and, in the case of civil proceedings, may institute them in their own name, and
(b)   they may, in their own name, make representations in the interests of the inhabitants at any public inquiry held by or on behalf of any Minister or public body under any enactment.

[. . .]

[. . .]

Byelaws

235 POWER OF COUNCILS TO MAKE BYELAWS FOR GOOD RULE AND GOVERNMENT AND SUPPRESSION OF NUISANCES

(1)   The council of a district [the council of a principal area in Wales] and the council of a London borough may make byelaws for the good rule and government of the whole or any part of the district [principal area] or borough, as the case may be, and for the prevention and suppression of nuisances therein.

(2)   The confirming authority in relation to byelaws made under this section shall be the Secretary of State.

(3)   Byelaws shall not be made under this section for any purpose as respects any area if provision for that purpose as respects that area is made by, or is or may be made under, any other enactment.

[. . .]

> *The amendment made to section 2, above, by the Localism Act 2011 Schedule 3 Part 2 and Schedule 25 Part 4, came into force on 4 May 2012*

HOUSE OF COMMONS DISQUALIFICATION ACT 1975
(c. 24)

An Act to consolidate certain enactments relating to disqualification for membership of the House of Commons.

[. . .]

1 DISQUALIFICATION OF HOLDERS OF CERTAIN OFFICES AND PLACES

(1)   Subject to the provisions of this Act, a person is disqualified for membership of the House of Commons who for the time being—
(za) is a Lord Spiritual;
(a)   holds any of the judicial offices specified in Part I of Schedule 1 to this Act;
(b)   is employed in the civil service of the Crown, whether in an established capacity or not, and whether for the whole or part of his time;
(c)   is a member of any of the regular armed forces of the Crown [. . .];
(d)   is a member of any police force maintained by a local policing body or a police authority;
[. . .]
(e)   is a member of the legislature of any country or territory outside the Commonwealth [(other than Ireland)]; or
(f)   holds any office described in Part II or Part III of Schedule 1.
[. . .]

(4)   Except as provided by this Act, a person shall not be disqualified for membership of the House of Commons by reason of his holding an office or place of profit under the Crown

or any other office or place; and a person shall not be disqualified for appointment to or for holding any office or place by reason of his being a member of that House.

2 MINISTERIAL OFFICES

(1)   Not more than ninety-five persons being the holders of offices specified in Schedule 2 to this Act (in this section referred to as Ministerial offices) shall be entitled to sit and vote in the House of Commons at any one time.

(2)   If at any time the number of members of the House of Commons who are holders of Ministerial offices exceeds the number entitled to sit and vote in that House under subsection (1) above, none except any who were both members of that House and holders of Ministerial offices before the excess occurred shall sit or vote therein until the number has been reduced, by death, resignation or otherwise, to the number entitled to sit and vote as aforesaid.

(3)   A person holding a Ministerial office is not disqualified by this Act by reason of any office held by him ex officio as the holder of that Ministerial office.

[. . .]

4 STEWARDSHIP OF CHILTERN HUNDREDS, ETC.

For the purposes of the provisions of this Act relating to the vacation of the seat of a member of the House of Commons who becomes disqualified by this Act for membership of that House, the office of steward or bailiff of Her Majesty's three Chiltern Hundreds of Stoke, Desborough and Burnham, or of the Manor of Northstead, shall be treated as included among the offices described in Part III of Schedule 1 to this Act.

[. . .]

6 EFFECTS OF DISQUALIFICATION AND PROVISION FOR RELIEF

(1)   Subject to any order made by the House of Commons under this section—
       (a) if any person disqualified by this Act for membership of that House, or for membership for a particular constituency, is elected as a member of that House, or as a member for that constituency, as the case may be, his election shall be void; and
       (b) if any person being a member of that House becomes disqualified by this Act for membership, or for membership for the constituency for which he is sitting, his seat shall be vacated.

(2)   If, in a case falling or alleged to fall within subsection (1) above, it appears to the House of Commons that the grounds of disqualification or alleged disqualification under this Act which subsisted or arose at the material time have been removed, and that it is otherwise proper so to do, that House may by order direct that any such disqualification incurred on those grounds at that time shall be disregarded for the purposes of this section.

[. . .]

7 JURISDICTION OF PRIVY COUNCIL AS TO DISQUALIFICATION

(1)   Any person who claims that a person purporting to be a member of the House of Commons is disqualified by this Act, or has been so disqualified at any time since his election, may apply to Her Majesty in Council, in accordance with such rules as Her Majesty in Council may prescribe, for a declaration to that effect.

[. . .]

SCHEDULE 2 MINISTERIAL OFFICES

Prime Minister and First Lord of the Treasury.

Lord President of the Council.

Lord Privy Seal.

Chancellor of the Duchy of Lancaster.

Paymaster General.

Secretary of State.

Chancellor of the Exchequer.

[. . .]

President of the Board of Trade.

Minister of State.

Chief Secretary to the Treasury.

Minister in charge of a public department of Her Majesty's Government in the United Kingdom (if not within the other provisions of this Schedule).

Attorney General.

[. . .]

Solicitor General.

[Advocate General for Scotland]

[. . .]

Parliamentary Secretary to the Treasury.

Financial Secretary to the Treasury.

Parliamentary Secretary in a Government Department other than the Treasury, or not in a department.

Junior Lord of the Treasury.

Treasurer of Her Majesty's Household.

Comptroller of Her Majesty's Household.

Vice-Chamberlain of Her Majesty's Household.

Assistant Government Whip.

As amended by the Police Reform and Social Responsibility Act 2011, Schedule 16, paragraph 123

MINISTERIAL AND OTHER SALARIES ACT 1975
(c. 27)

An Act to consolidate the enactments relating to the salaries of Ministers and Opposition Leaders and Chief Whips and to other matters connected therewith.

[. . .]

1 SALARIES

(1)   Subject to the provisions of this Act—
    (a)   there shall be paid to the holder of any Ministerial office specified in Schedule 1 to this Act such salary as is provided for by that Schedule; and
    (b)   there shall be paid to the Leaders and Whips of the Opposition such salaries as are provided for by Schedule 2 to this Act.

(2)   There shall be paid to the Lord Chancellor a salary (which shall be charged on and paid out of the Consolidated Fund of the United Kingdom) at such rate as together with any salary payable to him as Speaker of the House of Lords will amount to [[£2,500] a year more than the salary for the time being payable to the Lord Chief Justice], [. . .].

(3)   There shall be paid to the Speaker of the House of Commons a salary (which shall be charged on and paid out of the Consolidated Fund of the United Kingdom) of [£75,766] a year; and on a dissolution of Parliament the Speaker of the House of Commons at the time of the dissolution shall for this purpose be deemed to remain Speaker until a Speaker is chosen by the new Parliament.

(3A)   There shall be paid to the Speaker of the House of Lords a salary (which shall be paid out of money provided by Parliament) of [£101,038] a year.

[. . .]

2 OPPOSITION LEADERS AND WHIPS

(1)   In this Act "Leader of the Opposition" means, in relation to either House of Parliament, that Member of that House who is for the time being the Leader in that House of the party in opposition to Her Majesty's Government having the greatest numerical strength in the House of Commons; and "Chief Opposition Whip" means, in relation to either House of Parliament, the person for the time being nominated as such by the Leader of the Opposition in that House; and "Assistant Opposition Whip", in relation to the House of Commons, means a person for the time being nominated as such, and to be paid as such, by the Leader of the Opposition in the House of Commons.

    [. . .]

As amended by the Ministerial and other Salaries Act (Amendment) Order 2011

BRITISH NATIONALITY ACT 1981
(c. 61)

An Act to make fresh provision about citizenship and nationality, and to amend the Immigration Act 1971 as regards the right of abode in the United Kingdom.

[. . .]

Part I BRITISH CITIZENSHIP

Acquisition after commencement

1 ACQUISITION BY BIRTH OR ADOPTION

(1)   A person born in the United Kingdom after commencement [, or in a qualifying territory on or after the appointed day,] shall be a British citizen if at the time of the birth his father or mother is—
(a)   a British citizen; or
(b)   settled in the United Kingdom [or that territory].

[(1A) A person born in the United Kingdom or a qualifying territory on or after the relevant day shall be a British citizen if at the time of the birth his father or mother is a member of the armed forces.]

(2)   A new-born infant who, after commencement, is found abandoned in the United Kingdom [, or on or after the appointed day is found abandoned in a qualifying territory,] shall, unless the contrary is shown, be deemed for the purposes of subsection (1)—
(a)   to have been born in the United Kingdom after commencement [or in that territory on or after the appointed day]; and
(b)   to have been born to a parent who at the time of the birth was a British citizen or settled in the United Kingdom [or that territory].

(3)   A person born in the United Kingdom after commencement who is not a British citizen by virtue of subsection (1)[, (1A)] or (2) shall be entitled to be registered as a British citizen if, while he is a minor—
(a)   his father or mother becomes a British citizen or becomes settled in the United Kingdom; and
(b)   an application is made for his registration as a British citizen.

[(3A) A person born in the United Kingdom on or after the relevant day who is not a British citizen by virtue of subsection (1), (1A) or (2) shall be entitled to be registered as a British citizen if, while he is a minor—
(a)   his father or mother becomes a member of the armed forces; and
(b)   an application is made for his registration as a British citizen]

(4)   A person born in the United Kingdom after commencement who is not a British citizen by virtue of subsection (1)[, (1A)] or (2) shall be entitled, on an application for his registration as a British citizen made at any time after he has attained the age of ten years, to be registered as such a citizen if, as regards each of the first ten years of that person's life, the number of days on which he was absent from the United Kingdom in that year does not exceed 90.

[. . .]

2 ACQUISITION BY DESCENT

(1)   A person born outside the United Kingdom [and the qualifying territories] after
       commencement shall be a British citizen if at the time of the birth his father or mother—
       (a) is a British citizen otherwise than by descent; or
       (b) is a British citizen and is serving outside the United Kingdom [and the qualifying
            territories] in service to which this paragraph applies, his or her recruitment for that
            service having taken place in the United Kingdom [or a qualifying territory]; or
       (c) is a British citizen and is serving outside the United Kingdom [and the qualifying
            territories] in service under a Community institution, his or her recruitment for that
            service having taken place in a country which at the time of the recruitment was a
            member of the Communities.

(2)   Paragraph (b) of subsection (1) applies to—
       (a) Crown service under the government of the United Kingdom [or of a qualifying
            territory]; and
       (b) service of any description for the time being designated under subsection (3).

[. . .]

3 ACQUISITION BY REGISTRATION: MINORS

(1)   If while a person is a minor an application is made for his registration as a British citizen,
       the Secretary of State may, if he thinks fit, cause him to be registered as such a citizen.

(2)   A person born outside the United Kingdom [and the qualifying territories] shall be
       entitled, on an application for his registration as a British citizen made [while he is a
       minor], to be registered as such a citizen if the requirements specified in subsection (3) or,
       in the case of a person born stateless, the requirements specified in paragraphs (a) and (b)
       of that subsection, are fulfilled in the case of either that person's father or his mother ("the
       parent in question").

(3)   The requirements referred to in subsection (2) are—
       (a) that the parent in question was a British citizen by descent at the time of the birth;
            and
       (b) that the father or mother of the parent in question—
            (i)   was a British citizen otherwise than by descent at the time of the birth of the
                  parent in question; or
            (ii) became a British citizen otherwise than by descent at commencement, or would
                  have become such a citizen otherwise than by descent at commencement but for
                  his or her death; and
       (c) that, as regards some period of three years ending with a date not later than the date
            of the birth—
            (i)   the parent in question was in the United Kingdom [or a qualifying territory]
                  at the beginning of that period; and
            (ii) the number of days on which the parent in question was absent from the United
                  Kingdom [and the qualifying territories] in that period does not exceed 270.
       [. . .]

(5)   A person born outside the United Kingdom [and the qualifying territories] shall be
       entitled, on an application for his registration as a British citizen made while he is a minor,
       to be registered as such a citizen if the following requirements are satisfied, namely—
       (a) that at the time of that person's birth his father or mother was a British citizen by
            descent; and

(b) subject to subsection (6), that that person and his father and mother were in the United Kingdom [or a qualifying territory] at the beginning of the period of three years ending with the date of the application and that, in the case of each of them, the number of days on which the person in question was absent from the United Kingdom [and the qualifying territories] in that period does not exceed 270; and

(c) subject to subsection (6), that the consent of his father and mother to the registration has been signified in the prescribed manner.

(6) In the case of an application under subsection (5) for the registration of a person as a British citizen—

(a) if his father or mother died, or their marriage [or civil partnership] was terminated, on or before the date of the application, or his father and mother were legally separated on that date, the references to his father and mother in paragraph (b) of that subsection shall be read either as references to his father or as references to his mother; [and]

(b) if his father or mother died on or before that date, the reference to his father and mother in paragraph (c) of that subsection shall be read as a reference to either of them;

[. . .]

[. . .]

5 ACQUISITION BY REGISTRATION: NATIONALS FOR PURPOSES OF THE COMMUNITY TREATIES

A [British overseas territories citizen] who falls to be treated as a national of the United Kingdom for the purposes of the Community Treaties shall be entitled to be registered as a British citizen if an application is made for his registration as such a citizen.

6 ACQUISITION BY NATURALISATION

(1) If, on an application for naturalisation as a British citizen made by a person of full age and capacity, the Secretary of State is satisfied that the applicant fulfils the requirements of Schedule 1 for naturalisation as such a citizen under this subsection, he may, if he thinks fit, grant to him a certificate of naturalisation as such a citizen.

(2) If, on an application for naturalisation as a British citizen made by a person of full age and capacity who on the date of the application is married to a British citizen, [or is the civil partner of a British citizen] the Secretary of State is satisfied that the applicant fulfils the requirements of Schedule 1 for naturalisation as such a citizen under this subsection, he may, if he thinks fit, grant to him a certificate of naturalisation as such a citizen.

[. . .]

Acquisition at commencement

11 CITIZENS OF U.K. AND COLONIES WHO ARE TO BECOME BRITISH CITIZENS AT COMMENCEMENT

(1) Subject to subsection (2), a person who immediately before commencement—
(a) was a citizen of the United Kingdom and Colonies; and
(b) had the right of abode in the United Kingdom under the Immigration Act 1971 as then in force,
shall at commencement become a British citizen.

(2)   A person who was registered as a citizen of the United Kingdom and Colonies under
section 1 of the British Nationality (No. 2) Act 1964 (stateless persons) on the ground
mentioned in subsection (1)(a) of that section (namely that his mother was a citizen of the
United Kingdom and Colonies at the time when he was born) shall not become a British
citizen under subsection (1) unless—
(a)   his mother becomes a British citizen under subsection (1) or would have done so but
for her death; or
(b)   immediately before commencement he had the right of abode in the United Kingdom
by virtue of section 2(1)(c) of the Immigration Act 1971 as then in force (settlement in
United Kingdom, combined with five or more years' ordinary residence there as a
citizen of the United Kingdom and Colonies).

[. . .]

Part II [BRITISH OVERSEAS TERRITORIES CITIZENSHIP]

Acquisition after commencement

15 ACQUISITION BY BIRTH OR ADOPTION

(1)   A person born in a [British overseas territory] after commencement shall be a [British
overseas territories citizen] if at the time of the birth his father or mother is—
(a)   a [British overseas territories citizen]; or
(b)   settled in a [British overseas territory].

[. . .]

16 ACQUISITION BY DESCENT

(1)   A person born outside the [British overseas territories] after commencement shall be a
[British overseas territories citizen] if at the time of the birth his father or mother—
(a)   is such a citizen otherwise than by descent; or
(b)   is such a citizen and is serving outside the [British overseas territories] in service to
which this paragraph applies, his or her recruitment for that service having taken
place in a [British overseas territory].

[. . .]

Part III BRITISH OVERSEAS CITIZENSHIP

26 CITIZENS OF U.K. AND COLONIES WHO ARE TO BECOME
BRITISH OVERSEAS CITIZENS AT COMMENCEMENT

Any person who was a citizen of the United Kingdom and Colonies immediately before
commencement and who does not at commencement become either a British citizen or a [British
overseas territories citizen] shall at commencement become a British Overseas citizen.

[. . .]

Part V MISCELLANEOUS AND SUPPLEMENTARY

[. . .]

40 DEPRIVATION OF CITIZENSHIP

(1)   In this section a reference to a person's "citizenship status" is a reference to his status as—
(a)   a British citizen,

(b)   a British overseas territories citizen,

(c)   a British Overseas citizen,

(d)   a British National (Overseas),

(e)   a British protected person, or

(f)   a British subject.

[(2)   The Secretary of State may by order deprive a person of a citizenship status if the Secretary of State is satisfied that deprivation is conducive to the public good.]

(3)   The Secretary of State may by order deprive a person of a citizenship status which results from his registration or naturalisation if the Secretary of State is satisfied that the registration or naturalisation was obtained by means of—

(a)   fraud,

(b)   false representation, or

(c)   concealment of a material fact.

(4)   The Secretary of State may not make an order under subsection (2) if he is satisfied that the order would make a person stateless.

(5)   Before making an order under this section in respect of a person the Secretary of State must give the person written notice specifying—

(a)   that the Secretary of State has decided to make an order,

(b)   the reasons for the order, and

(c)   the person's right of appeal under section 40A (1) or under section 2B of the Special Immigration Appeals Commission Act 1997 (c. 68).

[. . .]

42 REGISTRATION AND NATURALISATION: CITIZENSHIP CEREMONY, OATH AND PLEDGE

(1)   A person of full age shall not be registered under this Act as a British citizen unless he has made the relevant citizenship oath and pledge specified in Schedule 5 at a citizenship ceremony.

(2)   A certificate of naturalisation as a British citizen shall not be granted under this Act to a person of full age unless he has made the relevant citizenship oath and pledge specified in Schedule 5 at a citizenship ceremony.

(3)   A person of full age shall not be registered under this Act as a British overseas territories citizen unless he has made the relevant citizenship oath and pledge specified in Schedule 5.

(4)   A certificate of naturalisation as a British overseas territories citizen shall not be granted under this Act to a person of full age unless he has made the relevant citizenship oath and pledge specified in Schedule 5.

(5)   A person of full age shall not be registered under this Act as a British Overseas citizen or a British subject unless he has made the relevant citizenship oath specified in Schedule 5.

[. . .]

44 DECISIONS INVOLVING EXERCISE OF DISCRETION

(1)   Any discretion vested by or under this Act in the Secretary of State, a Governor or a Lieutenant-Governor shall be exercised without regard to the race, colour or religion of any person who may be affected by its exercise.

[. . .]

[. . .]

SCHEDULES

SCHEDULE 1 REQUIREMENTS FOR NATURALISATION

NATURALISATION AS A BRITISH CITIZEN UNDER SECTION 6(1)

1   (1) Subject to paragraph 2, the requirements for naturalisation as a British citizen under
section 6(1) are, in the case of any person who applies for it—
    (a)   the requirements specified in sub-paragraph (2) of this paragraph, or the
alternative requirement specified in sub-paragraph (3) of this paragraph; and
    (b)   that he is of good character; and
    (c)   that he has a sufficient knowledge of the English, Welsh or Scottish Gaelic
language; and
    [(ca) that he has sufficient knowledge about life in the United Kingdom; and]
    (d)   that either—
        (i) his intentions are such that, in the event of a certificate of naturalisation as a
British citizen being granted to him, his home or (if he has more than one)
his principal home will be in the United Kingdom; or
        (ii) he intends, in the event of such a certificate being granted to him, to enter
into, or continue in, Crown service under the government of the United
Kingdom, or service under an international organisation of which the United
Kingdom or Her Majesty's government therein is a member, or service in the
employment of a company or association established in the United Kingdom.

  (2) The requirements referred to in sub-paragraph (1)(a) of this paragraph are—
    (a)   that the applicant was in the United Kingdom at the beginning of the period of
five years ending with the date of the application, and that the number of days on
which he was absent from the United Kingdom in that period does not exceed
450; and
    (b)   that the number of days on which he was absent from the United Kingdom in the
period of twelve months so ending does not exceed 90; and
    (c)   that he was not at any time in the period of twelve months so ending subject
under the immigration laws to any restriction on the period for which he might
remain in the United Kingdom; and
    (d)   that he was not at any time in the period of five years so ending in the United
Kingdom in breach of the immigration laws.

  (3) The alternative requirement referred to in sub-paragraph (1)(a) of this paragraph is
that on the date of the application he is serving outside the United Kingdom in Crown
service under the government of the United Kingdom.

[. . .]

NATURALISATION AS A BRITISH CITIZEN UNDER SECTION 6(2)

3   Subject to paragraph 4, the requirements for naturalisation as a British citizen under
section 6(2) are, in the case of any person who applies for it—
    (a)   that he was in the United Kingdom at the beginning of the period of three years
ending with the date of the application, and that the number of days on which he was
absent from the United Kingdom in that period does not exceed 270; and
    (b)   that the number of days on which he was absent from the United Kingdom in the
period of twelve months so ending does not exceed 90; and
    (c)   that on the date of the application he was not subject under the immigration laws to
any restriction on the period for which he might remain in the United Kingdom; and

(d) that he was not at any time in the period of three years ending with the date of the application in the United Kingdom in breach of the immigration laws; and

(e) the [requirements specified in paragraph 1(1)(b), (c) and (ca)].

[...]

SENIOR COURTS ACT 1981
(c. 54)

An Act to consolidate with amendments the Supreme Court of Judicature (Consolidation) Act 1925 and other enactments relating to the Senior Courts in England and Wales and the administration of justice therein; to repeal certain obsolete or unnecessary enactments so relating; to amend Part VIII of the Mental Health Act 1959, the Courts-Martial (Appeals) Act 1968, the Arbitration Act 1979 and the law relating to county courts; and for connected purposes.

[...]

Part I **CONSTITUTION OF [SENIOR COURTS]**
[...]

The High Court

4 THE HIGH COURT

(1) The High Court shall consist of—

[...]

(b)   the Lord Chief Justice;

[(ba)   the President of the Queen's Bench Division;

(c)   the President of the Family Division;

(d)   the Chancellor of the High Court;]

[(dd)   the Senior Presiding Judge]

[(ddd) the vice-president of the Queen's Bench Division;] and

(e)   not more than [108] puisne judges of that court.

(2) The puisne judges of the High Court shall be styled "Justices of the High Court".

(3) All the judges of the High Court shall, except where this Act expressly provides otherwise, have in all respects equal power, authority and jurisdiction.

[...]

10 APPOINTMENT OF JUDGES OF [SENIOR COURTS]

(1) Whenever the office of Lord Chief Justice, Master of the Rolls, [President of the Queen's Bench Division, President of the Family Division or Chancellor of the High Court] is vacant, Her Majesty [, on the recommendation of the Lord Chancellor] may by letters patent appoint a qualified person to that office.

(2) Subject to the limits on numbers for the time being imposed by sections 2(1) and 4(1), Her Majesty may [,on the recommendation of the Lord Chancellor] from time to time by letters patent appoint qualified persons as Lords Justices of Appeal or as puisne judges of the High Court.

(3) No person shall be qualified for appointment—
   (a) as Lord Chief Justice, Master of the Rolls, [President of the Queen's Bench Division, President of the Family Division or Chancellor of the High Court], unless he is qualified for appointment as a Lord Justice of Appeal or is a judge of the Court of Appeal;
   (b) as a Lord Justice of Appeal, [unless—
      [(i) he satisfies the judicial-appointment eligibility condition on a 7-year basis; or]
      (ii) he is a judge of the High Court;]; or
   (c) as a puisne judge of the High Court, [unless—
      [(i) he satisfies the judicial-appointment eligibility condition on a 7-year basis; or]
      (ii) he is a Circuit judge who has held that office for at least 2 years.]

[. . .]

11 TENURE OF OFFICE OF JUDGES OF [SENIOR COURTS]

(1) This section applies to the office of any judge of the [Senior Courts] [. . .]

(2) A person appointed to an office to which this section applies shall vacate it on the day on which he attains the age of [seventy] years unless by virtue of this section he has ceased to hold it before then.

(3) A person appointed to an office to which this section applies shall hold that office during good behaviour, subject to a power of removal by Her Majesty on an address presented to Her by both Houses of Parliament.

(3A) It is for the Lord Chancellor to recommend to Her Majesty the exercise of the power of removal under subsection (3).

[. . .]

(7) A person who holds an office to which this section applies may at any time resign it by giving the Lord Chancellor notice in writing to that effect.

(8) The Lord Chancellor, if satisfied by means of a medical certificate that a person holding an office to which this section applies—
   (a) is disabled by permanent infirmity from the performance of the duties of his office; and
   (b) is for the time being incapacitated from resigning his office,
   may, subject to subsection (9), by instrument under his hand declare that person's office to have been vacated; and the instrument shall have the like effect for all purposes as if that person had on the date of the instrument resigned his office.

[. . .]

Part II JURISDICTION

[. . .]

The High Court

General jurisdiction

19 GENERAL JURISDICTION OF HIGH COURT

(1) The High Court shall be a superior court of record.

   [. . .]

[. . .]

29 MANDATORY, PROHIBITING AND QUASHING ORDERS

(1) The orders of mandamus, prohibition and certiorari shall be known instead as mandatory, prohibiting and quashing orders respectively.

(1A) The High Court shall have jurisdiction to make mandatory, prohibiting and quashing orders in those classes of case in which, immediately before 1st May 2004, it had jurisdiction to make orders of mandamus, prohibition and certiorari respectively.

(2) Every such order shall be final, subject to any right of appeal therefrom.

(3) In relation to the jurisdiction of the Crown Court, other than its jurisdiction in matters relating to trial on indictment, the High Court shall have all such jurisdiction to make [mandatory, prohibiting or quashing orders] as the High Court possesses in relation to the jurisdiction of an inferior court.

[. . .]

(4) The power of the High Court under any enactment to require justices of the peace or a judge or officer of a county court to do any act relating to the duties of their respective offices, or to require a magistrates' court to state a case for the opinion of the High Court, in any case where the High Court formerly had by virtue of any enactment jurisdiction to make a rule absolute, or an order, for any of those purposes, shall be exercisable by [mandatory order].

[(5) In any statutory provision—
      (a) references to mandamus or to a writ or order of mandamus shall be read as references to a mandatory order;
      (b) references to prohibition or to a writ or order of prohibition shall be read as references to a prohibiting order;
      (c) references to certiorari or to a writ or order of certiorari shall be read as references to a quashing order; and
      (d) references to the issue or award of a writ of mandamus, prohibition or certiorari shall be read as references to the making of the corresponding mandatory, prohibiting or quashing order.]
[. . .]

31 APPLICATION FOR JUDICIAL REVIEW

(1) An application to the High Court for one or more of the following forms of relief, namely—
     [(a) mandatory, prohibiting or quashing order;]
      (b) a declaration or injunction under subsection (2); or
      (c) an injunction under section 30 restraining a person not entitled to do so from acting in an office to which that section applies,
     shall be made in accordance with rules of court by a procedure to be known as an application for judicial review.

(2) A declaration may be made or an injunction granted under this subsection in any case where an application for judicial review, seeking that relief, has been made and the High Court considers that, having regard to—
      (a) the nature of the matters in respect of which relief may be granted by [mandatory, prohibiting or quashing orders];
      (b) the nature of the persons and bodies against whom relief may be granted by such orders; and
      (c) all the circumstances of the case,

it would be just and convenient for the declaration to be made or the injunction to be granted, as the case may be.

(3)   No application for judicial review shall be made unless the leave of the High Court has been obtained in accordance with rules of court; and the court shall not grant leave to make such an application unless it considers that the applicant has a sufficient interest in the matter to which the application relates.

[(4)   On an application for judicial review the High Court may award to the applicant damages, restitution or the recovery of a sum due if—
(a)   the application includes a claim for such an award arising from any matter to which the application relates; and
(b)   the court is satisfied that such an award would have been made if the claim had been made in an action begun by the applicant at the time of making the application.]

[(5)   If, on an application for judicial review, the High Court quashes the decision to which the application relates, it may in addition—
(a)   remit the matter to the court, tribunal or authority which made the decision, with a direction to reconsider the matter and reach a decision in accordance with the findings of the High Court, or
(b)   substitute its own decision for the decision in question.

(5A)   But the power conferred by subsection (5)(b) is exercisable only if—
(a)   the decision in question was made by a court or tribunal,
(b)   the decision is quashed on the ground that there has been an error of law, and
(c)   without the error, there would have been only one decision which the court or tribunal could have reached.

(5B)   Unless the High Court otherwise directs, a decision substituted by it under subsection (5)(b) has effect as if it were a decision of the relevant court or tribunal.]

(6)   Where the High Court considers that there has been undue delay in making an application for judicial review, the court may refuse to grant—
(a)   leave for the making of the application; or
(b)   any relief sought on the application,
if it considers that the granting of the relief sought would be likely to cause substantial hardship to, or substantially prejudice the rights of, any person or would be detrimental to good administration.

(7)   Subsection (6) is without prejudice to any enactment or rule of court which has the effect of limiting the time within which an application for judicial review may be made.

[. . .]

CONTEMPT OF COURT ACT 1981

An Act to amend the law relating to contempt of court and related matters.

Strict liability

1 THE STRICT LIABILITY RULE

In this Act "the strict liability rule" means the rule of law whereby conduct may be treated as a contempt of court as tending to interfere with the course of justice in particular legal proceedings regardless of intent to do so.

2 LIMITATION OF SCOPE OF STRICT LIABILITY

(1)   The strict liability rule applies only in relation to publications, and for this purpose "publication" includes any speech, writing, programme included in a cable programme service or other communication in whatever form, which is addressed to the public at large or any section of the public.

(2)   The strict liability rule applies only to a publication which creates a substantial risk that the course of justice in the proceedings in question will be seriously impeded or prejudiced.

(3)   The strict liability rule applies to a publication only if the proceedings in question are active within the meaning of this section at the time of the publication.

(4)   Schedule 1 applies for determining the times at which proceedings are to be treated as active within the meaning of this section.

In this section "programme service" has the same meaning as in the Broadcasting Act 1990.

3 DEFENCE OF INNOCENT PUBLICATION OR DISTRIBUTION

(1)   A person is not guilty of contempt of court under the strict liability rule as the publisher of any matter to which that rule applies if at the time of publication (having taken all reasonable care) he does not know and has no reason to suspect that relevant proceedings are active.

(2)   A person is not guilty of contempt of court under the strict liability rule as the distributor of a publication containing any such matter if at the time of distribution (having taken all reasonable care) he does not know that it contains such matter and has no reason to suspect that it is likely to do so.

(3)   The burden of proof of any fact tending to establish a defence afforded by this section to any person lies upon that person.

(4)   Section 11 of the Administration of Justice Act 1960 is repealed.

4 CONTEMPORARY REPORTS OF PROCEEDINGS

(1)   Subject to this section a person is not guilty of contempt of court under the strict liability rule in respect of a fair and accurate report of legal proceedings held in public, published contemporaneously and in good faith.

(2)   In any such proceedings the court may, where it appears to be necessary for avoiding a substantial risk of prejudice to the administration of justice in those proceedings, or in any other proceedings pending or imminent, order that the publication of any report of the proceedings, or any part of the proceedings, be postponed for such period as the court thinks necessary for that purpose.

Where in proceedings for any offence which is an administration of justice offence for the purposes of section 54 of the Criminal Procedure and Investigations Act 1996 (acquittal tainted by an administration of justice offence) it appears to the court that there is a possibility that (by virtue of that section) proceedings may be taken against a person for an offence of which he has been acquitted, subsection (2) of this section shall apply as if those proceedings were pending or imminent.

(3)   For the purposes of subsection (1) of this section and of section 3 of the Law of Libel Amendment Act 1888 (privilege) a report of proceedings shall be treated as published contemporaneously—

(a) in the case of a report of which publication is postponed pursuant to an order under subsection (2) of this section, if published as soon as practicable after that order expires;

(b) in the case of a report of committal proceedings of which publication is permitted by virtue only of subsection (3) of section 8 of the Magistrates' Courts Act 1980, if published as soon as practicable after publication is so permitted.

(4) Subsection 9 of the said section 8 is repealed.

5 DISCUSSION OF PUBLIC AFFAIRS

A publication made as or as part of a discussion in good faith of public affairs or other matters of general public interest is not to be treated as a contempt of court under the strict liability rule if the risk of impediment or prejudice to particular legal proceedings is merely incidental to the discussion.

6 SAVINGS

Nothing in the foregoing provisions of this Act—

(a) prejudices any defence available at common law to a charge of contempt of court under the strict liability rule;

(b) implies that any publication is punishable as contempt of court under that rule which would not be so punishable apart from those provisions;

(c) restricts liability for contempt of court in respect of conduct intended to impede or prejudice the administration of justice.

7 CONSENT REQUIRED FOR INSTITUTION OF PROCEEDINGS

Proceedings for a contempt of court under the strict liability rule (other than Scottish proceedings) shall not be instituted except by or with the consent of the Attorney General or on the motion of a court having jurisdiction to deal with it.

Other aspects of law and procedure

8 CONFIDENTIALITY OF JURY'S DELIBERATIONS

(1) Subject to subsection (2) below, it is a contempt of court to obtain, disclose or solicit any particulars of statements made, opinions expressed, arguments advanced or votes cast by members of a jury in the course of their deliberations in any legal proceedings.

(2) This section does not apply to any disclosure of any particulars—

(a) in the proceedings in question for the purpose of enabling the jury to arrive at their verdict, or in connection with the delivery of that verdict, or

(b) in evidence in any subsequent proceedings for an offence alleged to have been committed in relation to the jury in the first mentioned proceedings,
or to the publication of any particulars so disclosed.

(3) Proceedings for a contempt of court under this section (other than Scottish proceedings) shall not be instituted except by or with the consent of the Attorney General or on the motion of a court having jurisdiction to deal with it.

9 USE OF TAPE RECORDERS

(1) Subject to subsection (4) below, it is a contempt of court—

    (a) to use in court, or bring into court for use, any tape recorder or other instrument for recording sound, except with the leave of the court;

    (b) to publish a recording of legal proceedings made by means of any such instrument, or any recording derived directly or indirectly from it, by playing it in the hearing of the public or any section of the public, or to dispose of it or any recording so derived, with a view to such publication;

    (c) to use any such recording in contravention of any conditions of leave granted under paragraph (a).

(2) Leave under paragraph (a) of subsection (1) may be granted or refused at the discretion of the court, and if granted may be granted subject to such conditions as the court thinks proper with respect to the use of any recording made pursuant to the leave; and where leave has been granted the court may at the like discretion withdraw or amend it either generally or in relation to any particular part of the proceedings.

(3) Without prejudice to any other power to deal with an act of contempt under paragraph (a) of subsection (1), the court may order the instrument, or any recording made with it, or both, to be forfeited; and any object so forfeited shall (unless the court otherwise determines on application by a person appearing to be the owner) be sold or otherwise disposed of in such manner as the court may direct.

(4) This section does not apply to the making or use of sound recordings for purposes of official transcripts of proceedings.

10 SOURCES OF INFORMATION

No court may require a person to disclose, nor is any person guilty of contempt of court for refusing to disclose, the source of information contained in a publication for which he is responsible, unless it be established to the satisfaction of the court that disclosure is necessary in the interests of justice or national security or for the prevention of disorder or crime.

REPRESENTATION OF THE PEOPLE ACT 1983
(c. 2)

An Act to consolidate the Representation of the People Acts of 1949, 1969, 1977, 1978, and 1980, the Electoral Registers Acts of 1949 and 1953, the Elections (Welsh Forms) Act 1964, Part III of the Local Government Act 1972, sections 6 to 10 of the Local Government (Scotland) Act 1973, the Representation of the People (Armed Forces) Act 1976, the Returning Officers (Scotland) Act 1977, section 3 of the Representation of the People Act 1981, section 62 of and Schedule 2 to the Mental Health (Amendment) Act 1982, and connected provisions; and to repeal as obsolete the Representation of the People Act 1979 and other enactments related to the Representation of the People Acts.

[. . .]

Part I **PARLIAMENTARY AND LOCAL GOVERNMENT FRANCHISE AND ITS EXERCISE**

Parliamentary and local government franchise

[1 PARLIAMENTARY ELECTORS

(1)   A person is entitled to vote as an elector at a parliamentary election in any constituency if on the date of the poll he—
(a)   is registered in the register of parliamentary electors for that constituency;
(b)   is not subject to any legal incapacity to vote (age apart);
(c)   is either a Commonwealth citizen or a citizen of the Republic of Ireland; and
(d)   is of voting age (that is, 18 years or over).

(2)   A person is not entitled to vote as an elector—
(a)   more than once in the same constituency at any parliamentary election; or
(b)   in more than one constituency at a general election.]

[. . .]

Part II THE ELECTION CAMPAIGN

[. . .]

75 PROHIBITION OF EXPENSES NOT AUTHORISED BY ELECTION AGENT

(1)   No expenses shall, with a view to promoting or procuring the election of a candidate [(or, in the case of an election of the London members of the London Assembly at an ordinary election, a registered political party or candidates of that party)] at an election, be incurred [after he becomes a candidate at that election] by any person other than the candidate, his election agent and persons authorised in writing by the election agent on account—
(a)   of holding public meetings or organising any public display; or
(b)   of issuing advertisements, circulars or publications; or
(c)   of otherwise presenting to the electors the candidate or his views or the extent or nature of his backing or disparaging another candidate [or
(d)   in the case of an election of the London members of the London Assembly at an ordinary election, of otherwise presenting to the electors the candidate's registered political party (if any) or the views of that party or the extent or nature of that party's backing or disparaging any other registered political party]
[. . .] this subsection shall not—
(i)   restrict the publication of any matter relating to the election in a newspaper or other periodical or in a broadcast made by the British Broadcasting Corporation or [or by Sianel Pedwar Cymru or in a programme included in any service licensed under Part I or III of the Broadcasting Act 1990 [or Part I or II of the Broadcasting Act 1996];]
[. . .]
(ii)   apply to any expenses [incurred by any person which do not exceed in the aggregate the permitted sum (and are not incurred by that person as part of a concerted plan of action),] or to expenses incurred by any person in travelling or in living away from home or similar personal expenses.

(1ZZA) Paragraph (c) or (d) of subsection (1) above does not restrict the publication of any matter relating to the election in—
(a) a newspaper or other periodical,
(b) a broadcast made by the British Broadcasting Corporation or by Sianel Pedwar Cymru, or
(c) a programme included in any service licensed under Part 1 or 3 of the Broadcasting Act 1990 or Part 1 or 2 of the Broadcasting Act 1996.

(1ZZB) Subsection (1) above does not apply to any expenses incurred by any person—
(a) which do not exceed in the aggregate the permitted sum (and are not incurred by that person as part of a concerted plan of action), or
(b) in travelling or in living away from home or similar personal expenses.

(1ZA)   For the purposes of [subsection (1ZZB)(a)] above, "the permitted sum" means—
(a) in respect of a candidate at a parliamentary election, £500;
(b) in respect of a candidate at a local government election, £50 together with an additional 0.5p for every entry in the register of local government electors for the electoral area in question as it has effect on the last day for publication of notice of the election;
and expenses shall be regarded as incurred by a person "as part of a concerted plan of action" if they are incurred by that person in pursuance of any plan or other arrangement whereby that person and one or more other persons are to incur, with a view to promoting or procuring the election of the same candidate, expenses which (disregarding [subsection (1ZZB)(a)] fall within subsection (1) above.
[. . .]

(2)   Where a person incurs any expenses required by this section to be authorised by the election agent—
(a) that person shall [within 21 days after the day on which the result of the election is declared deliver] to the appropriate officer a return of the amount of those expenses, stating the election at which and the candidate in whose support they were incurred, and
(b) the return shall be accompanied by a declaration made by that person (or in the case of an association or body of persons, by a director, general manager, secretary or other similar officer of the association or body) verifying the return and giving particulars of the matters for which the expenses were incurred.
but this subsection does not apply to any person engaged or employed for payment or promise of payment by the candidate or his election agent.

[. . .]

(5)   If a person—
(a) incurs, or aids, abets, counsels or procures any other person to incur, any expenses in contravention of this section, or
(b) knowingly makes the declaration required by subsection (2) falsely, he shall be guilty of a corrupt practice; and if a person fails to [deliver or] send any declaration or return or a copy of it as required by this section he shall be guilty of an illegal practice, but—
(i) the court before whom a person is convicted under this subsection may, if they think it just in the special circumstances of the case, mitigate or entirely remit any incapacity imposed by virtue of section 173 below; and
(ii) a candidate shall not be liable, nor shall his election be avoided, for a corrupt or illegal practice under this subsection committed by an agent without his consent or connivance.

[. . .]

93 BROADCASTING OF LOCAL ITEMS DURING ELECTION PERIOD

(1) Each broadcasting authority shall adopt a code of practice with respect to the participation of candidates at a parliamentary or local government election in items about the constituency or electoral area in question which are included in relevant services during the election period.

(2) The code for the time being adopted by a broadcasting authority under this section shall be either—
(a) a code drawn up by that authority, whether on their own or jointly with one or more other broadcasting authorities, or
(b) a code drawn up by one or more other such authorities;
and a broadcasting authority shall from time to time consider whether the code for the time being so adopted by them should be replaced by a further code falling within paragraph (a) or (b).

(3) Before drawing up a code under this section a broadcasting authority shall have regard to any views expressed by the Electoral Commission for the purposes of this subsection; and any such code may make different provision for different cases.

(4) [The Office of Communications shall] do all that they can to secure that the code for the time being adopted by them under this section is observed in the provision of relevant services; and the British Broadcasting Corporation and Sianel Pedwar Cymru shall each observe in the provision of relevant services the code so adopted by them.

(5) For the purposes of subsection (1) "the election period", in relation to an election, means the period beginning—
(a) (if a parliamentary general election) with the date of the dissolution of Parliament ,
(b) (if a parliamentary by-election) with the date of the issue of the writ for the election or any earlier date on which a certificate of the vacancy is notified in the London Gazette in accordance with the Recess Elections Act 1975, or
(c) (if a local government election) with the last date for publication of notice of the election,
and ending with the close of the poll.

(6) In this section—

"broadcasting authority" means the British Broadcasting Corporation, [the Office of Communications] or Sianel Pedwar Cymru;

"candidate", in relation to an election, means a candidate standing nominated at the election or included in a list of candidates submitted in connection with it;

[. . .]

Amended by the Fixed-Term Parliaments Act 2011, Schedule, paragraph 8

POLICE AND CRIMINAL EVIDENCE ACT 1984
(c. 60)

An Act to make further provision in relation to the powers and duties of the police, persons in police detention, criminal evidence, police discipline and complaints against the police; to provide for arrangements for obtaining the views of the community on policing and for a rank of deputy chief constable; to amend the law relating to the Police Federations and Police Forces and Police Cadets in Scotland; and for connected purposes.

[. . .]

Part I **POWERS TO STOP AND SEARCH**

1 POWER OF CONSTABLE TO STOP AND SEARCH PERSONS, VEHICLES ETC.

(1)   A constable may exercise any power conferred by this section—
   (a)   in any place to which at the time when he proposes to exercise the power the public or any section of the public has access, on payment or otherwise, as of right or by virtue of express or implied permission; or
   (b)   in any other place to which people have ready access at the time when he proposes to exercise the power but which is not a dwelling.

(2)   Subject to subsection (3) to (5) below, a constable—
   (a)   may search—
      (i)   any person or vehicle;
      (ii) anything which is in or on a vehicle,
      for stolen or prohibited articles [, any article to which subsection (8A) below applies or any firework to which subsection (8B) below applies]; and
   (b)   may detain a person or vehicle for the purpose of such a search.

(3)   This section does not give a constable power to search a person or vehicle or anything in or on a vehicle unless he has reasonable grounds for suspecting that he will find stolen or prohibited articles [, any article to which subsection (8A) below applies or any firework to which subsection (8B) below applies].

(4)   If a person is in a garden or yard occupied with and used for the purposes of a dwelling or on other land so occupied and used, a constable may not search him in the exercise of the power conferred by this section unless the constable has reasonable grounds for believing—
   (a)   that he does not reside in the dwelling; and
   (b)   that he is not in the place in question with the express or implied permission of a person who resides in the dwelling.

(5)   If a vehicle is in a garden or yard occupied with and used for the purposes of a dwelling or on other land so occupied and used, a constable may not search the vehicle or anything in or on it in the exercise of the power conferred by this section unless he has reasonable grounds for believing—
   (a)   that the person in charge of the vehicle does not reside in the dwelling; and
   (b)   that the vehicle is not in the place in question with the express or implied permission of a person who resides in the dwelling.

(6)   If in the course of such a search a constable discovers an article which he has reasonable grounds for suspecting to be a stolen or prohibited article [, an article to which subsection (8A) below applies or a firework to which subsection (8B) below applies], he may seize it.

(7)   An article is prohibited for the purposes of this Part of this Act if it is—
   (a)   an offensive weapon; or
   (b)   an article—
      (i)   made or adapted for use in the course of or in connection with an offence to which this sub-paragraph applies; or
      (ii) intended by the person having it with him for such use by him or by some other person.

(8)   The offences to which subsection (7)(b)(i) above applies are—
(a) burglary;
(b) theft;
(c) offences under section 12 of the Theft Act 1968 (taking motor vehicle or other conveyance without authority); [. . .]
[(d) fraud (contrary to section 1 of the Fraud Act 2006)] [; and
(e) offences under section 1 of the Criminal Damage Act 1971 (destroying or damaging property).]

[(8A) This subsection applies to any article in relation to which a person has committed, or is committing or is going to commit an offence under section 139 of the Criminal Justice Act 1988.]

[(8B) This subsection applies to any firework which a person possesses in contravention of a prohibition imposed by fireworks regulations.

(8C) In this section—
(a) "firework" shall be construed in accordance with the definition of "fireworks" in section 1(1) of the Fireworks Act 2003; and
(b) "fireworks regulations" has the same meaning as in that Act.]

(9)   In this Part of this Act "offensive weapon" means any article—
(a) made or adapted for use for causing injury to persons; or
(b) intended by the person having it with him for such use by him or by some other person.

2 PROVISIONS RELATING TO SEARCH UNDER SECTION 1 AND OTHER POWERS

(1)   A constable who detains a person or vehicle in the exercise—
(a) of the power conferred by section 1 above; or
(b) of any other power—
(i)   to search a person without first arresting him; or
(ii) to search a vehicle without making an arrest,
need not conduct a search if it appears to him subsequently—
(i)   that no search is required; or
(ii) that a search is impracticable.

(2)   If a constable contemplates a search, other than a search of an unattended vehicle, in the exercise—
(a) of the power conferred by section 1 above; or
(b) of any other power, except the power conferred by section 6 below and the power conferred by section 27(2) of the Aviation Security Act 1982—
(i)   to search a person without first arresting him; or
(ii) to search a vehicle without making an arrest,
it shall be his duty, subject to subsection (4) below, to take reasonable steps before he commences the search to bring to the attention of the appropriate person—
(i)   if the constable is not in uniform, documentary evidence that he is a constable; and
(ii) whether he is in uniform or not, the matters specified in subsection (3) below;
and the constable shall not commence the search until he has performed that duty.

(3)   The matters referred to in subsection (2)(ii) above are—
(a) the constable's name and the name of the police station to which he is attached;
(b) the object of the proposed search;
(c) the constable's grounds for proposing to make it; and
(d) the effect of section 3(7) or (8) below, as may be appropriate.

(4)   A constable need not bring the effect of section 3(7) or (8) below to the attention of the appropriate person if it appears to the constable that it will not be practicable to make the record in section 3(1) below.

(5)   In this section "the appropriate person" means—
      (a) if the constable proposes to search a person, that person; and
      (b) if he proposes to search a vehicle, or anything in or on a vehicle, the person in charge of the vehicle.

(6)   On completing a search of an unattended vehicle or anything in or on such a vehicle in the exercise of any such power as is mentioned in subsection (2) above a constable shall leave a notice—
      (a) stating that he has searched it;
      (b) giving the name of the police station to which he is attached;
      (c) stating that an application for compensation for any damage caused by the search may be made to that police station; and
      (d) stating the effect of section 3(8) below.

(7)   The constable shall leave the notice inside the vehicle unless it is not reasonably practicable to do so without damaging the vehicle.

(8)   The time for which a person or vehicle may be detained for the purposes of such a search is such time as is reasonably required to permit a search to be carried out either at the place where the person or vehicle was first detained or nearby.

(9)   Neither the power conferred by section 1 above nor any other power to detain and search a person without first arresting him or to detain and search a vehicle without making an arrest is to be construed—
      (a) as authorising a constable to require a person to remove any of his clothing in public other than an outer coat, jacket or gloves; or
      (b) as authorising a constable not in uniform to stop a vehicle.

[. . .]

3 DUTY TO MAKE RECORDS CONCERNING SEARCHES

(1)   Where a constable has carried out a search in the exercise of any such power as is mentioned in section 2(1) above, other than a search—
      (a) under section 6 below; or
      (b) under section 27(2) of the Aviation Security Act 1982, a record of the search shall be made in writing unless it is not practicable to do so.

(2)   If a record of a search is required to be made by subsection (1) above-
      (a) in a case where the search results in a person being arrested and taken to a police station, the constable shall secure that the record is made as part of the person's custody record;
      (b) in any other case, the constable shall make the record on the spot, or, if that is not practicable, as soon as practicable after the completion of the search

(6)   The record of a search of a person or a vehicle—
      (a) shall state—
           (i)   the object of the search;
           (ii) the grounds for making it;
           (iii) the date and time when it was made;
           (iv) the place where it was made;

(v) except in the case of a search of an unattended vehicle, the ethnic origins of the person searched or the person in charge of the vehicle searched (as the case may be) and

(b) shall identify the constable who carried out the search.

(6A) The requirement in subsection 6(a)(v) above for a record to state a person's ethnic origins is a requirement to state-
(a) the thnic origins of the person as described by the person, and
(b) if different, the ethnic origins of the person as perceived by the constable

(7) If a record of a search of a person has been made under his section, the person who was searched shall be entitled to a copy of the record if he asks for one before the end of the period specified in subsection (9) below.

(8) If—
(a) the owner of a vehicle which has been searched or the person who was in charge of the vehicle at the time when it was searched asked for a copy of the record of the search before the end of the period specified in subsection (9) below; and
(b) a record of the search of the vehicle has been made under this section,

(9) The period mentioned in subsections (7) and (8) above is the period of 3 months beginning with the date on which the search was made.

[. . .]

4 ROAD CHECKS

(1) This section shall have effect in relation to the conduct of road checks by police officers for the purpose of ascertaining whether a vehicle is carrying—
(a) a person who has committed an offence other than a road traffic offence or a [vehicle] excise offence;
(b) a person who is a witness to such an offence;
(c) a person intending to commit such an offence; or
(d) a person who is unlawfully at large.

(2) For the purposes of this section a road check consists of the exercise in a locality of the power conferred by [section 163 of the Road Traffic Act 1988.] in such a way as to stop during the period for which its exercise in that way in that locality continues all vehicles or vehicles selected by any criterion.

(3) Subject to subsection (5) below, there may only be such a road check if a police officer of the rank of superintendent or above authorises it in writing.

(4) An officer may only authorise a road check under subsection (3) above—
(a) for the purpose specified in subsection (1)(a) above, if he has reasonable grounds—
(i) for believing that the offence is [an indictable offence]; and
(ii) for suspecting that the person is, or is about to be, in the locality in which vehicles would be stopped if the road check were authorised;
(b) for the purpose specified in subsection (1)(b) above, if he has reasonable grounds for believing that the offence is [an indictable offence];
(c) for the purpose specified in subsection (1)(c) above, if he has reasonable grounds—
(i) for believing that the offence would be [an indictable offence]; and
(ii) for suspecting that the person is, or is about to be, in the locality in which vehicles would be stopped if the road check were authorised;
(d) for the purpose specified in subsection (1)(d) above, if he has reasonable grounds for suspecting that the person is, or is about to be, in that locality.

(5)   An officer below the rank of superintendent may authorise such a road check if it appears to him that it is required as a matter of urgency for one of the purposes specified in subsection (1) above.

(6)   If an authorisation is given under subsection (5) above, it shall be the duty of the officer who gives it—
   (a) to make a written record of the time at which he gives it; and
   (b) to cause an officer of the rank of superintendent or above to be informed that it has been given.

(7)   The duties imposed by subsection (6) above shall be performed as soon as it is practicable to do so.
       [. . .]

(15)   Where a vehicle is stopped in a road check, the person in charge of the vehicle at the time when it is stopped shall be entitled to obtain a written statement of the purpose of the road check if he applies for such a statement not later than the end of the period of twelve months from the day on which the vehicle was stopped.

(16)   Nothing in this section affects the exercise by police officers of any power to stop vehicles for purposes other than those specified in subsection (1) above.
       [. . .]

Part II **POWERS OF ENTRY, SEARCH AND SEIZURE**

Search warrants

8 POWER OF JUSTICE OF THE PEACE TO AUTHORISE ENTRY AND SEARCH OF PREMISES

(1)   If on an application made by a constable a justice of the peace is satisfied that there are reasonable grounds for believing—
   (a) that [an indictable offence] has been committed; and
   (b) that there is material on premises [mentioned in subsection (1A) below] which is likely to be of substantial value (whether by itself or together with other material) to the investigation of the offence; and
   (c) that the material is likely to be relevant evidence; and
   (d) that it does not consist of or include items subject to legal privilege, excluded material or special procedure material; and
   (e) that any of the conditions specified in subsection (3) below applies [in relation to each set of premises specified in the application],
   he may issue a warrant authorising a constable to enter and search the premises.

[(1A) The premises referred to in subsection (1)(b) above are—
   (a) one or more sets of premises specified in the application (in which case the application is for a "specific premises warrant"); or
   (b) any premises occupied or controlled by a person specified in the application, including such sets of premises as are so specified (in which case the application is for an "all premises warrant").

(1B) If the application is for an all premises warrant, the justice of the peace must also be satisfied—
   (a) that because of the particulars of the offence referred to in paragraph (a) of subsection (1) above, there are reasonable grounds for believing that it is necessary to

search premises occupied or controlled by the person in question which are not specified in the application in order to find the material referred to in paragraph (b) of that subsection; and

(b) that it is not reasonably practicable to specify in the application all the premises which he occupies or controls and which might need to be searched.]

[(1C) The warrant may authorise entry to and search of premises on more than one occasion if, on the application, the justice of the peace is satisfied that it is necessary to authorise multiple entries in order to achieve the purpose for which he issues the warrant.

(1D) If it authorises multiple entries, the number of entries authorised may be unlimited, or limited to a maximum.]

(2) A constable may seize and retain anything for which a search has been authorised under subsection (1) above.

(3) The conditions mentioned in subsection (1)(e) above are—
(a) that it is not practicable to communicate with any person entitled to grant entry to the premises;
(b) that it is practicable to communicate with a person entitled to grant entry to the premises but it is not practicable to communicate with any person entitled to grant access to the evidence;
(c) that entry to the premises will not be granted unless a warrant is produced;
(d) that the purpose of a search may be frustrated or seriously prejudiced unless a constable arriving at the premises can secure immediate entry to them.

(4) In this Act "relevant evidence", in relation to an offence, means anything that would be admissible in evidence at a trial for the offence.

(5) The power to issue a warrant conferred by this section is in addition to any such power otherwise conferred.

[. . .]

9 SPECIAL PROVISIONS AS TO ACCESS

(1) A constable may obtain access to excluded material or special procedure material for the purposes of a criminal investigation by making an application under Schedule 1 below and in accordance with that Schedule.

(2) Any Act (including a local Act) passed before this Act under which a search of premises for the purposes of a criminal investigation could be authorised by the issue of a warrant to a constable shall cease to have effect so far as it relates to the authorisation of searches—
(a) for items subject to legal privilege; or
(b) for excluded material; or
(c) for special procedure material consisting of documents or records other than documents.
[. . .]

10 MEANING OF "ITEMS SUBJECT TO LEGAL PRIVILEGE"

(1) Subject to subsection (2) below, in this Act "items subject to legal privilege" means—
(a) communications between a professional legal adviser and his client or any person representing his client made in connection with the giving of legal advice to the client;

(b)   communications between a professional legal adviser and his client or any person representing his client or between such an adviser or his client or any such representative and any other person made in connection with or in contemplation of legal proceedings and for the purposes of such proceedings; and

(c)   items enclosed with or referred to in such communications and made—
  (i)   in connection with the giving of legal advice; or
  (ii)   in connection with or in contemplation of legal proceedings and for the purposes of such proceedings,

when they are in the possession of a person who is entitled to possession of them.

(2)   Items held with the intention of furthering a criminal purpose are not items subject to legal privilege.

11 MEANING OF "EXCLUDED MATERIAL"

(1)   Subject to the following provisions of this section, in this Act "excluded material" means—
  (a)   personal records which a person has acquired or created in the course of any trade, business, profession or other occupation or for the purposes of any paid or unpaid office and which he holds in confidence;
  (b)   human tissue or tissue fluid which has been taken for the purposes of diagnosis or medical treatment and which a person holds in confidence;
  (c)   journalistic material which a person holds in confidence and which consists—
    (i)   of documents; or
    (ii)   of records other than documents.

(2)   A person holds material other than journalistic material in confidence for the purposes of this section if he holds it subject—
  (a)   to an express or implied undertaking to hold it in confidence; or
  (b)   to a restriction on disclosure or an obligation of secrecy contained in any enactment, including an enactment contained in an Act passed after this Act.

(3)   A person holds journalistic material in confidence for the purposes of this section if—
  (a)   he holds it subject to such an undertaking, restriction or obligation; and
  (b)   it has been continuously held (by one or more persons) subject to such an undertaking, restriction or obligation since it was first acquired or created for the purposes of journalism.

12 MEANING OF "PERSONAL RECORDS"

In this Part of this Act "personal records" means documentary and other records concerning an individual (whether living or dead) who can be identified from them and relating—

(a)   to his physical or mental health;

(b)   to spiritual counselling or assistance given or to be given to him; or

(c)   to counselling or assistance given or to be given to him, for the purposes of his personal welfare, by any voluntary organisation or by any individual who—
  (i)   by reason of his office or occupation has responsibilities for his personal welfare; or
  (ii)   by reason of an order of a court has responsibilities for his supervision.

13 MEANING OF "JOURNALISTIC MATERIAL"

(1)   Subject to subsection (2) below, in this Act "journalistic material" means material acquired or created for the purposes of journalism.

(2)   Material is only journalistic material for the purposes of this Act if it is in the possession of a person who acquired or created it for the purposes of journalism.

(3)   A person who receives material from someone who intends that the recipient shall use it for the purposes of journalism is to be taken to have acquired it for those purposes.

14 MEANING OF "SPECIAL PROCEDURE MATERIAL"

(1)   In this Act "special procedure material" means—
       (a) material to which subsection (2) below applies; and
       (b) journalistic material, other than excluded material.

(2)   Subject to the following provisions of this section, this subsection applies to material, other than items subject to legal privilege and excluded material, in the possession of a person who—
       (a) acquired or created it in the course of any trade, business, profession or other occupation or for the purpose of any paid or unpaid office; and
       (b) holds it subject—
            (i)   to an express or implied undertaking to hold it in confidence; or
            (ii) to a restriction or obligation such as is mentioned in section 11(2)(b) above.
       [. . .]

15 SEARCH WARRANTS—SAFEGUARDS

(1)   This section and section 16 below have effect in relation to the issue to constables under any enactment, including an enactment contained in an Act passed after this Act, of warrants to enter and search premises; and an entry on or search of premises under a warrant is unlawful unless it complies with this section and section 16 below.

(2)   Where a constable applies for any such warrant, it shall be his duty—
       (a) to state—
            (i)   the ground on which he makes the application; [. . .]
            (ii) the enactment under which the warrant would be issued; [and]
            [(iii) if the application is for a warrant authorising entry and search on more than one occasion, the ground on which he applies for such a warrant, and whether he seeks a warrant authorising an unlimited number of entries, or (if not) the maximum number of entries desired;]
       [(b) to specify the matters set out in subsection (2A) below; and]
       (c) to identify, so far as is practicable, the articles or persons to be sought.

(2A)   The matters which must be specified pursuant to subsection (2)(b) above are—
       [(a) if the application relates to one or more sets of premises specified in the application, each set of premises which it is desired to enter and search;
       (b) if the application relates to any premises occupied or controlled by a person specified in the application—
            (i)   as many sets of premises which it is desired to enter and search as it is reasonably practicable to specify;
            (ii) the person who is in occupation or control of those premises and any others which it is desired to enter and search;
            (iii) why it is necessary to search more premises than those specified under sub-paragraph (i); and
            (iv) why it is not reasonably practicable to specify all the premises which it is desired to enter and search.

(3)   An application for such a warrant shall be made ex parte and supported by an information in writing.

(4)   The constable shall answer on oath any question that the justice of the peace or judge hearing the application asks him.

(5)   A warrant shall authorise an entry on one occasion only [unless it specifies that it authorises multiple entries] .

[(5A) If it specifies that it authorises multiple entries, it must also specify whether the number of entries authorised is unlimited, or limited to a specified maximum.]

(6)   A warrant—
       (a) shall specify—
            (i)   the name of the person who applies for it;
            (ii) the date on which it is issued;
            (iii) the enactment under which it is issued; and
            [(iv) each set of premises to be searched, or (in the case of an all premises warrant) the person who is in occupation or control of premises to be searched, together with any premises under his occupation or control which can be specified and which are to be searched; and]
       (b) shall identify, so far as is practicable, the articles or persons to be sought.
       [. . .]

16 EXECUTION OF WARRANTS

(1)   A warrant to enter and search premises may be executed by any constable.

(2)   Such a warrant may authorise persons to accompany any constable who is executing it.

[(2A) A person so authorised has the same powers as the constable whom he accompanies in respect of—
       (a) the execution of the warrant, and
       (b) the seizure of anything to which the warrant relates.

(2B) But he may exercise those powers only in the company, and under the supervision, of a constable.]

(3)   Entry and search under a warrant must be within [three months] from the date of its issue.

[(3A) If the warrant is an all premises warrant, no premises which are not specified in it may be entered or searched unless a police officer of at least the rank of inspector has in writing authorised them to be entered.]

[(3B) No premises may be entered or searched for the second or any subsequent time under a warrant which authorises multiple entries unless a police officer of at least the rank of inspector has in writing authorised that entry to those premises.]

(4)   Entry and search under a warrant must be at a reasonable hour unless it appears to the constable executing it that the purpose of a search may be frustrated on an entry at a reasonable hour.

(5)   Where the occupier of premises which are to be entered and searched is present at the time when a constable seeks to execute a warrant to enter and search them, the constable—

   (a) shall identify himself to the occupier and, if not in uniform, shall produce to him
     . documentary evidence that he is a constable;

   (b) shall produce the warrant to him; and

   (c) shall supply him with a copy of it.

(6)   Where—

   (a) the occupier of such premises is not present at the time when a constable seeks to
      execute such a warrant; but

   (b) some other person who appears to the constable to be in charge of the premises is
      present,

   subsection (5) above shall have effect as if any reference to the occupier were a reference
   to that other person.

(7)   If there is no person present who appears to the constable to be in charge of the premises,
   he shall leave a copy of the warrant in a prominent place on the premises.

(8)   A search under a warrant may only be a search to the extent required for the purpose for
   which the warrant was issued.

(9)   A constable executing a warrant shall make an endorsement on it stating—

   (a) whether the articles or persons sought were found; and

   (b) whether any articles were seized, other than articles which were sought

   [and, unless the warrant is a [. . .] warrant specifying one set of premises only, he shall do
   so separately in respect of each set of premises entered and searched, which he shall in
   each case state in the endorsement.]

[. . .]

Entry and search without search warrant

17 ENTRY FOR PURPOSE OF ARREST ETC.

(1)   Subject to the following provisions of this section, and without prejudice to any other
   enactment, a constable may enter and search any premises for the purpose—

   (a) of executing—

     (i) a warrant of arrest issued in connection with or arising out of criminal
        proceedings; or

     (ii) a warrant of commitment issued under section 76 of the Magistrates' Courts
        Act 1980;

   (b) of arresting a person for an [indictable] offence;

   (c) of arresting a person for an offence under—

     (i) section 1 (prohibition of uniforms in connection with political objects), [. . .] of
        the Public Order Act 1936;

     [. . .]

     [(iii) section 4 of the Public Order Act 1986 (fear or provocation of violence);]

     [. . .]

     [(iv) section 76 of the Criminal Justice and Public Order Act 1994 (failure to comply
        with interim possession order);]

     [. . .]

   (d) of recapturing [any person whatever] who is unlawfully at large and whom he is
      pursuing; or

   (e) of saving life or limb or preventing serious damage to property.

(2)   Except for the purpose specified in paragraph (e) of subsection (1) above, the powers of
   entry and search conferred by this section—

(a) are only exercisable if the constable has reasonable grounds for believing that the person whom he is seeking is on the premises; and

(b) are limited, in relation to premises consisting of two or more separate dwellings, to powers to enter and search—

   (i) any parts of the premises which the occupiers of any dwelling comprised in the premises use in common with the occupiers of any other such dwelling; and

   (ii) any such dwelling in which the constable has reasonable grounds for believing that the person whom he is seeking may be.

(3) The powers of entry and search conferred by this section are only exercisable for the purposes specified in subsection (1)(c)(ii) [or (iv)] above by a constable in uniform.

(4) The power of search conferred by this section is only a power to search to the extent that is reasonably required for the purpose for which the power of entry is exercised.

(5) Subject to subsection (6) below, all the rules of common law under which a constable has power to enter premises without a warrant are hereby abolished.

(6) Nothing in subsection (5) above affects any power of entry to deal with or prevent a breach of the peace.

18 ENTRY AND SEARCH AFTER ARREST

(1) Subject to the following provisions of this section, a constable may enter and search any premises occupied or controlled by a person who is under arrest for an [indictable] offence, if he has reasonable grounds for suspecting that there is on the premises evidence, other than items subject to legal privilege, that relates—

(a) to that offence; or

(b) to some other [indictable] offence which is connected with or similar to that offence.

(2) A constable may seize and retain anything for which he may search under subsection (1) above.

(3) The power to search conferred by subsection (1) above is only a power to search to the extent that is reasonably required for the purpose of discovering such evidence.

(4) Subject to subsection (5) below, the powers conferred by this section may not be exercised unless an officer of the rank of inspector or above has authorised them in writing.

[(5) A constable may conduct a search under subsection (1)—

(a) before the person is taken to a police station or released on bail under section 30A, and

(b) without obtaining an authorisation under subsection (4),

if the condition in subsection (5A) is satisfied.

(5A) The condition is that the presence of the person at a place (other than a police station) is necessary for the effective investigation of the offence.]

(6) If a constable conducts a search by virtue of subsection (5) above, he shall inform an officer of the rank of inspector or above that he has made the search as soon as practicable after he has made it.

(7) An officer who—

(a) authorises a search; or

(b) is informed of a search under subsection (6) above, shall make a record in writing—

    (i)   of the grounds for the search; and

    (ii) of the nature of the evidence that was sought.

[. . .]

Seizure etc.

19 GENERAL POWER OF SEIZURE ETC.

(1)   The powers conferred by subsections (2), (3) and (4) below are exercisable by a constable who is lawfully on any premises.

(2)   The constable may seize anything which is on the premises if he has reasonable grounds for believing—

    (a)   that it has been obtained in consequence of the commission of an offence; and

    (b)   that it is necessary to seize it in order to prevent it being concealed, lost, damaged, altered or destroyed.

(3)   The constable may seize anything which is on the premises if he has reasonable grounds for believing—

    (a)   that it is evidence in relation to an offence which he is investigating or any other offence; and

    (b)   that it is necessary to seize it in order to prevent the evidence being concealed, lost, altered or destroyed.

(4)   The constable may require any information which is [stored in any electronic form] and is accessible from the premises to be produced in a form in which it can be taken away and in which it is visible and legible [or from which it can readily be produced in a visible and legible form] if he has reasonable grounds for believing—

    (a)   that—

        (i)   it is evidence in relation to an offence which he is investigating or any other offence; or

        (ii) it has been obtained in consequence of the commission of an offence; and

    (b)   that it is necessary to do so in order to prevent it being concealed, lost, tampered with or destroyed.

(5)   The powers conferred by this section are in addition to any power otherwise conferred.

[. . .]

20 EXTENSION OF POWERS OF SEIZURE TO COMPUTERISED INFORMATION

(1)   Every power of seizure which is conferred by an enactment to which this section applies on a constable who has entered premises in the exercise of a power conferred by an enactment shall be construed as including a power to require any information [stored in any electronic form] and accessible from the premises to be produced in a form in which it can be taken away and in which it is visible and legible [or from which it can readily be produced in a visible and legible form].

(2)   This section applies—

    (a)   to any enactment contained in an Act passed before this Act;

    (b)   to sections 8 and 18 above;

    (c)   to paragraph 13 of Schedule 1 to this Act; and

    (d)   to any enactment contained in an Act passed after this Act.

21 ACCESS AND COPYING

(1)   A constable who seizes anything in the exercise of a power conferred by any enactment, including an enactment contained in an Act passed after this Act, shall, if so requested by a person showing himself—
(a) to be the occupier of premises on which it was seized; or
(b) to have had custody or control of it immediately before the seizure,
provide that person with a record of what he seized.

(2)   The officer shall provide the record within a reasonable time from the making of the request for it.

(3)   Subject to subsection (8) below, if a request for permission to be granted access to anything which—
(a) has been seized by a constable; and
(b) is retained by the police for the purpose of investigating an offence,
is made to the officer in charge of the investigation by a person who had custody or control of the thing immediately before it was so seized or by someone acting on behalf of such a person, the officer shall allow the person who made the request access to it under the supervision of a constable.

(4)   Subject to subsection (8) below, if a request for a photograph or copy of any such thing is made to the officer in charge of the investigation by a person who had custody or control of the thing immediately before it was so seized, or by someone acting on behalf of such a person, the officer shall—
(a) allow the person who made the request access to it under the supervision of a constable for the purpose of photographing or copying it; or
(b) photograph or copy it, or cause it to be photographed or copied.

(5)   A constable may also photograph or copy, or have photographed or copied, anything which he has power to seize, without a request being made under subsection (4) above.

(6)   Where anything is photographed or copied under subsection (4)(b) above, the photograph or copy shall be supplied to the person who made the request.

(7)   The photograph or copy shall be so supplied within a reasonable time from the making of the request.

(8)   There is no duty under this section to grant access to, or to supply a photograph or copy of, anything if the officer in charge of the investigation for the purposes of which it was seized has reasonable grounds for believing that to do so would prejudice—
(a) that investigation;
(b) the investigation of an offence other than the offence for the purposes of investigating which the thing was seized; or
(c) any criminal proceedings which may be brought as a result of—
(i)   the investigation of which he is in charge; or
(ii) any such investigation as is mentioned in paragraph (b) above.

[(9)   The references to a constable in subsections (1), (2), (3)(a) and (5) include a person authorised under section 16(2) to accompany a constable executing a warrant.]

22 RETENTION

(1)   Subject to subsection (4) below, anything which has been seized by a constable or taken away by a constable following a requirement made by virtue of section 19 or 20 above may be retained so long as is necessary in all the circumstances.

(2)   Without prejudice to the generality of subsection (1) above—
(a) anything seized for the purposes of a criminal investigation may be retained, except as
provided by subsection (4) below—
(i)   for use as evidence at a trial for an offence; or
(ii) for forensic examination or for investigation in connection with an offence; and
(b) anything may be retained in order to establish its lawful owner, where there are
reasonable grounds for believing that it has been obtained in consequence of the
commission of an offence.

(3)   Nothing seized on the ground that it may be used—
(a) to cause physical injury to any person;
(b) to damage property;
(c) to interfere with evidence; or
(d) to assist in escape from police detention or lawful custody,
may be retained when the person from whom it was seized is no longer in police detention
or the custody of a court or is in the custody of a court but has been released on bail.

(4)   Nothing may be retained for either of the purposes mentioned in subsection (2)(a) above if
a photograph or copy would be sufficient for that purpose.

       [. . .]

[. . .]

Part III **ARREST**

[24 ARREST WITHOUT WARRANT: CONSTABLES

(1)   A constable may arrest without a warrant—
(a) anyone who is about to commit an offence;
(b) anyone who is in the act of committing an offence;
(c) anyone whom he has reasonable grounds for suspecting to be about to commit an
offence;
(d) anyone whom he has reasonable grounds for suspecting to be committing an offence.

(2)   If a constable has reasonable grounds for suspecting that an offence has been committed,
he may arrest without a warrant anyone whom he has reasonable grounds to suspect of
being guilty of it.

(3)   If an offence has been committed, a constable may arrest without a warrant—
(a) anyone who is guilty of the offence;
(b) anyone whom he has reasonable grounds for suspecting to be guilty of it.

(4)   But the power of summary arrest conferred by subsection (1), (2) or (3) is exercisable only
if the constable has reasonable grounds for believing that for any of the reasons
mentioned in subsection (5) it is necessary to arrest the person in question.

(5)   The reasons are—
(a) to enable the name of the person in question to be ascertained (in the case where the
constable does not know, and cannot readily ascertain, the person's name, or has
reasonable grounds for doubting whether a name given by the person as his name is
his real name);
(b) correspondingly as regards the person's address;
(c) to prevent the person in question—
(i)   causing physical injury to himself or any other person;
(ii) suffering physical injury;

(iii) causing loss of or damage to property;

(iv) committing an offence against public decency (subject to subsection (6)); or

(v) causing an unlawful obstruction of the highway;

(d) to protect a child or other vulnerable person from the person in question;

(e) to allow the prompt and effective investigation of the offence or of the conduct of the person in question;

(f) to prevent any prosecution for the offence from being hindered by the disappearance of the person in question.

(6) Subsection (5)(c)(iv) applies only where members of the public going about their normal business cannot reasonably be expected to avoid the person in question.]

24A ARREST WITHOUT WARRANT: OTHER PERSONS

(1) A person other than a constable may arrest without a warrant—

(a) anyone who is in the act of committing an indictable offence;

(b) anyone whom he has reasonable grounds for suspecting to be committing an indictable offence.

(2) Where an indictable offence has been committed, a person other than a constable may arrest without a warrant—

(a) anyone who is guilty of the offence;

(b) anyone whom he has reasonable grounds for suspecting to be guilty of it.

(3) But the power of summary arrest conferred by subsection (1) or (2) is exercisable only if—

(a) the person making the arrest has reasonable grounds for believing that for any of the reasons mentioned in subsection (4) it is necessary to arrest the person in question; and

(b) it appears to the person making the arrest that it is not reasonably practicable for a constable to make it instead.

(4) The reasons are to prevent the person in question—

(a) causing physical injury to himself or any other person;

(b) suffering physical injury;

(c) causing loss of or damage to property; or

(d) making off before a constable can assume responsibility for him.]

[. . .]

28 INFORMATION TO BE GIVEN ON ARREST

(1) Subject to subsection (5) below, where a person is arrested, otherwise than by being informed that he is under arrest, the arrest is not lawful unless the person arrested is informed that he is under arrest as soon as is practicable after his arrest.

(2) Where a person is arrested by a constable, subsection (1) above applies regardless of whether the fact of the arrest is obvious.

(3) Subject to subsection (5) below, no arrest is lawful unless the person arrested is informed of the ground for the arrest at the time of, or as soon as is practicable after, the arrest.

(4) Where a person is arrested by a constable, subsection (3) above applies regardless of whether the ground for the arrest is obvious.

(5) Nothing in this section is to be taken to require a person to be informed—

(a) that he is under arrest; or

(b) of the ground for the arrest,

if it was not reasonably practicable for him to be so informed by reason of his having escaped from arrest before the information could be given.

29 VOLUNTARY ATTENDANCE AT POLICE STATION ETC.

Where for the purpose of assisting with an investigation a person attends voluntarily at a police station or at any other place where a constable is present or accompanies a constable to a police station or any such other place without having been arrested—
(a)   he shall be entitled to leave at will unless he is placed under arrest;

(b)   he shall be informed at once that he is under arrest if a decision is taken by a constable to prevent him from leaving at will.

30 ARREST ELSEWHERE THAN AT POLICE STATION

[(1)   Subsection (1A) applies where a person is, at any place other than a police station—
(a)   arrested by a constable for an offence, or
(b)   taken into custody by a constable after being arrested for an offence by a person other than a constable.

(1A)   The person must be taken by a constable to a police station as soon as practicable after the arrest.

(1B)   Subsection (1A) has effect subject to section 30A (release on bail) and subsection (7) (release without bail).]

(2)   Subject to subsections (3) and (5) below, the police station to which an arrested person is taken under [subsection (1A)] above shall be a designated police station.

(3)   A constable to whom this subsection applies may take an arrested person to any police station unless it appears to the constable that it may be necessary to keep the arrested person in police detention for more than six hours.

(4)   Subsection (3) above applies—
(a)   to a constable who is working in a locality covered by a police station which is not a designated police station; and
(b)   to a constable belonging to a body of constables maintained by an authority other than a local policing body.

(5)   Any constable may take an arrested person to any police station if—
(a)   either of the following conditions is satisfied—
(i)   the constable has arrested him without the assistance of any other constable and no other constable is available to assist him;
(ii)   the constable has taken him into custody from a person other than a constable without the assistance of any other constable and no other constable is available to assist him; and
(b)   it appears to the constable that he will be unable to take the arrested person to a designated police station without the arrested person injuring himself, the constable or some other person.

(6)   If the first police station to which an arrested person is taken after his arrest is not a designated police station, he shall be taken to a designated police station not more than six hours after his arrival at the first police station unless he is released previously.

[(7)   A person arrested by a constable at any place other than a police station must be released without bail if the condition in subsection (7A) is satisfied.

(7A)   The condition is that, at any time before the person arrested reaches a police station, a constable is satisfied that there are no grounds for keeping him under arrest or releasing him on bail under section 30A.]

(8)   A constable who releases a person under subsection (7) above shall record the fact that he has done so.

(9)   The constable shall made the record as soon as is practicable after the release.

[(10)   Nothing in subsection (1A) or in section 30A prevents a constable delaying taking a person to a police station or releasing him on bail if the condition in subsection (10A) is satisfied.

(10A)   The condition is that the presence of the person at a place (other than a police station) is necessary in order to carry out such investigations as it is reasonable to carry out immediately.

(11)   Where there is any such delay the reasons for the delay must be recorded when the person first arrives at the police station or (as the case may be) is released on bail.]

[. . .]

30A BAIL ELSEWHERE THAN AT POLICE STATION

(1)   A constable may release on bail a person who is arrested or taken into custody in the circumstances mentioned in section 30(1).

(2)   A person may be released on bail under subsection (1) at any time before he arrives at a police station.

(3)   A person released on bail under subsection (1) must be required to attend a police station.

(3A)   Where a constable releases a person on bail under subsection (1)—
        (a) no recognizance for the person's surrender to custody shall be taken from the person,
        (b) no security for the person's surrender to custody shall be taken from the person or from anyone else on the person's behalf,
        (c) the person shall not be required to provide a surety or sureties for his surrender to custody, and
        (d) no requirement to reside in a bail hostel may be imposed as a condition of bail.

(3B)   Subject to subsection (3A), where a constable releases a person on bail under subsection (1) the constable may impose, as conditions of the bail, such requirements as appear to the constable to be necessary—
        (a) to secure that the person surrenders to custody,
        (b) to secure that the person does not commit an offence while on bail,
        (c) to secure that the person does not interfere with witnesses or otherwise obstruct the course of justice, whether in relation to himself or any other person, or
        (d) for the person's own protection or, if the person is under the age of 17, for the person's own welfare or in the person's own interests.

(4)   Where a person is released on bail under subsection (1), a requirement may be imposed on the person as a condition of bail only under the preceding provisions of this section.]

(5)   The police station which the person is required to attend may be any police station.

[30B BAIL UNDER SECTION 30A: NOTICES

(1)   Where a constable grants bail to a person under section 30A, he must give that person a notice in writing before he is released.

(2)   The notice must state—
(a) the offence for which he was arrested, and
(b) the ground on which he was arrested.

(3)   The notice must inform him that he is required to attend a police station.

(4)   It may also specify the police station which he is required to attend and the time when he is required to attend.

[. . .]

[. . .]

[30D FAILURE TO ANSWER TO BAIL UNDER SECTION 30A

(1)   A constable may arrest without a warrant a person who—
(a) has been released on bail under section 30A subject to a requirement to attend a specified police station, but
(b) fails to attend the police station at the specified time.
[. . .]

[. . .]

31 ARREST FOR FURTHER OFFENCE. WHERE—

(a)   a person—
(i)   has been arrested for an offence; and
(ii) is at a police station in consequence of that arrest; and

(b)   it appears to a constable that, if he were released from that arrest, he would be liable to arrest for some other offence,

He shall be arrested for that other offence.

32 SEARCH UPON ARREST

(1)   A constable may search an arrested person, in any case where the person to be searched has been arrested at a place other than a police station, if the constable has reasonable grounds for believing that the arrested person may present a danger to himself or others.

(2)   Subject to subsections (3) to (5) below, a constable shall also have power in any such case—
(a) to search the arrested person for anything—
(i)   which he might use to assist him to escape from lawful custody; or
(ii) which might be evidence relating to an offence; and
[(b) if the offence for which he has been arrested is an indictable offence, to enter and search any premises in which he was when arrested or immediately before he was arrested for evidence relating to the offence.]

(3)   The power to search conferred by subsection (2) above is only a power to search to the extent that is reasonably required for the purpose of discovering any such thing or any such evidence.

(4)   The powers conferred by this section to search a person are not to be construed as authorising a constable to require a person to remove any of his clothing in public other than an outer coat, jacket or gloves [but they do authorise a search of a person's mouth].

(5)   A constable may not search a person in the exercise of the power conferred by subsection (2)(a) above unless he has reasonable grounds for believing that the person to be searched may have concealed on him anything for which a search is permitted under that paragraph.

(6)   A constable may not search premises in the exercise of the power conferred by subsection (2)(b) above unless he has reasonable grounds for believing that there is evidence for which a search is permitted under that paragraph on the premises.

(7)   In so far as the power of search conferred by subsection (2)(b) above relates to premises consisting of two or more separate dwellings, it is limited to a power to search—
       (a)   any dwelling in which the arrest took place or in which the person arrested was immediately before his arrest; and
       (b)   any parts of the premises which the occupier of any such dwelling uses in common with the occupiers of any other dwellings comprised in the premises.

(8)   A constable searching a person in the exercise of the power conferred by subsection (1) above may seize and retain anything he finds, if he has reasonable grounds for believing that the person searched might use it to cause physical injury to himself or to any other person.

(9)   A constable searching a person in the exercise of the power conferred by subsection (2)(a) above may seize and retain anything he finds, other than an item subject to legal privilege, if he has reasonable grounds for believing—
       (a)   that he might use it to assist him to escape from lawful custody; or
       (b)   that it is evidence of an offence or has been obtained in consequence of the commission of an offence.
       [. . .]

[. . .]

Part IV DETENTION

Detention—conditions and duration

34 LIMITATIONS ON POLICE DETENTION

(1)   A person arrested for an offence shall not be kept in police detention except in accordance with the provisions of this Part of this Act.

(2)   Subject to subsection (3) below, if at any time a custody officer—
       (a)   becomes aware, in relation to any person in police detention, that the grounds for the detention of that person have ceased to apply; and
       (b)   is not aware of any other grounds on which the continued detention of that person could be justified under the provision of this Part of this Act,
       it shall be the duty of the custody officer, subject to subsection (4) below, to order his immediate release from custody.

(3)   No person in police detention shall be released except on the authority of a custody officer at the police station where his detention was authorised or, if it was authorised at more than one station, a custody officer at the station where it was last authorised.

(4)   A person who appears to the custody officer to have been unlawfully at large when he was arrested is not to be released under subsection (2) above.

       [. . .]

35 DESIGNATED POLICE STATIONS

(1)   The chief officer of police for each police area shall designate the police stations in his area which, subject to [sections 30(3) and (5), 30A (5) and 30D (2)], are to be the stations in that area to be used for the purpose of detaining arrested persons.

(2)   A chief officer's duty under subsection (1) above is to designate police stations appearing to him to provide enough accommodation for that purpose.

[. . .]

(3)   Without prejudice to section 12 of the Interpretation Act 1978 (continuity of duties) a chief officer—
(a) may designate a station which was not previously designated; and
(b) may direct that a designation of a station previously made shall cease to operate.
[. . .]

36 CUSTODY OFFICERS AT POLICE STATIONS

(1)   One or more custody officers shall be appointed for each designated police station.

(2)   A custody officer for [a police station designated under section 35(1) above] shall be appointed—
(a) by the chief officer of police for the area in which the designated police station is situated; or
(b) by such other police officer as the chief officer of police for that area may direct.
[. . .]

[(3) No officer may be appointed a custody officer unless the officer is of at least the rank of sergeant.]

(4)   An officer of any rank may perform the functions of a custody officer at a designated police station if a custody officer is not readily available to perform them.

(5)   Subject to the following provisions of this section and to section 39(2) below, none of the functions of a custody officer in relation to a person shall be performed by an officer who at the time when the function falls to be performed is involved in the investigation of an offence for which that person is in police detention at that time.

[. . .]

37 DUTIES OF CUSTODY OFFICER BEFORE CHARGE

(1)   Where—
(a) a person is arrested for an offence—
(i)   without a warrant; or
(ii) under a warrant not endorsed for bail, [. . .]
(b) [. . .]
the custody officer at each police station where he is detained after his arrest shall determine whether he has before him sufficient evidence to charge that person with the offence for which he was arrested and may detain him at the police station for such period as is necessary to enable him to do so.

(2)   If the custody officer determines that he does not have such evidence before him, the person arrested shall be released either on bail or without bail, unless the custody officer has reasonable grounds for believing that his detention without being charged is necessary to secure or preserve evidence relating to an offence for which he is under arrest or to obtain such evidence by questioning him.

(3)   If the custody officer has reasonable grounds for so believing, he may authorise the person arrested to be kept in police detention.

(4)   Where a custody officer authorises a person who has not been charged to be kept in police detention, he shall, as soon as is practicable, make a written record of the grounds for the detention.

(5)   Subject to subsection (6) below, the written record shall be made in the presence of the person arrested who shall at that time be informed by the custody officer of the grounds for his detention.

(6)   Subsection (5) above shall not apply where the person arrested is, at the time when the written record is made—
       (a)   incapable of understanding what is said to him;
       (b)   violent or likely to become violent; or
       (c)   in urgent need of medical attention.

(7)   Subject to section 41(7) below, if the custody officer determines that he has before him sufficient evidence to charge the person arrested with the offence for which he was arrested, the person arrested—
       [(a)   [shall be—
               (i)   released without charge and on bail, or
               (ii)   kept in police detention,
               for the purpose] of enabling the Director of Public Prosecutions to make a decision under section 37B below,
       (b)   shall be released without charge and on bail but not for that purpose,
       (c)   shall be released without charge and without bail, or
       (d)   shall be charged.]

[(7A) The decision as to how a person is to be dealt with under subsection (7) above shall be that of the custody officer.

(7B)   Where a person is [dealt with under subsection (7)(a)] above, it shall be the duty of the custody officer to inform him that he is being released [, or (as the case may be) detained,] to enable the Director of Public Prosecutions to make a decision under section 37B below.]

(8)   Where—
       (a)   a person is released under subsection (7)(b) [or (c)] above; and
       (b)   at the time of his release a decision whether he should be prosecuted for the offence for which he was arrested has not been taken,
       it shall be the duty of the custody officer so to inform him.

       [. . .]

(9)   If the person arrested is not in a fit state to be dealt with under subsection (7) above, he may be kept in police detention until he is.

(10)   The duty imposed on the custody officer under subsection (1) above shall be carried out by him as soon as practicable after the person arrested arrives at the police station or, in the case of a person arrested at the police station, as soon as practicable after the arrest.

       [. . .]

[. . .]

38 DUTIES OF CUSTODY OFFICER AFTER CHARGE

(1)   Where a person arrested for an offence otherwise than under a warrant endorsed for bail is charged with an offence, the custody officer shall [, subject to section 25 of the Criminal

Justice and Public Order Act 1994,] order his release from police detention, either on bail or without bail, unless—

(a) If the person arrested is not an arrested juvenile—

  (i)   his name or address cannot be ascertained or the custody officer has reasonable grounds for doubting whether a name or address furnished by him as his name or address is his real name or address;

  [(ii)   the custody officer has reasonable grounds for believing that the person arrested will fail to appear in court to answer to bail;

  (iii)   in the case of a person arrested for an imprisonable offence, the custody officer has reasonable grounds for believing that the detention of the person arrested is necessary to prevent him from committing an offence;

  [(iiia) in a case where a sample may be taken from the person under section 63B below, the custody officer has reasonable grounds for believing that the detention of the person is necessary to enable the sample to be taken from him;]

  (iv)   in the case of a person arrested for an offence which is not an imprisonable offence, the custody officer has reasonable grounds for believing that the detention of the person arrested is necessary to prevent him from causing physical injury to any other person or from causing loss of or damage to property;

  (v)   the custody officer has reasonable grounds for believing that the detention of the person arrested is necessary to prevent him from interfering with the administration of justice or with the investigation of offences or of a particular offence; or

  (vi)   the custody officer has reasonable grounds for believing that the detention of the person arrested is necessary for his own protection;

(b) if he is an arrested juvenile—

  (i)   any of the requirements of paragraph (a) above is satisfied [(but, in the case of paragraph (a)(iiia) above, only if the arrested juvenile has attained the minimum age)]; or

  (ii)   the custody officer has reasonable grounds for believing that he ought to be detained in his own interests

[(c) the offence with which the person is charged is murder.

(2)   If the release of a person arrested is not required by subsection (1) above, the custody officer may authorise him to be kept in police detention [but may not authorise a person to be kept in police detention by virtue of subsection (1)(a)(iiia) after the end of the period of six hours beginning when he was charged with the offence].

      [. . .]

(3)   Where a custody officer authorises a person who has been charged to be kept in police detention, he shall, as soon as practicable, make a written record of the grounds for the detention.

(4)   Subject to subsection (5) below, the written record shall be made in the presence of the person charged who shall at that time be informed by the custody officer of the grounds for his detention.

(5)   Subsection (4) above shall not apply where the person charged is, at the time when the written record is made—

(a) incapable of understanding what is said to him;

(b) violent or likely to become violent; or

(c) in urgent need of medical attention.

      [. . .]

39 RESPONSIBILITIES IN RELATION TO PERSONS DETAINED

(1) Subject to subsections (2) and (4) below, it shall be the duty of the custody officer at a police station to ensure—

(a) that all persons in police detention at that station are treated in accordance with this Act and any code of practice issued under it and relating to the treatment of persons in police detention; and

(b) that all matters relating to such persons which are required by this Act or by such codes of practice to be recorded are recorded in the custody records relating to such persons.

(2) If the custody officer, in accordance with any code of practice issued under this Act, transfers or permits the transfer of a person in police detention—

(a) to the custody of a police officer investigating an offence for which that person is in police detention; or

(b) to the custody of an officer who has charge of that person outside the police station,

the custody officer shall cease in relation to that person to be subject to the duty imposed on him by subsection (1)(a) above; and it shall be the duty of the officer to whom the transfer is made to ensure that he is treated in accordance with the provisions of this Act and of any such codes of practice as are mentioned in subsection (1) above.

[. . .]

40 REVIEW OF POLICE DETENTION

(1) Reviews of the detention of each person in police detention in connection with the investigation of an offence shall be carried out periodically in accordance with the following provisions of this section—

(a) in the case of a person who has been arrested and charged, by the custody officer; and

(b) in the case of a person who has been arrested but not charged, by an officer of at least the rank of inspector who has not been directly involved in the investigation.

(2) The officer to whom it falls to carry out a review is referred to in this section as a "review officer".

(3) Subject to subsection (4) below—

(a) the first review shall be not later than six hours after the detention was first authorised;

(b) the second review shall be not later than nine hours after the first;

(c) subsequent reviews shall be at intervals of not more than nine hours.

(4) A review may be postponed—

(a) if, having regard to all the circumstances prevailing at the latest time for it specified in subsection (3) above, it is not practicable to carry out the review at that time;

(b) without prejudice to the generality of paragraph (a) above—

(i) if at that time the person in detention is being questioned by a police officer and the review officer is satisfied that an interruption of the questioning for the purpose of carrying out the review would prejudice the investigation in connection with which he is being questioned; or

(ii) if at that time no review officer is readily available.

(5) If a review is postponed under subsection (4) above it shall be carried out as soon as practicable after the latest time specified for it in subsection (3) above.

(6) If a review is carried out after postponement under subsection (4) above, the fact that it

was so carried out shall not affect any requirement of this section as to the time at which any subsequent review is to be carried out.

[. . .]

[. . .]

41 LIMITS ON PERIOD OF DETENTION WITHOUT CHARGE

(1)   Subject to the following provisions of this section and to sections 42 and 43 below, a person shall not be kept in police detention for more than 24 hours without being charged.

(2)   The time from which the period of detention of a person is to be calculated (in this Act referred to as "the relevant time")—
   (a)   in the case of a person to whom this paragraph applies, shall be—
      (i)   the time at which that person arrives at the relevant police station; or
      (ii) the time 24 hours after the time of that person's arrest,
      whichever is the earlier;
   (b)   in the case of a person arrested outside England and Wales, shall be—
      (i)   the time at which that person arrives at the first police station to which he is taken in the police area in England or Wales in which the offence for which he was arrested is being investigated; or
      (ii) the time 24 hours after the time of that person's entry into England and Wales, whichever is the earlier;
   (c)   in the case of a person who—
      (i)   attends voluntarily at a police station; or
      (ii) accompanies a constable to a police station without having been arrested,
      and is arrested at the police station, the time of his arrest;
   [(ca) in the case of a person who attends a police station to answer to bail granted under section 30A, the time when he arrives at the police station;]
   (d)   in any other case, except where subsection (5) below applies, shall be the time at which the person arrested arrives at the first police station to which he is taken after his arrest.

[. . .]

(7)   Subject to subsection (8) below, a person who at the expiry of 24 hours after the relevant time is in police detention and has not been charged shall be released at that time either on bail or without bail.

(8)   Subsection (7) above does not apply to a person whose detention for more than 24 hours after the relevant time has been authorised or is otherwise permitted in accordance with section 42 or 43 below.

[. . .]

42 AUTHORISATION OF CONTINUED DETENTION

(1)   Where a police officer of the rank of superintendent or above who is responsible for the police station at which a person is detained has reasonable grounds for believing that—
   (a)   the detention of that person without charge is necessary to secure or preserve evidence relating to an offence for which he is under arrest or to obtain such evidence by questioning him;

        [(b) an offence for which he is under arrest is an [indictable] offence; and]

        (c)   the investigation is being conducted diligently and expeditiously,

            he may authorise the keeping of that person in police detention for a period expiring at or before 36 hours after the relevant time.

(2)   Where an officer such as is mentioned in subsection (1) above has authorised the keeping of a person in police detention for a period expiring less than 36 hours after the relevant time, such an officer may authorise the keeping of that person in police detention for a further period expiring not more than 36 hours after that time if the conditions specified in subsection (1) above are still satisfied when he gives the authorisation.

(3)   If it is proposed to transfer a person in police detention to another police area, the officer determining whether or not to authorise keeping him in detention under subsection (1) above shall have regard to the distance and the time the journey would take.

(4)   No authorisation under subsection (1) above shall be given in respect of any person—

        (a) more than 24 hours after the relevant time; or

        (b) before the second review of his detention under section 40 above has been carried out.

(5)   Where an officer authorises the keeping of a person in police detention under subsection (1) above, it shall be his duty—

        (a) to inform that person of the grounds for his continued detention; and

        (b) to record the grounds in that person's custody record.

(6)   Before determining whether to authorise the keeping of a person in detention under subsection (1) or (2) above, an officer shall give—

        (a) that person; or

        (b) any solicitor representing him who is available at the time when it falls to the officer to determine whether to give the authorisation,

        an opportunity to make representations to him about the detention.

        [. . .]

(9)   Where—

        (a) an officer authorises the keeping of a person in detention under subsection (1) above; and

        (b) at the time of the authorisation he has not yet exercised a right conferred on him by section 56 or 58 below,

        the officer—

        (i)   shall inform him of that right;

        (ii) shall decide whether he should be permitted to exercise it;

        (iii) shall record the decision in his custody record; and

        (iv) if the decision is to refuse to permit the exercise of the right, shall also record the grounds for the decision in that record.

(10) Where an officer has authorised the keeping of a person who has not been charged in detention under subsection (1) or (2) above, he shall be released from detention, either on bail or without bail, not later than 36 hours after the relevant time, unless—

        (a) he has been charged with an offence; or

        (b) his continued detention is authorised or otherwise permitted in accordance with section 43 below.

        [. . .]

43 WARRANTS OF FURTHER DETENTION

(1) Where, on an application on oath made by a constable and supported by an information, a magistrates' court is satisfied that there are reasonable grounds for believing that the further detention of the person to whom the application relates is justified, it may issue a warrant of further detention authorising the keeping of that person in police detention.

(2) A court may not hear an application for a warrant of further detention unless the person to whom the application relates—
(a) has been furnished with a copy of the information; and
(b) has been brought before the court for the hearing.

(3) The person to whom the application relates shall be entitled to be legally represented at the hearing and, if he is not so represented but wishes to be so represented—
(a) the court shall adjourn the hearing to enable him to obtain representation; and
(b) he may be kept in police detention during the adjournment.

(4) A person's further detention is only justified for the purposes of this section or section 44 below if—
(a) his detention without charge is necessary to secure or preserve evidence relating to an offence for which he is under arrest or to obtain such evidence by questioning him;
(b) an offence for which he is under arrest is [an indictable offence]; and
(c) the investigation is being conducted diligently and expeditiously.

(5) Subject to subsection (7) below, an application for a warrant of further detention may be made—
(a) at any time before the expiry of 36 hours after the relevant time; or
(b) in a case where—
    (i) it is not practicable for the magistrates' court to which the application will be made to sit at the expiry of 36 hours after the relevant time; but
    (ii) the court will sit during the 6 hours following the end of that period,
at any time before the expiry of the said 6 hours.

(6) In a case to which subsection (5)(b) above applies—
(a) the person to whom the application relates may be kept in police detention until the application is heard; and
(b) the custody officer shall make a note in that person's custody record—
    (i) of the fact that he was kept in police detention for more than 36 hours after the relevant time; and
    (ii) of the reason why he was so kept.

(7) If—
(a) an application for a warrant of further detention is made after the expiry of 36 hours after the relevant time; and
(b) it appears to the magistrates' court that it would have been reasonable for the police to make it before the expiry of that period,
the court shall dismiss the application.

(8) Where on an application such as is mentioned in subsection (1) above a magistrates' court is not satisfied that there are reasonable grounds for believing that the further detention of the person to whom the application relates is justified, it shall be its duty—
(a) to refuse the application; or
(b) to adjourn the hearing of it until a time not later than 36 hours after the relevan time.

(9) The person to whom the application relates may be kept in police detention during the adjournment.

(10) A warrant of further detention shall—
   (a) state the time at which it is issued;
   (b) authorise the keeping in police detention of the person to whom it relates for the period stated in it.

(11) Subject to subsection (12) below, the period stated in a warrant of further detention shall be such period as the magistrates' court thinks fit, having regard to the evidence before it.

(12) The period shall not be longer than 36 hours.

   [. . .]

(15) Where an application under this section is refused, the person to whom the application relates shall forthwith be charged or, subject to subsection (16) below, released, either on bail or without bail.

(16) A person need not be released under subsection (15) above—
   (a) before the expiry of 24 hours after the relevant time; or
   (b) before the expiry of any longer period for which his continued detention is or has been authorised under section 42 above.

(17) Where an application under this section is refused, no further application shall be made under this section in respect of the person to whom the refusal relates, unless supported by evidence which has come to light since the refusal.

(18) Where a warrant of further detention is issued, the person to whom it relates shall be released from police detention, either on bail or without bail, upon or before the expiry of the warrant unless he is charged.

   [. . .]

44 EXTENSION OF WARRANTS OF FURTHER DETENTION

(1) On an application on oath made by a constable and supported by an information a magistrates' court may extend a warrant of further detention issued under section 43 above if it is satisfied that there are reasonable grounds for believing that the further detention of the person to whom the application relates is justified.

(2) Subject to subsection (3) below, the period for which a warrant of further detention may be extended shall be such period as the court thinks fit, having regard to the evidence before it.

(3) The period shall not—
   (a) be longer than 36 hours; or
   (b) end later than 96 hours after the relevant time.
   [. . .]

Detention—miscellaneous

46 DETENTION AFTER CHARGE

(1) Where a person—
   (a) is charged with an offence; and
   (b) after being charged—
       (i) is kept in police detention; or
       (ii) is detained by a local authority in pursuance of arrangements made under section 38(6) above,

he shall be brought before a magistrates' court in accordance with the provisions of this section.

(2)   If he is to be brought before a magistrates' court [in the local justice] area in which the police station at which he was charged is situated, he shall be brought before such a court as soon as is practicable and in any event not later than the first sitting after he is charged with the offence.

(3)   If no magistrates' court [in that area] is due to sit either on the day on which he is charged or on the next day, the custody officer for the police station at which he was charged shall inform the [designated officer] for the area that there is a person in the area to whom subsection (2) above applies.

(4)   If the person charged is to be brought before a magistrates' court [in a local justice] area other than that in which the police station at which he was charged is situated, he shall be removed to that area as soon as is practicable and brought before such a court as soon as is practicable after his arrival in the area and in any event not later than the first sitting of a magistrates' court [in that area] after his arrival in the area.

(5)   If no magistrates' court [in that area] is due to sit either on the day on which he arrives in the area or on the next day—
      (a) he shall be taken to a police station in the area; and
      (b) the custody officer at that station shall inform the [designated officer] for the area that there is a person in the area to whom subsection (4) applies.

(6)   Subject to subsection (8) below, where [the designated officer for a local justice] area has been informed—
      (a) under subsection (3) above that there is a person in the area to whom subsection (2) above applies; or
      (b) under subsection (5) above that there is a person in the area to whom subsection (4) above applies,
      [the designated officer] shall arrange for a magistrates' court to sit not later than the day next following the relevant day.

(7)   In this section "the relevant day"—
      (a) in relation to a person who is to be brought before a magistrates' court [in the local justice] area in which the police station at which he was charged is situated, means the day on which he was charged; and
      (b) in relation to a person who is to be brought before a magistrates' court [in any other local justice] area, means the day on which he arrives in the area.
      [. . .]

[. . .]

Part V **QUESTIONING AND TREATMENT OF PERSONS BY POLICE**
[. . .]

54 SEARCHES OF DETAINED PERSONS

(1)   The custody officer at a police station shall ascertain [. . .] everything which a person has with him when he is—
      (a) brought to the station after being arrested elsewhere or after being committed to custody by an order of sentence of a court; or
      [(b) arrested at the station or detained there [, as a person falling within section 34(7), under section 37 above] [or as a person to whom section 46ZA (4) or (5) applies]].

[(2)   The custody officer may record or cause to be recorded all or any of the things which he ascertains under subsection (1).

(2A)   In the case of an arrested person, any such record may be made as part of his custody record.

(3)   Subject to subsection (4) below, a custody officer may seize and retain any such thing or cause any such thing to be seized and retained.

(4)   Clothes and personal effects may only be seized if the custody officer—
    (a)   believes that the person from whom they are seized may use them—
        (i)   to cause physical injury to himself or any other person;
        (ii)   to damage property;
        (iii)   to interfere with evidence; or
        (iv)   to assist him to escape; or
    (b)   has reasonable grounds for believing that they may be evidence relating to an offence.

(5)   Where anything is seized, the person from whom it is seized shall be told the reason for the seizure unless he is—
    (a)   violent or likely to become violent; or
    (b)   incapable of understanding what is said to him.

(6)   Subject to subsection (7) below, a person may be searched if the custody officer considers it necessary to enable him to carry out his duty under subsection (1) above and to the extent that the custody officer considers necessary for that purpose.

[(6A)   A person who is in custody at a police station or is in police detention otherwise than at a police station may at any time be searched in order to ascertain whether he has with him anything which he could use for any of the purposes specified in subsection (4)(a) above.

(6B)   Subject to subsection (6C) below, a constable may seize and retain, or cause to be seized and retained, anything found on such a search.

(6C)   A constable may only seize clothes and personal effects in the circumstances specified in subsection (4) above.]

(7)   An intimate search may not be conducted under this section.

(8)   A search under this section shall be carried out by a constable.

(9)   The constable carrying out a search shall be of the same sex as the person searched.

54A SEARCHES AND EXAMINATION TO ASCERTAIN IDENTITY

(1)   If an officer of at least the rank of inspector authorises it, a person who is detained in a police station may be searched or examined, or both—
    (a)   for the purpose of ascertaining whether he has any mark that would tend to identify him as a person involved in the commission of an offence; or
    (b)   for the purpose of facilitating the ascertainment of his identity.

(2)   An officer may only give an authorisation under subsection (1) for the purpose mentioned in paragraph (a) of that subsection if—
    (a)   the appropriate consent to a search or examination that would reveal whether the mark in question exists has been withheld; or
    (b)   it is not practicable to obtain such consent.

(3)   An officer may only give an authorisation under subsection (1) in a case in which subsection (2) does not apply if—

(a) the person in question has refused to identify himself; or

(b) the officer has reasonable grounds for suspecting that that person is not who he claims to be.

(4) An officer may give an authorisation under subsection (1) orally or in writing but, if he gives it orally, he shall confirm it in writing as soon as is practicable.

(5) Any identifying mark found on a search or examination under this section may be photographed—

(a) with the appropriate consent; or

(b) if the appropriate consent is withheld or it is not practicable to obtain it, without it.

(6) Where a search or examination may be carried out under this section, or a photograph may be taken under this section, the only persons entitled to carry out the search or examination, or to take the photograph, are [constables]

(7) A person may not under this section carry out a search or examination of a person of the opposite sex or take a photograph of any part of the body of a person of the opposite sex.

(8) An intimate search may not be carried out under this section.

(9) A photograph taken under this section—

(a) may be used by, or disclosed to, any person for any purpose related to the prevention or detection of crime, the investigation of an offence or the conduct of a prosecution; and

(b) after being so used or disclosed, may be retained but may not be used or disclosed except for a purpose so related.

[. . .]

55 INTIMATE SEARCHES

(1) Subject to the following provisions of this section, if an officer of at least the rank of [inspector] has reasonable grounds for believing—

(a) that a person who has been arrested and is in police detention may have concealed on him anything which—

(i) he could use to cause physical injury to himself or others; and

(ii) he might so use while he is in police detention or in the custody of a court; or

(b) that such a person—

(i) may have a Class A drug concealed on him; and

(ii) was in possession of it with the appropriate criminal intent before his arrest,

he may authorise [an intimate search] of that person.

(2) An officer may not authorise an intimate search of a person for anything unless he has reasonable grounds for believing that it cannot be found without his being intimately searched.

[. . .]

[(3A) A drug offence search shall not be carried out unless the appropriate consent has been given in writing.

[. . .]

(4) An intimate search which is only a drug offence search shall be by way of examination by a suitably qualified person.

(5) Except as provided by subsection (4) above, an intimate search shall be by way of examination by a suitably qualified person unless an officer of at least the rank of [inspector] considers that this is not practicable.

(6)   An intimate search which is not carried out as mentioned in subsection (5) above shall be carried out by a constable.

(7)   A constable may not carry out an intimate search of a person of the opposite sex.

(8)   No intimate search may be carried out except—
(a)   at a police station;
(b)   at a hospital;
(c)   at a registered medical practitioner's surgery; or
(d)   at some other place used for medical purposes.

(9)   An intimate search which is only a drug offence search may not be carried out at a police station.

(10)   If an intimate search of a person is carried out, the custody record relating to him shall state—
(a)   which parts of his body were searched; and
(b)   why they were searched.
[. . .]

(12)   The custody officer at a police station may seize and retain anything which is found on an intimate search of a person, or cause any such thing to be seized and retained—
(a)   if he believes that the person from whom it is seized may use it—
(i)   to cause physical injury to himself or any other person;
(ii)   to damage property;
(iii) to interfere with evidence; or
(iv)   to assist him to escape; or
(b)   if he has reasonable grounds for believing that it may be evidence relating to an offence.

(13)   Where anything is seized under this section, the person from whom it is seized shall be told the reason for the seizure unless he is—
(a)   violent or likely to become violent; or
(b)   incapable of understanding what is said to him.
[. . .]

56 RIGHT TO HAVE SOMEONE INFORMED WHEN ARRESTED

(1)   Where a person has been arrested and is being held in custody in a police station or other premises, he shall be entitled, if he so requests, to have one friend or relative or other person who is known to him or who is likely to take an interest in his welfare told, as soon as is practicable except to the extent that delay is permitted by this section, that he has been arrested and is being detained there.

(2)   Delay is only permitted—
(a)   in the case of a person who is in police detention for [an indictable offence]; and
(b)   if an officer of at least the rank of [inspector] authorises it.

(3)   In any case the person in custody must be permitted to exercise the right conferred by subsection (1) above within 36 hours from the relevant time, as defined in section 41(2) above.

(4)   An officer may give an authorisation under subsection (2) above orally or in writing but, if he gives it orally, he shall confirm it in writing as soon as is practicable.

(5)   [Subject to sub-section (5A) below] An officer may only authorise delay where he has reasonable grounds for believing that telling the named person of the arrest—

(a) will lead to interference with or harm to evidence connected with [an indictable offence] or interference with or physical injury to other persons; or

(b) will lead to the alerting of other persons suspected of having committed such an offence but not yet arrested for it; or

(c) will hinder the recovery of any property obtained as a result of such an offence.

[(5A) An officer may also authorise delay where he has reasonable grounds for believing that—

(a) the person detained for [the indictable offence] has benefited from his criminal conduct, and

(b) the recovery of the value of the property constituting the benefit will be hindered by telling the named person of the arrest.

[. . .]

(6) If a delay is authorised—

(a) the detained person shall be told the reason for it; and

(b) the reason shall be noted on his custody record.

(7) The duties imposed by subsection (6) above shall be performed as soon as is practicable.

(8) The rights conferred by this section on a person detained at a police station or other premises are exercisable whenever he is transferred from one place to another; and this section applies to each subsequent occasion on which they are exercisable as it applies to the first such occasion.

(9) There may be no further delay in permitting the exercise of the right conferred by subsection (1) above once the reason for authorising delay ceases to subsist.

[. . .]

[. . .]

58 ACCESS TO LEGAL ADVICE

(1) A person arrested and held in custody in a police station or other premises shall be entitled, if he so requests, to consult a solicitor privately at any time.

(2) Subject to subsection (3) below, a request under subsection (1) above and the time at which it was made shall be recorded in the custody record.

(3) Such a request need not be recorded in the custody record of a person who makes it at a time while he is at a court after being charged with an offence.

(4) If a person makes such a request, he must be permitted to consult a solicitor as soon as is practicable except to the extent that delay is permitted by this section.

(5) In any case he must be permitted to consult a solicitor within 36 hours from the relevant time, as defined in section 41(2) above.

(6) Delay in compliance with a request is only permitted—

(a) in the case of a person who is in police detention for [an indictable offence]; and

(b) if an officer of at least the rank of superintendent authorises it.

(7) An officer may give an authorisation under subsection (6) above orally or in writing but, if he gives it orally, he shall confirm it in writing as soon as is practicable.

(8) [Subject to sub-section (8A) below] An officer may only authorise delay where he has reasonable grounds for believing that the exercise of the right conferred by subsection (1) above at the time when the person detained desires to exercise it—

(a) will lead to interference with or harm to evidence connected with [an indictable offence] or interference with or physical injury to other persons; or

(b) will lead to the alerting of other persons suspected of having committed such an offence but not yet arrested for it; or

(c) will hinder the recovery of any property obtained as a result of such an offence.

[(8A) An officer may also authorise delay where he has reasonable grounds for believing that—

(a) the person detained for [the indictable offence] has benefited from his criminal conduct, and

(b) the recovery of the value of the property constituting the benefit will be hindered by the exercise of the right conferred by subsection (1) above.

(8B) For the purposes of subsection (8A) above the question whether a person has benefited from his criminal conduct is to be decided in accordance with Part 2 of the Proceeds of Crime Act 2002.]

(9)   If delay is authorised—

(a) the detained person shall be told the reasons for it; and

(b) the reason shall be noted on his custody record.

(10) The duties imposed by subsection (9) above shall be performed as soon as is practicable.

(11) There may be no further delay in permitting the exercise of the right conferred by subsection (1) above once the reason for authorising delay ceases to subsist.

[(12) Nothing in this section applies to a person arrested or detained under the terrorism provisions.]

[. . .]

60 TAPE-RECORDING OF INTERVIEWS

(1)   It shall be the duty of the Secretary of State—

(a) to issue a code of practice in connection with the tape-recording of interviews of persons suspected of the commission of criminal offences which are held by police officers at police stations; and

(b) to make an order requiring the tape-recording of interviews of persons suspected of the commission of criminal offences, or of such descriptions of criminal offences as may be specified in the order, which are so held, in accordance with the code as it has effect for the time being.

[. . .]

60A VISUAL RECORDING OF INTERVIEWS

(1)   The Secretary of State shall have power—

(a) to issue a code of practice for the visual recording of interviews held by police officers at police stations; and

(b) to make an order requiring the visual recording of interviews so held, and requiring the visual recording to be in accordance with the code for the time being in force under this section.

(2)   A requirement imposed by an order under this section may be imposed in relation to such cases or police stations in such areas, or both, as may be specified or described in the order.

[. . .]

61 FINGER-PRINTING

(1) Except as provided by this section no person's fingerprints may be taken without the appropriate consent.

(2) Consent to the taking of a person's fingerprints must be in writing if it is given at a time when he is at a police station.

[(3) The fingerprints of a person detained at a police station may be taken without the appropriate consent if—
   (a) he is detained in consequence of his arrest for a recordable offence; and
   (b) he has not had his fingerprints taken in the course of the investigation of the offence by the police.

(3A) Where a person mentioned in paragraph (a) of subsection (3) or (4) has already had his fingerprints taken in the course of the investigation of the offence by the police], that fact shall be disregarded for the purposes of that subsection if—
   (a) the fingerprints taken on the previous occasion do not constitute a complete set of his fingerprints; or
   (b) some or all of the fingerprints taken on the previous occasion are not of sufficient quality to allow satisfactory analysis, comparison or matching (whether in the case in question or generally).

(4) The fingerprints of a person detained at a police station may be taken without the appropriate consent if—
   (a) he has been charged with a recordable offence or informed that he will be reported for such an offence; and
   (b) he has not had his fingerprints taken in the course of the investigation of the offence by the police.
   [. . .]

(5A) The fingerprints of a person may be taken without the appropriate consent if (before or after the coming into force of this subsection) he has been arrested for a recordable offence and released and—
   (a) in the case of a person who is on bail, he has not had his fingerprints taken in the course of the investigation of the offence by the police; or
   (b) in any case, he has had his fingerprints taken in the course of that investigation but subsection (3A)(a) or (b) above applies."

(5B) The fingerprints of a person not detained at a police station may be taken without the appropriate consent if (before or after the coming into force of this subsection) he has been charged with a recordable offence or informed that he will be reported for such an offence and—
   (a) he has not had his fingerprints taken in the course of the investigation of the offence by the police; or
   (b) he has had his fingerprints taken in the course of that investigation but subsection (3A)(a) or (b) above applies."

(6) Subject to this section, the fingerprints of a person may be taken without the appropriate consent if (before or after the coming into force of this subsection)—
   (a) he has been convicted of a recordable offence,
   (b) he has been given a caution in respect of a recordable offence which, at the time of the caution, he has admitted, or
   (c) he has been warned or reprimanded under section 65 of the Crime and Disorder Act 1998 for a recordable offence, and
   either of the conditions mentioned in subsection (6ZA) below is met.

(6ZA) The conditions referred to in subsection (6) above are—
    (a) the person has not had his fingerprints taken since he was convicted, cautioned or warned or reprimanded;
    (b) he has had his fingerprints taken since then but subsection (3A)(a) or (b) above applies.

(6ZB) Fingerprints may only be taken as specified in subsection (6) above with the authorisation of an officer of at least the rank of inspector.

(6ZC) An officer may only give an authorisation under subsection (6ZB) above if the officer is satisfied that taking the fingerprints is necessary to assist in the prevention or detection of crime.

(6D) Subject to this section, the fingerprints of a person may be taken without the appropriate consent if—
    (a) under the law in force in a country or territory outside England and Wales the person has been convicted of an offence under that law (whether before or after the coming into force of this subsection and whether or not he has been punished for it);
    (b) the act constituting the offence would constitute a qualifying offence if done in England and Wales (whether or not it constituted such an offence when the person was convicted); and
    (c) either of the conditions mentioned in subsection (6E) below is met.

(6E) The conditions referred to in subsection (6D)(c) above are—
    (a) the person has not had his fingerprints taken on a previous occasion under subsection (6D) above;
    (b) he has had his fingerprints taken on a previous occasion under that subsection but subsection (3A)(a) or (b) above applies.

(6F) Fingerprints may only be taken as specified in subsection (6D) above with the authorisation of an officer of at least the rank of inspector.

(6G) An officer may only give an authorisation under subsection (6F) above if the officer is satisfied that taking the fingerprints is necessary to assist in the prevention or detection of crime."

(7) Where a person's fingerprints are taken without the appropriate consent by virtue of any power conferred by this section—
    (a) before the fingerprints are taken, the person shall be informed of—
        (i) the reason for taking the fingerprints;
        (ii) the power by virtue of which they are taken; and
        (iii) in a case where the authorisation of the court or an officer is required for the exercise of the power, the fact that the authorisation has been given; and
    (b) those matters shall be recorded as soon as practicable after the fingerprints are taken

(7A) If a person's fingerprints are taken at a police station (or, where by virtue of subsection (4A), (6A) or (6BA) the fingerprints are taken at a place other than a police station, the constable taking the fingerprints)". taking the fingerprints), whether with or without the appropriate consent—
    (a) before the fingerprints are taken, an officer shall inform him that they may be the subject of a speculative search; and
    (b) the fact that the person has been informed of this possibility shall be recorded as soon as is practicable after the fingerprints have been taken.
    [. . .]

[. . .]

64   RETENTION OF SAMPLES AND FINGERPRINTS, ETC GENERALLY

(1)   This section applies to the following material—
  (a)   fingerprints, samples or impressions of footwear—
    (i)   taken from a person under any power conferred by this Part of this Act, or
    (ii)   taken in connection with the investigation of an offence with the consent of the person from whom they were taken, and
  (b)   a DNA profile derived from a DNA sample falling within paragraph (a).

(2)   Material to which this section applies may be retained after it has fulfilled the purpose for which it was taken or derived.

(3)   This section is subject to sections 64ZA to 64ZJ.

(4)   This section and sections 64ZA to 64ZH do not apply to material to which paragraph 14 of Schedule 8 to the Terrorism Act 2000 applies.

(5)   Any reference in those sections to a person being arrested for or charged with an offence does not include a reference to a person—
  (a)   being arrested under section 41 of the Terrorism Act 2000, or
  (b)   being charged with an offence following an arrest under that section.

(6)   Nothing in this section, or sections 64ZA to 64ZN, affects any power conferred by—
  (a)   paragraph 18(2) of Schedule 2 to the Immigration Act 1971 (power to take reasonable steps to identify a person detained), or
  (b)   section 20 of the Immigration and Asylum Act 1999 (disclosure of police information to the Secretary of State for use for immigration purposes)."

64ZA   DESTRUCTION OF SAMPLES

(1)   A DNA sample to which section 64 applies must be destroyed—
  (a)   as soon as a DNA profile has been derived from the sample, or
  (b)   if sooner, before the end of the period of 6 months beginning with the date on which the sample was taken.

(2)   Any other sample to which section 64 applies must be destroyed before the end of the period of 6 months beginning with the date on which it was taken.

64ZB   DESTRUCTION OF DATA GIVEN VOLUNTARILY

(1)   This section applies to—
  (a)   fingerprints or impressions of footwear taken in connection with the investigation of an offence with the consent of the person from whom they were taken, and
  (b)   a DNA profile derived from a DNA sample taken in connection with the investigation of an offence with the consent of the person from whom the sample was taken.

(2)   Material to which this section applies must be destroyed as soon as it has fulfilled the purpose for which it was taken or derived, unless it is—
  (a)   material relating to a person who is convicted of the offence,
  (b)   material relating to a person who has previously been convicted of a recordable offence, other than a person who has only one exempt conviction,
  (c)   material in relation to which any of sections 64ZC to 64ZH applies, or
  (d)   material which is not required to be destroyed by virtue of consent given under section 64ZL.

(3)   If material to which this section applies leads to the person to whom the material relates being arrested for or charged with an offence other than the offence under investigation—
(a)   the material is not required to be destroyed by virtue of this section, and
(b)   sections 64ZD to 64ZH have effect in relation to the material as if the material was taken (or, in the case of a DNA profile, was derived from material taken) in connection with the investigation of the offence in respect of which the person is arrested or charged

64ZC   DESTRUCTION OF DATA RELATING TO A PERSON SUBJECT TO A CONTROL ORDER

(1)   This section applies to material falling within subsection (2) relating to a person who—
(a)   has no previous convictions or only one exempt conviction, and
(b)   is subject to a control order.

(2)   Material falls within this subsection if it is—
(a)   fingerprints taken from the person, or
(b)   a DNA profile derived from a DNA sample taken from the person.

(3)   The material must be destroyed before the end of the period of 2 years beginning with the date on which the person ceases to be subject to a control order.

(4)   This section ceases to have effect in relation to the material if the person is convicted—
(a)   in England and Wales or Northern Ireland of a recordable offence, or
(b)   in Scotland of an offence which is punishable by imprisonment,
before the material is required to be destroyed by virtue of this section.

(5)   For the purposes of subsection (1)—
(a)   a person has no previous convictions if the person has not previously been convicted—
(i)   in England and Wales or Northern Ireland of a recordable offence, or
(ii)   in Scotland of an offence which is punishable by imprisonment, and
(b)   if the person has been previously convicted of a recordable offence in England and Wales or Northern Ireland, the conviction is exempt if it is in respect of a recordable offence other than a qualifying offence, committed when the person is aged under 18.

(6)   For the purposes of that subsection—
(a)   a person is to be treated as having been convicted of an offence if—
(i)   he has been given a caution in England and Wales or Northern Ireland in respect of the offence which, at the time of the caution, he has admitted, or
(ii)   he has been warned or reprimanded under section 65 of the Crime and Disorder Act 1998 for the offence, and
(b)   if a person is convicted of more than one offence arising out of a single course of action, those convictions are to be treated as a single conviction.

(7)   In this section—
(a)   "recordable offence" has, in relation to a conviction in Northern Ireland, the meaning given by Article 2(2) of the Police and Criminal Evidence (Northern Ireland) Order 1989, and
(b)   "qualifying offence" has, in relation to a conviction in respect of a recordable offence committed in Northern Ireland, the meaning given by Article 53A of that Order.

64ZD DESTRUCTION OF DATA RELATING TO PERSONS NOT CONVICTED

(1) This section applies to material falling within subsection (2) relating to a person who—
  (a) has no previous convictions or only one exempt conviction,
  (b) is arrested for or charged with a recordable offence, and
  (c) is aged 18 or over at the time of the alleged offence.

(2) Material falls within this subsection if it is—
  (a) fingerprints or impressions of footwear taken from the person in connection with the investigation of the offence, or
  (b) a DNA profile derived from a DNA sample so taken.

(3) The material must be destroyed—
  (a) in the case of fingerprints or impressions of footwear, before the end of the period of 6 years beginning with the date on which the fingerprints or impressions were taken,
  (b) in the case of a DNA profile, before the end of the period of 6 years beginning with the date on which the DNA sample from which the profile was derived was taken (or, if the profile was derived from more than one DNA sample, the date on which the first of those samples was taken).

(4) But if, before the material is required to be destroyed by virtue of this section, the person is arrested for or charged with a recordable offence the material may be further retained until the end of the period of 6 years beginning with the date of the arrest or charge.

(5) This section ceases to have effect in relation to the material if the person is convicted of a recordable offence before the material is required to be destroyed by virtue of this section.

64ZE DESTRUCTION OF DATA RELATING TO PERSONS UNDER 18 NOT CONVICTED: RECORDABLE OFFENCES OTHER THAN QUALIFYING OFFENCES

(1) This section applies to material falling within subsection (2) relating to a person who—
  (a) has no previous convictions or only one exempt conviction,
  (b) is arrested for or charged with a recordable offence other than a qualifying offence, and
  (c) is aged under 18 at the time of the alleged offence.

(2) Material falls within this subsection if it is—
  (a) fingerprints or impressions of footwear taken from the person in connection with the investigation of the offence, or
  (b) a DNA profile derived from a DNA sample so taken.

(3) The material must be destroyed—
  (a) in the case of fingerprints or impressions of footwear, before the end of the period of 3 years beginning with the date on which the fingerprints or impressions were taken,
  (b) in the case of a DNA profile, before the end of the period of 3 years beginning with the date on which the DNA sample from which the profile was derived was taken (or, if the profile was derived from more than one DNA sample, the date on which the first of those samples was taken).

(4) But if, before the material is required to be destroyed by virtue of this section, the person is arrested for or charged with a recordable offence—
  (a) where the person is aged 18 or over at the time of the alleged offence, the material may be further retained until the end of the period of 6 years beginning with the date of the arrest or charge,

(b) where—
    (i) the alleged offence is not a qualifying offence, and
    (ii) the person is aged under 18 at the time of the alleged offence,
the material may be further retained until the end of the period of 3 years beginning with the date of the arrest or charge,

(c) where—
    (i) the alleged offence is a qualifying offence, and
    (ii) the person is aged under 16 at the time of the alleged offence,
the material may be further retained until the end of the period of 3 years beginning with the date of the arrest or charge,

(d) where—
    (i) the alleged offence is a qualifying offence, and
    (ii) the person is aged 16 or 17 at the time of the alleged offence,
the material may be further retained until the end of the period of 6 years beginning with the date of the arrest or charge,

(e) where—
    (i) the person is convicted of the offence,
    (ii) the offence is not a qualifying offence,
    (iii) the person is aged under 18 at the time of the offence, and
    (iv) the person has no previous convictions,
the material may be further retained until the end of the period of 5 years beginning with the date of the arrest or charge.

(5) This section ceases to have effect in relation to the material if, before the material is required to be destroyed by virtue of this section, the person—
    (a) is convicted of a recordable offence and is aged 18 or over at the time of the offence,
    (b) is convicted of a qualifying offence, or
    (c) having a previous exempt conviction, is convicted of a recordable offence.

64ZF DESTRUCTION OF DATA RELATING TO PERSONS UNDER 16 NOT CONVICTED: QUALIFYING OFFENCES

(1) This section applies to material falling within subsection (2) relating to a person who—
    (a) has no previous convictions or only one exempt conviction,
    (b) is arrested for or charged with a qualifying offence, and
    (c) is aged under 16 at the time of the alleged offence.

(2) Material falls within this subsection if it is—
    (a) fingerprints or impressions of footwear taken from the person in connection with the investigation of the offence, or
    (b) a DNA profile derived from a DNA sample so taken.

(3) The material must be destroyed—
    (a) in the case of fingerprints or impressions of footwear, before the end of the period of 3 years beginning with the date on which the fingerprints or impressions were taken,
    (b) in the case of a DNA profile, before the end of the period of 3 years beginning with the date on which the DNA sample from which the profile was derived was taken (or, if the profile was derived from more than one DNA sample, the date on which the first of those samples was taken).

(4) But if, before the material is required to be destroyed by virtue of this section, the person is arrested for or charged with a recordable offence—
    (a) where the person is aged 18 or over at the time of the alleged offence, the material may be further retained until the end of the period of 6 years beginning with the date of the arrest or charge,

(b) where—
    (i)   the alleged offence is not a qualifying offence, and
    (ii) the person is aged under 18 at the time of the alleged offence,
the material may be further retained until the end of the period of 3 years beginning with the date of the arrest or charge,
(c) where—
    (i)   the alleged offence is a qualifying offence, and
    (ii) the person is aged under 16 at the time of the alleged offence,
the material may be further retained until the end of the period of 3 years beginning with the date of the arrest or charge,
(d) where—
    (i)   the alleged offence is a qualifying offence, and
    (ii) the person is aged 16 or 17 at the time of the alleged offence,
the material may be further retained until the end of the period of 6 years beginning with the date of the arrest or charge,
(e) where—
    (i)   the person is convicted of the offence,
    (ii) the offence is not a qualifying offence,
    (iii) the person is aged under 18 at the time of the offence, and
    (iv) the person has no previous convictions,
the material may be further retained until the end of the period of 5 years beginning with the date of the arrest or charge.

(5)   This section ceases to have effect in relation to the material if, before the material is required to be destroyed by virtue of this section, the person—
(a) is convicted of a recordable offence and is aged 18 or over at the time of the offence,
(b) is convicted of a qualifying offence, or
(c) having a previous exempt conviction, is convicted of a recordable offence.

64ZG DESTRUCTION OF DATA RELATING TO PERSONS AGED 16 OR 17 NOT CONVICTED: QUALIFYING OFFENCES

(1)   This section applies to material falling within subsection (2) relating to a person who—
(a) has no previous convictions or only one exempt conviction,
(b) is arrested for or charged with a qualifying offence, and
(c) is aged 16 or 17 at the time of the alleged offence.

(2)   Material falls within this subsection if it is—
(a) fingerprints or impressions of footwear taken from the person in connection with the investigation of the offence, or
(b) a DNA profile derived from a DNA sample so taken.

(3)   The material must be destroyed—
(a) in the case of fingerprints or impressions of footwear, before the end of the period of 6 years beginning with the date on which the fingerprints or impressions were taken,
(b) in the case of a DNA profile, before the end of the period of 6 years beginning with the date on which the DNA sample from which the profile was derived was taken (or, if the profile was derived from more than one DNA sample, the date on which the first of those samples was taken).

(4)   But if, before the material is required to be destroyed by virtue of this section, the person is arrested for or charged with a recordable offence—

(a) where the person is aged 18 or over at the time of the alleged offence, the material may be further retained until the end of the period of 6 years beginning with the date of the arrest or charge,

(b) where—
    (i) the alleged offence is not a qualifying offence, and
    (ii) the person is aged under 18 at the time of the alleged offence,
the material may be further retained until the end of the period of 3 years beginning with the date of the arrest or charge,

(c) where—
    (i) the alleged offence is a qualifying offence, and
    (ii) the person is aged 16 or 17 at the time of the alleged offence,
the material may be further retained until the end of the period of 6 years beginning with the date of the arrest or charge,

(d) where—
    (i) the person is convicted of the offence,
    (ii) the offence is not a qualifying offence,
    (iii) the person is aged under 18 at the time of the offence, and
    (iv) the person has no previous convictions,
the material may be further retained until the end of the period of 5 years beginning with the date of the arrest or charge.

(5) This section ceases to have effect in relation to the material if, before the material is required to be destroyed by virtue of this section, the person—
    (a) is convicted of a recordable offence and is aged 18 or over at the time of the offence,
    (b) is convicted of a qualifying offence, or
    (c) having a previous exempt conviction, is convicted of a recordable offence.

64ZH DESTRUCTION OF DATA RELATING TO PERSONS UNDER 18 CONVICTED OF A RECORDABLE OFFENCE OTHER THAN A QUALIFYING OFFENCE

(1) This section applies to material falling within subsection (2) relating to a person who—
    (a) has no previous convictions,
    (b) is convicted of a recordable offence other than a qualifying offence, and
    (c) is aged under 18 at the time of the offence.

(2) Material falls within this subsection if it is—
    (a) fingerprints or impressions of footwear taken from the person in connection with the investigation of the offence, or
    (b) a DNA profile derived from a DNA sample so taken.

(3) The material must be destroyed—
    (a) in the case of fingerprints or impressions of footwear, before the end of the period of 5 years beginning with the date on which the fingerprints or impressions were taken,
    (b) in the case of a DNA profile, before the end of the period of 5 years beginning with the date on which the DNA sample from which the profile was derived was taken (or, if the profile was derived from more than one DNA sample, the date on which the first of those samples was taken).

(4) But if, before the material is required to be destroyed by virtue of this section, the person is arrested for or charged with a recordable offence—
    (a) where the person is aged 18 or over at the time of the alleged offence, the material may be further retained until the end of the period of 6 years beginning with the date of the arrest or charge,

(b) where—
    (i) the alleged offence is not a qualifying offence, and
    (ii) the person is aged under 18 at the time of the alleged offence,
the material may be further retained until the end of the period of 3 years beginning with the date of the arrest or charge,

(c) where—
    (i) the alleged offence is a qualifying offence, and
    (ii) the person is aged under 16 at the time of the alleged offence,
the material may be further retained until the end of the period of 3 years beginning with the date of the arrest or charge,

(d) where—
    (i) the alleged offence is a qualifying offence, and
    (ii) the person is aged 16 or 17 at the time of the alleged offence,
the material may be further retained until the end of the period of 6 years beginning with the date of the arrest or charge.

(5) This section ceases to have effect in relation to the material if the person is convicted of a further recordable offence before the material is required to be destroyed by virtue of this section.

64ZI SECTIONS 64ZB TO 64ZH: SUPPLEMENTARY PROVISION

(1) Any reference in section 64ZB or sections 64ZD to 64ZH to a person being charged with an offence includes a reference to a person being informed that he will be reported for an offence.

(2) For the purposes of those sections—
(a) a person has no previous convictions if the person has not previously been convicted of a recordable offence, and
(b) if the person has been previously convicted of a recordable offence, the conviction is exempt if it is in respect of a recordable offence other than a qualifying offence, committed when the person is aged under 18.

(3) For the purposes of those sections, a person is to be treated as having been convicted of an offence if—
(a) he has been given a caution in respect of the offence which, at the time of the caution, he has admitted, or
(b) he has been warned or reprimanded under section 65 of the Crime and Disorder Act 1998 for the offence.

(4) If a person is convicted of more than one offence arising out of a single course of action, those convictions are to be treated as a single conviction for the purpose of any provision of those sections relating to an exempt, first or subsequent conviction.

(5) Subject to the completion of any speculative search that the responsible chief officer of police considers necessary or desirable, material falling within any of sections 64ZD to 64ZH must be destroyed immediately if it appears to the chief officer that—
(a) the arrest was unlawful,
(b) the taking of the fingerprints, impressions of footwear or DNA sample concerned was unlawful,
(c) the arrest was based on mistaken identity, or
(d) other circumstances relating to the arrest or the alleged offence mean that it is appropriate to destroy the material.

(6)   "Responsible chief officer of police" means the chief officer of police for the police area—
    (a)   in which the samples, fingerprints or impressions of footwear were taken, or
    (b)   in the case of a DNA profile, in which the sample from which the DNA profile was derived was taken.

64ZJ DESTRUCTION OF FINGERPRINTS TAKEN UNDER SECTION 61(6A)

Fingerprints taken from a person by virtue of section 61(6A) (taking fingerprints for the purposes of identification) must be destroyed as soon as they have fulfilled the purpose for which they were taken.

64ZK RETENTION FOR PURPOSES OF NATIONAL SECURITY

(1)   Subsection (2) applies if the responsible chief officer of police determines that it is necessary for—
    (a)   a DNA profile to which section 64 applies, or
    (b)   fingerprints to which section 64 applies, other than fingerprints taken under section 61(6A),
to be retained for the purposes of national security.

(2)   Where this subsection applies—
    (a)   the material is not required to be destroyed in accordance with sections 64ZB to 64ZH, and
    (b)   section 64ZN(2) does not apply to the material,
for as long as the determination has effect.

(3)   A determination under subsection (1) has effect for a maximum of 2 years beginning with the date on which the material would otherwise be required to be destroyed, but a determination may be renewed.

(4)   "Responsible chief officer of police" means the chief officer of police for the police area—
    (a)   in which the fingerprints were taken, or
    (b)   in the case of a DNA profile, in which the sample from which the DNA profile was derived was taken.

64ZL RETENTION WITH CONSENT

(1)   If a person consents in writing to the retention of fingerprints, impressions of footwear or a DNA profile to which section 64 applies, other than fingerprints taken under section 61(6A)—
    (a)   the material is not required to be destroyed in accordance with sections 64ZB to 64ZH, and
    (b)   section 64ZN(2) does not apply to the material.

(2)   It is immaterial for the purposes of subsection (1) whether the consent is given at, before or after the time when the entitlement to the destruction of the material arises.

(3)   Consent given under this section can be withdrawn at any time.

64ZM DESTRUCTION OF COPIES, AND NOTIFICATION OF DESTRUCTION

(1)   If fingerprints or impressions of footwear are required to be destroyed by virtue of any of sections 64ZB to 64ZJ, any copies of the fingerprints or impressions of footwear must also be destroyed.

(2)   If a DNA profile is required to be destroyed by virtue of any of those sections, no copy may be kept except in a form which does not include information which identifies the person to whom the DNA profile relates.

(3)   If a person makes a request to the responsible chief officer of police to be notified when anything relating to the person is destroyed under any of sections 64ZA to 64ZJ, the responsible chief officer of police or a person authorised by the chief officer or on the chief officer's behalf must within three months of the request issue the person with a certificate recording the destruction.

(4)   "Responsible chief officer of police" means the chief officer of police for the police area—
    (a)   in which the samples, fingerprints or impressions of footwear which have been destroyed were taken, or
    (b)   in the case of a DNA profile which has been destroyed, in which the samples from which the DNA profile was derived were taken.

64ZN USE OF RETAINED MATERIAL

(1)   Any material to which section 64 applies which is retained after it has fulfilled the purpose for which it was taken or derived must not be used other than—
    (a)   in the interests of national security,
    (b)   for the purposes of a terrorist investigation,
    (c)   for purposes related to the prevention or detection of crime, the investigation of an offence or the conduct of a prosecution, or
    (d)   for purposes related to the identification of a deceased person or of the person to whom the material relates.

(2)   Material which is required to be destroyed by virtue of any of sections 64ZA to 64ZJ, or of section 64ZM, must not at any time after it is required to be destroyed be used—
    (a)   in evidence against the person to whom the material relates, or
    (b)   for the purposes of the investigation of any offence.

(3)   In this section—
    (a)   the reference to using material includes a reference to allowing any check to be made against it and to disclosing it to any person,
    (b)   the reference to crime includes a reference to any conduct which—
        (i)   constitutes one or more criminal offences (whether under the law of a part of the United Kingdom or of a country or territory outside the United Kingdom), or
        (ii)   is, or corresponds to, any conduct which, if it all took place in any one part of the United Kingdom, would constitute one or more criminal offences, and
    (c)   the references to an investigation and to a prosecution include references, respectively, to any investigation outside the United Kingdom of any crime or suspected crime and to a prosecution brought in respect of any crime in a country or territory outside the United Kingdom."

(a)   after the definition of "appropriate consent" there is inserted—
"DNA profile" means any information derived from a DNA sample;

"DNA sample" means any material that has come from a human body and consists of or includes human cells;

"terrorist investigation" has the meaning given by section 32 of the Terrorism Act 2000."

(2A)   In subsection (2), the reference to the destruction of a sample does not include a reference to the destruction of a sample under section 64ZA (requirement to destroy samples).

65 PART V—SUPPLEMENTARY

[(1)] —In this Part of this Act—

["analysis", in relation to a skin impression, includes comparison and matching;]

"appropriate consent" means—
(a) in relation to a person who has attained the age of 17 years, the consent of that person;
(b) in relation to a person who has not attained that age but has attained the age of 14 years, the consent of that person and his parent or guardian; and
(c) in relation to a person who has not attained the age of 14 years, the consent of his parent or guardian;

"DNA profile" means any information derived from a DNA sample;

"DNA sample" means any material that has come from a human body and consists of or includes human cells;

[. . .]

["fingerprints", in relation to any person, means a record (in any form and produced by any method) of the skin pattern and other physical characteristics or features of—
(a) any of that person's fingers; or
(b) either of his palms;]

["intimate sample" means—
(a) a sample of blood, semen or any other tissue fluid, urine or pubic hair;
(b) a dental impression;
[(c) a swab taken from any part of a person's genitals (including pubic hair) or from a person's body orifice other than the mouth;]]

["intimate search" means a search which consists of the physical examination of a person's body orifices other than the mouth;]

["non-intimate sample" means—
(a) a sample of hair other than pubic hair;
(b) a sample taken from a nail or from under a nail;
[(c) a swab taken from any part of a person's body other than a part from which a swab taken would be an intimate sample;]
(d) saliva;
[(e) a skin impression;]]
[. . .]

"offence", in relation to any country or territory outside England and Wales, includes an act punishable under the law of that country or territory, however it is described

["skin impression", in relation to any person, means any record (other than a fingerprint) which is a record (in any form and produced by any method) of the skin pattern and other physical characteristics or features of the whole or any part of his foot or of any other part of his body;]

[. . .]

"speculative search", in relation to a person's fingerprints or samples, means such a check against other fingerprints or samples or against information derived from other samples as is referred to in section 63A (1) above;

"sufficient" and "insufficient", in relation to a sample, means [(subject to subsection (2) below)]sufficient or insufficient (in point of quantity or quality) for the purpose of enabling information to be produced by the means of analysis used or to be used in relation to the sample.]

[. . .]

Part VI CODES OF PRACTICE—GENERAL

66 CODES OF PRACTICE

(1)   The Secretary of State shall issue codes of practice in connection with—
(a) the exercise by police officers of statutory powers—
(i)   to search a person without first arresting him; [. . .]
(ii) to search a vehicle without making an arrest; [. . .] or
(iii) to arrest a person;]
(b) the detention, treatment, questioning and identification of persons by police officers;
(c) searches of premises by police officers; and
(d) the seizure of property found by police officers on persons or premises.
[. . .]

67 CODES OF PRACTICE—SUPPLEMENTARY

(1)   In this section, "code" means a code of practice under section 60, 60A or 66.

(2)   The Secretary of State may at any time revise the whole or any part of a code.

(3)   A code may be made, or revised, so as to—
(a) apply only in relation to one or more specified areas,
(b) have effect only for a specified period,
(c) apply only in relation to specified offences or descriptions of offender.

[. . .]

(9)   Persons other than police officers who are charged with the duty of investigating offences or charging offenders shall in the discharge of that duty have regard to any relevant provision of [. . .] a code.

(9A) Persons on whom powers are conferred by—
(a) any designation under section 38 or 39 of the Police Reform Act 2002 (c. 30) (police powers for civilian staff), or
(b) any accreditation under section 41 of that Act (accreditation under community safety accreditation schemes),
shall have regard to any relevant provision of a code [. . .] in the exercise or performance of the powers and duties conferred or imposed on them by that designation or accreditation.]

(10)   A failure on the part—
(a) of a police officer to comply with any provision of [. . .] a code; [. . .]
(b) of any person other than a police officer who is charged with the duty of investigating offences or charging offenders to have regard to any relevant provision of [. . .] a code in the discharge of that duty, [, or
(c) of a person designated under section 38 or 39 or accredited under section 41 of the Police Reform Act 2002 (c. 30) to have regard to any relevant provision of [. . .] a code in the exercise or performance of the powers and duties conferred or imposed on him by that designation or accreditation,]
shall not of itself render him liable to any criminal or civil proceedings.

(11)   In all criminal and civil proceedings any [. . .] code shall be admissible in evidence; and if any provision of [. . .] a code appears to the court or tribunal conducting the proceedings to be relevant to any question arising in the proceedings it shall be taken into account in determining that question.

[. . .]

[. . .]

Part VIII EVIDENCE IN CRIMINAL PROCEEDINGS—GENERAL

[. . .]

Confessions

76 CONFESSIONS

(1)   In any proceedings a confession made by an accused person may be given in evidence against him in so far as it is relevant to any matter in issue in the proceedings and is not excluded by the court in pursuance of this section.

(2)   If, in any proceedings where the prosecution proposes to give in evidence a confession made by an accused person, it is represented to the court that the confession was or may have been obtained—
(a)   by oppression of the person who made it; or
(b)   in consequence of anything said or done which was likely, in the circumstances existing at the time, to render unreliable any confession which might be made by him in consequence thereof,
the court shall not allow the confession to be given in evidence against him except in so far as the prosecution proves to the court beyond reasonable doubt that the confession (notwithstanding that it may be true) was not obtained as aforesaid.

(3)   In any proceedings where the prosecution proposes to give in evidence a confession made by an accused person, the court may of its own motion require the prosecution, as a condition of allowing it to do so, to prove that the confession was not obtained as mentioned in subsection (2) above.

(4)   The fact that a confession is wholly or partly excluded in pursuance of this section shall not affect the admissibility in evidence—
(a)   of any facts discovered as a result of the confession; or
(b)   where the confession is relevant as showing that the accused speaks, writes or expresses himself in a particular way, of so much of the confession as is necessary to show that he does so.

(5)   Evidence that a fact to which this subsection applies was discovered as a result of a statement made by an accused person shall not be admissible unless evidence of how it was discovered is given by him or on his behalf.

(6)   Subsection (5) above applies—
(a)   to any fact discovered as a result of a confession which is wholly excluded in pursuance of this section; and
(b)   to any fact discovered as a result of a confession which is partly so excluded, if the fact is discovered as a result of the excluded part of the confession.

(7)   Nothing in Part VII of this Act shall prejudice the admissibility of a confession made by an accused person.

(8)   In this section "oppression" includes torture, inhuman or degrading treatment, and the use or threat of violence (whether or not amounting to torture).

[. . .]

[. . .]

Miscellaneous

78 EXCLUSION OF UNFAIR EVIDENCE

(1)   In any proceedings the court may refuse to allow evidence on which the prosecution proposes to rely to be given if it appears to the court that, having regard to all the circumstances, including the circumstances in which the evidence was obtained, the admission of the evidence would have such an adverse effect on the fairness of the proceedings that the court ought not to admit it.

[. . .]

[. . .]

Part VIII SUPPLEMENTARY

82 PART VIII—INTERPRETATION

(1)   In this Part of this Act—

"confession", includes any statement wholly or partly adverse to the person who made it, whether made to a person in authority or not and whether made in words or otherwise;

[. . .]

[. . .]

Part XI MISCELLANEOUS AND SUPPLEMENTARY

[. . .]

117 POWER OF CONSTABLE TO USE REASONABLE FORCE

Where any provision of this Act—

(a)   confers a power on a constable; and

(b)   does not provide that the power may only be exercised with the consent of some person, other than a police officer,

the officer may use reasonable force, if necessary, in the exercise of the power.
[. . .]

As amended by the Crime and Security Act 2010 ss1-6 and s14; Police Reform and Social Responsibility Act 2011, Schedule 16 paragraphs 161 and 163(3)

PUBLIC ORDER ACT 1986
(c. 64)

An Act to abolish the common law offences of riot, rout, unlawful assembly and affray and certain statutory offences relating to public order; to create new offences relating to public order; to control public processions and assemblies; to control the stirring up of racial hatred; to provide for the exclusion of certain offenders from sporting events; to create a new offence relating to the contamination of or interference with goods; to confer power to direct certain trespassers to leave land; to amend section 7 of the Conspiracy and Protection of Property Act 1875, section 1 of the Prevention of Crime Act 1953, Part V of the Criminal Justice (Scotland) Act 1980 and the Sporting Events (Control of Alcohol etc.) Act 1985; to repeal certain obsolete or unnecessary enactments; and for connected purposes.

[. . .]

Part I **NEW OFFENCES**

1 RIOT

(1)   Where 12 or more persons who are present together use or threaten unlawful violence for a common purpose and the conduct of them (taken together) is such as would cause a person of reasonable firmness present at the scene to fear for his personal safety, each of the persons using unlawful violence for the common purpose is guilty of riot.

(2)   It is immaterial whether or not the 12 or more use or threaten unlawful violence simultaneously.

(3)   The common purpose may be inferred from conduct.

(4)   No person of reasonable firmness need actually be, or be likely to be, present at the scene.

(5)   Riot may be committed in private as well as in public places.

[. . .]

2 VIOLENT DISORDER

(1)   Where 3 or more persons who are present together use or threaten unlawful violence and the conduct of them (taken together) is such as would cause a person of reasonable firmness present at the scene to fear for his personal safety, each of the persons using or threatening unlawful violence is guilty of violent disorder.

(2)   It is immaterial whether or not the 3 or more use or threaten unlawful violence simultaneously.

(3)   No person of reasonable firmness need actually be, or be likely to be, present at the scene.

(4)   Violent disorder may be committed in private as well as in public places.

[. . .]

3 AFFRAY

(1)   A person is guilty of affray if he uses or threatens unlawful violence towards another and his conduct is such as would cause a person of reasonable firmness present at the scene to fear for his personal safety.

(2)   Where 2 or more persons use or threaten the unlawful violence, it is the conduct of them taken together that must be considered for the purposes of subsection (1).

(3)   For the purposes of this section a threat cannot be made by the use of words alone.

(4)   No person of reasonable firmness need actually be, or be likely to be, present at the scene.

(5)   Affray may be committed in private as well as in public places.

[...]

4 FEAR OR PROVOCATION OF VIOLENCE

(1)   A person is guilty of an offence if he—
(a) uses towards another person threatening, abusive or insulting words or behaviour, or
(b) distributes or displays to another person any writing, sign or other visible representation which is threatening, abusive or insulting,
with intent to cause that person to believe that immediate unlawful violence will be used against him or another by any person, or to provoke the immediate use of unlawful violence by that person or another, or whereby that person is likely to believe that such violence will be used or it is likely that such violence will be provoked.

(2)   An offence under this section may be committed in a public or a private place, except that no offence is committed where the words or behaviour are used, or the writing, sign or other visible representation is distributed or displayed, by a person inside a dwelling and the other person is also inside that or another dwelling.

[...]

[4A INTENTIONAL HARASSMENT, ALARM OR DISTRESS

(1)   A person is guilty of an offence if, with intent to cause a person harassment, alarm or distress, he—
(a) uses threatening, abusive or insulting words or behaviour, or disorderly behaviour, or
(b) displays any writing, sign or other visible representation which is threatening, abusive or insulting,
thereby causing that or another person harassment, alarm or distress.

(2)   An offence under this section may be committed in a public or a private place, except that no offence is committed where the words or behaviour are used, or the writing, sign or other visible representation is displayed, by a person inside a dwelling and the person who is harassed, alarmed or distressed is also inside that or another dwelling.

(3)   It is a defence for the accused to prove—
(a) that he was inside a dwelling and had no reason to believe that the words or behaviour used, or the writing, sign or other visible representation displayed, would be heard or seen by a person outside that or any other dwelling, or
(b) that his conduct was reasonable.
[...]

5 HARASSMENT, ALARM OR DISTRESS

(1)   A person is guilty of an offence if he—
(a) uses threatening, abusive or insulting words or behaviour, or disorderly behaviour, or
(b) displays any writing, sign or other visible representation which is threatening, abusive or insulting,

within the hearing or sight of a person likely to be caused harassment, alarm or distress thereby.

(2)   An offence under this section may be committed in a public or a private place, except that no offence is committed where the words or behaviour are used, or the writing, sign or other visible representation is displayed, by a person inside a dwelling and the other person is also inside that or another dwelling.

(3)   It is a defence for the accused to prove—
   (a)   that he had no reason to believe that there was any person within hearing or sight who was likely to be caused harassment, alarm or distress, or
   (b)   that he was inside a dwelling and had no reason to believe that the words or behaviour used, or the writing, sign or other visible representation displayed, would be heard or seen by a person outside that or any other dwelling, or
   (c)   that his conduct was reasonable.
   [. . .]

6   MENTAL ELEMENT: MISCELLANEOUS

(1)   A person is guilty of riot only if he intends to use violence or is aware that his conduct may be violent.

(2)   A person is guilty of violent disorder or affray only if he intends to use or threaten violence or is aware that his conduct may be violent or threaten violence.

(3)   A person is guilty of an offence under section 4 only if he intends his words or behaviour, or the writing, sign or other visible representation, to be threatening, abusive or insulting, or is aware that it may be threatening, abusive or insulting.

(4)   A person is guilty of an offence under section 5 only if he intends his words or behaviour, or the writing, sign or other visible representation, to be threatening, abusive or insulting, or is aware that it may be threatening, abusive or insulting or (as the case may be) he intends his behaviour to be or is aware that it may be disorderly.

(5)   For the purposes of this section a person whose awareness is impaired by intoxication shall be taken to be aware of that of which he would be aware if not intoxicated, unless he shows either that his intoxication was not self-induced or that it was caused solely by the taking or administration of a substance in the course of medical treatment.

(6)   In subsection (5) "intoxication" means any intoxication, whether caused by drink, drugs or other means, or by a combination of means.

(7)   Subsections (1) and (2) do not affect the determination for the purposes of riot or violent disorder of the number of persons who use or threaten violence.
   [. . .]

8   INTERPRETATION

In this Part—

"dwelling" means any structure or part of a structure occupied as a person's home or as other living accommodation (whether the occupation is separate or shared with others) but does not include any part not so occupied, and for this purpose "structure" includes a tent, caravan, vehicle, vessel or other temporary or movable structure;

"violence" means any violent conduct, so that—
(a) except in the context of affray, it includes violent conduct towards property as well as violent conduct towards persons, and
(b) it is not restricted to conduct causing or intended to cause injury or damage but includes any other violent conduct (for example, throwing at or towards a person a missile of a kind capable of causing injury which does not hit or falls short).

9 OFFENCES ABOLISHED

(1) The common law offences of riot, rout, unlawful assembly and affray are abolished.

[. . .]

[. . .]

Part II PROCESSIONS AND ASSEMBLIES

11 ADVANCE NOTICE OF PUBLIC PROCESSIONS

(1) Written notice shall be given in accordance with this section of any proposal to hold a public procession intended—
(a) to demonstrate support for or opposition to the views or actions of any person or body of persons,
(b) to publicise a cause or campaign, or
(c) to mark or commemorate an event,
unless it is not reasonably practicable to give any advance notice of the procession.

(2) Subsection (1) does not apply where the procession is one commonly or customarily held in the police area (or areas) in which it is proposed to be held or is a funeral procession organised by a funeral director acting in the normal course of his business.

(3) The notice must specify the date when it is intended to hold the procession, the time when it is intended to start it, its proposed route, and the name and address of the person (or of one of the persons) proposing to organise it.

(4) Notice must be delivered to a police station—
(a) in the police area in which it is proposed the procession will start, or
(b) where it is proposed the procession will start in Scotland and cross into England, in the first police area in England on the proposed route.
[. . .]

(7) Where a public procession is held, each of the persons organising it is guilty of an offence if—
(a) the requirements of this section as to notice have not been satisfied, or
(b) the date when it is held, the time when it starts, or its route, differs from the date, time or route specified in the notice.

(8) It is a defence for the accused to prove that he did not know of, and neither suspected nor had reason to suspect, the failure to satisfy the requirements or (as the case may be) the difference of date, time or route.

(9) To the extent that an alleged offence turns on a difference of date, time or route, it is a defence for the accused to prove that the difference arose from circumstances beyond his control or from something done with the agreement of a police officer or by his direction.

[. . .]

12 IMPOSING CONDITIONS ON PUBLIC PROCESSIONS

(1)   If the senior police officer, having regard to the time or place at which and the circumstances in which any public procession is being held or is intended to be held and to its route or proposed route, reasonably believes that—

    (a) it may result in serious public disorder, serious damage to property or serious disruption to the life of the community, or

    (b) the purpose of the persons organising it is the intimidation of others with a view to compelling them not to do an act they have a right to do, or to do an act they have a right not to do,

he may give directions imposing on the persons organising or taking part in the procession such conditions as appear to him necessary to prevent such disorder, damage, disruption or intimidation, including conditions as to the route of the procession or prohibiting it from entering any public place specified in the directions.

(2)   In subsection (1) "the senior police officer" means—

    (a) in relation to a procession being held, or to a procession intended to be held in a case where persons are assembling with a view to taking part in it, the most senior in rank of the police officers present at the scene, and

    (b) in relation to a procession intended to be held in a case where paragraph (a) does not apply, the chief officer of police.

(3)   A direction given by a chief officer of police by virtue of subsection (2)(b) shall be given in writing.

(4)   A person who organises a public procession and knowingly fails to comply with a condition imposed under this section is guilty of an offence, but it is a defence for him to prove that the failure arose from circumstances beyond his control.

(5)   A person who takes part in a public procession and knowingly fails to comply with a condition imposed under this section is guilty of an offence, but it is a defence for him to prove that the failure arose from circumstances beyond his control.

(6)   A person who incites another to commit an offence under subsection (5) is guilty of an offence.

[. . .]

13 PROHIBITING PUBLIC PROCESSIONS

(1)   If at any time the chief officer of police reasonably believes that, because of particular circumstances existing in any district or part of a district, the powers under section 12 will not be sufficient to prevent the holding of public processions in that district or part from resulting in serious public disorder, he shall apply to the council of the district for an order prohibiting for such period not exceeding 3 months as may be specified in the application the holding of all public processions (or of any class of public procession so specified) in the district or part concerned.

(2)   On receiving such an application, a council may with the consent of the Secretary of State make an order either in the terms of the application or with such modifications as may be approved by the Secretary of State.

(3)   Subsection (1) does not apply in the City of London or the metropolitan police district.

(4)   If at any time the Commissioner of Police for the City of London or the Commissioner of Police of the Metropolis reasonably believes that, because of particular circumstances

existing in his police area or part of it, the powers under section 12 will not be sufficient to prevent the holding of public processions in that area or part from resulting in serious public disorder, he may with the consent of the Secretary of State make an order prohibiting for such period not exceeding 3 months as may be specified in the order the holding of all public processions (or of any class of public procession so specified) in the area or part concerned.

(5) An order made under this section may be revoked or varied by a subsequent order made in the same way, that is, in accordance with subsections (1) and (2) or subsection (4), as the case may be.

(6) Any order under this section shall, if not made in writing, be recorded in writing as soon as practicable after being made.

(7) A person who organises a public procession the holding of which he knows is prohibited by virtue of an order under this section is guilty of an offence.

(8) A person who takes part in a public procession the holding of which he knows is prohibited by virtue of an order under this section is guilty of an offence.

(9) A person who incites another to commit an offence under subsection (8) is guilty of an offence.

[. . .]

14 IMPOSING CONDITIONS ON PUBLIC ASSEMBLIES

(1) If the senior police officer, having regard to the time or place at which and the circumstances in which any public assembly is being held or is intended to be held, reasonably believes that—
  (a) it may result in serious public disorder, serious damage to property or serious disruption to the life of the community, or
  (b) the purpose of the persons organising it is the intimidation of others with a view to compelling them not to do an act they have a right to do, or to do an act they have a right not to do,
he may give directions imposing on the persons organising or taking part in the assembly such conditions as to the place at which the assembly may be (or continue to be) held, its maximum duration, or the maximum number of persons who may constitute it, as appear to him necessary to prevent such disorder, damage, disruption or intimidation.

(2) In subsection (1) "the senior police officer" means—
  (a) in relation to an assembly being held, the most senior in rank of the police officers present at the scene, and
  (b) in relation to an assembly intended to be held, the chief officer of police.

(3) A direction given by a chief officer of police by virtue of subsection (2)(b) shall be given in writing.

(4) A person who organises a public assembly and knowingly fails to comply with a condition imposed under this section is guilty of an offence, but it is a defence for him to prove that the failure arose from circumstances beyond his control.

(5) A person who takes part in a public assembly and knowingly fails to comply with a condition imposed under this section is guilty of an offence, but it is a defence for him to prove that the failure arose from circumstances beyond his control.

(6)   A person who incites another to commit an offence under subsection (5) is guilty of an offence.

[. . .]

[14A PROHIBITING TRESPASSORY ASSEMBLIES

(1)   If at any time the chief officer of police reasonably believes that an assembly is intended to be held in any district at a place on land to which the public has no right of access or only a limited right of access and that the assembly—
(a) is likely to be held without the permission of the occupier of the land or to conduct itself in such a way as to exceed the limits of any permission of his or the limits of the public's right of access, and
(b) may result—
    (i)   in serious disruption to the life of the community, or
    (ii) where the land, or a building or monument on it, is of historical, architectural, archaeological or scientific importance, in significant damage to the land, building or monument,
he may apply to the council of the district for an order prohibiting for a specified period the holding of all trespassory assemblies in the district or a part of it, as specified.

(2)   On receiving such an application, a council may—
(a) in England and Wales, with the consent of the Secretary of State make an order either in the terms of the application or with such modifications as may be approved by the Secretary of State; or
(b) in Scotland, make an order in the terms of the application.
[. . .]

(5)   An order prohibiting the holding of trespassory assemblies operates to prohibit any assembly which—
(a) is held on land to which the public has no right of access or only a limited right of access, and
(b) takes place in the prohibited circumstances, that is to say, without the permission of the occupier of the land or so as to exceed the limits of any permission of his or the limits of the public's right of access.

(6)   No order under this section shall prohibit the holding of assemblies for a period exceeding 4 days or in an area exceeding an area represented by a circle with a radius of 5 miles from a specified centre.

[. . .]

(9)   In this section and sections 14B and 14C—

"assembly" means an assembly of 20 or more persons;

"land" means land in the open air;

"limited", in relation to a right of access by the public to land, means that their use of it is restricted to use for a particular purpose (as in the case of a highway or road) or is subject to other restrictions;

[. . .]

"public" includes a section of the public; and

"specified" means specified in an order under this section.

[. . .]

[14B OFFENCES IN CONNECTION WITH TRESPASSORY ASSEMBLIES AND ARREST THEREFOR

(1)   A person who organises an assembly the holding of which he knows is prohibited by an order under section 14A is guilty of an offence.

(2)   A person who takes part in an assembly which he knows is prohibited by an order under section 14A is guilty of an offence.

(3)   In England and Wales, a person who incites another to commit an offence under subsection (2) is guilty of an offence.

[. . .]

[14C STOPPING PERSONS FROM PROCEEDING TO TRESPASSORY ASSEMBLIES

(1)   If a constable in uniform reasonably believes that a person is on his way to an assembly within the area to which an order under section 14A applies which the constable reasonably believes is likely to be an assembly which is prohibited by that order, he may, subject to subsection (2) below—
(a) stop that person, and
(b) direct him not to proceed in the direction of the assembly.

(2)   The power conferred by subsection (1) may only be exercised within the area to which the order applies.

(3)   A person who fails to comply with a direction under subsection (1) which he knows has been given to him is guilty of an offence.

[. . .]

[. . .]

16 INTERPRETATION

In this Part—
[. . .]
"public assembly" means an assembly of 20 or more persons in a public place which is wholly or partly open to the air;

"public place" means—
(a) any highway, or in Scotland any road within the meaning of the Roads (Scotland) Act 1984, and
(b) any place to which at the material time the public or any section of the public has access, on payment or otherwise, as of right or by virtue of express or implied permission;
"public procession" means a procession in a public place.

Part III RACIAL HATRED

Meaning of "racial hatred"

17 MEANING OF "RACIAL HATRED"

In this Part "racial hatred" means hatred against a group of persons [. . .] defined by reference to colour, race, nationality (including citizenship) or ethnic or national origins.

Acts intended or likely to stir up racial hatred

18 USE OF WORDS OR BEHAVIOUR OR DISPLAY OF WRITTEN MATERIAL

(1)   A person who uses threatening, abusive or insulting words or behaviour, or displays any written material which is threatening, abusive or insulting, is guilty of an offence if—
(a)   he intends thereby to stir up racial hatred, or
(b)   having regard to all the circumstances racial hatred is likely to be stirred up thereby.

(2)   An offence under this section may be committed in a public or a private place, except that no offence is committed where the words or behaviour are used, or the written material is displayed, by a person inside a dwelling and are not heard or seen except by other persons in that or another dwelling.

[. . .]

(4)   In proceedings for an offence under this section it is a defence for the accused to prove that he was inside a dwelling and had no reason to believe that the words or behaviour used, or the written material displayed, would be heard or seen by a person outside that or any other dwelling.

(5)   A person who is not shown to have intended to stir up racial hatred is not guilty of an offence under this section if he did not intend his words or behaviour, or the written material, to be, and was not aware that it might be, threatening, abusive or insulting.

(6)   This section does not apply to words or behaviour used, or written material displayed, solely for the purpose of being included in a programme [included in a programme service].

19 PUBLISHING OR DISTRIBUTING WRITTEN MATERIAL

(1)   A person who publishes or distributes written material which is threatening, abusive or insulting is guilty of an offence if—
(a)   he intends thereby to stir up racial hatred, or
(b)   having regard to all the circumstances racial hatred is likely to be stirred up thereby.

(2)   In proceedings for an offence under this section it is a defence for an accused who is not shown to have intended to stir up racial hatred to prove that he was not aware of the content of the material and did not suspect, and had no reason to suspect, that it was threatening, abusive or insulting.

(3)   References in this Part to the publication or distribution of written material are to its publication or distribution to the public or a section of the public.

20 PUBLIC PERFORMANCE OF PLAY

(1)   If a public performance of a play is given which involves the use of threatening, abusive or insulting words or behaviour, any person who presents or directs the performance is guilty of an offence if—
(a)   he intends thereby to stir up racial hatred, or
(b)   having regard to all the circumstances (and, in particular, taking the performance as a whole) racial hatred is likely to be stirred up thereby.
[. . .]

[. . .]

Supplementary provisions

26 SAVINGS FOR REPORTS OF PARLIAMENTARY OR JUDICIAL PROCEEDINGS

(1)   Nothing in this Part applies to a fair and accurate report of proceedings in Parliament [or in the Scottish Parliament].

(2)   Nothing in this Part applies to a fair and accurate report of proceedings publicly heard before a court or tribunal exercising judicial authority where the report is published contemporaneously with the proceedings or, if it is not reasonably practicable or would be unlawful to publish a report of them contemporaneously, as soon as publication is reasonably practicable and lawful.

27 PROCEDURE AND PUNISHMENT

(1)   No proceedings for an offence under this Part may be instituted in England and Wales except by or with the consent of the Attorney General.

(2)   For the purposes of the rules in England and Wales against charging more than one offence in the same count or information, each of sections 18 to 23 creates one offence.

(3)   A person guilty of an offence under this Part is liable—
   (a)   on conviction on indictment to imprisonment for a term not exceeding [seven years] or a fine or both;
   (b)   on summary conviction to imprisonment for a term not exceeding six months or a fine not exceeding the statutory maximum or both.
   [. . .]

Part 3A HATRED AGAINST PERSONS ON RELIGIOUS GROUNDS [OR GROUNDS OF SEXUAL ORIENTATION]

[*Meaning of "religious hatred"* [and "hatred on the grounds of sexual orientation"]]

[29A MEANING OF "RELIGIOUS HATRED"

In this Part "religious hatred" means hatred against a group of persons defined by reference to religious belief or lack of religious belief.]

[29AB MEANING OF "HATRED ON THE GROUNDS OF SEXUAL ORIENTATION"

In this Part "hatred on the grounds of sexual orientation" means hatred against a group of persons defined by reference to sexual orientation (whether towards persons of the same sex, the opposite sex or both)]

[*Acts intended to stir up religious hatred* [or hatred on the grounds of sexual orientation]]

[29B USE OF WORDS OR BEHAVIOUR OR DISPLAY OF WRITTEN MATERIAL

(1)   A person who uses threatening words or behaviour, or displays any written material which is threatening, is guilty of an offence if he intends thereby to stir up religious hatred [or hatred on the grounds of sexual orientation].

(2)   An offence under this section may be committed in a public or a private place, except that no offence is committed where the words or behaviour are used, or the written material is displayed, by a person inside a dwelling and are not heard or seen except by other persons in that or another dwelling.

[. . .]

(4)   In proceedings for an offence under this section it is a defence for the accused to prove that he was inside a dwelling and had no reason to believe that the words or behaviour used, or the written material displayed, would be heard or seen by a person outside that or any other dwelling.

(5)   This section does not apply to words or behaviour used, or written material displayed, solely for the purpose of being included in a programme service.]

[. . .]

[29J PROTECTION OF FREEDOM OF EXPRESSION

Nothing in this Part shall be read or given effect in a way which prohibits or restricts discussion, criticism or expressions of antipathy, dislike, ridicule, insult or abuse of particular religions or the beliefs or practices of their adherents, or of any other belief system or the beliefs or practices of its adherents, or proselytising or urging adherents of a different religion or belief system to cease practising their religion or belief system.]

[29JA PROTECTION OF FREEDOM OF EXPRESSION (SEXUAL ORIENTATION)

In this Part, for the avoidance of doubt, the discussion or criticism of sexual conduct or practices or the urging of persons to refrain from or modify such conduct or practices shall not be taken of itself to be threatening or intended to stir up hatred]

[. . .]

Part V **MISCELLANEOUS AND GENERAL**

[. . .]

40 AMENDMENTS, REPEALS AND SAVINGS

[. . .]

(4)   Nothing in this Act affects the common law powers in England and Wales to deal with or prevent a breach of the peace.

OFFICIAL SECRETS ACT 1989
(c. 6)

An Act to replace section 2 of the Official Secrets Act 1911 by provisions protecting more limited classes of official information.

[. . .]

1 SECURITY AND INTELLIGENCE

(1)   A person who is or has been—
(a)   a member of the security and intelligence services; or
(b)   a person notified that he is subject to the provisions of this subsection,
is guilty of an offence if without lawful authority he discloses any information, document or other article relating to security or intelligence which is or has been in his possession by virtue of his position as a member of any of those services or in the course of his work while the notification is or was in force.

(2)   The reference in subsection (1) above to disclosing information relating to security or intelligence includes a reference to making any statement which purports to be a disclosure of such information or is intended to be taken by those to whom it is addressed as being such a disclosure.

(3)   A person who is or has been a Crown servant or government contractor is guilty of an offence if without lawful authority he makes a damaging disclosure of any information, document or other article relating to security or intelligence which is or has been in his possession by virtue of his position as such but otherwise than as mentioned in subsection (1) above.

(4)   For the purposes of subsection (3) above a disclosure is damaging if—
(a)   it causes damage to the work of, or of any part of, the security and intelligence services; or
(b)   it is of information or a document or other article which is such that its unauthorised disclosure would be likely to cause such damage or which falls within a class or description of information, documents or articles the unauthorised disclosure of which would be likely to have that effect.

(5)   It is a defence for a person charged with an offence under this section to prove that at the time of the alleged offence he did not know, and had no reasonable cause to believe, that the information, document or article in question related to security or intelligence or, in the case of an offence under subsection (3), that the disclosure would be damaging within the meaning of that subsection.

(6)   Notification that a person is subject to subsection (1) above shall be effected by a notice in writing served on him by a Minister of the Crown; and such a notice may be served if, in the Minister's opinion, the work undertaken by the person in question is or includes work connected with the security and intelligence services and its nature is such that the interests of national security require that he should be subject to the provisions of that subsection.

[. . .]

2 DEFENCE

(1)   A person who is or has been a Crown servant or government contractor is guilty of an offence if without lawful authority he makes a damaging disclosure of any information, document or other article relating to defence which is or has been in his possession by virtue of his position as such.

(2)   For the purposes of subsection (1) above a disclosure is damaging if—
(a)   it damages the capability of, or of any part of, the armed forces of the Crown to carry out their tasks or leads to loss of life or injury to members of those forces or serious damage to the equipment or installations of those forces; or

(b) otherwise than as mentioned in paragraph (a) above, it endangers the interests of the United Kingdom abroad, seriously obstructs the promotion or protection by the United Kingdom of those interests or endangers the safety of British citizens abroad; or

(c) it is of information or of a document or article which is such that its unauthorised disclosure would be likely to have any of those effects.

(3) It is a defence for a person charged with an offence under this section to prove that at the time of the alleged offence he did not know, and had no reasonable cause to believe, that the information, document or article in question related to defence or that its disclosure would be damaging within the meaning of subsection (1) above.

[. . .]

3 INTERNATIONAL RELATIONS

(1) A person who is or has been a Crown servant or government contractor is guilty of an offence if without lawful authority he makes a damaging disclosure of—
(a) any information, document or other article relating to international relations; or
(b) any confidential information, document or other article which was obtained from a State other than the United Kingdom or an international organisation,
being information or a document or article which is or has been in his possession by virtue of his position as a Crown servant or government contractor.

(2) For the purposes of subsection (1) above a disclosure is damaging if—
(a) it endangers the interests of the United Kingdom abroad, seriously obstructs the promotion or protection by the United Kingdom of those interests or endangers the safety of British citizens abroad; or
(b) it is of information or of a document or article which is such that its unauthorised disclosure would be likely to have any of those effects.

(3) In the case of information or a document or article within subsection (1)(b) above—
(a) the fact that it is confidential, or
(b) its nature or contents,
may be sufficient to establish for the purposes of subsection (2)(b) above that the information, document or article is such that its unauthorised disclosure would be likely to have any of the effects there mentioned.

(4) It is a defence for a person charged with an offence under this section to prove that at the time of the alleged offence he did not know, and had no reasonable cause to believe, that the information, document or article in question was such as is mentioned in subsection (1) above or that its disclosure would be damaging within the meaning of that subsection.

[. . .]

[. . .]

7 AUTHORISED DISCLOSURES

(1) For the purposes of this Act a disclosure by—
(a) a Crown servant; or
(b) a person, not being a Crown servant or government contractor, in whose case a notification for the purposes of section 1(1) above is in force,

is made with lawful authority if, and only if, it is made in accordance with his official duty.

[. . .]

(4) It is a defence for a person charged with an offence under any of the foregoing provisions of this Act to prove that at the time of the alleged offence he believed that he had lawful authority to make the disclosure in question and had no reasonable cause to believe otherwise.

[. . .]

8 SAFEGUARDING OF INFORMATION

(1) Where a Crown servant or government contractor, by virtue of his position as such, has in his possession or under his control any document or other article which it would be an offence under any of the foregoing provisions of this Act for him to disclose without lawful authority he is guilty of an offence if—
   (a) being a Crown servant, he retains the document or article contrary to his official duty; or
   (b) being a government contractor, he fails to comply with an official direction for the return or disposal of the document or article,
   or if he fails to take such care to prevent the unauthorised disclosure of the document or article as a person in his position may reasonably be expected to take.

(2) It is a defence for a Crown servant charged with an offence under subsection (1)(a) above to prove that at the time of the alleged offence he believed that he was acting in accordance with his official duty and had no reasonable cause to believe otherwise.

[. . .]

(4) Where a person has in his possession or under his control any document or other article which it would be an offence under section 5 above for him to disclose without lawful authority, he is guilty of an offence if—
   (a) he fails to comply with an official direction for its return or disposal; or
   (b) where he obtained it from a Crown servant or government contractor on terms requiring it to be held in confidence or in circumstances in which that servant or contractor could reasonably expect that it would be so held, he fails to take such care to prevent its unauthorised disclosure as a person in his position may reasonably be expected to take.

(5) Where a person has in his possession or under his control any document or other article which it would be an offence under section 6 above for him to disclose without lawful authority, he is guilty of an offence if he fails to comply with an official direction for its return or disposal.

(6) A person is guilty of an offence if he discloses any official information, document or other article which can be used for the purpose of obtaining access to any information, document or other article protected against disclosure by the foregoing provisions of this Act and the circumstances in which it is disclosed are such that it would be reasonable to expect that it might be used for that purpose without authority.

(7) For the purposes of subsection (6) above a person discloses information or a document or article which is official if—
   (a) he has or has had it in his possession by virtue of his position as a Crown servant or government contractor; or

(b) he knows or has reasonable cause to believe that a Crown servant or government contractor has or has had it in his possession by virtue of his position as such.

[...]

[...]

11 ARREST, SEARCH AND TRIAL

[...]

(3)   Section 9(1) of the Official Secrets Act 1911 (search warrants) shall have effect as if references to offences under that Act included references to offences under any provision of this Act other than section 8(1), (4) or (5); and the following provisions of the Police and Criminal Evidence Act 1984, that is to say—
(a) section 9(2) (which excludes items subject to legal privilege and certain other material from powers of search conferred by previous enactments); and
(b) paragraph 3(b) of Schedule 1 (which prescribes access conditions for the special procedure laid down in that Schedule),
shall apply to section 9(1) of the said Act of 1911 as extended by this subsection as they apply to that section as originally enacted.

[...]

12 "CROWN SERVANT" AND "GOVERNMENT CONTRACTOR"

(1)   In this Act "Crown servant" means—
(a) a Minister of the Crown;
[...]
(c) any person employed in the civil service of the Crown, including Her Majesty's Diplomatic Service, Her Majesty's Overseas Civil Service, the civil service of Northern Ireland and the Northern Ireland Court Service;
(d) any member of the naval, military or air forces of the Crown, including any person employed by an association established for the purposes of [Part XI of the Reserve Forces Act 1996];
(e) any constable and any other person employed or appointed in or for the purposes of any police force [(including the Police Service of Northern Ireland and the Police Service of Northern Ireland Reserve)] [or of the Serious Organised Crime Agency];
[...]

(2)   In this Act "government contractor" means, subject to subsection (3) below, any person who is not a Crown servant but who provides, or is employed in the provision of, goods or services—
(a) for the purposes of any Minister or person mentioned in paragraph (a) [, (ab)] or (b) of subsection (1) above, [of any office-holder in the Scottish Administration,] of any of the services, forces or bodies mentioned in that subsection or of the holder of any office prescribed under that subsection;
[...] or
(b) under an agreement or arrangement certified by the Secretary of State as being one to which the government of a State other than the United Kingdom or an international organisation is a party or which is subordinate to, or made for the purposes of implementing, any such agreement or arrangement.
[...]

[...]

SECURITY SERVICE ACT 1989
(c. 5)

An Act to place the Security Service on a statutory basis; to enable certain actions to be taken on the authority of warrants issued by the Secretary of State, with provision for the issue of such warrants to be kept under review by a Commissioner; to establish a procedure for the investigation by a Tribunal or, in some cases, by the Commissioner of complaints about the Service; and for connected purposes.

[. . .]

1 THE SECURITY SERVICE

(1)   There shall continue to be a Security Service (in this Act referred to as "the Service") under the authority of the Secretary of State.

(2)   The function of the Service shall be the protection of national security and, in particular, its protection against threats from espionage, terrorism and sabotage, from the activities of agents of foreign powers and from actions intended to overthrow or undermine parliamentary democracy by political, industrial or violent means.

(3)   It shall also be the function of the Service to safeguard the economic well-being of the United Kingdom against threats posed by the actions or intentions of persons outside the British Islands.

[(4)   It shall also be the function of the Service to act in support of the activities of police forces [, the Serious Organised Crime Agency] and other law enforcement agencies in the prevention and detection of serious crime.]

[. . .]

2 THE DIRECTOR-GENERAL

(1)   The operations of the Service shall continue to be under the control of a Director-General appointed by the Secretary of State.

(2)   The Director-General shall be responsible for the efficiency of the Service and it shall be his duty to ensure—
    (a)   that there are arrangements for securing that no information is obtained by the Service except so far as necessary for the proper discharge of its functions or disclosed by it except so far as necessary for that purpose or for the purpose of [the prevention or detection of] serious crime [or for the purpose of any criminal proceedings]; and
    (b)   that the Service does not take any action to further the interests of any political party; and
    (c)   that there are arrangements, agreed with [the Director General of the Serious Organised Crime Agency], for co-ordinating the activities of the Service in pursuance of section 1(4) of this Act with the activities of police forces, the Serious Organised Crime Agency, and other law enforcement agencies.

(3)   The arrangements mentioned in subsection (2)(a) above shall be such as to ensure that information in the possession of the Service is not disclosed for use in determining whether a person should be employed, or continue to be employed, by any person, or in

any office or capacity, except in accordance with provisions in that behalf approved by the Secretary of State.

[. . .]

CRIMINAL JUSTICE AND PUBLIC ORDER ACT 1994
(c. 33)

An Act to make further provision in relation to criminal justice (including employment in the prison service); to amend or extend the criminal law and powers for preventing crime and enforcing that law; to amend the Video Recordings Act 1984; and for purposes connected with those purposes.

[. . .]

Part IV **POLICE POWERS**

[. . .]

Powers of police to stop and search

60 POWERS TO STOP AND SEARCH IN ANTICIPATION OF [, OR AFTER,] VIOLENCE

[(1) If a police officer of or above the rank of inspector reasonably believes—
    (a) that incidents involving serious violence may take place in any locality in his police

        area, and that it is expedient to give an authorisation under this section to prevent their occurrence [;]
    [(aa) that—
        (i) an incident involving serious violence has taken place in England and Wales in his police area;
        (ii) a dangerous instrument or offensive weapon used in the incident is being carried in any locality in his police area by a person; and
        (iii) it is expedient to give an authorisation under this section to find the instrument or weapon; or]
    (b) that persons are carrying dangerous instruments or offensive weapons in any locality in his police area without good reason,
    he may give an authorisation that the powers conferred by this section are to be exercisable at any place within that locality for a specified period not exceeding 24 hours.]

    [. . .]

(3) If it appears to [an officer of or above the rank of] superintendent that it is expedient to do so, having regard to offences which have, or are reasonably suspected to have, been committed in connection with any [activity] falling within the authorisation, he may direct that the authorisation shall continue in being for a further [24] hours.

[(3A) If an inspector gives an authorisation under subsection (1) he must, as soon as it is practicable to do so, cause an officer of or above the rank of superintendent to be informed.]

(4) This section confers on any constable in uniform power—
    (a) to stop any pedestrian and search him or anything carried by him for offensive weapons or dangerous instruments;

(b) to stop any vehicle and search the vehicle, its driver and any passenger for offensive weapons or dangerous instruments.

[. . .]

(5)   A constable may, in the exercise of [the powers conferred by subsection (4) above], stop any person or vehicle and make any search he thinks fit whether or not he has any grounds for suspecting that the person or vehicle is carrying weapons or articles of that kind.

(6)   If in the course of a search under this section a constable discovers a dangerous instrument or an article which he has reasonable grounds for suspecting to be an offensive weapon, he may seize it.

(7)   This section applies (with the necessary modifications) to ships, aircraft and hovercraft as it applies to vehicles.

[. . .]

(10)   Where a vehicle is stopped by a constable under this section, the driver shall be entitled to obtain a written statement that the vehicle was stopped under the powers conferred by this section if he applies for such a statement not later than the end of the period of twelve months from the day on which the vehicle was stopped [. . .]

[(10A) A person who is searched by a constable under this section shall be entitled to obtain a written statement that he was searched under the powers conferred by this section if he applies for such a statement not later than the end of the period of twelve months from the day on which he was searched.]

[. . .]

[. . .]

Part V PUBLIC ORDER: COLLECTIVE TRESPASS OR NUISANCE ON LAND

Powers to remove trespassers on land

61 POWER TO REMOVE TRESPASSERS ON LAND

(1)   If the senior police officer present at the scene reasonably believes that two or more persons are trespassing on land and are present there with the common purpose of residing there for any period, that reasonable steps have been taken by or on behalf of the occupier to ask them to leave and—
(a) that any of those persons has caused damage to the land or to property on the land or used threatening, abusive or insulting words or behaviour towards the occupier, a member of his family or an employee or agent of his, or
(b) that those persons have between them six or more vehicles on the land,
he may direct those persons, or any of them, to leave the land and to remove any vehicles or other property they have with them on the land.

(2)   Where the persons in question are reasonably believed by the senior police officer to be persons who were not originally trespassers but have become trespassers on the land, the officer must reasonably believe that the other conditions specified in subsection (1) are satisfied after those persons became trespassers before he can exercise the power conferred by that subsection.

(3)   A direction under subsection (1) above, if not communicated to the persons referred to in subsection (1) by the police officer giving the direction, may be communicated to them by any constable at the scene.

(4)   If a person knowing that a direction under subsection (1) above has been given which
applies to him—
(a) fails to leave the land as soon as reasonably practicable, or
(b) having left again enters the land as a trespasser within the period of three months
beginning with the day on which the direction was given,
he commits an offence and is liable on summary conviction to imprisonment for a term
not exceeding three months or a fine not exceeding level 4 on the standard scale, or both.

[. . .]

(6)   In proceedings for an offence under this section it is a defence for the accused to show—
(a) that he was not trespassing on the land, or
(b) that he had a reasonable excuse for failing to leave the land as soon as reasonably
practicable or, as the case may be, for again entering the land as a trespasser.
[. . .]

62 SUPPLEMENTARY POWERS OF SEIZURE

(1)   If a direction has been given under section 61 and a constable reasonably suspects that
any person to whom the direction applies has, without reasonable excuse—
(a) failed to remove any vehicle on the land which appears to the constable to belong to
him or to be in his possession or under his control; or
(b) entered the land as a trespasser with a vehicle within the period of three months
beginning with the day on which the direction was given,
the constable may seize and remove that vehicle.

[. . .]

[. . .]

Disruptive trespassers

68 OFFENCE OF AGGRAVATED TRESPASS

(1)   A person commits the offence of aggravated trespass if he trespasses on land [. . .] and,
in relation to any lawful activity which persons are engaging in or are about to engage
in on that or adjoining land [. . .], does there anything which is intended by him to have
the effect—
(a) of intimidating those persons or any of them so as to deter them or any of them from
engaging in that activity,
(b) of obstructing that activity, or
(c) of disrupting that activity.
[. . .]

69 POWERS TO REMOVE PERSONS COMMITTING OR PARTICIPATING
IN AGGRAVATED TRESPASS

(1)   If the senior police officer present at the scene reasonably believes—
(a) that a person is committing, has committed or intends to commit the offence of
aggravated trespass on land [. . .]; or
(b) that two or more persons are trespassing on land [. . .] and are present there with the
common purpose of intimidating persons so as to deter them from engaging in a
lawful activity or of obstructing or disrupting a lawful activity,

he may direct that person or (as the case may be) those persons (or any of them) to leave the land.

(2) A direction under subsection (1) above, if not communicated to the persons referred to in subsection (1) by the police officer giving the direction, may be communicated to them by any constable at the scene.

(3) If a person knowing that a direction under subsection (1) above has been given which applies to him—
   (a) fails to leave the land as soon as practicable, or
   (b) having left again enters the land as a trespasser within the period of three months beginning with the day on which the direction was given,
   he commits an offence and is liable on summary conviction to imprisonment for a term not exceeding three months or a fine not exceeding level 4 on the standard scale, or both.

(4) In proceedings for an offence under subsection (3) it is a defence for the accused to show—
   (a) that he was not trespassing on the land, or
   (b) that he had a reasonable excuse for failing to leave the land as soon as practicable or, as the case may be, for again entering the land as a trespasser.
   [. . .]

INTELLIGENCE SERVICES ACT 1994
(c. 13)

An Act to make provision about the Secret Intelligence Service and the Government Communications Headquarters, including provision for the issue of warrants and authorisations enabling certain actions to be taken and for the issue of such warrants and authorisations to be kept under review; to make further provision about warrants issued on applications by the Security Service; to establish a procedure for the investigation of complaints about the Secret Intelligence Service and the Government Communications Headquarters; to make provision for the establishment of an Intelligence and Security Committee to scrutinise all three of those bodies; and for connected purposes.

[. . .]

The Secret Intelligence Service

1 THE SECRET INTELLIGENCE SERVICE

(1) There shall continue to be a Secret Intelligence Service (in this Act referred to as "the Intelligence Service") under the authority of the Secretary of State; and, subject to subsection (2) below, its functions shall be—
   (a) to obtain and provide information relating to the actions or intentions of persons outside the British Islands; and
   (b) to perform other tasks relating to the actions or intentions of such persons.

(2) The functions of the Intelligence Service shall be exercisable only—
   (a) in the interests of national security, with particular reference to the defence and foreign policies of Her Majesty's Government in the United Kingdom; or
   (b) in the interests of the economic well-being of the United Kingdom; or
   (c) in support of the prevention or detection of serious crime.

2 THE CHIEF OF THE INTELLIGENCE SERVICE

(1)   The operations of the Intelligence Service shall continue to be under the control of a Chief of that Service appointed by the Secretary of State.

(2)   The Chief of the Intelligence Service shall be responsible for the efficiency of that Service and it shall be his duty to ensure—
    (a) that there are arrangements for securing that no information is obtained by the Intelligence Service except so far as necessary for the proper discharge of its functions and that no information is disclosed by it except so far as necessary—
        (i)   for that purpose;
        (ii) in the interests of national security;
        (iii) for the purpose of the prevention or detection of serious crime; or
        (iv) for the purpose of any criminal proceedings; and
    (b) that the Intelligence Service does not take any action to further the interests of any United Kingdom political party.

(3)   Without prejudice to the generality of subsection (2)(a) above, the disclosure of information shall be regarded as necessary for the proper discharge of the functions of the Intelligence Service if it consists of—
    (a) the disclosure of records subject to and in accordance with the Public Records Act 1958; or
    (b) the disclosure, subject to and in accordance with arrangements approved by the Secretary of State, of information to the Comptroller and Auditor General for the purposes of his functions.

[. . .]

GCHQ

3 THE GOVERNMENT COMMUNICATIONS HEADQUARTERS

(1)   There shall continue to be a Government Communications Headquarters under the authority of the Secretary of State; and, subject to subsection (2) below, its functions shall be—
    (a) to monitor or interfere with electromagnetic, acoustic and other emissions and any equipment producing such emissions and to obtain and provide information derived from or related to such emissions or equipment and from encrypted material; and
    (b) to provide advice and assistance about—
        (i)   languages, including terminology used for technical matters, and
        (ii) cryptography and other matters relating to the protection of information and other material,
    to the armed forces of the Crown, to Her Majesty's Government in the United Kingdom or to a Northern Ireland Department or to any other organisation which is determined for the purposes of this section in such manner as may be specified by the Prime Minister.

(2)   The functions referred to in subsection (1)(a) above shall be exercisable only—
    (a) in the interests of national security, with particular reference to the defence and foreign policies of Her Majesty's Government in the United Kingdom; or
    (b) in the interests of the economic well-being of the United Kingdom in relation to the actions or intentions of persons outside the British Islands; or
    (c) in support of the prevention or detection of serious crime.
    [. . .]

4 THE DIRECTOR OF GCHQ

(1)   The operations of GCHQ shall continue to be under the control of a Director appointed by the Secretary of State.

(2)   The Director shall be responsible for the efficiency of GCHQ and it shall be his duty to ensure—

(a)   that there are arrangements for securing that no information is obtained by GCHQ except so far as necessary for the proper discharge of its functions and that no information is disclosed by it except so far as necessary for that purpose or for the purpose of any criminal proceedings; and

(b)   that GCHQ does not take any action to further the interests of any United Kingdom political party.

[. . .]

The Intelligence and Security Committee

10 THE INTELLIGENCE AND SECURITY COMMITTEE

(1)   There shall be a Committee, to be known as the Intelligence and Security Committee and in this section referred to as "the Committee", to examine the expenditure, administration and policy of—

(a)   the Security Service;

(b)   the Intelligence Service; and

(c)   GCHQ.

(2)   The Committee shall consist of nine members—

(a)   who shall be drawn both from the members of the House of Commons and from the members of the House of Lords; and

(b)   none of whom shall be a Minister of the Crown.

(3)   The members of the Committee shall be appointed by the Prime Minister after consultation with the Leader of the Opposition, within the meaning of the Ministerial and other Salaries Act 1975; and one of those members shall be so appointed as Chairman of the Committee.

[. . .]

POLICE ACT 1996
(c. 16)

An Act to consolidate the Police Act 1964, Part IX of the Police and Criminal Evidence Act 1984, Chapter I of Part I of the Police and Magistrates' Courts Act 1994 and certain other enactments relating to the police.

[. . .]

Part I ORGANISATION OF POLICE FORCES

Police areas

1 POLICE AREAS

(1)   England and Wales shall be divided into police areas.

(2)   The police areas referred to in subsection (1) shall be—

(a) those listed in Schedule 1 (subject to any amendment made to that Schedule by an order under section 32 below, section 58 of the Local Government Act 1972, [or section 17 of the Local Government Act 1992 or Part 1 of the Local Government and Public Involvement in Health Act 2007]),

(b) the metropolitan police district, and

(c) the City of London police area.

(3) References in Schedule 1 to any local government area are to that area as it is for the time being, [. . .]

Forces outside London

2 MAINTENANCE OF POLICE FORCES

A police force shall be maintained for every police area for the time being listed in Schedule 1.

3 ESTABLISHMENT OF POLICE AUTHORITIES

(1) There shall be a police authority for every police area for the time being listed in Schedule 1.

(2) A police authority established under this section for any area shall be a body corporate to be known by the name of the area with the addition of the words "Police Authority".

4 MEMBERSHIP OF POLICE AUTHORITIES ETC.

(1) Subject to subsection (2), each police authority established under section 3 shall consist of seventeen members.

[. . .]

[. . .]

[The metropolitan police force]

5A MAINTENANCE OF THE METROPOLITAN POLICE FORCE

A police force shall be maintained for the metropolitan police district.

5B ESTABLISHMENT OF THE METROPOLITAN POLICE AUTHORITY

(1) There shall be a police authority for the metropolitan police district.

(2) The police authority established under this section shall be a body corporate to be known as the Metropolitan Police Authority.

5C MEMBERSHIP ETC OF THE METROPOLITAN POLICE AUTHORITY

(1) The Metropolitan Police Authority shall consist of twenty three members (subject to subsection (2)).

[. . .]

[The metropolitan police and forces outside London]

6 GENERAL FUNCTIONS OF POLICE AUTHORITIES

(1)   Every police authority established under section 3 [—]
[(a) shall secure the maintenance of an efficient and effective police force for its area, and
(b) shall hold the chief officer of police of that force to account for the exercise of his functions and those of persons under his direction and control.]

(2)   In discharging its functions, every police authority established under section 3 shall have regard to—
(a) any [strategic priorities determined by the Secretary of State under section 37A]
[(aa)   the views of people in the authority's area about policing in that area,]
(b) any objectives determined by the authority [by virtue of section 6ZB],
(c) any performance targets established by the authority, whether in compliance with a direction under section 38 or otherwise, and
[(d) any plan issued by the authority by virtue of section 6ZB.]

(3)   In discharging any function to which a code of practice issued under section 39 relates, a police authority established under section 3 shall have regard to the code.

[. . .]

[6ZA POWER TO CONFER PARTICULAR FUNCTIONS ON POLICE AUTHORITIES

(1)   The Secretary of State may by order confer particular functions on police authorities.

(2)   Without prejudice to the generality of subsection (1), an order under this section may contain provision requiring a police authority—
(a) to monitor the performance of the police force maintained for its area in—
(i) complying with any duty imposed on the force by or under this Act, the Human Rights Act 1998 or any other enactment;
(ii) carrying out any plan issued by virtue of section 6ZB;
(b) to secure that arrangements are made for that force to co-operate with other police forces whenever necessary or expedient;
(c) to promote diversity within that force and within the authority.
[. . .]

[6ZB PLANS BY POLICE AUTHORITIES

(1)   Before the beginning of each financial year every police authority shall issue a plan (a "policing plan") setting out—
(a) the authority's objectives ("policing objectives") for the policing of its area during that year; and
(b) the proposed arrangements for the policing of that area for the period of three years beginning with that year.
[. . .]

[. . .]

[9A GENERAL FUNCTIONS OF THE COMMISSIONER OF POLICE OF THE METROPOLIS

(1)   The metropolitan police force shall be under the direction and control of the Commissioner of Police of the Metropolis appointed under section 9B.

[(1A) Subsection (1) is subject to any provision included in a police force collaboration agreement by virtue of section 23(4).]

(2) In discharging his functions, the Commissioner of Police of the Metropolis shall have regard to—
[(a) any arrangements involving the metropolitan police force that are made by virtue of section 6ZA(2)(b);
(b) the policing plan issued by the Metropolitan Police Authority under section 6ZB.]

[9B APPOINTMENT OF COMMISSIONER OF POLICE OF THE METROPOLIS

(1) There shall be a Commissioner of Police of the Metropolis.

(2) Any appointment of a Commissioner of Police of the Metropolis shall be made by Her Majesty by warrant under Her sign manual.

(3) A person appointed as Commissioner of Police of the Metropolis shall hold office at Her Majesty's pleasure.

(4) Any appointment of a Commissioner of Police of the Metropolis shall be subject to regulations under section 50.

(5) Before recommending to Her Majesty that She appoint a person as the Commissioner of Police of the Metropolis, the Secretary of State shall have regard to—
(a) any recommendations made to him by the Metropolitan Police Authority; and
(b) any representations made to him by the Mayor of London.

[. . .]

[9E REMOVAL OF COMMISSIONER OR DEPUTY COMMISSIONER

(1) The Metropolitan Police Authority, acting with the approval of the Secretary of State, may call upon the Commissioner of Police of the Metropolis [in the interests of efficiency or effectiveness, to retire or to resign].

(2) Before seeking the approval of the Secretary of State under subsection (1), the Metropolitan Police Authority shall give the Commissioner of Police of the Metropolis (—)
[(a) an explanation in writing of the Authority's grounds for calling upon him, in the interests of efficiency or effectiveness, to retire or to resign; and
(b) an opportunity to make representations;
and the Authority shall consider any representations made by or on behalf of the Commissioner.

The opportunity given to the Commissioner to make representations must include the opportunity to make them in person.]

[. . .]

[. . .]

10 GENERAL FUNCTIONS OF CHIEF CONSTABLES

(1) A police force maintained under section 2 shall be under the direction and control of the chief constable appointed under section 11.

[(1A) Subsection (1) is subject to any provision included in a police force collaboration agreement by virtue of section 23(4).]

(2)   In discharging his functions, every chief constable shall have regard to [—]
[(a) any arrangements involving his force that are made by virtue of section 6ZA(2)(b);
(b) the policing plan issued by the police authority for his area under section 6ZB.]

11 APPOINTMENT AND REMOVAL OF CHIEF CONSTABLES

(1)   The chief constable of a police force maintained under section 2 shall be appointed by the police authority responsible for maintaining the force, but subject to the approval of the Secretary of State and to regulations under section 50.

(2)   Without prejudice to any regulations under section 50 or under the Police Pensions Act 1976, the police authority, acting with the approval of the Secretary of State, may call upon the chief constable [in the interests of efficiency or effectiveness, to retire or to resign].

(3)   Before seeking the approval of the Secretary of State under subsection (2), the police authority shall give the chief constable [—]
[(a) an explanation in writing of the authority's grounds for calling upon him, in the interests of efficiency or effectiveness, to retire or to resign; and
(b) an opportunity to make representations;
and the authority shall consider any representations made by or on behalf of the chief officer.

The opportunity given to the chief constable to make representations must include the opportunity to make them in person.]

[. . .]

20 QUESTIONS ON POLICE MATTERS AT COUNCIL MEETINGS

(1)   Every relevant council shall make arrangements (whether by standing orders or otherwise) for enabling questions on the discharge of the functions of a police authority [established under section 3] to be put by members of the council at a meeting of the council for answer by a person nominated by the authority for that purpose.

[. . .]

General provisions

22 REPORTS BY CHIEF CONSTABLES TO POLICE AUTHORITIES

(1)   Every [chief officer of police of a police force] shall, as soon as possible after the end of each financial year, submit to the police authority a general report on the policing during that year of the area for which his force is maintained.

(2)   A [chief officer] shall arrange for a report submitted by him under subsection (1) to be published in such manner as appears to him to be appropriate.

(3)   The [chief officer of police] of a police force shall, whenever so required by the police authority, submit to that authority a report on such matters as may be specified in the requirement, being matters connected with the policing of the area for which the force is maintained.

[. . .]

(5)   If it appears to the [chief officer] that a report in compliance with subsection (3) would contain information which in the public interest ought not to be disclosed, or is not needed for the discharge of the functions of the police authority, he may request that authority to refer the requirement to submit the report to the Secretary of State; and in any such case the requirement shall be of no effect unless it is confirmed by the Secretary of State.

[. . .]

30 JURISDICTION OF CONSTABLES

(1)   A member of a police force shall have all the powers and privileges of a constable throughout England and Wales and the adjacent United Kingdom waters.

[(2)   A special constable shall have all the powers and privileges of a constable throughout England and Wales and the adjacent United Kingdom waters.]

[. . .]

[. . .]

Alteration of police areas

32 POWER TO ALTER POLICE AREAS BY ORDER

(1)   The Secretary of State may by order make alterations in police areas in England and Wales other than the City of London police area.

(2)   The alterations that may be made by an order under this section include alterations that result in a reduction or an increase in the number of police areas, but not alterations that result in the abolition of the metropolitan police district.

(3)   The Secretary of State shall not exercise his power under this section to make alterations unless either—
(a) he has received a request to make the alterations from the police authority for each of the areas [. . .] affected by them, or
(b) it appears to him to be expedient to make the alterations in the interests of efficiency or effectiveness.
[. . .]

[. . .]

Part II CENTRAL SUPERVISION, DIRECTION AND FACILITIES

Functions of Secretary of State

36 GENERAL DUTY OF SECRETARY OF STATE

(1)   The Secretary of State shall exercise his powers under the provisions of this Act referred to in subsection (2) in such manner and to such extent as appears to him to be best calculated to promote the efficiency and effectiveness of the police.

(2)   The provisions of this Act mentioned in subsection (1) are—
(a) Part I;
(b) this Part;
(c) Part III (other than sections 61 and 62);
(d) in Chapter II of Part IV, [sections 84 and 85] and Schedule 6; and
(e) in Part V, section 95.
[. . .]

38 SETTING OF PERFORMANCE TARGETS

(1)   Where [a strategic priority has been determined under section 37A], the Secretary of State may direct police authorities to establish levels of performance ("performance targets") to be aimed at in seeking [to give effect to that priority].

[. . .]

[. . .]

[40 POWER TO GIVE DIRECTIONS TO A POLICE FORCE

(1)   Where the Secretary of State is satisfied that the whole or any part of a police force is failing to discharge any of its functions in an effective manner, whether generally or in particular respects, he may direct the police authority responsible for maintaining the force to take specified measures for the purpose of remedying the failure.

(2)   Where the Secretary of State is satisfied that the whole or a part of a police force will fail to discharge any of its functions in an effective manner, whether generally or in particular respects, unless remedial measures are taken, he may direct the police authority responsible for maintaining the force to take specified measures in order to prevent such a failure occurring.

(3)   The measures that may be specified in a direction under subsection (1) or (2) include the submission to the Secretary of State of an action plan setting out the measures which the person or persons submitting the plan propose to take for the purpose of remedying the failure in question or (as the case may be) preventing such a failure occurring.

(4)   The Secretary of State shall not give a direction under this section in relation to any police force unless—
(a)   the police authority responsible for maintaining the force and the chief officer of police of that force have each been given such information about the Secretary of State's grounds for proposing to give that direction as he considers appropriate for enabling them to make representations or proposals under the following paragraphs of this subsection;
(b)   that police authority and chief officer have each been given an opportunity of making representations about those grounds;
(c)   that police authority and chief officer have each had an opportunity of making proposals for the taking of remedial measures that would make the giving of the direction unnecessary; and
(d)   the Secretary of State has considered any such representations and any such proposals.

(5)   Subsection (4) does not apply if the Secretary of State is satisfied that—
(a)   the police authority responsible for maintaining the force and the chief officer of police of that force have already been made aware of the matters constituting the Secretary of State's grounds for proposing to give a direction under this section;
(b)   the information they had about those matters was sufficient to enable them to identify remedial measures that would have made the giving of the direction unnecessary; and
(c)   they have each had a reasonable opportunity to take such measures.

(6)   The Secretary of State shall not give a direction under this section unless Her Majesty's Chief Inspector of Constabulary has been given—
(a)   the same information about the grounds for proposing to give that direction as is required to be given under subsection (4)(a) (or would be so required but for subsection (5)); and

(b) an opportunity of making written observations about those grounds.
The Secretary of State shall publish any such observations in such manner as appears to him to be appropriate.

(7)   A police authority that is given a direction under this section shall comply with it.]

[40A POWER TO GIVE DIRECTIONS IN RELATION TO LOCAL POLICING BODY

(1)   Where the Secretary of State is satisfied that a local policing body is failing to discharge any of its functions in an effective manner, whether generally or in particular respects, he may direct the local policing body to take specified measures for the purpose of remedying the failure.

(2)   Where the Secretary of State is satisfied that a local policing body will fail to discharge any of its functions in an effective manner, whether generally or in particular respects, unless remedial measures are taken, he may direct the local policing body to take specified measures in order to prevent such a failure occurring.

[. . .]

[. . .]

41 DIRECTIONS AS TO MINIMUM BUDGET

(1)   The power of the Secretary of State to give directions under [section 40 or 40A] to a police authority established under section 3 shall include power to direct the authority that the amount of its budget requirement for any financial year (under section 43 of the Local Government Finance Act 1992) shall not be less than an amount specified in the direction.

[. . .]

50 REGULATIONS FOR POLICE FORCES

(1)   Subject to the provisions of this section, the Secretary of State may make regulations as to the government, administration and conditions of service of police forces.

(2)   Without prejudice to the generality of subsection (1), regulations under this section may make provision with respect to—
(a) the ranks to be held by members of police forces;
(b) the qualifications for appointment and promotion of members of police forces;
(c) periods of service on probation;
(d) voluntary retirement of members of police forces;
(e) the conduct, efficiency and effectiveness of members of police forces and the maintenance of discipline;
(f) the suspension of members of a police force from membership of that force and from their office as constable;
(g) the maintenance of personal records of members of police forces;
(h) the duties which are or are not to be performed by members of police forces;
(i) the treatment as occasions of police duty of attendance at meetings of the Police Federations and of any body recognised by the Secretary of State for the purposes of section 64;
(j) the hours of duty, leave, pay and allowances of members of police forces; and
(k) the issue, use and return of police clothing, personal equipment and accoutrements.

(3)   Without prejudice to the powers conferred by this section, regulations under this section shall—
(a) establish, or
(b) make provision for the establishment of,
procedures for the taking of disciplinary proceedings in respect of the conduct, efficiency and effectiveness of members of police forces, including procedures for cases in which such persons may be dealt with by dismissal.]

[. . .]

[. . .]

Inspectors of constabulary

54 APPOINTMENT AND FUNCTIONS OF INSPECTORS OF CONSTABULARY

(1)   Her Majesty may appoint such number of inspectors (to be known as "Her Majesty's Inspectors of Constabulary") as the Secretary of State may with the consent of the Treasury determine, and of the persons so appointed one may be appointed as chief inspector of constabulary.

(2)   The inspectors of constabulary shall inspect, and report on the efficiency and effectiveness of, every police force maintained for a police area [. . .]

[. . .]

55 PUBLICATION OF REPORTS

(1)   The inspectors of constabulary must arrange for any report prepared under section 54 to be published in such manner as appears to the inspectors to be appropriate.

(2)   "(2)But the inspectors of constabulary must exclude from publication under subsection (1) anything that the inspectors consider—
(a) would be against the interests of national security, or
(b) might jeopardise the safety of any person.

(2A) The inspectors must disclose to the Secretary of State anything excluded from publication by virtue of subsection (2). [. . .]

[. . .]

Part III POLICE REPRESENTATIVE INSTITUTIONS

59 POLICE FEDERATIONS

(1)   There shall continue to be a Police Federation for England and Wales and a Police Federation for Scotland for the purpose of representing members of the police forces in those countries respectively in all matters affecting their welfare and efficiency, except for—
(a) questions of promotion affecting individuals, and
(b) (subject to subsection (2)) questions of discipline affecting individuals.

(2)   A Police Federation may represent a member of a police force at any proceedings brought under regulations made in accordance with section 50(3) above or section 26(2A) of the Police (Scotland) Act 1967 or on an appeal from any such proceedings.

(3)   Except on an appeal to a police appeals tribunal or as [provided in regulations made in accordance with] section 84, a member of a police force may only be represented under subsection (2) by another member of a police force.

(4)   The Police Federations shall act through local and central representative bodies.

(5)   The Police Federations and every branch of a Federation shall be entirely independent of, and subject to subsection (6) unassociated with, any body or person outside the police service, but may employ persons outside the police service in an administrative or advisory capacity.

(6)   The Secretary of State—
(a)   may authorise a Police Federation or a branch of a Federation to be associated with a person or body outside the police service in such cases and manner, and subject to such conditions and restrictions, as he may specify, and
(b)   may vary or withdraw an authorisation previously given;
and anything for the time being so authorised shall not be precluded by subsection (5).

[. . .]

60 REGULATIONS FOR POLICE FEDERATIONS

(1)   The Secretary of State may by regulations—
(a)   prescribe the constitution and proceedings of the Police Federations, or
(b)   authorise the Federations to make rules concerning such matters relating to their constitution and proceedings as may be specified in the regulations.

(2)   Without prejudice to the generality of subsection (1), regulations under this section may make provision—
(a)   with respect to the membership of the Federations;
(b)   with respect to the raising of funds by the Federations by voluntary subscription and the use and management of funds derived from such subscriptions;
(c)   with respect to the manner in which representations may be made by committees or bodies of the Federations to local policing bodies, police authorities, chief officers of police and the Secretary of State;
[. . .]
[. . .]

64 MEMBERSHIP OF TRADE UNIONS

(1)   Subject to the following provisions of this section, a member of a police force shall not be a member of any trade union, or of any association having for its objects, or one of its objects, to control or influence the pay, pensions or conditions of service of any police force.

(2)   Where a person was a member of a trade union before becoming a member of a police force, he may, with the consent of the chief officer of police, continue to be a member of that union during the time of his service in the police force.

[. . .]

Part IV COMPLAINTS, DISCIPLINARY PROCEEDINGS ETC.

[. . .]

Chapter II Disciplinary and other proceedings

84 REPRESENTATION ETC. AT DISCIPLINARY AND OTHER PROCEEDINGS

(1)   The Secretary of State shall by regulations make provision for or in connection with—
    (a) enabling the officer concerned or a relevant authority to be represented in proceedings conducted under regulations made in pursuance of section 50(3) or section 51(2A);
    (b) enabling the panel conducting such proceedings to receive advice from a relevant lawyer or another person falling within any prescribed description of persons.

(2)   Regulations under this section may in particular make provision—
    (a) specifying the circumstances in which the officer concerned or a relevant authority is entitled to be legally represented (by a relevant lawyer);
    (b) specifying the circumstances in which the officer concerned or a relevant authority is entitled to be represented by a person (other than a relevant lawyer) who falls within any prescribed description of persons;
    (c) for securing that—
        (i)   a relevant authority may be legally represented, and
        (ii) the panel conducting the proceedings may receive advice from a relevant lawyer,
    whether or not the officer concerned is legally represented.

(3)   Without prejudice to the powers conferred by this section, regulations under this section shall, in relation to cases where the officer concerned is entitled to legal or other representation, make provision—
    (a) for securing that the officer is notified of his right to such representation;
    (b) specifying when the officer is to be so notified;
    (c) for securing that proceedings at which the officer may be dismissed are not to take place unless the officer has been notified of his right to such representation.

(4)   In this section—

"the officer concerned", in relation to proceedings within subsection (1)(a), means the member of a police force or special constable to whom the proceedings relate;

"the panel", in relation to proceedings within subsection (1)(a), means the panel of persons, or the person, prescribed for the purpose of conducting the proceedings;

"prescribed" means prescribed by regulations under this section;

"relevant authority" means—
    (a) where the officer concerned is a member of a police force (other than the chief officer of police), or a special constable, the chief officer of police of the police force of which the officer is a member, or for which the officer is appointed as a special constable;
    (b) where the officer concerned is the chief officer of police, the local policing body for the police force of which the officer is a member;

"relevant lawyer" means a person who, for the purposes of the Legal Services Act 2007, is an authorised person in relation to an activity which constitutes the exercise of a right of audience (within the meaning of that Act);

"senior officer" means a member of a police force holding a rank above that of chief superintendent.

(5) But in prescribed circumstances "relevant authority" also includes the Independent Police Complaints Commission.

(6) Regulations under this section may make different provision for different cases and circumstances.

(7) A statutory instrument containing regulations under this section shall be subject to annulment in pursuance of a resolution of either House of Parliament.

(8) Subsection (7) does not apply to a statutory instrument containing (whether alone or with other provision) any regulations under this section coming into force at a time that is the earliest time at which any regulations under this section are to come into force since the commencement of paragraph 7 of Schedule 22 to the Criminal Justice and Immigration Act 2008.

[. . .]

85 APPEALS AGAINST DISMISSAL, ETC.

[(1) The Secretary of State shall by rules make provision specifying the cases in which a member of a police force or a special constable may appeal to a police appeals tribunal.

(2) A police appeals tribunal may, on the determination of an appeal under this section, make an order dealing with the appellant in any way in which he could have been dealt with by the person who made the decision appealed against.]

[. . .]

[. . .]

88 LIABILITY FOR WRONGFUL ACTS OF CONSTABLES

(1) The chief officer of police for a police area shall be liable in respect of [any unlawful conduct of] constables under his direction and control in the performance or purported performance of their functions in like manner as a master is liable in respect of torts committed by his servants in the course of their employment, and accordingly shall [, in the case of a tort,] be treated for all purposes as a joint tortfeasor.

[. . .]

(3) Any proceedings in respect of a claim made by virtue of this section shall be brought against the chief officer of police for the time being or, in the case of a vacancy in that office, against the person for the time being performing the functions of the chief officer of police; and references in subsections (1) and (2) to the chief officer of police shall be construed accordingly.

[. . .]

Part V MISCELLANEOUS AND GENERAL

Offences

89 ASSAULTS ON CONSTABLES

(1) Any person who assaults a constable in the execution of his duty, or a person assisting a constable in the execution of his duty, shall be guilty of an offence and liable on summary

conviction to imprisonment for a term not exceeding six months or to a fine not exceeding level 5 on the standard scale, or to both.

(2)   Any person who resists or wilfully obstructs a constable in the execution of his duty, or a person assisting a constable in the execution of his duty, shall be guilty of an offence and liable on summary conviction to imprisonment for a term not exceeding one month or to a fine not exceeding level 3 on the standard scale, or to both.

[. . .]

90 IMPERSONATION, ETC.

(1)   Any person who with intent to deceive impersonates a member of a police force or special constable, or makes any statement or does any act calculated falsely to suggest that he is such a member or constable, shall be guilty of an offence and liable on summary conviction to imprisonment for a term not exceeding six months or to a fine not exceeding level 5 on the standard scale, or to both.

(2)   Any person who, not being a constable, wears any article of police uniform in circumstances where it gives him an appearance so nearly resembling that of a member of a police force as to be calculated to deceive shall be guilty of an offence and liable on summary conviction to a fine not exceeding level 3 on the standard scale.

(3)   Any person who, not being a member of a police force or special constable, has in his possession any article of police uniform shall, unless he proves that he obtained possession of that article lawfully and has possession of it for a lawful purpose, be guilty of an offence and liable on summary conviction to a fine not exceeding level 1 on the standard scale.

(4)   In this section—
    (a)   "article of police uniform" means any article of uniform or any distinctive badge or mark or document of identification usually issued to members of police forces or special constables, or anything having the appearance of such an article, badge, mark or document,
    [. . .]
[. . .]

93 ACCEPTANCE OF GIFTS AND LOANS

(1)   A local policing body may, in connection with the discharge of any of its functions, accept gifts of money, and gifts or loans of other property, on such terms as appear to the body to be appropriate. [. . .]
[. . .]

Miscellaneous

96 ARRANGEMENTS FOR OBTAINING THE VIEWS OF THE COMMUNITY ON POLICING

(1)   Arrangements shall be made for each police area for obtaining—
    (a)   the views of people in that area about matters concerning the policing of the area, and
    (b)   their co-operation with the police in preventing crime [and anti-social behaviour] in that area; and for obtaining the views of victims of crime in that area about matters concerning the policing of the area.
    [. . .]
[. . .]

As amended by the Police Reform and Social Responsibility Act 2011, s 14, 25, 84, 91, Schedule 16 paragraph 40

POLICE ACT 1997
(c. 50)

An Act to make provision for the National Criminal Intelligence Service and the National Crime Squad; to make provision about entry on and interference with property and with wireless telegraphy in the course of the prevention or detection of serious crime; to make provision for the Police Information Technology Organisation; to provide for the issue of certificates about criminal records; to make provision about the administration and organisation of the police; to repeal certain enactments about rehabilitation of offenders; and for connected purposes.

[. . .]

Part II THE NATIONAL CRIME SQUAD

[. . .]

76 REPORTS FROM NCS SERVICE AUTHORITY

(1)   The Secretary of State may require the NCS Service Authority to submit to him a report on such matters connected with the discharge of the Authority's functions, or otherwise with the activities of the National Crime Squad, as may be specified in the requirement.

(2)   A report submitted under subsection (1) shall be in such form as the Secretary of State may specify.

(3)   The Secretary of State may arrange, or require the Authority to arrange, for a report under this section to be published in such manner as appears to him to be appropriate.

[. . .]

Part III AUTHORISATION OF ACTION IN RESPECT OF PROPERTY

The Commissioners

91 THE COMMISSIONERS

(1)   The Prime Minister [after consultation with the Scottish Ministers], shall appoint for the purposes of this Part—
(a) a Chief Commissioner, and
(b) such number of other Commissioners as the Prime Minister thinks fit.

(2)   The persons appointed under subsection (1) shall be persons who hold or have held high judicial office within the meaning of [Part 3 of the Constitutional Reform Act 2005 or are or have been members of the Judicial Committee of the Privy Council].

(3)   Subject to subsections (4) to (7), each Commissioner shall hold and vacate office in accordance with the terms of his appointment.

(4)   Each Commissioner shall be appointed for a term of three years.

(5)   A person who ceases to be a Commissioner (otherwise than under subsection (7)) may be reappointed under this section.

[(6)   Subject to subsection (7), a Commissioner shall not be removed from office before the end of the term for which he is appointed unless—
(a)   a resolution approving his removal has been passed by each House of Parliament; and
(b)   a resolution approving his removal has been passed by the Scottish Parliament.]
[. . .]

[. . .]

Authorisations

92 EFFECT OF AUTHORISATION UNDER PART III

No entry on or interference with property or with wireless telegraphy shall be unlawful if it is authorised by an authorisation having effect under this Part.

93 AUTHORISATIONS TO INTERFERE WITH PROPERTY ETC.

(1)   Where subsection (2) applies, an authorising officer may authorise—
(a)   the taking of such action, in respect of such property in the relevant area, as he may specify,
[(ab) the taking of such action falling within subsection (1A), in respect of property outside the relevant area, as he may specify, or]
(b)   the taking of such action in the relevant area as he may specify, in respect of wireless telegraphy.

(1A) The action falling within this subsection is action for maintaining or retrieving any equipment, apparatus or device the placing or use of which in the relevant area has been authorised under this Part or Part II of the Regulation of Investigatory Powers Act 2000 or under any enactment contained in or made under an Act of the Scottish Parliament which makes provision equivalent to that made by Part II of that Act of 2000.

[. . .]

(2)   This subsection applies where the authorising officer believes—
(a)   that it is necessary for the action specified to be taken [for the purpose of preventing or detecting] serious crime, and
[(b) that the taking of the action is proportionate to what the action seeks to achieve.
[. . .]

(2B) The matters to be taken into account in considering whether the requirements of subsection (2) are satisfied in the case of any authorisation shall include whether what it is thought necessary to achieve by the authorised action could reasonably be achieved by other means.

(3)   An authorising officer shall not give an authorisation under this section except on an application made—
(za) if the authorising officer is within subsection (5)(a) to (c)—
(i)   by a member of the officer's police force; or
(ii) in a case where the chief officer of police of that force ("the authorising force") has made an agreement under section 23(1) of the Police Act 1996 with the chief officer of police of one or more other police forces, by a member of a collaborative force;

(a) if the authorising officer is within [subsection (5)(d)] to [(ea) or (ee)], by a member of his police force,

[. . .]

(4) For the purposes of subsection (2), conduct which constitutes one or more offences shall be regarded as serious crime if, and only if,—

(a) it involves the use of violence, results in substantial financial gain or is conduct by a large number of persons in pursuit of a common purpose, or

(b) the offence or one of the offences is an offence for which a person who has attained the age of twenty-one and has no previous convictions could reasonably be expected to be sentenced to imprisonment for a term of three years or more,

and, where the authorising officer is within subsection (5)(h), it relates to an assigned matter within the meaning of section 1(1) of the Customs and Excise Management Act 1979.

(5) In this section "authorising officer" means—

(a) the chief constable of a police force maintained under section 2 of the Police Act 1996 (maintenance of police forces for areas in England and Wales except London);

(b) the Commissioner, or an Assistant Commissioner, of Police of the Metropolis;

(c) the Commissioner of Police for the City of London;

(d) the chief constable of a police force maintained under or by virtue of section 1 of the Police (Scotland) Act 1967 (maintenance of police forces for areas in Scotland);

(e) the Chief Constable or a Deputy Chief Constable of the [Police Service of Northern Ireland];

(ea) the Chief Constable of the Ministry of Defence Police;

[. . .]

(f) the Director General of the Serious Organised Crime Agency, or any member of the staff of that Agency who is designated for the purposes of this paragraph by that Director General;

[. . .]

(7) The powers conferred by, or by virtue of, this section are additional to any other powers which a person has as a constable either at common law or under or by virtue of any other enactment and are not to be taken to affect any of those other powers.

[. . .]

95 AUTHORISATIONS: FORM AND DURATION, ETC.

(1) An authorisation shall be in writing, except that in an urgent case an authorisation (other than one given by virtue of section 94) may be given orally.

(2) An authorisation shall, unless renewed under subsection (3), cease to have effect—

(a) if given orally or by virtue of section 94, at the end of the period of 72 hours beginning with the time when it took effect;

(b) in any other case, at the end of the period of three months beginning with the day on which it took effect.

(3) If at any time before an authorisation would cease to have effect the authorising officer who gave the authorisation, or in whose absence it was given, considers it necessary for the authorisation to continue to have effect for the purpose for which it was issued, he may, in writing, renew it for a period of three months beginning with the day on which it would cease to have effect.

(4)   A person shall cancel an authorisation given by him if satisfied that [the authorisation is one in relation to which the requirements of paragraphs (a) and (b) of section 93(2) are no longer satisfied.

[. . .]

[. . .]

Authorisations requiring approval

97 AUTHORISATIONS REQUIRING APPROVAL

(1)   An authorisation to which this section applies shall not take effect until—
   (a) it has been approved in accordance with this section by a Commissioner appointed under section 91(1)(b), and
   (b) the person who gave the authorisation has been notified under subsection (4).

(2)   Subject to subsection (3), this section applies to an authorisation if, at the time it is given, the person who gives it believes—
   (a) that any of the property specified in the authorisation—
       (i)   is used wholly or mainly as a dwelling or as a bedroom in a hotel, or
       (ii) constitutes office premises, or
   (b) that the action authorised by it is likely to result in any person acquiring knowledge of—
       (i)   matters subject to legal privilege,
       (ii) confidential personal information, or
       (iii) confidential journalistic material.

(3)   This section does not apply to an authorisation where the person who gives it believes that the case is one of urgency.

(4)   Where a Commissioner receives a notice under section 96 which specifies that this section applies to the authorisation, he shall as soon as is reasonably practicable—
   (a) decide whether to approve the authorisation or refuse approval, and
   (b) give written notice of his decision to the person who gave the authorisation.

(5)   A Commissioner shall approve an authorisation if, and only if, he is satisfied that there are reasonable grounds for believing the matters specified in section 93(2).

(6)   Where a Commissioner refuses to approve an authorisation, he shall, as soon as is reasonably practicable, make a report of his findings to the authorising officer who gave it or in whose absence it was given. [. . .]

[. . .]

98 MATTERS SUBJECT TO LEGAL PRIVILEGE

(1)   Subject to subsection (5) below, in section 97 "matters subject to legal privilege" means matters to which subsection (2), (3) or (4) below applies.

(2)   This subsection applies to communications between a professional legal adviser and—
   (a) his client, or
   (b) any person representing his client,
   which are made in connection with the giving of legal advice to the client.

(3)   This subsection applies to communications—
   (a) between a professional legal adviser and his client or any person representing his client, or

(b) between a professional legal adviser or his client or any such representative and any other person,

which are made in connection with or in contemplation of legal proceedings and for the purposes of such proceedings.

(4) This subsection applies to items enclosed with or referred to in communications of the kind mentioned in subsection (2) or (3) and made—
 (a) in connection with the giving of legal advice, or
 (b) in connection with or in contemplation of legal proceedings and for the purposes of such proceedings.

(5) For the purposes of section 97—
 (a) communications and items are not matters subject to legal privilege when they are in the possession of a person who is not entitled to possession of them, and
 (b) communications and items held, or oral communications made, with the intention of furthering a criminal purpose are not matters subject to legal privilege.

99 CONFIDENTIAL PERSONAL INFORMATION

(1) In section 97 "confidential personal information" means—
 (a) personal information which a person has acquired or created in the course of any trade, business, profession or other occupation or for the purposes of any paid or unpaid office, and which he holds in confidence, and
 (b) communications as a result of which personal information—
  (i) is acquired or created as mentioned in paragraph (a), and
  (ii) is held in confidence.

(2) For the purposes of this section "personal information" means information concerning an individual (whether living or dead) who can be identified from it and relating—
 (a) to his physical or mental health, or
 (b) to spiritual counselling or assistance given or to be given to him.

(3) A person holds information in confidence for the purposes of this section if he holds it subject—
 (a) to an express or implied undertaking to hold it in confidence, or
 (b) to a restriction on disclosure or an obligation of secrecy contained in any enactment (including an enactment contained in an Act passed after this Act).

100 CONFIDENTIAL JOURNALISTIC MATERIAL

(1) In section 97 "confidential journalistic material" means—
 (a) material acquired or created for the purposes of journalism which—
  (i) is in the possession of persons who acquired or created it for those purposes,
  (ii) is held subject to an undertaking, restriction or obligation of the kind mentioned in section 99(3), and
  (iii) has been continuously held (by one or more persons) subject to such an undertaking, restriction or obligation since it was first acquired or created for the purposes of journalism, and
 (b) communications as a result of which information is acquired for the purposes of journalism and held as mentioned in paragraph (a)(ii).

(2) For the purposes of subsection (1), a person who receives material, or acquires information, from someone who intends that the recipient shall use it for the purposes of journalism is to be taken to have acquired it for those purposes.

[. . .]

Complaints etc.

103 QUASHING OF AUTHORISATIONS ETC.

(1)   Where, at any time, a Commissioner appointed under section 91(1)(b) is satisfied that, at the time an authorisation was given or renewed, there were no reasonable grounds for believing the matters specified in section 93(2), he may quash the authorisation or, as the case may be, renewal.

(2)   Where, in the case of an authorisation or renewal to which section 97 does not apply, a Commissioner appointed under section 91(1)(b) is at any time satisfied that, at the time the authorisation was given or, as the case may be, renewed,—
     (a) there were reasonable grounds for believing any of the matters specified in subsection (2) of section 97, and
     (b) there were no reasonable grounds for believing the case to be one of urgency for the purposes of subsection (3) of that section,
     he may quash the authorisation or, as the case may be, renewal.

(3)   Where a Commissioner quashes an authorisation or renewal under subsection (1) or (2), he may order the destruction of any records relating to information obtained by virtue of the authorisation (or, in the case of a renewal, relating wholly or partly to information so obtained after the renewal) other than records required for pending criminal or civil proceedings.

     [. . .]

CIVIL PROCEDURE RULES 1998/3132

[. . .]

Part 54 JUDICIAL REVIEW

54.1 SCOPE AND INTERPRETATION

(1)   This Section of this Part contains rules about judicial review.

(2)   In this Section—
     (a) a "claim for judicial review" means a claim to review the lawfulness of—
          (i)   an enactment; or
          (ii) a decision, action or failure to act in relation to the exercise of a public function.
          [. . .]
     (e) "the judicial review procedure" means the Part 8 procedure as modified by this Section;
     (f) "interested party" means any person (other than the claimant and defendant) who is directly affected by the claim; and
     (g) "court" means the High Court, unless otherwise stated.
     (Rule 8.1(6)(b) provides that a rule or practice direction may, in relation to a specified type of proceedings, disapply or modify any of the rules set out in Part 8 as they apply to those proceedings)

54.2 WHEN THIS SECTION MUST BE USED

The judicial review procedure must be used in a claim for judicial review where the claimant is seeking—

(a)   a mandatory order;

(b)   a prohibiting order;

(c)   a quashing order; or

(d)   an injunction under section 30 of the [Senior Courts Act 1981] (restraining a person from acting in any office in which he is not entitled to act).

54.3 WHEN THIS SECTION MAY BE USED

(1)   The judicial review procedure may be used in a claim for judicial review where the claimant is seeking—
(a) a declaration; or
(b) an injunction.
(Section 31(2) of the [Senior Courts Act 1981] sets out the circumstances in which the court may grant a declaration or injunction in a claim for judicial review)

(Where the claimant is seeking a declaration or injunction in addition to one of the remedies listed in rule 54.2, the judicial review procedure must be used)

(2)   A claim for judicial review may include a claim for damages, restitution or the recovery of a sum due but may not seek such a remedy alone.

(Section 31(4) of the [Senior Courts Act] sets out the circumstances in which the court may award damages, restitution or the recovery of a sum due on a claim for judicial review)

54.4 PERMISSION REQUIRED

The court's permission to proceed is required in a claim for judicial review whether started under this Section or transferred to the Administrative Court.

54.5 TIME LIMIT FOR FILING CLAIM FORM

(1)   The claim form must be filed—
(a) promptly; and
(b) in any event not later than 3 months after the grounds to make the claim first arose.

(2)   The time limit in this rule may not be extended by agreement between the parties.

(3)   This rule does not apply when any other enactment specifies a shorter time limit for making the claim for judicial review.

54.6 CLAIM FORM

(1)   In addition to the matters set out in rule 8.2 (contents of the claim form) the claimant must also state—
(a) the name and address of any person he considers to be an interested party;
(b) that he is requesting permission to proceed with a claim for judicial review; and
(c) any remedy (including any interim remedy) he is claiming.
(Part 25 sets out how to apply for an interim remedy)

(2)   The claim form must be accompanied by the documents required by [Practice Direction 54A].

54.7 SERVICE OF CLAIM FORM

The claim form must be served on—

(a)   the defendant; and

(b)   unless the court otherwise directs, any person the claimant considers to be an interested party,

within 7 days after the date of issue.

54.8 ACKNOWLEDGMENT OF SERVICE

(1)   Any person served with the claim form who wishes to take part in the judicial review must file an acknowledgment of service in the relevant practice form in accordance with the following provisions of this rule.

(2)   Any acknowledgment of service must be—
(a)   filed not more than 21 days after service of the claim form; and
(b)   served on—
(i)   the claimant; and
(ii)   subject to any direction under rule 54.7(b), any other person named in the claim form,
as soon as practicable and, in any event, not later than 7 days after it is filed.

(3)   The time limits under this rule may not be extended by agreement between the parties.

(4)   The acknowledgment of service—
(a)   must—
(i)   where the person filing it intends to contest the claim, set out a summary of his grounds for doing so; and
(ii)   state the name and address of any person the person filing it considers to be an interested party; and
(b)   may include or be accompanied by an application for directions.
[. . .]

[. . .]

54.17 COURT'S POWERS TO HEAR ANY PERSON

(1)   Any person may apply for permission—
(a)   to file evidence; or
(b)   make representations at the hearing of the judicial review.

(2)   An application under paragraph (1) should be made promptly.

54.18 JUDICIAL REVIEW MAY BE DECIDED WITHOUT A HEARING

The court may decide the claim for judicial review without a hearing where all the parties agree.

54.19 COURT'S POWERS IN RESPECT OF QUASHING ORDERS

(1)   This rule applies where the court makes a quashing order in respect of the decision to which the claim relates.

(2)   The court may—
    (a) (i)   remit the matter to the decision-maker; and
       (ii) direct it to reconsider the matter and reach a decision in accordance with the judgment of the court; or
    (b) in so far as any enactment permits, substitute its own decision for the decision to which the claim relates.
    (Section 31 of the [Senior Courts Act 1981] enables the High Court, subject to certain conditions, to substitute its own decision for the decision in question.)

54.20 TRANSFER

The court may—

(a)   order a claim to continue as if it had not been started under this Section; and

(b)   where it does so, give directions about the future management of the claim.

(Part 30 (transfer) applies to transfers to and from the Administrative Court)

[. . .]

CRIME AND DISORDER ACT 1998
(c. 37)

An Act to make provision for preventing crime and disorder; to create certain racially-aggravated offences; to abolish the rebuttable presumption that a child is doli incapax and to make provision as to the effect of a child's failure to give evidence at his trial; to abolish the death penalty for treason and piracy; to make changes to the criminal justice system; to make further provision for dealing with offenders; to make further provision with respect to remands and committals for trial and the release and recall of prisoners; to amend Chapter I of Part II of the Crime (Sentences) Act 1997 and to repeal Chapter I of Part III of the Crime and Punishment (Scotland) Act 1997; to make amendments designed to facilitate, or otherwise desirable in connection with, the consolidation of certain enactments; and for connected purposes.

[. . .]

Part I PREVENTION OF CRIME AND DISORDER

Chapter I England and Wales

Crime and disorder: general

1 ANTI-SOCIAL BEHAVIOUR ORDERS

(1)   An application for an order under this section may be made by a relevant authority if it appears to the authority that the following conditions are fulfilled with respect to any person aged 10 or over, namely—
    (a) that the person has acted, since the commencement date, in an anti-social manner, that is to say, in a manner that caused or was likely to cause harassment, alarm or distress to one or more persons not of the same household as himself; and
    (b) that such an order is necessary to protect relevant persons from further anti-social acts by him;

(c) Before making an application under subsection (1) in respect of a person under the age of 16, the relevant authority must prepare a report on the person's family circumstances in accordance with regulations made by the Secretary of State;

[. . .]

(3) Such an application shall be made by complaint to [a magistrates' court]

(4) If, on such an application, it is proved that the conditions mentioned in subsection (1) above are fulfilled, the magistrates' court may make an order under this section (an "anti-social behaviour order") which prohibits the defendant from doing anything described in the order.

(5) For the purpose of determining whether the condition mentioned in subsection (1)(a) above is fulfilled, the court shall disregard any act of the defendant which he shows was reasonable in the circumstances.

[. . .]

(6) The prohibitions that may be imposed by an anti-social behaviour order are those necessary for the purpose of protecting persons (whether relevant persons or persons elsewhere in England and Wales) from further anti-social acts by the defendant.

(7) An anti-social behaviour order shall have effect for a period (not less than two years) specified in the order or until further order.

(8) Subject to subsection (9) below, the applicant or the defendant may apply by complaint to the court which made an anti-social behaviour order for it to be varied or discharged by a further order.

(9) Except with the consent of both parties, no anti-social behaviour order shall be discharged before the end of the period of two years beginning with the date of service of the order.

[. . .]

[. . .]

1C ORDERS ON CONVICTION IN CRIMINAL PROCEEDINGS

(1) This section applies where a person (the "offender") is convicted of a relevant offence.

(2) If the court considers—
(a) that the offender has acted, at any time since the commencement date, in an anti-social manner, that is to say in a manner that caused or was likely to cause harassment, alarm or distress to one or more persons not of the same household as himself, and
(b) that an order under this section is necessary to protect persons in any place in England and Wales from further anti-social acts by him,
it may make an order which prohibits the offender from doing anything described in the order.

(3) The court may make an order under this section [—]
[(a) if the prosecutor asks it to do so, or
(b) if the court thinks it is appropriate to do so.]
[. . .]

(4) An order under this section shall not be made except—
(a) in addition to a sentence imposed in respect of the relevant offence; or
(b) in addition to an order discharging him conditionally.
[. . .]

(5)   An order under this section takes effect on the day on which it is made, but the court may provide in any such order that such requirements of the order as it may specify shall, during any period when the offender is detained in legal custody, be suspended until his release from that custody.

[. . .]

[. . .]

11 CHILD SAFETY ORDERS

(1)   Subject to subsection (2) below, if a magistrates' court, on the application of a local authority, is satisfied that one or more of the conditions specified in subsection (3) below are fulfilled with respect to a child under the age of 10, it may make an order (a "child safety order") which—
      (a) places the child, for a period (not exceeding the permitted maximum) specified in the order, under the supervision of the responsible officer; and
      (b) requires the child to comply with such requirements as are so specified.

(2)   A court shall not make a child safety order unless it has been notified by the Secretary of State that arrangements for implementing such orders are available in the area in which it appears that the child resides or will reside and the notice has not been withdrawn.

(3)   The conditions are—
      (a) that the child has committed an act which, if he had been aged 10 or over, would have constituted an offence;
      (b) that a child safety order is necessary for the purpose of preventing the commission by the child of such an act as is mentioned in paragraph (a) above;
          [. . .]
      (d) that the child has acted in a manner that caused or was likely to cause harassment, alarm or distress to one or more persons not of the same household as himself.

(4)   The maximum period permitted for the purposes of subsection (1)(a) above is [twelve months].

(5)   The requirements that may be specified under subsection (1)(b) above are those which the court considers desirable in the interests of—
      (a) securing that the child receives appropriate care, protection and support and is subject to proper control; or
      (b) preventing any repetition of the kind of behaviour which led to the child safety order being made.

(6)   Proceedings under this section or section 12 below shall be family proceedings for the purposes of the 1989 Act or section 65 of the Magistrates' Courts Act 1980 ("the 1980 Act"); and the standard of proof applicable to such proceedings shall be that applicable to civil proceedings.

(7)   In this section "local authority" has the same meaning as in the 1989 Act.

(8)   In this section and section 12 below, "responsible officer", in relation to a child safety order, means one of the following who is specified in the order, namely—
      (a) a social worker of a local authority [. . .]; and
      (b) a member of a youth offending team.
          [. . .]

[. . .]

Part II **CRIMINAL LAW**

Racially or religiously aggravated offences: England and Wales

28 MEANING OF "[RACIALLY OR RELIGIOUSLY AGGRAVATED]"

(1)   An offence is [racially or religiously aggravated] for the purposes of sections 29 to 32
       below if—
       (a) at the time of committing the offence, or immediately before or after doing so, the
            offender demonstrates towards the victim of the offence hostility based on the victim's
            membership (or presumed membership) of a [racial or religious group]; or
       (b) the offence is motivated (wholly or partly) by hostility towards members of a [racial
            or religious group] based on their membership of that group.

(2)   In subsection (1)(a) above—

       "membership", in relation to a [racial or religious group], includes association with
       members of that group;

       "presumed" means presumed by the offender.

(3)   It is immaterial for the purposes of paragraph (a) or (b) of subsection (1) above whether
       or not the offender's hostility is also based, to any extent, [on any other factor not
       mentioned in that paragraph.]

(4)   In this section "racial group" means a group of persons defined by reference to race,
       colour, nationality (including citizenship) or ethnic or national origins.

[(5)   In this section "religious group" means a group of persons defined by reference to
       religious belief or lack of religious belief.]

29 RACIALLY OR RELIGIOUSLY AGGRAVATED ASSAULTS

(1)   A person is guilty of an offence under this section if he commits—
       (a) an offence under section 20 of the Offences Against the Person Act 1861 (malicious
            wounding or grievous bodily harm);
       (b) an offence under section 47 of that Act (actual bodily harm); or
       (c) common assault,
       which is [racially or religiously aggravated] for the purposes of this section.

       [. . .]

30 RACIALLY OR RELIGIOUSLY AGGRAVATED CRIMINAL DAMAGE

(1)   A person is guilty of an offence under this section if he commits an offence under section 1(1)
       of the Criminal Damage Act 1971 (destroying or damaging property belonging to another)
       which is [racially or religiously aggravated] for the purposes of this section.

       [. . .]

31 RACIALLY OR RELIGIOUSLY AGGRAVATED PUBLIC ORDER
   OFFENCES

(1)   A person is guilty of an offence under this section if he commits—
       (a) an offence under section 4 of the Public Order Act 1986 (fear or provocation of
            violence);

(b) an offence under section 4A of that Act (intentional harassment, alarm or distress); or
(c) an offence under section 5 of that Act (harassment, alarm or distress),
which is [racially or religiously aggravated] for the purposes of this section.

[. . .]

32 RACIALLY OR RELIGIOUSLY AGGRAVATED HARASSMENT ETC.

(1) A person is guilty of an offence under this section if he commits—
(a) an offence under section 2 of the Protection from Harassment Act 1997 (offence of harassment); or
(b) an offence under section 4 of that Act (putting people in fear of violence),
which is [racially or religiously aggravated] for the purposes of this section.

[. . .]

As amended by the Crime and Security Act 2010 s 4

DATA PROTECTION ACT 1998
(c. 29)

An Act to make new provision for the regulation of the processing of information relating to individuals, including the obtaining, holding, use or disclosure of such information.

[. . .]

Part I PRELIMINARY

1 BASIC INTERPRETATIVE PROVISIONS

(1) In this Act, unless the context otherwise requires—

"data" means information which—
(a) is being processed by means of equipment operating automatically in response to instructions given for that purpose,
(b) is recorded with the intention that it should be processed by means of such equipment,
(c) is recorded as part of a relevant filing system or with the intention that it should form part of a relevant filing system, [. . .]
(d) does not fall within paragraph (a), (b) or (c) but forms part of an accessible record as defined by section 68; [or
(e) is recorded information held by a public authority and does not fall within any of paragraphs (a) to (d);]

"data controller" means, subject to subsection (4), a person who (either alone or jointly or in common with other persons) determines the purposes for which and the manner in which any personal data are, or are to be, processed;

"data processor", in relation to personal data, means any person (other than an employee of the data controller) who processes the data on behalf of the data controller;

"data subject" means an individual who is the subject of personal data;

"personal data" means data which relate to a living individual who can be identified—
(a) from those data, or
(b) from those data and other information which is in the possession of, or is likely to come into the possession of, the data controller,
and includes any expression of opinion about the individual and any indication of the intentions of the data controller or any other person in respect of the individual;

"processing", in relation to information or data, means obtaining, recording or holding the information or data or carrying out any operation or set of operations on the information or data, including—
(a) organisation, adaptation or alteration of the information or data,
(b) retrieval, consultation or use of the information or data,
(c) disclosure of the information or data by transmission, dissemination or otherwise making available, or
(d) alignment, combination, blocking, erasure or destruction of the information or data;
"public authority" means a public authority as defined by the Freedom of Information Act 2000 or a Scottish public authority as defined by the Freedom of Information (Scotland) Act 2002;
[. . .]

(4) Where personal data are processed only for purposes for which they are required by or under any enactment to be processed, the person on whom the obligation to process the data is imposed by or under that enactment is for the purposes of this Act the data controller.

[. . .]

2 SENSITIVE PERSONAL DATA

In this Act "sensitive personal data" means personal data consisting of information as to—
(a) the racial or ethnic origin of the data subject,

(b) his political opinions,

(c) his religious beliefs or other beliefs of a similar nature,

(d) whether he is a member of a trade union (within the meaning of the Trade Union and Labour Relations (Consolidation) Act 1992),

(e) his physical or mental health or condition,

(f) his sexual life,

(g) the commission or alleged commission by him of any offence, or

(h) any proceedings for any offence committed or alleged to have been committed by him, the disposal of such proceedings or the sentence of any court in such proceedings.

3 THE SPECIAL PURPOSES

In this Act "the special purposes" means any one or more of the following—
(a) the purposes of journalism,

(b) artistic purposes, and

(c) literary purposes.

[. . .]

4 THE DATA PROTECTION PRINCIPLES

(1)   References in this Act to the data protection principles are to the principles set out in Part I of Schedule 1.

(2)   Those principles are to be interpreted in accordance with Part II of Schedule 1.

(3)   Schedule 2 (which applies to all personal data) and Schedule 3 (which applies only to sensitive personal data) set out conditions applying for the purposes of the first principle; and Schedule 4 sets out cases in which the eighth principle does not apply.

(4)   Subject to section 27(1), it shall be the duty of a data controller to comply with the data protection principles in relation to all personal data with respect to which he is the data controller.

6 THE COMMISSIONER [. . .]

(1)   For the purposes of this Act and of the Freedom of Information Act 2000 there shall be an officer known as the Information Commissioner (in this Act referred to as "the Commissioner").

[. . .]

[. . .]

Part II RIGHTS OF DATA SUBJECTS AND OTHERS

7 RIGHT OF ACCESS TO PERSONAL DATA

(1)   Subject to the following provisions of this section and to [sections 8, 9 and 9A], an individual is entitled—
(a) to be informed by any data controller whether personal data of which that individual is the data subject are being processed by or on behalf of that data controller,
(b) if that is the case, to be given by the data controller a description of—
(i)   the personal data of which that individual is the data subject,
(ii) the purposes for which they are being or are to be processed, and
(iii) the recipients or classes of recipients to whom they are or may be disclosed,
(c) to have communicated to him in an intelligible form—
(i)   the information constituting any personal data of which that individual is the data subject, and
(ii) any information available to the data controller as to the source of those data
[ ]

[. . .]

Part IV EXEMPTIONS

[. . .]

28 NATIONAL SECURITY

(1)   Personal data are exempt from any of the provisions of—
(a) the data protection principles,
(b) Parts II, III and V, and
(c) [sections 54A and] 55,
if the exemption from that provision is required for the purpose of safeguarding national security.

(2)   Subject to subsection (4), a certificate signed by a Minister of the Crown certifying that exemption from all or any of the provisions mentioned in subsection (1) is or at any time was required for the purpose there mentioned in respect of any personal data shall be conclusive evidence of that fact.

   [. . .]

(4)   Any person directly affected by the issuing of a certificate under subsection (2) may appeal to the Tribunal against the certificate.

(5)   If on an appeal under subsection (4), the Tribunal finds that, applying the principles applied by the court on an application for judicial review, the Minister did not have reasonable grounds for issuing the certificate, the Tribunal may allow the appeal and quash the certificate.

   [. . .]

[. . .]

35 DISCLOSURES REQUIRED BY LAW OR MADE IN CONNECTION WITH LEGAL PROCEEDINGS ETC.

(1)   Personal data are exempt from the non-disclosure provisions where the disclosure is required by or under any enactment, by any rule of law or by the order of a court.

(2)   Personal data are exempt from the non-disclosure provisions where the disclosure is necessary—
   (a) for the purpose of, or in connection with, any legal proceedings (including prospective legal proceedings), or
   (b) for the purpose of obtaining legal advice,
   or is otherwise necessary for the purposes of establishing, exercising or defending legal rights.

[. . .]

HUMAN RIGHTS ACT 1998
(c. 42)

An Act to give further effect to rights and freedoms guaranteed under the European Convention on Human Rights; to make provision with respect to holders of certain judicial offices who become judges of the European Court of Human Rights; and for connected purposes.

[. . .]

Introduction

1 THE CONVENTION RIGHTS

(1)   In this Act "the Convention rights" means the rights and fundamental freedoms set out in—
   (a) Articles 2 to 12 and 14 of the Convention,
   (b) Articles 1 to 3 of the First Protocol, and
   (c) Article 1 of the Thirteenth Protocol],
   as read with Articles 16 to 18 of the Convention.

(2)   Those Articles are to have effect for the purposes of this Act subject to any designated derogation or reservation (as to which see sections 14 and 15).

(3)   The Articles are set out in Schedule 1.

(4)   The [Secretary of State] may by order make such amendments to this Act as he considers appropriate to reflect the effect, in relation to the United Kingdom, of a protocol.

(5)   In subsection (4) "protocol" means a protocol to the Convention—
(a) which the United Kingdom has ratified; or
(b) which the United Kingdom has signed with a view to ratification.

(6)   No amendment may be made by an order under subsection (4) so as to come into force before the protocol concerned is in force in relation to the United Kingdom.

2 INTERPRETATION OF CONVENTION RIGHTS

(1)   A court or tribunal determining a question which has arisen in connection with a Convention right must take into account any—
(a) judgment, decision, declaration or advisory opinion of the European Court of Human Rights,
(b) opinion of the Commission given in a report adopted under Article 31 of the Convention,
(c) decision of the Commission in connection with Article 26 or 27(2) of the Convention, or
(d) decision of the Committee of Ministers taken under Article 46 of the Convention,
whenever made or given, so far as, in the opinion of the court or tribunal, it is relevant to the proceedings in which that question has arisen.

(2)   Evidence of any judgment, decision, declaration or opinion of which account may have to be taken under this section is to be given in proceedings before any court or tribunal in such manner as may be provided by rules.

(3)   In this section "rules" means rules of court or, in the case of proceedings before a tribunal, rules made for the purposes of this section—
(a) by [. . .] [the Lord Chancellor or] the Secretary of State, in relation to any proceedings outside Scotland;
(b) by the Secretary of State, in relation to proceedings in Scotland; or
(c) by a Northern Ireland department, in relation to proceedings before a tribunal in Northern Ireland—
(i)   which deals with transferred matters; and
(ii) for which no rules made under paragraph (a) are in force.

Legislation

3 INTERPRETATION OF LEGISLATION

(1)   So far as it is possible to do so, primary legislation and subordinate legislation must be read and given effect in a way which is compatible with the Convention rights.

(2)   This section—
(a) applies to primary legislation and subordinate legislation whenever enacted;
(b) does not affect the validity, continuing operation or enforcement of any incompatible primary legislation; and

(c) does not affect the validity, continuing operation or enforcement of any incompatible subordinate legislation if (disregarding any possibility of revocation) primary legislation prevents removal of the incompatibility.

4 DECLARATION OF INCOMPATIBILITY

(1) Subsection (2) applies in any proceedings in which a court determines whether a provision of primary legislation is compatible with a Convention right.

(2) If the court is satisfied that the provision is incompatible with a Convention right, it may make a declaration of that incompatibility.

(3) Subsection (4) applies in any proceedings in which a court determines whether a provision of subordinate legislation, made in the exercise of a power conferred by primary legislation, is compatible with a Convention right.

(4) If the court is satisfied—
(a) that the provision is incompatible with a Convention right, and
(b) that (disregarding any possibility of revocation) the primary legislation concerned prevents removal of the incompatibility,
it may make a declaration of that incompatibility.

(5) In this section "court" means—
[(a) the Supreme Court;]
(b) the Judicial Committee of the Privy Council;
(c) the [Court Martial Appeal Court];
(d) in Scotland, the High Court of Justiciary sitting otherwise than as a trial court or the Court of Session;
(e) in England and Wales or Northern Ireland, the High Court or the Court of Appeal.
[(f) the Court of Protection, in any matter being dealt with by the President of the Family Division, the Vice-Chancellor or a puisne judge of the High Court.]

(6) A declaration under this section ("a declaration of incompatibility")—
(a) does not affect the validity, continuing operation or enforcement of the provision in respect of which it is given; and
(b) is not binding on the parties to the proceedings in which it is made.

5 RIGHT OF CROWN TO INTERVENE

(1) Where a court is considering whether to make a declaration of incompatibility, the Crown is entitled to notice in accordance with rules of court.

(2) In any case to which subsection (1) applies—
(a) a Minister of the Crown (or a person nominated by him),
(b) a member of the Scottish Executive,
(c) a Northern Ireland Minister,
(d) a Northern Ireland department,
is entitled, on giving notice in accordance with rules of court, to be joined as a party to the proceedings.

(3) Notice under subsection (2) may be given at any time during the proceedings.

(4) A person who has been made a party to criminal proceedings (other than in Scotland) as the result of a notice under subsection (2) may, with leave, appeal to the [Supreme Court] against any declaration of incompatibility made in the proceedings.

(5)   In subsection (4)—

"criminal proceedings" includes all proceedings before the [Court Martial Appeal Court]; and

"leave" means leave granted by the court making the declaration of incompatibility or by the [Supreme Court].

Public authorities

6 ACTS OF PUBLIC AUTHORITIES

(1)   It is unlawful for a public authority to act in a way which is incompatible with a Convention right.

(2)   Subsection (1) does not apply to an act if—
  (a) as the result of one or more provisions of primary legislation, the authority could not have acted differently; or
  (b) in the case of one or more provisions of, or made under, primary legislation which cannot be read or given effect in a way which is compatible with the Convention rights, the authority was acting so as to give effect to or enforce those provisions.

(3)   In this section "public authority" includes—
  (a) a court or tribunal, and
  (b) any person certain of whose functions are functions of a public nature,
  but does not include either House of Parliament or a person exercising functions in connection with proceedings in Parliament.

  [. . .]

(5)   In relation to a particular act, a person is not a public authority by virtue only of subsection (3)(b) if the nature of the act is private.

(6)   "An act" includes a failure to act but does not include a failure to—
  (a) introduce in, or lay before, Parliament a proposal for legislation; or
  (b) make any primary legislation or remedial order.

7 PROCEEDINGS

(1)   A person who claims that a public authority has acted (or proposes to act) in a way which is made unlawful by section 6(1) may—
  (a) bring proceedings against the authority under this Act in the appropriate court or tribunal, or
  (b) rely on the Convention right or rights concerned in any legal proceedings,
  but only if he is (or would be) a victim of the unlawful act.

(2)   In subsection (1)(a) "appropriate court or tribunal" means such court or tribunal as may be determined in accordance with rules; and proceedings against an authority include a counterclaim or similar proceeding.

(3)   If the proceedings are brought on an application for judicial review, the applicant is to be taken to have a sufficient interest in relation to the unlawful act only if he is, or would be, a victim of that act.

(4)   If the proceedings are made by way of a petition for judicial review in Scotland, the applicant shall be taken to have title and interest to sue in relation to the unlawful act only if he is, or would be, a victim of that act.

(5)   Proceedings under subsection (1)(a) must be brought before the end of—
    (a) the period of one year beginning with the date on which the act complained of took place; or
    (b) such longer period as the court or tribunal considers equitable having regard to all the circumstances,
but that is subject to any rule imposing a stricter time limit in relation to the procedure in question.

(6)   In subsection (1)(b) "legal proceedings" includes—
    (a) proceedings brought by or at the instigation of a public authority; and
    (b) an appeal against the decision of a court or tribunal.

(7)   For the purposes of this section, a person is a victim of an unlawful act only if he would be a victim for the purposes of Article 34 of the Convention if proceedings were brought in the European Court of Human Rights in respect of that act.

(8)   Nothing in this Act creates a criminal offence.

(9)   In this section "rules" means—
    (a) in relation to proceedings before a court or tribunal outside Scotland, rules made by [. . .] [the Lord Chancellor or] the Secretary of State for the purposes of this section or rules of court,
    (b) in relation to proceedings before a court or tribunal in Scotland, rules made by the Secretary of State for those purposes,
    (c) in relation to proceedings before a tribunal in Northern Ireland—
        (i)   which deals with transferred matters; and
        (ii) for which no rules made under paragraph (a) are in force, rules made by a Northern Ireland department for those purposes,
    and includes provision made by order under section 1 of the Courts and Legal Services Act 1990.

(10)   In making rules, regard must be had to section 9.

(11)   The Minister who has power to make rules in relation to a particular tribunal may, to the extent he considers it necessary to ensure that the tribunal can provide an appropriate remedy in relation to an act (or proposed act) of a public authority which is (or would be) unlawful as a result of section 6(1), by order add to—
    (a) the relief or remedies which the tribunal may grant; or
    (b) the grounds on which it may grant any of them.

(12)   An order made under subsection (11) may contain such incidental, supplemental, consequential or transitional provision as the Minister making it considers appropriate.

(13)   "The Minister" includes the Northern Ireland department concerned.

8 JUDICIAL REMEDIES

(1)   In relation to any act (or proposed act) of a public authority which the court finds is (or would be) unlawful, it may grant such relief or remedy, or make such order, within its powers as it considers just and appropriate.

(2)   But damages may be awarded only by a court which has power to award damages, or to order the payment of compensation, in civil proceedings.

(3)   No award of damages is to be made unless, taking account of all the circumstances of the case, including—

(a) any other relief or remedy granted, or order made, in relation to the act in question (by that or any other court), and

(b) the consequences of any decision (of that or any other court) in respect of that act, the court is satisfied that the award is necessary to afford just satisfaction to the person in whose favour it is made.

(4)   In determining—
(a) whether to award damages, or
(b) the amount of an award,
the court must take into account the principles applied by the European Court of Human Rights in relation to the award of compensation under Article 41 of the Convention.

(5)   A public authority against which damages are awarded is to be treated—
(a) in Scotland, for the purposes of section 3 of the Law Reform (Miscellaneous Provisions)(Scotland) Act 1940 as if the award were made in an action of damages in which the authority has been found liable in respect of loss or damage to the person to whom the award is made;
(b) for the purposes of the Civil Liability (Contribution) Act 1978 as liable in respect of damage suffered by the person to whom the award is made.

(6)   In this section—

"court" includes a tribunal;

"damages" means damages for an unlawful act of a public authority; and

"unlawful" means unlawful under section 6(1).

9 JUDICIAL ACTS

(1)   Proceedings under section 7(1)(a) in respect of a judicial act may be brought only—
(a) by exercising a right of appeal;
(b) on an application (in Scotland a petition) for judicial review; or
(c) in such other forum as may be prescribed by rules.

(2)   That does not affect any rule of law which prevents a court from being the subject of judicial review.

(3)   In proceedings under this Act in respect of a judicial act done in good faith, damages may not be awarded otherwise than to compensate a person to the extent required by Article 5(5) of the Convention.

(4)   An award of damages permitted by subsection (3) is to be made against the Crown; but no award may be made unless the appropriate person, if not a party to the proceedings, is joined.

(5)   In this section—

"appropriate person" means the Minister responsible for the court concerned, or a person or government department nominated by him;

"court" includes a tribunal;

"judge" includes a member of a tribunal, a justice of the peace (or, in Northern Ireland, a lay magistrate)] and a clerk or other officer entitled to exercise the jurisdiction of a court;

"judicial act" means a judicial act of a court and includes an act done on the instructions, or on behalf, of a judge; and

"rules" has the same meaning as in section 7(9).

Remedial action

10 POWER TO TAKE REMEDIAL ACTION

(1) This section applies if—
   (a) a provision of legislation has been declared under section 4 to be incompatible with a Convention right and, if an appeal lies—
      (i) all persons who may appeal have stated in writing that they do not intend to do so;
      (ii) the time for bringing an appeal has expired and no appeal has been brought within that time; or
      (iii) an appeal brought within that time has been determined or abandoned; or
   (b) it appears to a Minister of the Crown or Her Majesty in Council that, having regard to a finding of the European Court of Human Rights made after the coming into force of this section in proceedings against the United Kingdom, a provision of legislation is incompatible with an obligation of the United Kingdom arising from the Convention.

(2) If a Minister of the Crown considers that there are compelling reasons for proceeding under this section, he may by order make such amendments to the legislation as he considers necessary to remove the incompatibility.

(3) If, in the case of subordinate legislation, a Minister of the Crown considers—
   (a) that it is necessary to amend the primary legislation under which the subordinate legislation in question was made, in order to enable the incompatibility to be removed, and
   (b) that there are compelling reasons for proceeding under this section,
   he may by order make such amendments to the primary legislation as he considers necessary.

(4) This section also applies where the provision in question is in subordinate legislation and has been quashed, or declared invalid, by reason of incompatibility with a Convention right and the Minister proposes to proceed under paragraph 2(b) of Schedule 2.

(5) If the legislation is an Order in Council, the power conferred by subsection (2) or (3) is exercisable by Her Majesty in Council.

(6) In this section "legislation" does not include a Measure of the Church Assembly or of the General Synod of the Church of England.

(7) Schedule 2 makes further provision about remedial orders.

Other rights and proceedings

11 SAFEGUARD FOR EXISTING HUMAN RIGHTS

A person's reliance on a Convention right does not restrict—

(a) any other right or freedom conferred on him by or under any law having effect in any part of the United Kingdom; or

(b) his right to make any claim or bring any proceedings which he could make or bring apart from sections 7 to 9.

12 FREEDOM OF EXPRESSION

(1) This section applies if a court is considering whether to grant any relief which, if granted, might affect the exercise of the Convention right to freedom of expression.

(2)   If the person against whom the application for relief is made ("the respondent") is neither present nor represented, no such relief is to be granted unless the court is satisfied—
    (a)   that the applicant has taken all practicable steps to notify the respondent; or
    (b)   that there are compelling reasons why the respondent should not be notified.

(3)   No such relief is to be granted so as to restrain publication before trial unless the court is satisfied that the applicant is likely to establish that publication should not be allowed.

(4)   The court must have particular regard to the importance of the Convention right to freedom of expression and, where the proceedings relate to material which the respondent claims, or which appears to the court, to be journalistic, literary or artistic material (or to conduct connected with such material), to—
    (a)   the extent to which—
        (i)   the material has, or is about to, become available to the public; or
        (ii)   it is, or would be, in the public interest for the material to be published;
    (b)   any relevant privacy code.

(5)   In this section—

"court" includes a tribunal; and

"relief" includes any remedy or order (other than in criminal proceedings).

13 FREEDOM OF THOUGHT, CONSCIENCE AND RELIGION

(1)   If a court's determination of any question arising under this Act might affect the exercise by a religious organisation (itself or its members collectively) of the Convention right to freedom of thought, conscience and religion, it must have particular regard to the importance of that right.

(2)   In this section "court" includes a tribunal.

Derogations and reservations

14 DEROGATIONS

(1)   In this Act "designated derogation" means—

[. . .]

any derogation by the United Kingdom from an Article of the Convention, or of any protocol to the Convention, which is designated for the purposes of this Act in an order made by the [Secretary of State]

(2)   [. . .]

(3)   If a designated derogation is amended or replaced it ceases to be a designated derogation.

(4)   But subsection (3) does not prevent the [Secretary of State] from exercising his power under subsection (1) [. . .] to make a fresh designation order in respect of the Article concerned.

(5)   The [Secretary of State] must by order make such amendments to Schedule 3 as he considers appropriate to reflect—
    (a)   any designation order; or
    (b)   the effect of subsection (3).

(6)   A designation order may be made in anticipation of the making by the United Kingdom of a proposed derogation.

15 RESERVATIONS

(1)   In this Act "designated reservation" means—
  (a) the United Kingdom's reservation to Article 2 of the First Protocol to the Convention; and
  (b) any other reservation by the United Kingdom to an Article of the Convention, or of any protocol to the Convention, which is designated for the purposes of this Act in an order made by the [Secretary of State].

(2)   The text of the reservation referred to in subsection (1)(a) is set out in Part II of Schedule 3.

(3)   If a designated reservation is withdrawn wholly or in part it ceases to be a designated reservation.

(4)   But subsection (3) does not prevent the [Secretary of State] from exercising his power under subsection (1)(b) to make a fresh designation order in respect of the Article concerned.

(5)   [Secretary of State] must by order make such amendments to this Act as he considers appropriate to reflect—
  (a) any designation order; or
  (b) the effect of subsection (3).

16 PERIOD FOR WHICH DESIGNATED DEROGATIONS HAVE EFFECT

(1)   If it has not already been withdrawn by the United Kingdom, a designated derogation ceases to have effect for the purposes of this Act—[. . .] at the end of the period of five years beginning with the date on which the order designating it was made.

(2)   At any time before the period—
  (a) fixed by subsection (1) [. . .], or
  (b) extended by an order under this subsection,
  comes to an end, the [Secretary of State] may by order extend it by a further period of five years.

(3)   An order under section 14(1) [. . .] ceases to have effect at the end of the period for consideration, unless a resolution has been passed by each House approving the order.

(4)   Subsection (3) does not affect—
  (a) anything done in reliance on the order; or
  (b) the power to make a fresh order under section 14(1) [. . .]

(5)   In subsection (3) "period for consideration" means the period of forty days beginning with the day on which the order was made.

(6)   In calculating the period for consideration, no account is to be taken of any time during which—
  (a) Parliament is dissolved or prorogued; or
  (b) both Houses are adjourned for more than four days.

(7)   If a designated derogation is withdrawn by the United Kingdom, the [. . .] [Secretary of State] must by order make such amendments to this Act as he considers are required to reflect that withdrawal.

17 PERIODIC REVIEW OF DESIGNATED RESERVATIONS

(1)   The appropriate Minister must review the designated reservation referred to in
section 15(1)(a)—
(a) before the end of the period of five years beginning with the date on which
section 1(2) came into force; and
(b) if that designation is still in force, before the end of the period of five years beginning
with the date on which the last report relating to it was laid under subsection (3).

(2)   The appropriate Minister must review each of the other designated reservations (if any)—
(a) before the end of the period of five years beginning with the date on which the order
designating the reservation first came into force; and
(b) if the designation is still in force, before the end of the period of five years beginning
with the date on which the last report relating to it was laid under subsection (3).

(3)   The Minister conducting a review under this section must prepare a report on the result of
the review and lay a copy of it before each House of Parliament.

Judges of the European Court of Human Rights

18 APPOINTMENT TO EUROPEAN COURT OF HUMAN RIGHTS

(1)   In this section "judicial office" means the office of—
(a) Lord Justice of Appeal, Justice of the High Court or Circuit judge, in England
and Wales;
(b) judge of the Court of Session or sheriff, in Scotland;
(c) Lord Justice of Appeal, judge of the High Court or county court judge, in
Northern Ireland.

(2)   The holder of a judicial office may become a judge of the European Court of Human
Rights ("the Court") without being required to relinquish his office.

(3)   But he is not required to perform the duties of his judicial office while he is a judge of
the Court.

(4)   In respect of any period during which he is a judge of the Court—
(a) a Lord Justice of Appeal or Justice of the High Court is not to count as a judge of the
relevant court for the purposes of section 2(1) or 4(1) of the [Senior Courts Act 1981]
(maximum number of judges) nor as a judge of the [Senior Courts] for the purposes
of section 12(1) to (6) of that Act (salaries etc.);
(b) a judge of the Court of Session is not to count as a judge of that court for the
purposes of section 1(1) of the Court of Session Act 1988 (maximum number of
judges) or of section 9(1)(c) of the Administration of Justice Act 1973 ("the 1973
Act")(salaries etc.);
(c) a Lord Justice of Appeal or judge of the High Court in Northern Ireland is not to
count as a judge of the relevant court for the purposes of section 2(1) or 3(1) of the
Judicature (Northern Ireland) Act 1978 (maximum number of judges) nor as a judge
of the [Court of Judicature] of Northern Ireland for the purposes of section 9(1)(d) of
the 1973 Act (salaries etc.);
(d) a Circuit judge is not to count as such for the purposes of section 18 of the Courts
Act 1971 (salaries etc.);
(e) a sheriff is not to count as such for the purposes of section 14 of the Sheriff Courts
(Scotland) Act 1907 (salaries etc.);
(f) a county court judge of Northern Ireland is not to count as such for the purposes of
section 106 of the County Courts Act (Northern Ireland) 1959 (salaries etc.).

(5)   If a sheriff principal is appointed a judge of the Court, section 11(1) of the Sheriff Courts (Scotland) Act 1971 (temporary appointment of sheriff principal) applies, while he holds that appointment, as if his office is vacant.

(6)   Schedule 4 makes provision about judicial pensions in relation to the holder of a judicial office who serves as a judge of the Court.

(7)   The Lord Chancellor or the Secretary of State may by order make such transitional provision (including, in particular, provision for a temporary increase in the maximum number of judges) as he considers appropriate in relation to any holder of a judicial office who has completed his service as a judge of the Court.

(7A) The following paragraphs apply to the making of an order under subsection (7) in relation to any holder of a judicial office listed in subsection (1)(a)—
      (a) before deciding what transitional provision it is appropriate to make, the person making the order must consult the Lord Chief Justice of England and Wales;
      (b) before making the order, that person must consult the Lord Chief Justice of England and Wales.

(7B) The following paragraphs apply to the making of an order under subsection (7) in relation to any holder of a judicial office listed in subsection (1)(c)—
      (a) before deciding what transitional provision it is appropriate to make, the person making the order must consult the Lord Chief Justice of Northern Ireland;
      (b) before making the order, that person must consult the Lord Chief Justice of Northern Ireland.

(7C) The Lord Chief Justice of England and Wales may nominate a judicial office holder (within the meaning of section 109(4) of the Constitutional Reform Act 2005) to exercise his functions under this section.

(7D) The Lord Chief Justice of Northern Ireland may nominate any of the following to exercise his functions under this section—
      (a) the holder of one of the offices listed in Schedule 1 to the Justice (Northern Ireland) Act 2002;
      (b) a Lord Justice of Appeal (as defined in section 88 of that Act).]

Parliamentary procedure

19 STATEMENTS OF COMPATIBILITY

(1)   A Minister of the Crown in charge of a Bill in either House of Parliament must, before Second Reading of the Bill—
      (a) make a statement to the effect that in his view the provisions of the Bill are compatible with the Convention rights ("a statement of compatibility"); or
      (b) make a statement to the effect that although he is unable to make a statement of compatibility the government nevertheless wishes the House to proceed with the Bill.

(2)   The statement must be in writing and be published in such manner as the Minister making it considers appropriate.

Supplemental

20 ORDERS ETC. UNDER THIS ACT

(1)   Any power of a Minister of the Crown to make an order under this Act is exercisable by statutory instrument.

(2)   The power of [. . .] [the Lord Chancellor or] the Secretary of State to make rules (other than rules of court) under section 2(3) or 7(9) is exercisable by statutory instrument.

(3)   Any statutory instrument made under section 14, 15 or 16(7) must be laid before Parliament.

(4)   No order may be made by [. . .] [the Lord Chancellor or] the Secretary of State under section 1(4), 7(11) or 16(2) unless a draft of the order has been laid before, and approved by, each House of Parliament.

(5)   Any statutory instrument made under section 18(7) or Schedule 4, or to which subsection (2) applies, shall be subject to annulment in pursuance of a resolution of either House of Parliament.

(6)   The power of a Northern Ireland department to make—
(a) rules under section 2(3)(c) or 7(9)(c), or
(b) an order under section 7(11),
is exercisable by statutory rule for the purposes of the Statutory Rules (Northern Ireland) Order 1979.

(7)   Any rules made under section 2(3)(c) or 7(9)(c) shall be subject to negative resolution; and section 41(6) of the Interpretation Act (Northern Ireland) 1954 (meaning of "subject to negative resolution") shall apply as if the power to make the rules were conferred by an Act of the Northern Ireland Assembly.

(8)   No order may be made by a Northern Ireland department under section 7(11) unless a draft of the order has been laid before, and approved by, the Northern Ireland Assembly.

21 INTERPRETATION, ETC.

(1)   In this Act—

"amend" includes repeal and apply (with or without modifications);

"the appropriate Minister" means the Minister of the Crown having charge of the appropriate authorised government department (within the meaning of the Crown Proceedings Act 1947);

"the Commission" means the European Commission of Human Rights;

"the Convention" means the Convention for the Protection of Human Rights and Fundamental Freedoms, agreed by the Council of Europe at Rome on 4th November 1950 as it has effect for the time being in relation to the United Kingdom;

"declaration of incompatibility" means a declaration under section 4;

"Minister of the Crown" has the same meaning as in the Ministers of the Crown Act 1975;

"Northern Ireland Minister" includes the First Minister and the deputy First Minister in Northern Ireland;

"primary legislation" means any—
(a) public general Act;
(b) local and personal Act;
(c) private Act;
(d) Measure of the Church Assembly;
(e) Measure of the General Synod of the Church of England;

    (f)   Order in Council—
        (i)   made in exercise of Her Majesty's Royal Prerogative;
        (ii) made under section 38(1)(a) of the Northern Ireland Constitution Act 1973 or the corresponding provision of the Northern Ireland Act 1998; or
        (iii) amending an Act of a kind mentioned in paragraph (a), (b) or (c);
           and includes an order or other instrument made under primary legislation (otherwise than by the [Welsh Ministers, the First Minister for Wales, the Counsel General to the Welsh Assembly Government,] a member of the Scottish Executive, a Northern Ireland Minister or a Northern Ireland department) to the extent to which it operates to bring one or more provisions of that legislation into force or amends any primary legislation;

"the First Protocol" means the protocol to the Convention agreed at Paris on 20th March 1952;

[. . .]

"the Eleventh Protocol" means the protocol to the Convention (restructuring the control machinery established by the Convention) agreed at Strasbourg on 11th May 1994;

["the Thirteenth Protocol" means the protocol to the Convention (concerning the abolition of the death penalty in all circumstances) agreed at Vilnius on 3rd May 2002;]

"remedial order" means an order under section 10;

"subordinate legislation" means any—
    (a)   Order in Council other than one—
        (i)   made in exercise of Her Majesty's Royal Prerogative;
        (ii) made under section 38(1)(a) of the Northern Ireland Constitution Act 1973 or the corresponding provision of the Northern Ireland Act 1998; or
        (iii) amending an Act of a kind mentioned in the definition of primary legislation;
    (b)   Act of the Scottish Parliament;
    [(ba) Measure of the National Assembly for Wales;
    (bb) Act of the National Assembly for Wales;]
    (c)   Act of the Parliament of Northern Ireland;
    (d)   Measure of the Assembly established under section 1 of the Northern Ireland Assembly Act 1973;
    (e)   Act of the Northern Ireland Assembly;
    (f)   order, rules, regulations, scheme, warrant, byelaw or other instrument made under primary legislation (except to the extent to which it operates to bring one or more provisions of that legislation into force or amends any primary legislation);
    (g)   order, rules, regulations, scheme, warrant, byelaw or other instrument made under legislation mentioned in paragraph (b), (c), (d) or (e) or made under an Order in Council applying only to Northern Ireland;
    (h)   order, rules, regulations, scheme, warrant, byelaw or other instrument made by a member of the Scottish Executive [, Welsh Ministers, the First Minister for Wales, the Counsel General to the Welsh Assembly Government,] a Northern Ireland Minister or a Northern Ireland department in exercise of prerogative or other executive functions of Her Majesty which are exercisable by such a person on behalf of Her Majesty;

"transferred matters" has the same meaning as in the Northern Ireland Act 1998; and

"tribunal" means any tribunal in which legal proceedings may be brought.

(2)   The references in paragraphs (b) and (c) of section 2(1) to Articles are to Articles of the Convention as they had effect immediately before the coming into force of the Eleventh Protocol.

(3)   The reference in paragraph (d) of section 2(1) to Article 46 includes a reference to Articles 32 and 54 of the Convention as they had effect immediately before the coming into force of the Eleventh Protocol.

(4)   The references in section 2(1) to a report or decision of the Commission or a decision of the Committee of Ministers include references to a report or decision made as provided by paragraphs 3, 4 and 6 of Article 5 of the Eleventh Protocol (transitional provisions).

[. . .]

22   SHORT TITLE, COMMENCEMENT, APPLICATION AND EXTENT

(1)   This Act may be cited as the Human Rights Act 1998.

(2)   Sections 18, 20 and 21(5) and this section come into force on the passing of this Act.

(3)   The other provisions of this Act come into force on such day as the Secretary of State may by order appoint; and different days may be appointed for different purposes.

(4)   Paragraph (b) of subsection (1) of section 7 applies to proceedings brought by or at the instigation of a public authority whenever the act in question took place; but otherwise that subsection does not apply to an act taking place before the coming into force of that section.

(5)   This Act binds the Crown.

(6)   This Act extends to Northern Ireland.

[. . .]

[. . .]

NORTHERN IRELAND ACT 1998
(c. 47)

An Act to make new provision for the government of Northern Ireland for the purpose of implementing the agreement reached at multi-party talks on Northern Ireland set out in Command Paper 3883.

[. . .]

Part I   PRELIMINARY

1   STATUS OF NORTHERN IRELAND

(1)   It is hereby declared that Northern Ireland in its entirety remains part of the United Kingdom and shall not cease to be so without the consent of a majority of the people of Northern Ireland voting in a poll held for the purposes of this section in accordance with Schedule 1.

(2)   But if the wish expressed by a majority in such a poll is that Northern Ireland should cease to be part of the United Kingdom and form part of a united Ireland, the Secretary of State shall lay before Parliament such proposals to give effect to that wish as may be agreed between Her Majesty's Government in the United Kingdom and the Government of Ireland.

[. . .]

Part II **LEGISLATIVE POWERS**

General

5 ACTS OF THE NORTHERN IRELAND ASSEMBLY

(1)   Subject to sections 6 to 8, the Assembly may make laws, to be known as Acts.

(2)   A Bill shall become an Act when it has been passed by the Assembly and has received Royal Assent.

(3)   A Bill receives Royal Assent at the beginning of the day on which Letters Patent under the Great Seal of Northern Ireland signed with Her Majesty's own hand signifying Her Assent are notified to the Presiding Officer.

[. . .]

6 LEGISLATIVE COMPETENCE

(1)   A provision of an Act is not law if it is outside the legislative competence of the Assembly.

(2)   A provision is outside that competence if any of the following paragraphs apply—
    (a) it would form part of the law of a country or territory other than Northern Ireland, or confer or remove functions exercisable otherwise than in or as regards Northern Ireland;
    (b) it deals with an excepted matter and is not ancillary to other provisions (whether in the Act or previously enacted) dealing with reserved or transferred matters;
    (c) it is incompatible with any of the Convention rights;
    (d) it is incompatible with Community law;
    (e) it discriminates against any person or class of person on the ground of religious belief or political opinion;
    (f) it modifies an enactment in breach of section 7.

(3)   For the purposes of this Act, a provision is ancillary to other provisions if it is a provision—
    (a) which provides for the enforcement of those other provisions or is otherwise necessary or expedient for making those other provisions effective; or
    (b) which is otherwise incidental to, or consequential on, those provisions;
and references in this Act to provisions previously enacted are references to provisions contained in, or in any instrument made under, other Northern Ireland legislation or an Act of Parliament.

[. . .]

7 ENTRENCHED ENACTMENTS

(1)   Subject to subsection (2), the following enactments shall not be modified by an Act of the Assembly or subordinate legislation made, confirmed or approved by a Minister or Northern Ireland department—
    (a) the European Communities Act 1972;
    (b) the Human Rights Act 1998; and
    (c) section 43(1) to (6) and (8), section 67, sections 84 to [86B], section 95(3) and (4) and section 98 and
    (d) section 1 and section 84 of the Justice (Northern Ireland) Act 2002.
    [. . .]

[. . .]

Scrutiny and stages of Bills

9 SCRUTINY BY MINISTERS

(1)   A Minister in charge of a Bill shall, on or before introduction of it in the Assembly, make a statement to the effect that in his view the Bill would be within the legislative competence of the Assembly.

[. . .]

10 SCRUTINY BY PRESIDING OFFICER

(1)   Standing orders shall ensure that a Bill is not introduced in the Assembly if the Presiding Officer decides that any provision of it would not be within the legislative competence of the Assembly.

(2)   Subject to subsection (3)—
    (a)   the Presiding Officer shall consider a Bill both on its introduction and before the Assembly enters on its final stage; and
    (b)   if he considers that the Bill contains—
        (i)   any provision which deals with an excepted matter and is ancillary to other provisions (whether in the Bill or previously enacted) dealing with reserved or transferred matters; or
        (ii)   any provision which deals with a reserved matter,
    he shall refer it to the Secretary of State; and
    (c)   the Assembly shall not proceed with the Bill or, as the case may be, enter on its final stage unless—
        (i)   the Secretary of State's consent to the consideration of the Bill by the Assembly is signified; or
        (ii)   the Assembly is informed that in his opinion the Bill does not contain any such provision as is mentioned in paragraph (b)(i) or (ii).

(3)   Subsection (2)(b) and (c) shall not apply—
    (a)   where, in the opinion of the Presiding Officer, each provision of the Bill which deals with an excepted or reserved matter is ancillary to other provisions (whether in the Bill or previously enacted) dealing with transferred matters only; or
    (b)   on the introduction of a Bill, where the Bill has been endorsed with a statement that the Secretary of State has consented to the Assembly considering the Bill.

[. . .]

11 SCRUTINY BY THE [SUPREME COURT]

(1)   The Attorney General for Northern Ireland may refer the question of whether a provision of a Bill would be within the legislative competence of the Assembly to the [Supreme Court] for decision.

[. . .]

[. . .]

Royal Assent

14 SUBMISSION BY SECRETARY OF STATE

(1)   It shall be the Secretary of State who submits Bills for Royal Assent.

[. . .]

[. . .]

Part III **EXECUTIVE AUTHORITIES**

Authorities

16A APPOINTMENT OF FIRST MINISTER, DEPUTY FIRST MINISTER AND NORTHERN IRELAND MINISTERS FOLLOWING ASSEMBLY ELECTION

(1)   This section applies where an Assembly is elected under section 31 or 32.

(2)   All Northern Ireland Ministers shall cease to hold office.

(3)   Within a period of seven days beginning with the first meeting of the Assembly—
   (a)   the offices of First Minister and deputy First Minister shall be filled by applying subsections (4) to (7); and
   (b)   the Ministerial offices to be held by Northern Ireland Ministers shall be filled by applying section 18(2) to (6).

(4)   The nominating officer of the largest political party of the largest political designation shall nominate a member of the Assembly to be the First Minister.

(5)   The nominating officer of the largest political party of the second largest political designation shall nominate a member of the Assembly to be the deputy First Minister.

(6)   If the persons nominated do not take up office within a period specified in standing orders, further nominations shall be made under subsections (4) and (5).

(7)   Subsections (4) to (6) shall be applied as many times as may be necessary to secure that the offices of First Minister and deputy First Minister are filled.

[. . .]

16B VACANCIES IN THE OFFICE OF FIRST MINISTER OR DEPUTY FIRST MINISTER

(1)   The First Minister or the deputy First Minister—
   (a)   may at any time resign by notice in writing to the Presiding Officer; and
   (b)   shall cease to hold office if he ceases to be a member of the Assembly otherwise than by virtue of a dissolution.

(2)   If either the First Minister or the deputy First Minister ceases to hold office at any time, whether by resignation or otherwise, the other—
   (a)   shall also cease to hold office at that time; but
   (b)   may continue to exercise the functions of his office until immediately before those offices are filled in accordance with this section.

(3)   Where the offices of the First Minister and the deputy First Minister become vacant at any time, they shall be filled by applying subsections (4) to (7) within a period of seven days beginning with that time.

(4)   The nominating officer of the largest political party of the largest political designation shall nominate a member of the Assembly to be the First Minister.

(5)   The nominating officer of the largest political party of the second largest political designation shall nominate a member of the Assembly to be the deputy First Minister.

(6)   If the persons nominated do not take up office within a period specified in standing orders, further nominations shall be made under subsections (4) and (5).

(7) Subsections (4) to (6) shall be applied as many times as may be necessary to secure that the offices of First Minister and deputy First Minister are filled.

[. . .]

16C SECTIONS 16A AND 16B: SUPPLEMENTARY

(1) In sections 16A and 16B and this section "nominating officer", in relation to a party, means—
   (a) the person registered under Part 2 of the Political Parties, Elections and Referendums Act 2000 as the party's nominating officer; or
   (b) a member of the Assembly nominated by him for the purposes of this section.

(2) For the purposes of sections 16A and 16B and this section—
   (a) the size of a political party is to be determined by reference to the number of seats in the Assembly which were held by members of the party on the day on which the Assembly first met following its election; but
   (b) if two or more parties are taken by virtue of paragraph (a) to be of the same size, the respective sizes of those parties is to be determined by reference to the number of first preference votes cast for the parties at the last general election of members of the Assembly;
   (this is subject to subsections (7) and (8)).

(3) For the purposes of sections 16A and 16B and this section, a political party to which one or more members of the Assembly belong is to be taken—
   (a) to be of the political designation "Nationalist" if, at the relevant time (see subsection (11)), more than half of the members of the Assembly who belonged to the party were designated Nationalists;
   (b) to be of the political designation "Unionist" if, at the relevant time, more than half of the members of the Assembly who belonged to the party were designated Unionists;
   (c) otherwise, to be of the political designation "Other".

(4) For the purposes of sections 16A and 16B and this section—
   (a) the size of the political designation "Nationalist" is to be taken to be equal to the number of members of the Assembly who, at the relevant time, were designated Nationalists;
   (b) the size of the political designation "Unionist" is to be taken to be equal to the number of members of the Assembly who, at the relevant time, were designated Unionists;
   (c) the size of the political designation "Other" is to be taken to be equal to the number of members of the Assembly who, at the relevant time, were neither designated Nationalists nor designated Unionists.

[. . .]

17 MINISTERIAL OFFICES

(1) The First Minister and the deputy First Minister acting jointly may at any time, and shall where subsection (2) applies, determine—
   (a) the number of Ministerial offices to be held by Northern Ireland Ministers; and
   (b) the functions to be exercisable by the holder of each such office.

(2) This subsection applies where provision is made by an Act of the Assembly for establishing a new Northern Ireland department or dissolving an existing one.

(3) In making a determination under subsection (1), the First Minister and the deputy First Minister shall ensure that the functions exercisable by those in charge of the different

Northern Ireland departments existing at the date of the determination are exercisable by the holders of different Ministerial offices.

(4)   The number of Ministerial offices shall not exceed 10 or such greater number as the Secretary of State may by order provide.

(5)   A determination under subsection (1) shall not have effect unless it is approved by a resolution of the Assembly passed with cross-community support.

18 NORTHERN IRELAND MINISTERS

(1)   Where—
(a) an Assembly is elected under section 31 or 32;
(b) a determination under section 17(1) takes effect;
(c) a resolution which causes one or more Ministerial offices to become vacant is passed under section 30(2);
(d) ;
(da) a period of exclusion under section 30(2) comes to an end; or
(e) such other circumstances obtain as may be specified in standing orders,
all Northern Ireland Ministers shall cease to hold office and the Ministerial offices shall be filled by applying subsections (2) to (6) within a period so specified.

(2)   The nominating officer of the political party for which the formula in subsection (5) gives the highest figure may select a Ministerial office and nominate a person to hold it who is a member of the party and of the Assembly.

(3)   If—
(a) the nominating officer does not exercise the power conferred by subsection (2) within a period specified in standing orders; or
(b) the nominated person does not take up the selected Ministerial office within that period,
that power shall become exercisable by the nominating officer of the political party for which the formula in subsection (5) gives the next highest figure.

(4)   Subsections (2) and (3) shall be applied as many times as may be necessary to secure that each of the Ministerial offices is filled.

(5)   The formula is—

$$\frac{S}{1 + M}$$

where—

S = the number of seats in the Assembly which were held by members of the party on the day on which the Assembly first met following its election;

M = the number of Ministerial offices (if any) which are held by members of the party.

(6)   Where the figures given by the formula for two or more political parties are equal, each of those figures shall be recalculated with S being equal to the number of first preference votes cast for the party at the last general election of members of the Assembly.

(7)   The holding of office as First Minister or deputy First Minister shall not prevent a person being nominated to hold a Ministerial office.

[. . .]

(9)   A Northern Ireland Minister shall cease to hold office if—
(a) he resigns by notice in writing to the First Minister and the deputy First Minister;

(b) he ceases to be a member of the Assembly otherwise than by virtue of a dissolution; or

(c) he is dismissed by the nominating officer who nominated him (or that officer's successor) and the Presiding Officer is notified of his dismissal.

[. . .]

[. . .]

20   THE EXECUTIVE COMMITTEE

(1) There shall be an Executive Committee of each Assembly consisting of the First Minister, the deputy First Minister and the Northern Ireland Ministers.

(2) The First Minister and the deputy First Minister shall be chairmen of the Committee.

(3) The Committee shall have the functions set out in paragraphs 19 and 20 of Strand One of the Belfast Agreement.

[. . .]

Functions

22   STATUTORY FUNCTIONS

(1) An Act of the Assembly or other enactment may confer functions on a Minister (but not a junior Minister) or a Northern Ireland department by name.

(2) Functions conferred on a Northern Ireland department by an enactment passed or made before the appointed day shall, except as provided by an Act of the Assembly or other subsequent enactment, continue to be exercisable by that department.

[. . .]

24   COMMUNITY LAW, CONVENTION RIGHTS ETC.

(1) A Minister or Northern Ireland department has no power to make, confirm or approve any subordinate legislation, or to do any act, so far as the legislation or act—
(a) is incompatible with any of the Convention rights;
(b) is incompatible with Community law;
(c) discriminates against a person or class of person on the ground of religious belief or political opinion;
(d) in the case of an act, aids or incites another person to discriminate against a person or class of person on that ground; or
(e) in the case of legislation, modifies an enactment in breach of section 7.
[. . .]

[. . .]

Part IV   THE NORTHERN IRELAND ASSEMBLY

[. . .]

Presiding Officer and Commission

39   PRESIDING OFFICER

(1) Each Assembly shall as its first business elect from among its members a Presiding Officer and deputies.

[. . .]

Proceedings etc.

[. . .]

42 PETITIONS OF CONCERN

(1)   If 30 members petition the Assembly expressing their concern about a matter which is to be voted on by the Assembly, the vote on that matter shall require cross-community support.

[. . .]

[. . .]

Part VII HUMAN RIGHTS AND EQUAL OPPORTUNITIES

Human rights

68 THE NORTHERN IRELAND HUMAN RIGHTS COMMISSION

(1)   There shall be a body corporate to be known as the Northern Ireland Human Rights Commission.

(2)   The Commission shall consist of a Chief Commissioner and other Commissioners appointed by the Secretary of State.

(3)   In making appointments under this section, the Secretary of State shall as far as practicable secure that the Commissioners, as a group, are representative of the community in Northern Ireland.

[. . .]

69 THE COMMISSION'S FUNCTIONS

(1)   The Commission shall keep under review the adequacy and effectiveness in Northern Ireland of law and practice relating to the protection of human rights.

(2)   The Commission shall, before the end of the period of two years beginning with the commencement of this section, make to the Secretary of State such recommendations as it thinks fit for improving—
       (a) its effectiveness;
       (b) the adequacy and effectiveness of the functions conferred on it by this Part; and
       (c) the adequacy and effectiveness of the provisions of this Part relating to it.

(3)   The Commission shall advise the Secretary of State and the Executive Committee of the Assembly of legislative and other measures which ought to be taken to protect human rights—
       (a) as soon as reasonably practicable after receipt of a general or specific request for advice; and
       (b) on such other occasions as the Commission thinks appropriate.

(4)   The Commission shall advise the Assembly whether a Bill is compatible with human rights—
       (a) as soon as reasonably practicable after receipt of a request for advice; and
       (b) on such other occasions as the Commission thinks appropriate.

(5)   The Commission may—
       (a) give assistance to individuals in accordance with section 70; and

(b) bring proceedings involving law or practice relating to the protection of human rights.

(6) The Commission shall promote understanding and awareness of the importance of human rights in Northern Ireland; and for this purpose it may undertake, commission or provide financial or other assistance for—
(a) research; and
(b) educational activities.
[. . .]

(8) For the purpose of exercising its functions under this section the Commission may conduct such investigations as it considers necessary or expedient.

[. . .]

70 ASSISTANCE BY COMMISSION

(1) This section applies to—
(a) proceedings involving law or practice relating to the protection of human rights which a person in Northern Ireland has commenced, or wishes to commence; or
(b) proceedings in the course of which such a person relies, or wishes to rely, on such law or practice.

(2) Where the person applies to the Northern Ireland Human Rights Commission for assistance in relation to proceedings to which this section applies, the Commission may grant the application on any of the following grounds—
(a) that the case raises a question of principle;
(b) that it would be unreasonable to expect the person to deal with the case without assistance because of its complexity, or because of the person's position in relation to another person involved, or for some other reason;
(c) that there are other special circumstances which make it appropriate for the Commission to provide assistance.

(3) Where the Commission grants an application under subsection (2) it may—
(a) provide, or arrange for the provision of, legal advice;
(b) arrange for the provision of legal representation;
(c) provide any other assistance which it thinks appropriate.
[. . .]

71 RESTRICTIONS ON APPLICATION OF RIGHTS

(1) Nothing in section 6(2)(c), 24(1)(a) or 69(5)(b) shall enable a person—
(a) to bring any proceedings in a court or tribunal on the ground that any legislation or act is incompatible with the Convention rights; or
(b) to rely on any of the Convention rights in any such proceedings,
unless he would be a victim for the purposes of article 34 of the Convention if proceedings in respect of the legislation or act were brought in the European Court of Human Rights.

[. . .]

[. . .]

80 LEGISLATIVE POWER TO REMEDY ULTRA VIRES ACTS

(1)   The Secretary of State may by order make such provision as he considers necessary or expedient in consequence of—

    (a)   any provision of an Act of the Assembly which is not, or may not be, within the legislative competence of the Assembly; or

    (b)   any purported exercise by a Minister or Northern Ireland department of his or its functions which is not, or may not be, a valid exercise of those functions.

    [. . .]

[. . .]

As amended by The Northern Ireland (Monitoring Commission etc.) Act 2003 (Cessation of Provisions) Order 2011, article 5(b)

SCOTLAND ACT 1998
(c. 46)

An Act to provide for the establishment of a Scottish Parliament and Administration and other changes in the government of Scotland; to provide for changes in the constitution and functions of certain public authorities; to provide for the variation of the basic rate of income tax in relation to income of Scottish taxpayers in accordance with a resolution of the Scottish Parliament; to amend the law about parliamentary constituencies in Scotland; and for connected purposes.

[. . .]

Part I THE SCOTTISH PARLIAMENT

The Scottish Parliament

1 THE SCOTTISH PARLIAMENT

(1)   There shall be a Scottish Parliament.

(2)   One member of the Parliament shall be returned for each constituency (under the simple majority system) at an election held in the constituency.

(3)   Members of the Parliament for each region shall be returned at a general election under the additional member system of proportional representation provided for in this Part and vacancies among such members shall be filled in accordance with this Part.

(4)   The validity of any proceedings of the Parliament is not affected by any vacancy in its membership.

    [. . .]

General elections

2 ORDINARY GENERAL ELECTIONS

(1)   The day on which the poll at the first ordinary general election for membership of the Parliament shall be held, and the day, time and place for the meeting of the Parliament following that poll, shall be appointed by order made by the Secretary of State.

(2)   The poll at subsequent ordinary general elections shall be held on the first Thursday in May in the fourth calendar year following that in which the previous ordinary general election was held, unless the day of the poll is determined by a proclamation under subsection (5).

[. . .]

(5)   If the Presiding Officer proposes a day for the holding of the poll which is not more than one month earlier, nor more than one month later, than the first Thursday in May, Her Majesty may by proclamation under the Scottish Seal—
(a) dissolve the Parliament,
(b) require the poll at the election to be held on the day proposed, and
(c) require the Parliament to meet within the period of seven days beginning immediately after the day of the poll.

[. . .]

5 CANDIDATES

(1)   At a general election, the candidates may stand for return as constituency members or regional members.

(2)   A person may not be a candidate to be a constituency member for more than one constituency.

(3)   The candidates to be regional members shall be those included in a list submitted under subsection (4) or individual candidates.

(4)   Any registered political party may submit to the regional returning officer a list of candidates to be regional members for a particular region (referred to in this Act, in relation to the region, as the party's "regional list").

(5)   A registered political party's regional list has effect in relation to the general election and any vacancy occurring among the regional members after that election and before the next general election.

(6)   Not more than twelve persons may be included in the list (but the list may include only one person).

[. . .]

6 POLL FOR REGIONAL MEMBERS

(1)   This section and sections 7 and 8 are about the return of regional members at a general election.

(2)   In each of the constituencies for the Parliament, a poll shall be held at which each person entitled to vote as elector may give a vote (referred to in this Act as a "regional vote") for—
(a) a registered political party which has submitted a regional list, or
(b) an individual candidate to be a regional member for the region.
[. . .]

7 CALCULATION OF REGIONAL FIGURES

(1)   The persons who are to be returned as constituency members for constituencies included in the region must be determined before the persons who are to be returned as the regional members for the region.

(2) For each registered political party which has submitted a regional list, the regional figure for the purposes of section 8 is—

(a) the total number of regional votes given for the party in all the constituencies included in the region, divided by

(b) the aggregate of one plus the number of candidates of the party returned as constituency members for any of those constituencies.

(3) Each time a seat is allocated to the party under section 8, that figure shall be recalculated by increasing (or further increasing) the aggregate in subsection (2)(b) by one.

(4) For each individual candidate to be a regional member for the region, the regional figure for the purposes of section 8 is the total number of regional votes given for him in all the constituencies included in the region.

8 ALLOCATION OF SEATS TO REGIONAL MEMBERS

(1) The first regional member seat shall be allocated to the registered political party or individual candidate with the highest regional figure.

(2) The second and subsequent regional member seats shall be allocated to the registered political party or individual candidate with the highest regional figure, after any recalculation required by section 7(3) has been carried out.

(3) An individual candidate already returned as a constituency or regional member shall be disregarded.

(4) Seats for the region which are allocated to a registered political party shall be filled by the persons in the party's regional list in the order in which they appear in the list.

(5) For the purposes of this section and section 10, a person in a registered political party's regional list who is returned as a member of the Parliament shall be treated as ceasing to be in the list (even if his return is void).

(6) Once a party's regional list has been exhausted (by the return of persons included in it as constituency members or by the previous application of subsection (1) or (2)) the party shall be disregarded.

(7) If (on the application of subsection (1) or any application of subsection (2)) the highest regional figure is the regional figure of two or more parties or individual candidates,

(a) the subsection in question shall apply to each of them; or

(b) if paragraph (a) would result in more than the correct number of seats for the region being allocated, the subsection in question shall apply as if the regional figure for each of those parties or candidates had been adjusted in accordance with subsection (8).

(8) The regional figure for a party or candidate is adjusted in accordance with this subsection by—

(a) adding one vote to the total number of regional votes given for the party or candidate in all the constituencies included in the region; and

(b) (in the case of a party) recalculating the regional figure accordingly.

(9) If, on the application of the subsection in question in accordance with subsection (7)(b), seats would be allocated to two or more parties or individual candidates and that would result in more than the correct number of seats for the region being allocated, the regional returning officer shall decide between them by lot.

[. . .]

Presiding Officer and administration

19 PRESIDING OFFICER

(1)   The Parliament shall, at its first meeting following a general election, elect from among its members a Presiding Officer and two deputies.

(2)   A person elected Presiding Officer or deputy shall hold office until the conclusion of the next election for Presiding Officer under subsection (1) unless he previously resigns, ceases to be a member of the Parliament otherwise than by virtue of a dissolution or is removed from office by resolution of the Parliament.

(3)   If the Presiding Officer or a deputy ceases to hold office before the Parliament is dissolved, the Parliament shall elect another from among its members to fill his place.

(4)   The Presiding Officer's functions may be exercised by a deputy if the office of Presiding Officer is vacant or the Presiding Officer is for any reason unable to act.

(5)   The Presiding Officer may (subject to standing orders) authorise any deputy to exercise functions on his behalf.

[. . .]

(7)   The validity of any act of the Presiding Officer or a deputy is not affected by any defect in his election.

[. . .]

Proceedings etc.

22 STANDING ORDERS

(1)   The proceedings of the Parliament shall be regulated by standing orders.

[. . .]

[. . .]

Legislation

28 ACTS OF THE SCOTTISH PARLIAMENT

(1)   Subject to section 29, the Parliament may make laws, to be known as Acts of the Scottish Parliament.

(2)   Proposed Acts of the Scottish Parliament shall be known as Bills; and a Bill shall become an Act of the Scottish Parliament when it has been passed by the Parliament and has received Royal Assent.

(3)   A Bill receives Royal Assent at the beginning of the day on which Letters Patent under the Scottish Seal signed with Her Majesty's own hand signifying Her Assent are recorded in the Register of the Great Seal.

(4)   The date of Royal Assent shall be written on the Act of the Scottish Parliament by the Clerk, and shall form part of the Act.

(5)   The validity of an Act of the Scottish Parliament is not affected by any invalidity in the proceedings of the Parliament leading to its enactment.

(6)   Every Act of the Scottish Parliament shall be judicially noticed.

(7)   This section does not affect the power of the Parliament of the United Kingdom to make laws for Scotland.

29 LEGISLATIVE COMPETENCE

(1)   An Act of the Scottish Parliament is not law so far as any provision of the Act is outside the legislative competence of the Parliament.

(2)   A provision is outside that competence so far as any of the following paragraphs apply—
(a) it would form part of the law of a country or territory other than Scotland, or confer or remove functions exercisable otherwise than in or as regards Scotland,
(b) it relates to reserved matters,
(c) it is in breach of the restrictions in Schedule 4,
(d) it is incompatible with any of the Convention rights or with Community law,
(e) it would remove the Lord Advocate from his position as head of the systems of criminal prosecution and investigation of deaths in Scotland.

(3)   For the purposes of this section, the question whether a provision of an Act of the Scottish Parliament relates to a reserved matter is to be determined, subject to subsection (4), by reference to the purpose of the provision, having regard (among other things) to its effect in all the circumstances.

(4)   A provision which—
(a) would otherwise not relate to reserved matters, but
(b) makes modifications of Scots private law, or Scots criminal law, as it applies to reserved matters,
is to be treated as relating to reserved matters unless the purpose of the provision is to make the law in question apply consistently to reserved matters and otherwise.

30 LEGISLATIVE COMPETENCE: SUPPLEMENTARY

(1)   Schedule 5 (which defines reserved matters) shall have effect.

[. . .]

31 SCRUTINY OF BILLS BEFORE INTRODUCTION

(1)   A member of the Scottish Executive in charge of a Bill shall, on or before introduction of the Bill in the Parliament, state that in his view the provisions of the Bill would be within the legislative competence of the Parliament.

(2)   The Presiding Officer shall, on or before the introduction of a Bill in the Parliament, decide whether or not in his view the provisions of the Bill would be within the legislative competence of the Parliament and state his decision.

[. . .]

32 SUBMISSION OF BILLS FOR ROYAL ASSENT

(1)   It is for the Presiding Officer to submit Bills for Royal Assent.

(2)   The Presiding Officer shall not submit a Bill for Royal Assent at any time when—
(a) the Advocate General, the Lord Advocate or the Attorney General is entitled to make a reference in relation to the Bill under section 33,

(b) any such reference has been made but has not been decided or otherwise disposed of by the [Supreme Court], or

(c) an order may be made in relation to the Bill under section 35.

(3) The Presiding Officer shall not submit a Bill in its unamended form for Royal Assent if—

(a) the [Supreme Court has] decided that the Bill or any provision of it would not be within the legislative competence of the Parliament, or

(b) a reference made in relation to the Bill under section 33 has been withdrawn following a request for withdrawal of the reference under section 34(2)(b).

(4) In this Act—

"Advocate General" means the Advocate General for Scotland,

[. . .]

33 SCRUTINY OF BILLS BY THE [SUPREME COURT]

(1) The Advocate General, the Lord Advocate or the Attorney General may refer the question of whether a Bill or any provision of a Bill would be within the legislative competence of the Parliament to the [Supreme Court] for decision.

(2) Subject to subsection (3), he may make a reference in relation to a Bill at any time during—

(a) the period of four weeks beginning with the passing of the Bill, and

(b) any period of four weeks beginning with any subsequent approval of the Bill in accordance with standing orders made by virtue of section 36(5).

(3) He shall not make a reference in relation to a Bill if he has notified the Presiding Officer that he does not intend to make a reference in relation to the Bill, unless the Bill has been approved as mentioned in subsection (2)(b) since the notification.

[. . .]

Other provisions

37 ACTS OF UNION

The Union with Scotland Act 1706 and the Union with England Act 1707 have effect subject to this Act.

[. . .]

Part II **THE SCOTTISH ADMINISTRATION**

Ministers and their staff

44 THE SCOTTISH GOVERNMENT

(1) There shall be a Scottish Government , whose members shall be—

(a) the First Minister,

(b) such Ministers as the First Minister may appoint under section 47, and

(c) the Lord Advocate and the Solicitor General for Scotland.

(2) The members of the Scottish Government are referred to collectively as the Scottish Ministers.

(3) A person who holds a Ministerial office may not be appointed a member of the Scottish Government ; and if a member of the Scottish Government is appointed to a Ministerial office he shall cease to hold office as a member of the Scottish Executive.

[. . .]

45 THE FIRST MINISTER

(1)   The First Minister shall be appointed by Her Majesty from among the members of the Parliament and shall hold office at Her Majesty's pleasure.

(2)   The First Minister may at any time tender his resignation to Her Majesty and shall do so if the Parliament resolves that the Scottish Government no longer enjoys the confidence of the Parliament.

(3)   The First Minister shall cease to hold office if a person is appointed in his place.

(4)   If the office of First Minister is vacant or he is for any reason unable to act, the functions exercisable by him shall be exercisable by a person designated by the Presiding Officer.

(5)   A person shall be so designated only if—
       (a)   he is a member of the Parliament, or
       (b)   if the Parliament has been dissolved, he is a person who ceased to be a member by virtue of the dissolution.
       [. . .]

46 CHOICE OF THE FIRST MINISTER

(1)   If one of the following events occurs, the Parliament shall within the period allowed nominate one of its members for appointment as First Minister.

(2)   The events are—
       (a)   the holding of a poll at a general election,
       (b)   the First Minister tendering his resignation to Her Majesty,
       (c)   the office of First Minister becoming vacant (otherwise than in consequence of his so tendering his resignation),
       (d)   the First Minister ceasing to be a member of the Parliament otherwise than by virtue of a dissolution.

(3)   The period allowed is the period of 28 days which begins with the day on which the event in question occurs; but—
       (a)   if another of those events occurs within the period allowed, that period shall be extended (subject to paragraph (b)) so that it ends with the period of 28 days beginning with the day on which that other event occurred, and
       (b)   the period shall end if the Parliament passes a resolution under section 3(1)(a) or when Her Majesty appoints a person as First Minister.

(4)   The Presiding Officer shall recommend to Her Majesty the appointment of any member of the Parliament who is nominated by the Parliament under this section.

47 MINISTERS

(1)   The First Minister may, with the approval of Her Majesty, appoint Ministers from among the members of the Parliament.

(2)   The First Minister shall not seek Her Majesty's approval for any appointment under this section without the agreement of the Parliament.

(3)   A Minister appointed under this section—
       (a)   shall hold office at Her Majesty's pleasure,
       (b)   may be removed from office by the First Minister,
       (c)   may at any time resign and shall do so if the Parliament resolves that the Scottish Executive no longer enjoys the confidence of the Parliament,

(d) if he resigns, shall cease to hold office immediately, and
(e) shall cease to hold office if he ceases to be a member of the Parliament otherwise than by virtue of a dissolution.
[. . .]

Ministerial functions

[. . .]

53 GENERAL TRANSFER OF FUNCTIONS

(1) The functions mentioned in subsection (2) shall, so far as they are exercisable within devolved competence, be exercisable by the Scottish Ministers instead of by a Minister of the Crown.

(2) Those functions are—
(a) those of Her Majesty's prerogative and other executive functions which are exercisable on behalf of Her Majesty by a Minister of the Crown,
(b) other functions conferred on a Minister of the Crown by a prerogative instrument, and
(c) functions conferred on a Minister of the Crown by any pre-commencement enactment,
but do not include any retained functions of the Lord Advocate.
[. . .]

[. . .]

57 COMMUNITY LAW AND CONVENTION RIGHTS

(1) Despite the transfer to the Scottish Ministers by virtue of section 53 of functions in relation to observing and implementing obligations under Community law, any function of a Minister of the Crown in relation to any matter shall continue to be exercisable by him as regards Scotland for the purposes specified in section 2(2) of the European Communities Act 1972.

[. . .]

58 POWER TO PREVENT OR REQUIRE ACTION

(1) If the Secretary of State has reasonable grounds to believe that any action proposed to be taken by a member of the Scottish Government would be incompatible with any international obligations, he may by order direct that the proposed action shall not be taken.

(2) If the Secretary of State has reasonable grounds to believe that any action capable of being taken by a member of the Scottish Government is required for the purpose of giving effect to any such obligations, he may by order direct that the action shall be taken.

[. . .]

[. . .]

Part 4A

Chapter 1 **INTRODUCTORY**

80A OVERVIEW OF PART 4A

(1)   In this Part—
       (a) Chapter 2 confers on the Scottish Parliament power to set a rate of income tax to be
            paid by Scottish taxpayers
[. . .]

80B POWER TO ADD NEW DEVOLVED TAXES

(1)   Her Majesty may by Order in Council amend this Part so as to—
       (a) specify, as an additional devolved tax, a tax of any description, or
       (b) make any other modifications of the provisions relating to devolved taxes which She
            considers necessary or expedient.
[. . .]

Chapter 2 **INCOME TAX**

80C POWER TO SET SCOTTISH RATE FOR SCOTTISH TAXPAYERS

(1)   The Scottish Parliament may by resolution (a "Scottish rate resolution") set the Scottish
       rate for the purpose of calculating the rates of income tax to be paid by Scottish
       taxpayers.

(2)   Section 6(2B) of the Income Tax Act 2007 provides for the calculation of those rates.

[. . .]

(8)   Standing orders must provide that only a member of the Scottish Government may move a
       motion for a Scottish rate resolution.

Miscellaneous

91 MALADMINISTRATION

(1)   The Parliament shall make provision for the investigation of relevant complaints made to
       its members in respect of any action taken by or on behalf of—
       (a) a member of the Scottish Government in the exercise of functions conferred on the
            Scottish Ministers, or
       (b) any other office-holder in the Scottish Administration.

(2)   For the purposes of subsection (1), a complaint is a relevant complaint if it is a complaint
       of a kind which could be investigated under the Parliamentary Commissioner Act 1967 if
       it were made to a member of the House of Commons in respect of a government
       department or other authority to which that Act applies.

(3)   The Parliament may make provision for the investigation of complaints in
       respect of—
       (a) any action taken by or on behalf of an office-holder in the Scottish Administration,
       (b) any action taken by or on behalf of the Parliamentary corporation,
       (c) any action taken by or on behalf of a Scottish public authority with mixed functions
            or no reserved functions, or

(d) any action concerning Scotland and not relating to reserved matters which is taken by or on behalf of a cross-border public authority.

[...]

[...]

100 HUMAN RIGHTS

(1) This Act does not enable a person—
(a) to bring any proceedings in a court or tribunal on the ground that an act is incompatible with the Convention rights, or
(b) to rely on any of the Convention rights in any such proceedings,
unless he would be a victim for the purposes of Article 34 of the Convention (within the meaning of the Human Rights Act 1998) if proceedings in respect of the act were brought in the European Court of Human Rights.

(2) Subsection (1) does not apply to the Lord Advocate, the Advocate General, the Attorney General or the Attorney General for Northern Ireland.

(3) This Act does not enable a court or tribunal to award any damages in respect of an act which is incompatible with any of the Convention rights which it could not award if section 8(3) and (4) of the Human Rights Act 1998 applied.

[...]

101 INTERPRETATION OF ACTS OF THE SCOTTISH PARLIAMENT ETC.

(1) This section applies to—
(a) any provision of an Act of the Scottish Parliament, or of a Bill for such an Act, and
(b) any provision of subordinate legislation made, confirmed or approved, or purporting to be made, confirmed or approved, by a member of the Scottish Executive,
which could be read in such a way as to be outside competence.

(2) Such a provision is to be read as narrowly as is required for it to be within comp etence, if such a reading is possible, and is to have effect accordingly.

[...]

102 POWERS OF COURTS OR TRIBUNALS TO VARY RETROSPECTIVE DECISIONS

(1) This section applies where any court or tribunal decides that—
(a) an Act of the Scottish Parliament or any provision of such an Act is not within the legislative competence of the Parliament, or
(b) a member of the Scottish Government does not have the power to make, confirm or approve a provision of subordinate legislation that he has purported to make, confirm or approve.

(2) The court or tribunal may make an order—
(a) removing or limiting any retrospective effect of the decision, or
(b) suspending the effect of the decision for any period and on any conditions to allow the defect to be corrected.

(3) In deciding whether to make an order under this section, the court or tribunal shall (among other things) have regard to the extent to which persons who are not parties to the proceedings would otherwise be adversely affected.

(4)   Where a court or tribunal is considering whether to make an order under this section, it shall order intimation of that fact to be given to—

(a) the Lord Advocate, and

(b) the appropriate law officer, where the decision mentioned in subsection (1) relates to a devolution issue (within the meaning of Schedule 6),

unless the person to whom the intimation would be given is a party to the proceedings.

(5)   A person to whom intimation is given under subsection (4) may take part as a party in the proceedings so far as they relate to the making of the order.

[. . .]

[. . .]

SCHEDULE 4   ENACTMENTS ETC. PROTECTED FROM MODIFICATION

Part I   THE PROTECTED PROVISIONS

Particular enactments

1.   (1) An Act of the Scottish Parliament cannot modify, or confer power by subordinate legislation to modify, any of the following provisions.

(2) The provisions are—

(a) Articles 4 and 6 of the Union with Scotland Act 1706 and of the Union with England Act 1707 so far as they relate to freedom of trade,

(b) the Private Legislation Procedure (Scotland) Act 1936,

(c) the following provisions of the European Communities Act 1972—

Section 1 and Schedule 1,

Section 2, other than subsection (2), the words following "such Community obligation" in subsection (3) and the words "subject to Schedule 2 to this Act" in subsection (4),

Section 3(1) and (2),

Section 11(2),

(d) paragraphs 5(3)(b) and 15(4)(b) of Schedule 32 to the Local Government, Planning and Land Act 1980 (designation of enterprise zones),

[. . .]

(f) the Human Rights Act 1998.

The law on reserved matters

2.   (1) An Act of the Scottish Parliament cannot modify, or confer power by subordinate legislation to modify, the law on reserved matters.

(2) In this paragraph, "the law on reserved matters" means—

(a) any enactment the subject-matter of which is a reserved matter and which is comprised in an Act of Parliament or subordinate legislation under an Act of Parliament, and

(b) any rule of law which is not contained in an enactment and the subject-matter of which is a reserved matter,

and in this sub-paragraph "Act of Parliament" does not include this Act.

[. . .]

3.   (1) Paragraph 2 does not apply to modifications which—

(a) are incidental to, or consequential on, provision made (whether by virtue of the Act in question or another enactment) which does not relate to reserved matters, and

(b) do not have a greater effect on reserved matters than is necessary to give effect to the purpose of the provision.

(2) In determining for the purposes of sub-paragraph (1)(b) what is necessary to give effect to the purpose of a provision, any power to make laws other than the power of the Parliament is to be disregarded.

[. . .]

SCHEDULE 5 RESERVED MATTERS

Part I GENERAL RESERVATIONS

The Constitution
1. The following aspects of the constitution are reserved matters, that is—
    (a) the Crown, including succession to the Crown and a regency,
    (b) the Union of the Kingdoms of Scotland and England,
    (c) the Parliament of the United Kingdom,
    (d) the continued existence of the High Court of Justiciary as a criminal court of first instance and of appeal,
    (e) the continued existence of the Court of Session as a civil court of first instance and of appeal.
    [. . .]

Political parties
6. The registration and funding of political parties is a reserved matter [but this paragraph does not reserve making payments to any political party for the purpose of assisting members of the Parliament who are connected with the party to perform their Parliamentary duties.

Foreign affairs etc.
7. (1) International relations, including relations with territories outside the United Kingdom, the European Communities (and their institutions) and other international organisations, regulation of international trade, and international development assistance and co-operation are reserved matters.

    (2) Sub-paragraph (1) does not reserve—
        (a) observing and implementing international obligations, obligations under the Human Rights Convention and obligations under Community law,
        (b) assisting Ministers of the Crown in relation to any matter to which that sub-paragraph applies.

Public service
8. (1) The Civil Service of the State is a reserved matter.

    (2) Sub-paragraph (1) does not reserve the subject-matter of—
        (a) Part I of the Sheriff Courts and Legal Officers (Scotland) Act 1927 (appointment of sheriff clerks and procurators fiscal etc.),
        (b) Part III of the Administration of Justice (Scotland) Act 1933 (officers of the High Court of Justiciary and of the Court of Session).

Defence
9. (1) The following are reserved matters—
        (a) the defence of the realm,

(b) the naval, military or air forces of the Crown, including reserve forces,

(c) visiting forces,

(d) international headquarters and defence organisations,

(e) trading with the enemy and enemy property.

(2) Sub-paragraph (1) does not reserve—

    (a) the exercise of civil defence functions by any person otherwise than as a member of any force or organisation referred to in sub-paragraph (1)(b) to (d) or any other force or organisation reserved by virtue of sub-paragraph (1)(a),

    (b) the conferral of enforcement powers in relation to sea fishing.

Treason

10. Treason (including constructive treason), treason felony and misprision of treason are reserved matters.

Part II SPECIFIC RESERVATIONS

Preliminary

1. The matters to which any of the Sections in this Part apply are reserved matters for the purposes of this Act.

2. A Section applies to any matter described or referred to in it when read with any illustrations, exceptions or interpretation provisions in that Section.

3. Any illustrations, exceptions or interpretation provisions in a Section relate only to that Section (so that an entry under the heading "exceptions" does not affect any other Section).

Reservations

Head A – Financial and Economic Matters

[. . .]

Head B – Home Affairs

[. . .]

Head C – Trade and Industry

[. . .]

Head D – Energy

[. . .]

Head E – Transport

[. . .]

Head F – Social Security

[. . .]

Head G – Regulation of the Professions

[. . .]

Head H – Employment

[. . .]

Head J – Health and Medicines

[. . .]

Head K – Media and Culture

[. . .]

Head L – Miscellaneous

[. . .]

As amended by the Scottish Parliament (Elections etc) Order 2010

As amended by the Scotland Act 2012, ss 23, 25, which provisions came into force 1st July 2012

HOUSE OF LORDS ACT 1999
(c. 34)

An Act to restrict membership of the House of Lords by virtue of a hereditary peerage; to make related provision about disqualifications for voting at elections to, and for membership of, the House of Commons; and for connected purposes.

[. . .]

1 EXCLUSION OF HEREDITARY PEERS

No-one shall be a member of the House of Lords by virtue of a hereditary peerage.

2 EXCEPTION FROM SECTION 1

(1)   Section 1 shall not apply in relation to anyone excepted from it by or in accordance with Standing Orders of the House.

(2)   At any one time 90 people shall be excepted from section 1; but anyone excepted as holder of the office of Earl Marshal, or as performing the office of Lord Great Chamberlain, shall not count towards that limit.

(3)   Once excepted from section 1, a person shall continue to be so throughout his life (until an Act of Parliament provides to the contrary).

(4)   Standing Orders shall make provision for filling vacancies among the people excepted from section 1; and in any case where—
(a)   the vacancy arises on a death occurring after the end of the first Session of the next Parliament after that in which this Act is passed, and
(b)   the deceased person was excepted in consequence of an election,
that provision shall require the holding of a by-election.

(5)   A person may be excepted from section 1 by or in accordance with Standing Orders made in anticipation of the enactment or commencement of this section.

[. . .]

3 REMOVAL OF DISQUALIFICATIONS IN RELATION TO THE HOUSE OF COMMONS

(1)   The holder of a hereditary peerage shall not be disqualified by virtue of that peerage for—
    (a)   voting at elections to the House of Commons, or
    (b)   being, or being elected as, a member of that House.

(2)   Subsection (1) shall not apply in relation to anyone excepted from section 1 by virtue of section 2.

[. . .]

6 INTERPRETATION AND SHORT TITLE

(1)   In this Act "hereditary peerage" includes the principality of Wales and the earldom of Chester.

    [. . .]

FREEDOM OF INFORMATION ACT 2000
(c. 36)

An Act to make provision for the disclosure of information held by public authorities or by persons providing services for them and to amend the Data Protection Act 1998 and the Public Records Act 1958; and for connected purposes.

[. . .]

Part I ACCESS TO INFORMATION HELD BY PUBLIC AUTHORITIES

Right to information

1 GENERAL RIGHT OF ACCESS TO INFORMATION HELD BY PUBLIC AUTHORITIES

(1)   Any person making a request for information to a public authority is entitled—
    (a)   to be informed in writing by the public authority whether it holds information of the description specified in the request, and
    (b)   if that is the case, to have that information communicated to him.

(2)   Subsection (1) has effect subject to the following provisions of this section and to the provisions of sections 2, 9, 12 and 14.

(3)   Where a public authority—
    (a)   reasonably requires further information in order to identify and locate the information requested, and
    (b)   has informed the applicant of that requirement,
the authority is not obliged to comply with subsection (1) unless it is supplied with that further information.

(4)   The information—
    (a)   in respect of which the applicant is to be informed under subsection (1)(a), or
    (b)   which is to be communicated under subsection (1)(b),
is the information in question held at the time when the request is received, except that account may be taken of any amendment or deletion made between that time and the time

when the information is to be communicated under subsection (1) (b), being an amendment or deletion that would have been made regardless of the receipt of the request.

(5)   A public authority is to be taken to have complied with subsection (1)(a) in relation to any information if it has communicated the information to the applicant in accordance with subsection (1)(b).

(6)   In this Act, the duty of a public authority to comply with subsection (1)(a) is referred to as "the duty to confirm or deny".

2 EFFECT OF THE EXEMPTIONS IN PART II

(1)   Where any provision of Part II states that the duty to confirm or deny does not arise in relation to any information, the effect of the provision is that where either—
(a) the provision confers absolute exemption, or
(b) in all the circumstances of the case, the public interest in maintaining the exclusion of the duty to confirm or deny outweighs the public interest in disclosing whether the public authority holds the information,
section 1(1)(a) does not apply.

(2)   In respect of any information which is exempt information by virtue of any provision of Part II, section 1(1)(b) does not apply if or to the extent that—
(a) the information is exempt information by virtue of a provision conferring absolute exemption, or
(b) in all the circumstances of the case, the public interest in maintaining the exemption outweighs the public interest in disclosing the information.

(3)   For the purposes of this section, the following provisions of Part II (and no others) are to be regarded as conferring absolute exemption—
(a) section 21,
(b) section 23,
(c) section 32,
(d) section 34,
(e) section 36 so far as relating to information held by the House of Commons or the House of Lords,
(ea) in section 37, paragraphs (a) to (ab) of subsection (1), and subsection (2) so far as relating to those paragraphs,
(f) in section 40—
(i)   subsection (1), and
(ii) subsection (2) so far as relating to cases where the first condition referred to in that subsection is satisfied by virtue of subsection (3)(a)(i) or (b) of that section,
(g) section 41, and
(h) section 44.
[. . .]
[. . .]

8 REQUEST FOR INFORMATION

(1)   In this Act any reference to a "request for information" is a reference to such a request which—
(a) is in writing,
(b) states the name of the applicant and an address for correspondence, and
(c) describes the information requested.

(2)   For the purposes of subsection (1)(a), a request is to be treated as made in writing where the text of the request—
(a) is transmitted by electronic means,
(b) is received in legible form, and
(c) is capable of being used for subsequent reference.

[. . .]

10 TIME FOR COMPLIANCE WITH REQUEST

(1)   Subject to subsections (2) and (3), a public authority must comply with section 1(1) promptly and in any event not later than the twentieth working day following the date of receipt.

[. . .]

11 MEANS BY WHICH COMMUNICATION TO BE MADE

(1)   Where, on making his request for information, the applicant expresses a preference for communication by any one or more of the following means, namely—
(a) the provision to the applicant of a copy of the information in permanent form or in another form acceptable to the applicant,
(b) the provision to the applicant of a reasonable opportunity to inspect a record containing the information, and
(c) the provision to the applicant of a digest or summary of the information in permanent form or in another form acceptable to the applicant,
the public authority shall so far as reasonably practicable give effect to that preference.

[. . .]

12 EXEMPTION WHERE COST OF COMPLIANCE EXCEEDS APPROPRIATE LIMIT

(1)   Section 1(1) does not oblige a public authority to comply with a request for information if the authority estimates that the cost of complying with the request would exceed the appropriate limit.

(2)   Subsection (1) does not exempt the public authority from its obligation to comply with paragraph (a) of section 1(1) unless the estimated cost of complying with that paragraph alone would exceed the appropriate limit.

(3)   In subsections (1) and (2) "the appropriate limit" means such amount as may be prescribed, and different amounts may be prescribed in relation to different cases.

[. . .]

[. . .]

Refusal of request

17 REFUSAL OF REQUEST

(1)   A public authority which, in relation to any request for information, is to any extent relying on a claim that any provision of Part II relating to the duty to confirm or deny is relevant to the request or on a claim that information is exempt information must, within the time for complying with section 1(1), give the applicant a notice which—

(a) states that fact,

(b) specifies the exemption in question, and

(c) states (if that would not otherwise be apparent) why the exemption applies.

[. . .]

(3) A public authority which, in relation to any request for information, is to any extent relying on a claim that subsection (1)(b) or (2)(b) of section 2 applies must, either in the notice under subsection (1) or in a separate notice given within such time as is reasonable in the circumstances, state the reasons for claiming—

(a) that, in all the circumstances of the case, the public interest in maintaining the exclusion of the duty to confirm or deny outweighs the public interest in disclosing whether the authority holds the information, or

(b) that, in all the circumstances of the case, the public interest in maintaining the exemption outweighs the public interest in disclosing the information.

(4) A public authority is not obliged to make a statement under subsection (1)(c) or (3) if, or to the extent that, the statement would involve the disclosure of information which would itself be exempt information.

(5) A public authority which, in relation to any request for information, is relying on a claim that section 12 or 14 applies must, within the time for complying with section 1(1), give the applicant a notice stating that fact.

[. . .]

The Information Commissioner [. . .]

18 THE INFORMATION COMMISSIONER [. . .]

(1) The Data Protection Commissioner shall be known instead as the Information Commissioner.

[. . .]

(3) In this Act—

(a) the Information Commissioner is referred to as "the Commissioner", [. . .]

[. . .]

[. . .]

Part II EXEMPT INFORMATION

21 INFORMATION ACCESSIBLE TO APPLICANT BY OTHER MEANS

(1) Information which is reasonably accessible to the applicant otherwise than under section 1 is exempt information.

(2) For the purposes of subsection (1)—

(a) information may be reasonably accessible to the applicant even though it is accessible only on payment, and

(b) information is to be taken to be reasonably accessible to the applicant if it is information which the public authority or any other person is obliged by or under any enactment to communicate (otherwise than by making the information available for inspection) to members of the public on request, whether free of charge or on payment.

(3)   For the purposes of subsection (1), information which is held by a public authority and does not fall within subsection (2)(b) is not to be regarded as reasonably accessible to the applicant merely because the information is available from the public authority itself on request, unless the information is made available in accordance with the authority's publication scheme and any payment required is specified in, or determined in accordance with, the scheme.

[. . .]

23 INFORMATION SUPPLIED BY, OR RELATING TO, BODIES DEALING WITH SECURITY MATTERS

(1)   Information held by a public authority is exempt information if it was directly or indirectly supplied to the public authority by, or relates to, any of the bodies specified in subsection (3).

(2)   A certificate signed by a Minister of the Crown certifying that the information to which it applies was directly or indirectly supplied by, or relates to, any of the bodies specified in subsection (3) shall, subject to section 60, be conclusive evidence of that fact.

(3)   The bodies referred to in subsections (1) and (2) are—
(a) the Security Service,
(b) the Secret Intelligence Service,
(c) the Government Communications Headquarters,
(d) the special forces,
[. . .]

24 NATIONAL SECURITY

(1)   Information which does not fall within section 23(1) is exempt information if exemption from section 1(1)(b) is required for the purpose of safeguarding national security.

(2)   The duty to confirm or deny does not arise if, or to the extent that, exemption from section 1(1)(a) is required for the purpose of safeguarding national security.

(3)   A certificate signed by a Minister of the Crown certifying that exemption from section 1(1)(b), or from section 1(1)(a) and (b), is, or at any time was, required for the purpose of safeguarding national security shall, subject to section 60, be conclusive evidence of that fact.

(4)   A certificate under subsection (3) may identify the information to which it applies by means of a general description and may be expressed to have prospective effect.

[. . .]

26 DEFENCE

(1)   Information is exempt information if its disclosure under this Act would, or would be likely to, prejudice—
(a) the defence of the British Islands or of any colony, or
(b) the capability, effectiveness or security of any relevant forces.

(2)   In subsection (1)(b) "relevant forces" means—
(a) the armed forces of the Crown, and
(b) any forces co-operating with those forces,
or any part of any of those forces.

(3) The duty to confirm or deny does not arise if, or to the extent that, compliance with section 1(1)(a) would, or would be likely to, prejudice any of the matters mentioned in subsection (1).

27 INTERNATIONAL RELATIONS

(1) Information is exempt information if its disclosure under this Act would, or would be likely to, prejudice—
(a) relations between the United Kingdom and any other State,
(b) relations between the United Kingdom and any international organisation or international court,
(c) the interests of the United Kingdom abroad, or
(d) the promotion or protection by the United Kingdom of its interests abroad.

(2) Information is also exempt information if it is confidential information obtained from a State other than the United Kingdom or from an international organisation or international court.

(3) For the purposes of this section, any information obtained from a State, organisation or court is confidential at any time while the terms on which it was obtained require it to be held in confidence or while the circumstances in which it was obtained make it reasonable for the State, organisation or court to expect that it will be so held.

(4) The duty to confirm or deny does not arise if, or to the extent that, compliance with section 1(1)(a)—
(a) would, or would be likely to, prejudice any of the matters mentioned in subsection (1), or
(b) would involve the disclosure of any information (whether or not already recorded) which is confidential information obtained from a State other than the United Kingdom or from an international organisation or international court.
[. . .]

28 RELATIONS WITHIN THE UNITED KINGDOM

(1) Information is exempt information if its disclosure under this Act would, or would be likely to, prejudice relations between any administration in the United Kingdom and any other such administration.

(2) In subsection (1) "administration in the United Kingdom" means—
(a) the government of the United Kingdom,
(b) the Scottish Administration,
(c) the Executive Committee of the Northern Ireland Assembly, or
[(d) the Welsh Assembly Government.]

(3) The duty to confirm or deny does not arise if, or to the extent that, compliance with section 1(1)(a) would, or would be likely to, prejudice any of the matters mentioned in subsection (1).

29 THE ECONOMY

(1) Information is exempt information if its disclosure under this Act would, or would be likely to, prejudice—
(a) the economic interests of the United Kingdom or of any part of the United Kingdom, or
(b) the financial interests of any administration in the United Kingdom, as defined by section 28(2).

(2)   The duty to confirm or deny does not arise if, or to the extent that, compliance with section 1(1)(a) would, or would be likely to, prejudice any of the matters mentioned in subsection (1).

30 INVESTIGATIONS AND PROCEEDINGS CONDUCTED BY PUBLIC AUTHORITIES

(1)   Information held by a public authority is exempt information if it has at any time been held by the authority for the purposes of—

(a)   any investigation which the public authority has a duty to conduct with a view to it being ascertained—
(i)   whether a person should be charged with an offence, or
(ii)   whether a person charged with an offence is guilty of it,

(b)   any investigation which is conducted by the authority and in the circumstances may lead to a decision by the authority to institute criminal proceedings which the authority has power to conduct, or

(c)   any criminal proceedings which the authority has power to conduct.

(2)   Information held by a public authority is exempt information if—

(a)   it was obtained or recorded by the authority for the purposes of its functions relating to—
(i)   investigations falling within subsection (1)(a) or (b),
(ii)   criminal proceedings which the authority has power to conduct,
(iii) investigations (other than investigations falling within subsection (1)(a) or (b)) which are conducted by the authority for any of the purposes specified in section 31(2) and either by virtue of Her Majesty's prerogative or by virtue of powers conferred by or under any enactment, or
(iv)   civil proceedings which are brought by or on behalf of the authority and arise out of such investigations, and

(b)   it relates to the obtaining of information from confidential sources.
[. . .]

31 LAW ENFORCEMENT

(1)   Information which is not exempt information by virtue of section 30 is exempt information if its disclosure under this Act would, or would be likely to, prejudice—

(a)   the prevention or detection of crime,
(b)   the apprehension or prosecution of offenders,
(c)   the administration of justice,
(d)   the assessment or collection of any tax or duty or of any imposition of a similar nature,
(e)   the operation of the immigration controls,
(f)   the maintenance of security and good order in prisons or in other institutions where persons are lawfully detained,
(g)   the exercise by any public authority of its functions for any of the purposes specified in subsection (2),
(h)   any civil proceedings which are brought by or on behalf of a public authority and arise out of an investigation conducted, for any of the purposes specified in subsection (2), by or on behalf of the authority by virtue of Her Majesty's prerogative or by virtue of powers conferred by or under an enactment, or
(i)   any inquiry held under the Fatal Accidents and Sudden Deaths Inquiries (Scotland) Act 1976 to the extent that the inquiry arises out of an investigation conducted, for

any of the purposes specified in subsection (2), by or on behalf of the authority by virtue of Her Majesty's prerogative or by virtue of powers conferred by or under an enactment.

(2)   The purposes referred to in subsection (1)(g) to (i) are—
(a)   the purpose of ascertaining whether any person has failed to comply with the law,
(b)   the purpose of ascertaining whether any person is responsible for any conduct which is improper,
(c)   the purpose of ascertaining whether circumstances which would justify regulatory action in pursuance of any enactment exist or may arise,
(d)   the purpose of ascertaining a person's fitness or competence in relation to the management of bodies corporate or in relation to any profession or other activity which he is, or seeks to become, authorised to carry on,
(e)   the purpose of ascertaining the cause of an accident,
(f)   the purpose of protecting charities against misconduct or mismanagement (whether by trustees or other persons) in their administration,
(g)   the purpose of protecting the property of charities from loss or misapplication,
(h)   the purpose of recovering the property of charities,
(i)   the purpose of securing the health, safety and welfare of persons at work, and
(j)   the purpose of protecting persons other than persons at work against risk to health or safety arising out of or in connection with the actions of persons at work.

(3)   The duty to confirm or deny does not arise if, or to the extent that, compliance with section 1(1)(a) would, or would be likely to, prejudice any of the matters mentioned in subsection (1).

[. . .]

34 PARLIAMENTARY PRIVILEGE

(1)   Information is exempt information if exemption from section 1(1)(b) is required for the purpose of avoiding an infringement of the privileges of either House of Parliament.

(2)   The duty to confirm or deny does not apply if, or to the extent that, exemption from section 1(1)(a) is required for the purpose of avoiding an infringement of the privileges of either House of Parliament.

(3)   A certificate signed by the appropriate authority certifying that exemption from section 1(1)(b), or from section 1(1)(a) and (b), is, or at any time was, required for the purpose of avoiding an infringement of the privileges of either House of Parliament shall be conclusive evidence of that fact.

(4)   In subsection (3) "the appropriate authority" means—
(a)   in relation to the House of Commons, the Speaker of that House, and
(b)   in relation to the House of Lords, the Clerk of the Parliaments.

35 FORMULATION OF GOVERNMENT POLICY, ETC.

(1)   Information held by a government department or by the [Welsh Assembly Government] is exempt information if it relates to—
(a)   the formulation or development of government policy,
(b)   Ministerial communications,
(c)   the provision of advice by any of the Law Officers or any request for the provision of such advice, or
(d)   the operation of any Ministerial private office.

(2)   Once a decision as to government policy has been taken, any statistical information used to provide an informed background to the taking of the decision is not to be regarded—
(a)   for the purposes of subsection (1)(a), as relating to the formulation or development of government policy, or
(b)   for the purposes of subsection (1)(b), as relating to Ministerial communications.

(3)   The duty to confirm or deny does not arise in relation to information which is (or if it were held by the public authority would be) exempt information by virtue of subsection (1).

(4)   In making any determination required by section 2(1)(b) or (2)(b) in relation to information which is exempt information by virtue of subsection (1)(a), regard shall be had to the particular public interest in the disclosure of factual information which has been used, or is intended to be used, to provide an informed background to decision-taking.

[. . .]

36   PREJUDICE TO EFFECTIVE CONDUCT OF PUBLIC AFFAIRS

(1)   This section applies to—
(a)   information which is held by a government department or by [the Welsh Assembly Government] and is not exempt information by virtue of section 35, and
(b)   information which is held by any other public authority.

(2)   Information to which this section applies is exempt information if, in the reasonable opinion of a qualified person, disclosure of the information under this Act—
(a)   would, or would be likely to, prejudice—
(i)   the maintenance of the convention of the collective responsibility of Ministers of the Crown, or
(ii)   the work of the Executive Committee of the Northern Ireland Assembly, or
[(iii) the work of the Cabinet of the Welsh Assembly Government]
(b)   would, or would be likely to, inhibit—
(i)   the free and frank provision of advice, or
(ii)   the free and frank exchange of views for the purposes of deliberation, or
(c)   would otherwise prejudice, or would be likely otherwise to prejudice, the effective conduct of public affairs.

(3)   The duty to confirm or deny does not arise in relation to information to which this section applies (or would apply if held by the public authority) if, or to the extent that, in the reasonable opinion of a qualified person, compliance with section 1(1)(a) would, or would be likely to, have any of the effects mentioned in subsection (2).

(4)   In relation to statistical information, subsections (2) and (3) shall have effect with the omission of the words "in the reasonable opinion of a qualified person".

[. . .]

[. . .]

42   LEGAL PROFESSIONAL PRIVILEGE

(1)   Information in respect of which a claim to legal professional privilege or, in Scotland, to confidentiality of communications could be maintained in legal proceedings is exempt information.

(2)   The duty to confirm or deny does not arise if, or to the extent that, compliance with section 1(1)(a) would involve the disclosure of any information (whether or not already recorded) in respect of which such a claim could be maintained in legal proceedings.

[. . .]

Part IV ENFORCEMENT

50 APPLICATION FOR DECISION BY COMMISSIONER

(1)   Any person (in this section referred to as "the complainant") may apply to the Commissioner for a decision whether, in any specified respect, a request for information made by the complainant to a public authority has been dealt with in accordance with the requirements of Part I.

(2)   On receiving an application under this section, the Commissioner shall make a decision unless it appears to him—
   (a) that the complainant has not exhausted any complaints procedure which is provided by the public authority in conformity with the code of practice under section 45,
   (b) that there has been undue delay in making the application,
   (c) that the application is frivolous or vexatious, or
   (d) that the application has been withdrawn or abandoned.

(3)   Where the Commissioner has received an application under this section, he shall either—
   (a) notify the complainant that he has not made any decision under this section as a result of the application and of his grounds for not doing so, or
   (b) serve notice of his decision (in this Act referred to as a "decision notice") on the complainant and the public authority.

(4)   Where the Commissioner decides that a public authority—
   (a) has failed to communicate information, or to provide confirmation or denial, in a case where it is required to do so by section 1(1), or
   (b) has failed to comply with any of the requirements of sections 11 and 17,
   the decision notice must specify the steps which must be taken by the authority for complying with that requirement and the period within which they must be taken.

(5)   A decision notice must contain particulars of the right of appeal conferred by section 57.

[. . .]

As amended by the Constitutional Reform and Governance Act 2010 Schedule 7 Paragraph 2

LOCAL GOVERNMENT ACT 2000
(c. 22)

An Act to make provision with respect to the functions and procedures of local authorities and provision with respect to local authority elections; to make provision with respect to grants and housing benefit in respect of certain welfare services; to amend section 29 of the Children Act 1989; and for connected purposes.

[. . .]

Part I **PROMOTION OF ECONOMIC, SOCIAL OR ENVIRONMENTAL WELL-BEING ETC.**

Interpretation

1 MEANING OF "LOCAL AUTHORITY" IN PART I

In this Part "local authority" means—
(a)   in relation to England—
    (i)   a county council,
    (ii)   a district council,
    (iii) a London borough council,
    (iv) the Common Council of the City of London in its capacity as a local authority,

[. . .]

Promotion of well-being

2 PROMOTION OF WELL-BEING

(1)   Every local authority in Wales are to have power to do anything which they consider is likely to achieve any one or more of the following objects—
    (a)   the promotion or improvement of the economic well-being of their area,
    (b)   the promotion or improvement of the social well-being of their area, and
    (c)   the promotion or improvement of the environmental well-being of their area.

    [. . .]

Part II **ARRANGEMENTS WITH RESPECT TO EXECUTIVES ETC.**

Executive arrangements

10 EXECUTIVE ARRANGEMENTS

(1)   In this Part "executive arrangements" means arrangements by a local authority in Wales —
    (a)   for and in connection with the creation and operation of an executive of the authority in Wales, and
    (b)   under which certain functions of the authority are the responsibility of the executive.
[. . .]

Local authority executives

11 LOCAL AUTHORITY EXECUTIVES

(1)   The executive of a local authority must take a form specified in subsections (2) to (5) that is applicable to the authority.

(2)   The executive may consist of—]
    (a)   an elected mayor of the authority, and
    (b)   two or more councillors of the authority appointed to the executive by the elected mayor.
Such an executive is referred to in this Part as a mayor and cabinet executive.

(3)   In the case of any local authority in Wales, the executive may consist of—
    (a)   a councillor of the authority (referred to in this Part as the executive leader) elected as leader of the executive by the authority, and

(b) two or more councillors of the authority appointed to the executive by one of the following—
(i)   the executive leader, or
(ii) the authority.
Such an executive is referred to in this Part as a [leader and cabinet executive (Wales)].

(4) In the case of any local authority in Wales, the executive may consist of—]
(a) an elected mayor of the authority, and
(b) an officer of the authority (referred to in this Part as the council manager) appointed to the executive by the authority.
Such an executive is referred to in this Part as a mayor and council manager executive.

(5) The executive] may take any such form as may be prescribed in regulations made by the Welsh Ministers.

[. . .]

(7) A local authority executive may not include the chairman or vice-chairman of the authority.

(8) The number of members of a mayor and cabinet executive or a leader and cabinet (Wales) executive may not exceed 10.

(9) The Welsh Ministers may by regulations specify a different maximum number of members of an executive to which subsection (8) applies, but the power under this subsection may not be exercised so as to provide for a maximum number which exceeds 10.

[. . .]

Executive functions

13 FUNCTIONS WHICH ARE THE RESPONSIBILITY OF AN EXECUTIVE

(1) This section has effect for the purposes of determining the functions of a local authority which are the responsibility of an executive of the authority under executive arrangements.

(2) Subject to any provision made by this Act or by any enactment which is passed or made after the day on which this Act is passed, any function of a local authority which is not specified in regulations under subsection (3) is to be the responsibility of an executive of the authority under executive arrangements.

(3) The Welsh Ministers may by regulations make provision for any function of a local authority specified in the regulations—
(a) to be a function which is not to be the responsibility of an executive of the authority under executive arrangements,
(b) to be a function which may be the responsibility of such an executive under such arrangements, or
(c) to be a function which—
(i)   to the extent provided by the regulations is to be the responsibility of such an executive under such arrangements, and
(ii) to the extent provided by the regulations is not to be the responsibility of such an executive under such arrangements.

(4) Executive arrangements must make provision for any function of a local authority falling within subsection (3)(b)—

(a) to be a function which is to be the responsibility of an executive of the authority,

(b) to be a function which is not to be the responsibility of such an executive, or

(c) to be a function which—

(i) to the extent provided by the arrangements is to be the responsibility of such an executive, and

(ii) to the extent provided by the arrangements is not to be the responsibility of such an executive.

[. . .]

Provisions with respect to executive arrangements

14 DISCHARGE OF FUNCTIONS: MAYOR AND CABINET EXECUTIVE

[(1) Subject to any provision made under section 18, 19 or 20, any functions which, under executive arrangements, are the responsibility of a mayor and cabinet executive are to be discharged in accordance with this section

(2) The elected mayor—

(a) may discharge any of those functions, or

(b) may arrange for the discharge of any of those functions—

(i) by the executive,

(ii) by another member of the executive,

(iii) by a committee of the executive, or

(iv) by an officer of the authority.

[. . .]

22 ACCESS TO INFORMATION ETC.

(1) Meetings of a local authority executive, or a committee of such an executive, are to be open to the public or held in private.

(2) Subject to regulations under subsection (9), it is for a local authority executive to decide which of its meetings, and which of the meetings of any committee of the executive, are to be open to the public and which of those meetings are to be held in private.

(3) A written record must be kept of prescribed decisions made at meetings of local authorities executives, or committees of such executives, which are held in private.

(4) A written record must be kept of prescribed decisions made by individual members of local authority executives.

(5) Written records under subsection (3) or (4) must include reasons for the decisions to which they relate.

(6) Written records under subsections (3) and (4), together with such reports, background papers or other documents as may be prescribed, must be made available to members of the public in accordance with regulations made by the Welsh Ministers.

(7) Regulations under subsection (6) may make provision for or in connection with preventing the whole or part of any record or document containing prescribed information from being made available to members of the public.

[. . .]

Part 1A **ARRANGEMENTS WITH RESPECT TO LOCAL AUTHORITY GOVERNANCE IN ENGLAND**

Chapter 1 **PERMITTED FORMS OF GOVERNANCE**

9B PERMITTED FORMS OF GOVERNANCE FOR LOCAL AUTHORITIES IN ENGLAND

(1)   A local authority must operate—
 (a)   executive arrangements,
 (b)   a committee system, or
 (c)   prescribed arrangements.

(2)   Executive arrangements must conform with any provisions made by or under this Part which relate to such arrangements (see, in particular, Chapter 2).

(3)   A committee system must conform with any provisions made by or under this Part which relate to such a system (see, in particular, Chapter 3).

(4)   In this Part—
"a committee system" means the arrangements made by a local authority, which does not operate executive arrangements or prescribed arrangements, for or in connection with the discharge of its functions in accordance with—
 (a)   Part 6 of the Local Government Act 1972, and
 (b)   this Part;
"executive arrangements" means arrangements by a local authority—
 (a)   for and in connection with the creation and operation of an executive of the authority, and
 (b)   under which certain functions of the authority are the responsibility of the executive;
"prescribed arrangements" means such arrangements as may be prescribed in regulations made by the Secretary of State under section 9BA.

9BA POWER OF SECRETARY OF STATE TO PRESCRIBE ADDITIONAL PERMITTED GOVERNANCE ARRANGEMENTS

(1)   The Secretary of State may by regulations make provision prescribing arrangements that local authorities may operate for and in connection with the discharge of their functions.

[. . .]

Chapter 2 **EXECUTIVE ARRANGEMENTS**

Local authority executives

9C LOCAL AUTHORITY EXECUTIVES

(1)   The executive of a local authority must take a form specified in subsection (2) or (3).

(2)   The executive may consist of—
 (a)   an elected mayor of the authority, and
 (b)   two or more councillors of the authority appointed to the executive by the elected mayor.
Such an executive is referred to in this Part as a mayor and cabinet executive.

(3)   The executive may consist of—
    (a)   a councillor of the authority (referred to in this Part as the executive leader) elected as leader of the executive by the authority, and
    (b)   two or more councillors of the authority appointed to the executive by the executive leader.
    Such an executive is referred to in this Part as a leader and cabinet executive (England).

[. . .]

Executive functions

9D   FUNCTIONS WHICH ARE THE RESPONSIBILITY OF AN EXECUTIVE

(1)   This section has effect for the purposes of determining which of the functions of a local authority that operates executive arrangements are the responsibility of an executive of the authority under those arrangements.

(2)   Subject to any provision made by this Act or by any enactment which is passed or made after the day on which this Act is passed, any function of the local authority which is not specified in regulations under subsection (3) is to be the responsibility of an executive of the authority under executive arrangements.

(3)   The Secretary of State may by regulations make provision for any function of a local authority specified in the regulations—
    (a)   to be a function which is not to be the responsibility of an executive of the authority under executive arrangements,
    (b)   to be a function which may be the responsibility of such an executive under such arrangements, or
    (c)   to be a function which—
        (i)   to the extent provided by the regulations, is to be the responsibility of such an executive under such arrangements, and
        (ii)   to the extent provided by the regulations, is not to be the responsibility of such an executive under such arrangements.

(4)   Executive arrangements must make provision for any function of a local authority falling within subsection (3)(b)—
    (a)   to be a function which is to be the responsibility of an executive of the authority,
    (b)   to be a function which is not to be the responsibility of such an executive, or
    (c)   to be a function which—
        (i)   to the extent provided by the arrangements, is to be the responsibility of such an executive, and
        (ii)   to the extent provided by the arrangements, is not to be the responsibility of such executive.

(5)   The power under subsection (3)(c) or (4)(c) includes power in relation to any function of a local authority that operates executive arrangements—
    (a)   to designate any action in connection with the discharge of that function which is to be the responsibility of an executive of the local authority, and
    (b)   to designate any action in connection with the discharge of that function which is not to be the responsibility of such an executive.

(6)   The Secretary of State may by regulations specify cases or circumstances in which any function of a local authority which, by virtue of the preceding provisions of this section, would otherwise be the responsibility of an executive of the authority to any extent is not to be the responsibility of such an executive to that or any particular extent.

(7) A function of a local authority may, by virtue of this section, be the responsibility of an executive of the authority to any extent notwithstanding that section 101 of the Local Government Act 1972, or any provision of that section, does not apply to that function.

(8) Any reference in this section to a function specified in regulations includes a reference to a function of a description specified in regulations.

(9) In this section—
"action" in relation to any function includes any action (of whatever nature and whether or not separately identified by any enactment) involving—
(a) the taking of any step in the course of, or otherwise for the purposes of or in connection with, the discharge of the function,
(b) the doing of anything incidental or conducive to the discharge of the function, or
(c) the doing of anything expedient in connection with the discharge of the function or any action falling within paragraph (a) or (b);
"function" means a function of any nature, whether conferred or otherwise arising before, on or after the passing of this Act.
[. . .]

Discharge of functions

9E DISCHARGE OF FUNCTIONS: GENERAL

(1) Subject to any provision made under section 9EA or 9EB, any functions which, under executive arrangements, are the responsibility of—
(a) a mayor and cabinet executive, or
(b) a leader and cabinet executive (England),
are to be discharged in accordance with this section.

(2) The senior executive member—
(a) may discharge any of those functions, or
(b) may arrange for the discharge of any of those functions—
(i) by the executive,
(ii) by another member of the executive,
(iii) by a committee of the executive,
(iv) by an area committee, or
(v) by an officer of the authority.

(3) Where by virtue of this section any functions may be discharged by a local authority executive, then, unless the senior executive member otherwise directs, the executive may arrange for the discharge of any of those functions—
(a) by a committee of the executive,
(b) by an area committee, or
(c) by an officer of the authority.

(4) Where by virtue of this section any functions may be discharged by a member of a local authority executive, then, unless the senior executive member otherwise directs, the member who may discharge the functions may arrange for the discharge of any of those functions—
(a) by an area committee, or
(b) by an officer of the authority.

(5) Where by virtue of this section any functions may be discharged by a committee of a local authority executive, then, unless the senior executive member otherwise directs, the committee may arrange for the discharge of any of those functions—
(a) by an area committee, or
(b) by an officer of the authority.

(6)   Where by virtue of this section any functions may be discharged by an area committee, then, unless the senior executive member otherwise directs, the committee may arrange for the discharge of any of those functions by an officer of the authority.

(7)   Any arrangements made by virtue of this section by a senior executive member, executive, member or committee for the discharge of any functions by an executive, member, committee or officer are not to prevent the senior executive member, executive, member or committee by whom the arrangements are made from exercising those functions.

(8)   In this section—
"area committee", in relation to a local authority, means a committee or sub-committee of the authority which satisfies the conditions in subsection (9);
"senior executive member" means—
(a)   in the case of a mayor and cabinet executive, the elected mayor;
(b)   in the case of a leader and cabinet executive (England), the executive leader.

(9)   A committee or sub-committee of a local authority satisfies the conditions in this subsection if—
(a)   the committee or sub-committee is established to discharge functions in respect of part of the area of the authority, and
(b)   the members of the committee or sub-committee who are members of the authority are elected for electoral divisions or wards which fall wholly or partly within that part.
[. . .]

Part III CONDUCT OF LOCAL GOVERNMENT MEMBERS AND EMPLOYEES

Chapter I CONDUCT OF MEMBERS

[. . .]

52 DUTY TO COMPLY WITH CODE OF CONDUCT

(1)   A person who is a member or co-opted member of a relevant authority at a time when the authority adopt a code of conduct under section 51 for the first time—
(a)   must, before the end of the period of two months beginning with the date on which the code of conduct is adopted, give to the authority a written undertaking that in performing his functions he will observe the authority's code of conduct for the time being under section 51, and
(b)   if he fails to do so, is to cease to be a member or co-opted member at the end of that period.
[. . .]

Chapter II INVESTIGATIONS, ETC.: ENGLAND

Standards Board for England

57 STANDARDS BOARD FOR ENGLAND

(1)   There is to be a body corporate known as the Standards Board for England.

(2)   The Standards Board for England is to consist of not less than three members appointed by the Secretary of State.

(3)   The Standards Board for England is to have the functions conferred on it by this Part and such other functions as may be conferred on it by order made by the Secretary of State under this subsection.

(4)   In exercising its functions the Standards Board for England must have regard to the need to promote and maintain high standards of conduct by members and co-opted members of relevant authorities in England.

(5)   The Standards Board for England—
    (a)   must appoint employees known as ethical standards officers who are to have the functions conferred on them by this Part,
    [(aa) may issue guidance to ethical standards officers with respect to the exercise by those officers of their functions,]
    (b)   may issue guidance to relevant authorities in England and police authorities in Wales on matters relating to the conduct of members and co-opted members of such authorities,
    (c)   may issue guidance to relevant authorities in England and police authorities in Wales in relation to the qualifications or experience which monitoring officers should possess, and
    (d)   may arrange for any such guidance to be made public.

As amended by the Localism Act 2011, Schedule 1, paragraph 3, Schedule 2, paragraph 1, Schedule 3, paragraphs 9, 10, 11, 13, 14, 28, Schedule 4, paragraph 17, Schedule 25, Part 4

POLITICAL PARTIES, ELECTIONS AND REFERENDUMS ACT 2000
(c. 41)

An Act to establish an Electoral Commission; to make provision about the registration and finances of political parties; to make provision about donations and expenditure for political purposes; to make provision about election and referendum campaigns and the conduct of referendums; to make provision about election petitions and other legal proceedings in connection with elections; to reduce the qualifying periods set out in sections 1 and 3 of the Representation of the People Act 1985; to make pre-consolidation amendments relating to European Parliamentary Elections; and for connected purposes.

[. . .]

Part I **THE ELECTORAL COMMISSION**

Establishment of Electoral Commission and bodies with related functions

1 ESTABLISHMENT OF THE ELECTORAL COMMISSION

(1)   There shall be a body corporate to be known as the Electoral Commission or, in Welsh, Comisiwn Etholiadol (in this Act referred to as "the Commission").

(2)   The Commission shall consist of members to be known as Electoral Commissioners.

(3)   There shall be not less than five, but not more than nine, Electoral Commissioners.

(4)   The Electoral Commissioners shall be appointed by Her Majesty (in accordance with section 3).

(5)   Her Majesty shall (in accordance with section 3 [but subject to section 3A(6)]) appoint one of the Electoral Commissioners to be the chairman of the Commission.

[. . .]

2 SPEAKER'S COMMITTEE

(1)   There shall be a Committee (to be known as "the Speaker's Committee") to perform the functions conferred on the Committee by this Act.

(2)   The Speaker's Committee shall consist of the Speaker of the House of Commons, who shall be the chairman of the Committee, and the following other members, namely—
   (a) the Member of the House of Commons who is for the time being the Chairman of the Home Affairs Select Committee of the House of Commons;
   [(b) the Lord Chancellor;]
   (c) a Member of the House of Commons who is a Minister of the Crown with responsibilities in relation to local government; and
   (d) five Members of the House of Commons who are not Ministers of the Crown.
   [. . .]

[. . .]

Part II REGISTRATION OF POLITICAL PARTIES

Requirement for registration

22 PARTIES TO BE REGISTERED IN ORDER TO FIELD CANDIDATES AT ELECTIONS

(1)   Subject to subsection (4), no nomination may be made in relation to a relevant election unless the nomination is in respect of—
   (a) a person who stands for election in the name of a qualifying registered party; or
   (b) a person who does not purport to represent any party; or
   (c) a qualifying registered party, where the election is one for which registered parties may be nominated.

(2)   For the purposes of subsection (1) a party (other than a minor party) is a "qualifying registered party" in relation to a relevant election if—
   (a) the constituency, local government area or electoral region in which the election is held—
      (i)   is in England, Scotland or Wales, or
      (ii) is the electoral region of Scotland or Wales,
      and the party was, [on the day ("the relevant day") which is two days before the last day for the delivery of nomination papers at that election], registered in respect of that part of Great Britain in the Great Britain register maintained by the Commission under section 23, or
   (b) the constituency, district electoral area or electoral region in which the election is held—
      (i)   is in Northern Ireland, or
      (ii) is the electoral region of Northern Ireland,
      and the party was, [on the relevant day], registered in the Northern Ireland register maintained by the Commission under that section.
   [. . .]

(4)   Subsection (1) does not apply in relation to any parish or community election.

(5)   The following elections are relevant elections for the purposes of this Part—
      (a)   parliamentary elections,
      (b)   elections to the European Parliament,
      (c)   elections to the Scottish Parliament,
      (d)   elections to the National Assembly for Wales,
      (e)   elections to the Northern Ireland Assembly,
      (f)   local government elections, and
      (g)   local elections in Northern Ireland.
      [. . .]

The registers of political parties

23 THE NEW REGISTERS

(1)   In place of the register of political parties maintained by the registrar of companies under
      the Registration of Political Parties Act 1998, there shall be the new registers of political
      parties mentioned in subsection (2) which—
      (a)   shall be maintained by the Commission, and
      (b)   (subject to the provisions of this section) shall be so maintained in such form as the
            Commission may determine.
      [. . .]

[. . .]

Supplemental

37 PARTY POLITICAL BROADCASTS

(1)   A broadcaster shall not include in its broadcasting services any party political broadcast
      made on behalf of a party which is not a registered party.

(2)   In this Act "broadcaster" means—
      (a)   the holder of a licence under the Broadcasting Act 1990 or 1996,
      (b)   the British Broadcasting Corporation, or
      (c)   Sianel Pedwar Cymru.
[. . .]

Chapter II **RESTRICTIONS ON DONATIONS TO REGISTERED PARTIES**

Permissible donations

54 PERMISSIBLE DONORS

(1)   A donation received by a registered party must not be accepted by the party if—
      (a)   the person by whom the donation would be made is not, at the time of its receipt by
            the party, a permissible donor; or
      (b)   the party is (whether because the donation is given anonymously or by reason of any
            deception or concealment or otherwise) unable to ascertain the identity of that
            person.

(2)   For the purposes of this Part the following are permissible donors—
      (a)   an individual registered in an electoral register;
      (b)   a company—
            (i)   registered under the Companies Act 2006, and
            (ii) incorporated within the United Kingdom or another member State,
            which carries on business in the United Kingdom;

(c) a registered party [, other than a Gibraltar party whose entry in the register includes a statement that it intends to contest one or more elections to the European Parliament in the combined region];

(d) a trade union entered in the list kept under the Trade Union and Labour Relations (Consolidation) Act 1992 or the Industrial Relations (Northern Ireland) Order 1992;

(e) a building society (within the meaning of the Building Societies Act 1986);

(f) a limited liability partnership registered under the Limited Liability Partnerships Act 2000[. . .] which carries on business in the United Kingdom;

(g) a friendly society registered under the Friendly Societies Act 1974 or a society registered (or deemed to be registered) under the Industrial and Provident Societies Act 1965 or the Industrial and Provident Societies Act (Northern Ireland) 1969; and

(h) any unincorporated association of two or more persons which does not fall within any of the preceding paragraphs but which carries on business or other activities wholly or mainly in the United Kingdom and whose main office is there.

[. . .]

(4) Where any person ("the principal donor") causes an amount ("the principal donation") to be received by a registered party by way of a donation—
(a) on behalf of himself and one or more other persons, or
(b) on behalf of two or more other persons,
then for the purposes of this Part each individual contribution by a person falling within paragraph (a) or (b) of more than [£500] shall be treated as if it were a separate donation received from that person.

(5) In relation to each such separate donation, the principal donor must ensure that, at the time when the principal donation is received by the party, the party is given—
(a) (except in the case of a donation which the principal donor is treated as making) all such details in respect of the person treated as making the donation as are required by virtue of paragraph 2or 2A of Schedule 6 to be given in respect of the donor of a recordable donation; and
(b) (in any case) all such details in respect of the donation as are required by virtue of paragraph 4 of Schedule 6 to be given in respect of a recordable donation.

(6) Where—
(a) any person ("the agent") causes an amount to be received by a registered party by way of a donation on behalf of another person ("the donor"), and
(b) the amount of that donation is more than [£500],
the agent must ensure that, at the time when the donation is received by the party, the party is given all such details in respect of the donor as are required by virtue of paragraph 2or 2A of Schedule 6 to be given in respect of the donor of a recordable donation.

(7) A person commits an offence if, without reasonable excuse, he fails to comply with subsection (5) or (6).

(8) In this section "electoral register" means any of the following—
(a) a register of parliamentary or local government electors maintained under section 9 of the Representation of the People Act 1983;
(b) a register of relevant citizens of the European Union prepared under [the European Parliamentary Elections (Franchise of Relevant Citizens of the Union) Regulations 2001]; or
(c) a register of peers prepared under regulations under section 3 of the Representation of the People Act 1985.

[. . .]

56 ACCEPTANCE OR RETURN OF DONATIONS: GENERAL

(1) Where—
  (a) a donation is received by a registered party, and
  (b) it is not immediately decided that the party should (for whatever reason) refuse the donation,
  all reasonable steps must be taken forthwith by or on behalf of the party to verify (or, so far as any of the following is not apparent, ascertain) the identity of the donor, whether he is a permissible donor, and (if that appears to be the case) all such details in respect of him as are required by virtue of [paragraph 2or 2A of Schedule 6] to be given in respect of the donor of a recordable donation.

(2) If a registered party receives a donation which it is prohibited from accepting by virtue of section 54(1), or which it is decided that the party should for any other reason refuse, then—
  (a) unless the donation falls within section 54(1)(b), the donation, or a payment of an equivalent amount, must be sent back to the person who made the donation or any person appearing to be acting on his behalf,
  (b) if the donation falls within that provision, the required steps (as defined by section 57(1)) must be taken in relation to the donation,
  within the period of 30 days beginning with the date when the donation is received by the party.

(3) Where—
  (a) subsection (2)(a) applies in relation to a donation, and
  (b) the donation is not dealt with in accordance with that provision,
  the party and the treasurer of the party are each guilty of an offence.

[. . .]

(4) Where—
  (a) subsection (2)(b) applies in relation to a donation, and
  (b) the donation is not dealt with in accordance with that provision,
  the treasurer of the party is guilty of an offence.

(5) For the purposes of this Part a donation received by a registered party shall be taken to have been accepted by the party unless—
  (a) the steps mentioned in paragraph (a) or (b) of subsection (2) are taken in relation to the donation within the period of 30 days mentioned in that subsection; and
  (b) a record can be produced of the receipt of the donation and—
    (i) of the return of the donation, or the equivalent amount, as mentioned in subsection (2)(a), or
    (ii) of the required steps being taken in relation to the donation as mentioned in subsection (2)(b),
  as the case may be.

  [. . .]

[. . .]

REGULATION OF INVESTIGATORY POWERS ACT 2000
(c. 23)

An Act to make provision for and about the interception of communications, the acquisition and disclosure of data relating to communications, the carrying out of surveillance, the use of covert human intelligence sources and the acquisition of the means by which electronic data protected by encryption or passwords may be decrypted or accessed; to provide for Commissioners and a tribunal with functions and jurisdiction in relation to those matters, to entries on and interferences with property or with wireless telegraphy and to the carrying out of their functions by the Security Service, the Secret Intelligence Service and the Government Communications Headquarters; and for connected purposes.

[. . .]

Part I **COMMUNICATIONS**

Chapter I **INTERCEPTION**

Unlawful and authorised interception

1   UNLAWFUL INTERCEPTION

(1)   It shall be an offence for a person intentionally and without lawful authority to intercept, at any place in the United Kingdom, any communication in the course of its transmission by means of—
(a)   a public postal service; or
(b)   a public telecommunication system.

(1A)   The Interception of Communications Commissioner may serve a monetary penalty notice on a person if the Commissioner—
(a)   considers that the person—
(i)   has without lawful authority intercepted, at any place in the United Kingdom, any communication in the course of its transmission by means of a public telecommunication system, and
(ii)   was not, at the time of the interception, making an attempt to act in accordance with an interception warrant which might, in the opinion of the Commissioner, explain the interception concerned, and
(b)   does not consider that the person has committed an offence under subsection (1).
[ ]

(2)   It shall be an offence for a person—
(a)   intentionally and without lawful authority, and
(b)   otherwise than in circumstances in which his conduct is excluded by subsection (6) from criminal liability under this subsection,
to intercept, at any place in the United Kingdom, any communication in the course of its transmission by means of a private telecommunication system.

(3)   Any interception of a communication which is carried out at any place in the United Kingdom by, or with the express or implied consent of, a person having the right to control the operation or the use of a private telecommunication system shall be actionable at the suit or instance of the sender or recipient, or intended recipient, of the communication if it is without lawful authority and is either—
(a)   an interception of that communication in the course of its transmission by means of that private system; or
(b)   an interception of that communication in the course of its transmission, by means of a public telecommunication system, to or from apparatus comprised in that private telecommunication system.
[. . .]

(5)   Conduct has lawful authority for the purposes of this section if, and only if—
(a)   it is authorised by or under section 3 or 4;

(b) it takes place in accordance with a warrant under section 5 ("an interception warrant"); or

(c) it is in exercise, in relation to any stored communication, of any statutory power that is exercised (apart from this section) for the purpose of obtaining information or of taking possession of any document or other property;

and conduct (whether or not prohibited by this section) which has lawful authority for the purposes of this section by virtue of paragraph (a) or (b) shall also be taken to be lawful for all other purposes.

[. . .]

[. . .]

3 LAWFUL INTERCEPTION WITHOUT AN INTERCEPTION WARRANT

(1) Conduct by any person consisting in the interception of a communication is authorised by this section if the communication is one which is both—

(a) a communication sent by a person who has consented to the interception; and

(b) a communication the intended recipient of which has so consented.

[. . .]

4 POWER TO PROVIDE FOR LAWFUL INTERCEPTION

(1) Conduct by any person ("the interceptor") consisting in the interception of a communication in the course of its transmission by means of a telecommunication system is authorised by this section if—

(a) the interception is carried out for the purpose of obtaining information about the communications of a person who, or who the interceptor has reasonable grounds for believing, is in a country or territory outside the United Kingdom;

(b) the interception relates to the use of a telecommunications service provided to persons in that country or territory which is either—

(i)   a public telecommunications service; or

(ii) a telecommunications service that would be a public telecommunications service if the persons to whom it is offered or provided were members of the public in a part of the United Kingdom;

(c) the person who provides that service (whether the interceptor or another person) is required by the law of that country or territory to carry out, secure or facilitate the interception in question;

(d) the situation is one in relation to which such further conditions as may be prescribed by regulations made by the Secretary of State are required to be satisfied before conduct may be treated as authorised by virtue of this subsection; and

(e) the conditions so prescribed are satisfied in relation to that situation.

[. . .]

5 INTERCEPTION WITH A WARRANT

(1) Subject to the following provisions of this Chapter, the Secretary of State may issue a warrant authorising or requiring the person to whom it is addressed, by any such conduct as may be described in the warrant, to secure any one or more of the following—

(a) the interception in the course of their transmission by means of a postal service or telecommunication system of the communications described in the warrant;

(b) the making, in accordance with an international mutual assistance agreement, of a request for the provision of such assistance in connection with, or in the form of, an interception of communications as may be so described;

(c) the provision, in accordance with an international mutual assistance agreement, to the competent authorities of a country or territory outside the United Kingdom of any such assistance in connection with, or in the form of, an interception of communications as may be so described;

(d) the disclosure, in such manner as may be so described, of intercepted material obtained by any interception authorised or required by the warrant, and of related communications data.

(2) The Secretary of State shall not issue an interception warrant unless he believes—
(a) that the warrant is necessary on grounds falling within subsection (3); and
(b) that the conduct authorised by the warrant is proportionate to what is sought to be achieved by that conduct.

(3) Subject to the following provisions of this section, a warrant is necessary on grounds falling within this subsection if it is necessary—
(a) in the interests of national security;
(b) for the purpose of preventing or detecting serious crime;
(c) for the purpose of safeguarding the economic well-being of the United Kingdom; or
(d) for the purpose, in circumstances appearing to the Secretary of State to be equivalent to those in which he would issue a warrant by virtue of paragraph (b), of giving effect to the provisions of any international mutual assistance agreement.
[. . .]

[. . .]

Restrictions on use of intercepted material etc.

15 GENERAL SAFEGUARDS

(1) Subject to subsection (6), it shall be the duty of the Secretary of State to ensure, in relation to all interception warrants, that such arrangements are in force as he considers necessary for securing—
(a) that the requirements of subsections (2) and (3) are satisfied in relation to the intercepted material and any related communications data; and
(b) in the case of warrants in relation to which there are section 8(4) certificates, that the requirements of section 16 are also satisfied.

(2) The requirements of this subsection are satisfied in relation to the intercepted material and any related communications data if each of the following—
(a) the number of persons to whom any of the material or data is disclosed or otherwise made available,
(b) the extent to which any of the material or data is disclosed or otherwise made available,
(c) the extent to which any of the material or data is copied, and
(d) the number of copies that are made,
is limited to the minimum that is necessary for the authorised purposes.

(3) The requirements of this subsection are satisfied in relation to the intercepted material and any related communications data if each copy made of any of the material or data (if not destroyed earlier) is destroyed as soon as there are no longer any grounds for retaining it as necessary for any of the authorised purposes.

[. . .]

Part IV SCRUTINY ETC. OF INVESTIGATORY POWERS AND OF THE FUNCTIONS OF THE INTELLIGENCE SERVICES

[. . .]

59 INTELLIGENCE SERVICES COMMISSIONER

(1)   The Prime Minister shall appoint a Commissioner to be known as the Intelligence Services Commissioner.

(2)   Subject to subsection (4), the Intelligence Services Commissioner shall keep under review, so far as they are not required to be kept under review by the Interception of Communications Commissioner—

    (a)   the exercise by the Secretary of State of his powers under sections 5 to 7of [,or the Scottish Ministers (by virtue of provision made under section 63 of the Scotland Act 1998) of their powers under section s 5 and 6(3) and (4) of] the Intelligence Services Act 1994 (warrants for interference with wireless telegraphy, entry and interference with property etc.);

    (b)   the exercise and performance by the Secretary of State [or the Scottish Ministers (by virtue of provision made under section 63 of the Scotland Act 1998),], in connection with or in relation to—

        (i)   the activities of the intelligence services, and

        (ii)   the activities in places other than Northern Ireland of the officials of the Ministry of Defence and of members of Her Majesty's forces,

    of the powers and duties conferred or imposed on him by Parts II and III of this Act [or on them by Part II of this Act];

    (c)   the exercise and performance by members of the intelligence services of the powers and duties conferred or imposed on them by or under Parts II and III of this Act;

    [. . .]

[. . .]

The Tribunal

65 THE TRIBUNAL

(1)   There shall, for the purpose of exercising the jurisdiction conferred on them by this section, be a tribunal consisting of such number of members as Her Majesty may by Letters Patent appoint.

(2)   The jurisdiction of the Tribunal shall be—

    (a)   to be the only appropriate tribunal for the purposes of section 7 of the Human Rights Act 1998 in relation to any proceedings under subsection (1)(a) of that section (proceedings for actions incompatible with Convention rights) which fall within subsection (3) of this section;

    (b)   to consider and determine any complaints made to them which, in accordance with subsection (4), are complaints for which the Tribunal is the appropriate forum;

    (c)   to consider and determine any reference to them by any person that he has suffered detriment as a consequence of any prohibition or restriction, by virtue of section 17, on his relying in, or for the purposes of, any civil proceedings on any matter; and

    (d)   to hear and determine any other such proceedings falling within subsection (3) as may be allocated to them in accordance with provision made by the Secretary of State by order.

(3)   Proceedings fall within this subsection if—

    (a)   they are proceedings against any of the intelligence services;

(b)   they are proceedings against any other person in respect of any conduct, or proposed conduct, by or on behalf of any of those services;

(c)   they are proceedings brought by virtue of section 55(4); or

(d)   they are proceedings relating to the taking place in any challengeable circumstances of any conduct falling within subsection (5).

(4)   The Tribunal is the appropriate forum for any complaint if it is a complaint by a person who is aggrieved by any conduct falling within subsection (5) which he believes—

(a)   to have taken place in relation to him, to any of his property, to any communications sent by or to him, or intended for him, or to his use of any postal service, telecommunications service or telecommunication system; and

(b)   to have taken place in challengeable circumstances or to have been carried out by or on behalf of any of the intelligence services.

[. . .]

(5)   Subject to subsection (6), conduct falls within this subsection if (whenever it occurred) it is—

(a)   conduct by or on behalf of any of the intelligence services;

(b)   conduct for or in connection with the interception of communications in the course of their transmission by means of a postal service or telecommunication system;

(c)   conduct to which Chapter II of Part I applies;

[(ca) the carrying out of surveillance by a foreign police or customs officer (within the meaning of section 76A);]

(d)   [other] conduct to which Part II applies;

(e)   the giving of a notice under section 49 or any disclosure or use of a key to protected information;

(f)   any entry on or interference with property or any interference with wireless telegraphy.

[. . .]

Amended by the Paragraph 14(2) of the Schedule to the Identity Documents Act 2010

As amended by the The Regulation of Investigatory Powers (Monetary Penalty Notices and Consents for Interceptions) Regulations 2011, regulations 2, 3

TERRORISM ACT 2000
(c. 11)

An Act to make provision about terrorism; and to make temporary provision for Northern Ireland about the prosecution and punishment of certain offences, the preservation of peace and the maintenance of order.

[. . .]

Part I INTRODUCTORY

1 TERRORISM: INTERPRETATION

(1)   In this Act "terrorism" means the use or threat of action where—

(a)   the action falls within subsection (2),

(b)   the use or threat is designed to influence the government [or an international governmental organisation] or to intimidate the public or a section of the public, and

(c) the use or threat is made for the purpose of advancing a political, religious [, racial] or ideological cause.

(2) Action falls within this subsection if it—
(a) involves serious violence against a person,
(b) involves serious damage to property,
(c) endangers a person's life, other than that of the person committing the action,
(d) creates a serious risk to the health or safety of the public or a section of the public, or
(e) is designed seriously to interfere with or seriously to disrupt an electronic system.

(3) The use or threat of action falling within subsection (2) which involves the use of firearms or explosives is terrorism whether or not subsection (1)(b) is satisfied.

[. . .]

[. . .]

Part II PROSCRIBED ORGANISATIONS

Procedure

3 PROSCRIPTION

(1) For the purposes of this Act an organisation is proscribed if—
(a) it is listed in Schedule 2, or
(b) it operates under the same name as an organisation listed in that Schedule.

[. . .]

[(5A) The cases in which an organisation promotes or encourages terrorism for the purposes of subsection (5)(c) include any case in which activities of the organisation—
(a) include the unlawful glorification of the commission or preparation (whether in the past, in the future or generally) of acts of terrorism; or
(b) are carried out in a manner that ensures that the organisation is associated with statements containing any such glorification.

(5B) The glorification of any conduct is unlawful for the purposes of subsection (5A) if there are persons who may become aware of it who could reasonably be expected to infer that what is being glorified, is being glorified as—
(a) conduct that should be emulated in existing circumstances, or
(b) conduct that is illustrative of a type of conduct that should be so emulated.

(5C) In this section—

"glorification" includes any form of praise or celebration, and cognate expressions are to be construed accordingly;

"statement" includes a communication without words consisting of sounds or images or both.]

[. . .]

[. . .]

Offences

11 MEMBERSHIP

(1) A person commits an offence if he belongs or professes to belong to a proscribed organisation.

(2)   It is a defence for a person charged with an offence under subsection (1) to prove—
    (a)   that the organisation was not proscribed on the last (or only) occasion on which he became a member or began to profess to be a member, and
    (b)   that he has not taken part in the activities of the organisation at any time while it was proscribed.

[. . .]

12 SUPPORT

(1)   A person commits an offence if—
    (a)   he invites support for a proscribed organisation, and
    (b)   the support is not, or is not restricted to, the provision of money or other property (within the meaning of section 15).

(2)   A person commits an offence if he arranges, manages or assists in arranging or managing a meeting which he knows is—
    (a)   to support a proscribed organisation,
    (b)   to further the activities of a proscribed organisation, or
    (c)   to be addressed by a person who belongs or professes to belong to a proscribed organisation.

(3)   A person commits an offence if he addresses a meeting and the purpose of his address is to encourage support for a proscribed organisation or to further its activities.

(4)   Where a person is charged with an offence under subsection (2)(c) in respect of a private meeting it is a defence for him to prove that he had no reasonable cause to believe that the address mentioned in subsection (2)(c) would support a proscribed organisation or further its activities.

    [. . .]

[. . .]

Part III TERRORIST PROPERTY

[. . .]

Offences

15 FUND-RAISING

(1)   A person commits an offence if he—
    (a)   invites another to provide money or other property, and
    (b)   intends that it should be used, or has reasonable cause to suspect that it may be used, for the purposes of terrorism.

(2)   A person commits an offence if he—
    (a)   receives money or other property, and
    (b)   intends that it should be used, or has reasonable cause to suspect that it may be used, for the purposes of terrorism.

(3)   A person commits an offence if he—
    (a)   provides money or other property, and
    (b)   knows or has reasonable cause to suspect that it will or may be used for the purposes of terrorism.
    [. . .]

[. . .]

19 DISCLOSURE OF INFORMATION: DUTY

(1)   This section applies where a person—
    (a) believes or suspects that another person has committed an offence under any of sections 15 to 18, and
    (b) bases his belief or suspicion on information which [comes to his attention—
        (i)   in the course of a trade, profession or business, or
        (ii) in the course of his employment (whether or not in the course of a trade, profession or business).]

(1A)   But this section does not apply if the information came to the person in the course of a business in the regulated sector.

(2)   The person commits an offence if he does not disclose to a constable as soon as is reasonably practicable—
    (a) his belief or suspicion, and
    (b) the information on which it is based.

(3)   It is a defence for a person charged with an offence under subsection (2) to prove that he had a reasonable excuse for not making the disclosure.

(4)   Where—
    (a) a person is in employment,
    (b) his employer has established a procedure for the making of disclosures of the matters specified in subsection (2), and
    (c) he is charged with an offence under that subsection,
    it is a defence for him to prove that he disclosed the matters specified in that subsection in accordance with the procedure.

(5)   Subsection (2) does not require disclosure by a professional legal adviser of—
    (a) information which he obtains in privileged circumstances, or
    (b) a belief or suspicion based on information which he obtains in privileged circumstances.

(6)   For the purpose of subsection (5) information is obtained by an adviser in privileged circumstances if it comes to him, otherwise than with a view to furthering a criminal purpose—
    (a) from a client or a client's representative, in connection with the provision of legal advice by the adviser to the client,
    (b) from a person seeking legal advice from the adviser, or from the person's representative, or
    (c) from any person, for the purpose of actual or contemplated legal proceedings.
        [. . .]

[. . .]

Part V COUNTER-TERRORIST POWERS

Suspected terrorists

40 TERRORIST: INTERPRETATION

(1)   In this Part "terrorist" means a person who—
    (a) has committed an offence under any of sections 11, 12, 15 to 18, 54 and 56 to 63, or
    (b) is or has been concerned in the commission, preparation or instigation of acts of terrorism.
        [. . .]

41 ARREST WITHOUT WARRANT

(1) A constable may arrest without a warrant a person whom he reasonably suspects to be a terrorist.

(2) Where a person is arrested under this section the provisions of Schedule 8 (detention: treatment, review and extension) shall apply.

(3) Subject to subsections (4) to (7), a person detained under this section shall (unless detained under any other power) be released not later than the end of the period of 48 hours beginning—
(a) with the time of his arrest under this section, or
(b) if he was being detained under Schedule 7 when he was arrested under this section, with the time when his examination under that Schedule began.

(4) If on a review of a person's detention under Part II of Schedule 8 the review officer does not authorise continued detention, the person shall (unless detained in accordance with subsection (5) or (6) or under any other power) be released.

(5) Where a police officer intends to make an application for a warrant under paragraph 29 of Schedule 8 extending a person's detention, the person may be detained pending the making of the application.

(6) Where an application has been made under paragraph 29 or 36 of Schedule 8 in respect of a person's detention, he may be detained pending the conclusion of proceedings on the application.

(7) Where an application under paragraph 29 or 36 of Schedule 8 is granted in respect of a person's detention, he may be detained, subject to paragraph 37 of that Schedule, during the period specified in the warrant.

[. . .]

42 SEARCH OF PREMISES

(1) A justice of the peace may on the application of a constable issue a warrant in relation to specified premises if he is satisfied that there are reasonable grounds for suspecting that a person whom the constable reasonably suspects to be a person falling within section 40(1)(b) is to be found there.

(2) A warrant under this section shall authorise any constable to enter and search the specified premises for the purpose of arresting the person referred to in subsection (1) under section 41.

[. . .]

43 SEARCH OF PERSONS

(1) A constable may stop and search a person whom he reasonably suspects to be a terrorist to discover whether he has in his possession anything which may constitute evidence that he is a terrorist.

(2) A constable may search a person arrested under section 41 to discover whether he has in his possession anything which may constitute evidence that he is a terrorist.

(3) A search of a person under this section must be carried out by someone of the same sex.

(4)   A constable may seize and retain anything which he discovers in the course of a search of a person under subsection (1) or (2) and which he reasonably suspects may constitute evidence that the person is a terrorist.

[. . .]

[. . .]

Inciting terrorism overseas

59 ENGLAND AND WALES

(1)   A person commits an offence if—
   (a) he incites another person to commit an act of terrorism wholly or partly outside the United Kingdom, and
   (b) the act would, if committed in England and Wales, constitute one of the offences listed in subsection (2).

(2)   Those offences are—
   (a) murder,
   (b) an offence under section 18 of the Offences against the Person Act 1861 (wounding with intent),
   (c) an offence under section 23 or 24 of that Act (poison),
   (d) an offence under section 28 or 29 of that Act (explosions), and
   (e) an offence under section 1(2) of the Criminal Damage Act 1971 (endangering life by damaging property).
      [. . .]

[. . .]

Terrorist bombing and finance offences

62 TERRORIST BOMBING: JURISDICTION

(1)   If—
   (a) a person does anything outside the United Kingdom as an act of terrorism or for the purposes of terrorism, and
   (b) his action would have constituted the commission of one of the offences listed in subsection (2) if it had been done in the United Kingdom,
   he shall be guilty of the offence.

(2)   The offences referred to in subsection (1)(b) are—
   (a) an offence under section 2, 3 or 5 of the Explosive Substances Act 1883 (causing explosions, &c.),
   (b) an offence under section 1 of the Biological Weapons Act 1974 (biological weapons), and
   (c) an offence under section 2 of the Chemical Weapons Act 1996 (chemical weapons).
      [. . .]

[. . .]

Part VIII **GENERAL**

114 POLICE POWERS

(1)   A power conferred by virtue of this Act on a constable—

(a) is additional to powers which he has at common law or by virtue of any other enactment, and

(b) shall not be taken to affect those powers.

(2)   A constable may if necessary use reasonable force for the purpose of exercising a power conferred on him by virtue of this Act (apart from paragraphs 2 and 3 of Schedule 7).

[. . .]

[. . .]

ANTI-TERRORISM, CRIME AND SECURITY ACT 2001
(c. 24)

An Act to amend the Terrorism Act 2000; to make further provision about terrorism and security; to provide for the freezing of assets; to make provision about immigration and asylum; to amend or extend the criminal law and powers for preventing crime and enforcing that law; to make provision about the control of pathogens and toxins; to provide for the retention of communications data; to provide for implementation of Title VI of the Treaty on European Union; and for connected purposes.

[. . .]

Part 1 TERRORIST PROPERTY

1 FORFEITURE OF TERRORIST CASH

(1)   Schedule 1 (which makes provision for enabling cash which—
(a) is intended to be used for the purposes of terrorism,
(b) consists of resources of an organisation which is a proscribed organisation, or
(c) is, or represents, property obtained through terrorism,
to be forfeited in civil proceedings before a magistrates' court or (in Scotland) the sheriff) is to have effect.

(2)   The powers conferred by Schedule 1 are exercisable in relation to any cash whether or not any proceedings have been brought for an offence in connection with the cash.

[. . .]

Part 2 FREEZING ORDERS

Orders

4 POWER TO MAKE ORDER

(1)   The Treasury may make a freezing order if the following two conditions are satisfied.

(2)   The first condition is that the Treasury reasonably believe that—
(a) action to the detriment of the United Kingdom's economy (or part of it) has been or is likely to be taken by a person or persons, or
(b) action constituting a threat to the life or property of one or more nationals of the United Kingdom or residents of the United Kingdom has been or is likely to be taken by a person or persons.

(3)   If one person is believed to have taken or to be likely to take the action the second condition is that the person is—
(a) the government of a country or territory outside the United Kingdom, or
(b) a resident of a country or territory outside the United Kingdom.

(4)   If two or more persons are believed to have taken or to be likely to take the action the second condition is that each of them falls within paragraph (a) or (b) of subsection (3); and different persons may fall within different paragraphs.

5 CONTENTS OF ORDER

(1)   A freezing order is an order which prohibits persons from making funds available to or for the benefit of a person or persons specified in the order.

(2)   The order must provide that these are the persons who are prohibited—
(a) all persons in the United Kingdom, and
(b) all persons elsewhere who are nationals of the United Kingdom or are bodies incorporated under the law of any part of the United Kingdom or are Scottish partnerships.

(3)   The order may specify the following (and only the following) as the person or persons to whom or for whose benefit funds are not to be made available—
(a) the person or persons reasonably believed by the Treasury to have taken or to be likely to take the action referred to in section 4;
(b) any person the Treasury reasonably believe has provided or is likely to provide assistance (directly or indirectly) to that person or any of those persons.

(4)   A person may be specified under subsection (3) by—
(a) being named in the order, or
(b) falling within a description of persons set out in the order.

(5)   The description must be such that a reasonable person would know whether he fell within it.

(6)   Funds are financial assets and economic benefits of any kind.

[. . .]

Orders: procedure etc.

10 PROCEDURE FOR MAKING FREEZING ORDERS

(1)   A power to make a freezing order is exercisable by statutory instrument.

(2)   A freezing order—
(a) must be laid before Parliament after being made;
(b) ceases to have effect at the end of the relevant period unless before the end of that period the order is approved by a resolution of each House of Parliament (but without that affecting anything done under the order or the power to make a new order).

(3)   The relevant period is a period of 28 days starting with the day on which the order is made.

[. . .]

[. . .]

Miscellaneous

15 THE CROWN

(1) A freezing order binds the Crown, subject to the following provisions of this section.

(2) No contravention by the Crown of a provision of a freezing order makes the Crown criminally liable; but the High Court or in Scotland the Court of Session may, on the application of a person appearing to the Court to have an interest, declare unlawful any act or omission of the Crown which constitutes such a contravention.

[. . .]

CRIMINAL JUSTICE AND POLICE ACT 2001
(c. 16)

An Act to make provision for combatting crime and disorder; to make provision about the disclosure of information relating to criminal matters and about powers of search and seizure; to amend the Police and Criminal Evidence Act 1984, the Police and Criminal Evidence (Northern Ireland) Order 1989 and the Terrorism Act 2000; to make provision about the police, the National Criminal Intelligence Service and the National Crime Squad; to make provision about the powers of the courts in relation to criminal matters; and for connected purposes.

[. . .]

Part 1 PROVISIONS FOR COMBATTING CRIME AND DISORDER

[. . .]

Chapter 3 OTHER PROVISIONS FOR COMBATTING CRIME AND DISORDER

[. . .]

Travel restrictions on drug trafficking offenders

33 POWER TO MAKE TRAVEL RESTRICTION ORDERS

(1) This section applies where—
  (a) a person ("the offender") has been convicted by any court of a post-commencement drug trafficking offence;
  (b) the court has determined that it would be appropriate to impose a sentence of imprisonment for that offence; and
  (c) the term of imprisonment which the court considers appropriate is a term of four years or more.

(2) It shall be the duty of the court, on sentencing the offender—
  (a) to consider whether it would be appropriate for the sentence for the offence to include the making of a travel restriction order in relation to the offender;
  (b) if the court determines that it is so appropriate, to make such travel restriction order in relation to the offender as the court thinks suitable in all the circumstances (including any other convictions of the offender for post-commencement drug trafficking offences in respect of which the court is also passing sentence); and
  (c) if the court determines that it is not so appropriate, to state its reasons for not making a travel restriction order.

(3)   A travel restriction order is an order that prohibits the offender from leaving the United Kingdom at any time in the period which—
   (a) begins with the offender's release from custody; and
   (b) continues after that time for such period of not less than two years as may be specified in the order.

(4)   A travel restriction order may contain a direction to the offender to deliver up, or cause to be delivered up, to the court any UK passport held by him; and where such a direction is given, the court shall send any passport delivered up in pursuance of the direction to the Secretary of State at such address as the Secretary of State may determine.

(5)   Where the offender's passport is held by the Secretary of State by reason of the making of any direction contained in a travel restriction order, the Secretary of State (without prejudice to any other power or duty of his to retain the passport)—
   (a) may retain it for so long as the prohibition imposed by the order applies to the offender, and is not for the time being suspended; and
   (b) shall not return the passport after the prohibition has ceased to apply, or when it is suspended, except where the passport has not expired and an application for its return is made to him by the offender.

(6)   In this section "post-commencement"—
   (a) except in relation to an offence that is a drug trafficking offence by virtue of an order under section 34(1)(c), means committed after the coming into force of this section; and
   (b) in relation to an offence that is a drug trafficking offence by virtue of such an order, means committed after the coming into force of that order.

(7)   References in this section to the offender's release from custody are references to his first release from custody after the imposition of the travel restriction order which is neither—
   (a) a release on bail; nor
   (b) a temporary release for a fixed period.

[(8)   (8) In this section "UK passport" means a United Kingdom passport within the meaning of the Immigration Act 1971 (see section 33(1)).

[. . .]

Further provision about intimidation etc.

42 POLICE DIRECTIONS STOPPING THE HARASSMENT ETC. OF A PERSON IN HIS HOME

(1)   Subject to the following provisions of this section, a constable who is at the scene may give a direction under this section to any person if—
   (a) that person is present outside or in the vicinity of any premises that are used by any individual ("the resident") as his dwelling;
   (b) that constable believes, on reasonable grounds, that that person is present there for the purpose (by his presence or otherwise) of representing to the resident or another individual (whether or not one who uses the premises as his dwelling), or of persuading the resident or such another individual—
      (i)   that he should not do something that he is entitled or required to do; or
      (ii) that he should do something that he is not under any obligation to do; and
   (c) that constable also believes, on reasonable grounds, that the presence of that person (either alone or together with that of any other persons who are also present)—

(i)   amounts to, or is likely to result in, the harassment of the resident; or

(ii) is likely to cause alarm or distress to the resident.

(2)   A direction under this section is a direction requiring the person to whom it is given to do all such things as the constable giving it may specify as the things he considers necessary to prevent one or both of the following—

(a) the harassment of the resident; or

(b) the causing of any alarm or distress to the resident.

[. . .]

(4)   The requirements that may be imposed by a direction under this section include—

(a) a requirement to leave the vicinity of the premises in question, and

(b) a requirement to leave that vicinity and not to return to it within such period as the constable may specify, not being longer than 3 months;

and (in either case) the requirement to leave the vicinity may be to do so immediately or after a specified period of time.

(5)   A direction under this section may make exceptions to any requirement imposed by the direction, and may make any such exception subject to such conditions as the constable giving the direction thinks fit; and those conditions may include—

(a) conditions as to the distance from the premises in question at which, or otherwise as to the location where, persons who do not leave their vicinity must remain; and

(b) conditions as to the number or identity of the persons who are authorised by the exception to remain in the vicinity of those premises.

[. . .]

[. . .]

Part 2 POWERS OF SEIZURE

Additional powers of seizure

[. . .]

50 ADDITIONAL POWERS OF SEIZURE FROM PREMISES

(1)   Where—

(a) a person who is lawfully on any premises finds anything on those premises that he has reasonable grounds for believing may be or may contain something for which he is authorised to search on those premises,

(b) a power of seizure to which this section applies or the power conferred by subsection (2) would entitle him, if he found it, to seize whatever it is that he has grounds for believing that thing to be or to contain, and

(c) in all the circumstances, it is not reasonably practicable for it to be determined, on those premises—

(i)   whether what he has found is something that he is entitled to seize, or

(ii) the extent to which what he has found contains something that he is entitled to seize,

that person's powers of seizure shall include power under this section to seize so much of what he has found as it is necessary to remove from the premises to enable that to be determined.

(2)   Where—

(a) a person who is lawfully on any premises finds anything on those premises ("the seizable property") which he would be entitled to seize but for its being comprised in something else that he has (apart from this subsection) no power to seize,

      (b) the power under which that person would have power to seize the seizable property is a power to which this section applies, and

      (c) in all the circumstances it is not reasonably practicable for the seizable property to be separated, on those premises, from that in which it is comprised,

that person's powers of seizure shall include power under this section to seize both the seizable property and that from which it is not reasonably practicable to separate it.

(3)   The factors to be taken into account in considering, for the purposes of this section, whether or not it is reasonably practicable on particular premises for something to be determined, or for something to be separated from something else, shall be confined to the following—

      (a) how long it would take to carry out the determination or separation on those premises;

      (b) the number of persons that would be required to carry out that determination or separation on those premises within a reasonable period;

      (c) whether the determination or separation would (or would if carried out on those premises) involve damage to property;

      (d) the apparatus or equipment that it would be necessary or appropriate to use for the carrying out of the determination or separation; and

      (e) in the case of separation, whether the separation—

         (i) would be likely, or

         (ii) if carried out by the only means that are reasonably practicable on those premises, would be likely,

           to prejudice the use of some or all of the separated seizable property for a purpose for which something seized under the power in question is capable of being used.

[. . .]

51 ADDITIONAL POWERS OF SEIZURE FROM THE PERSON

(1)   Where—

      (a) a person carrying out a lawful search of any person finds something that he has reasonable grounds for believing may be or may contain something for which he is authorised to search,

      (b) a power of seizure to which this section applies or the power conferred by subsection (2) would entitle him, if he found it, to seize whatever it is that he has grounds for believing that thing to be or to contain, and

      (c) in all the circumstances it is not reasonably practicable for it to be determined, at the time and place of the search—

         (i) whether what he has found is something that he is entitled to seize, or

         (ii) the extent to which what he has found contains something that he is entitled to seize,

that person's powers of seizure shall include power under this section to seize so much of what he has found as it is necessary to remove from that place to enable that to be determined.

(2)   Where—

      (a) a person carrying out a lawful search of any person finds something ("the seizable property") which he would be entitled to seize but for its being comprised in something else that he has (apart from this subsection) no power to seize,

      (b) the power under which that person would have power to seize the seizable property is a power to which this section applies, and

      (c) in all the circumstances it is not reasonably practicable for the seizable property to be separated, at the time and place of the search, from that in which it is comprised, that person's powers of seizure shall include power under this section to seize both the seizable property and that from which it is not reasonably practicable to separate it.

(3)   The factors to be taken into account in considering, for the purposes of this section, whether or not it is reasonably practicable, at the time and place of a search, for something to be determined, or for something to be separated from something else, shall be confined to the following—
    (a) how long it would take to carry out the determination or separation at that time and place;
    (b) the number of persons that would be required to carry out that determination or separation at that time and place within a reasonable period;
    (c) whether the determination or separation would (or would if carried out at that time and place) involve damage to property;
    (d) the apparatus or equipment that it would be necessary or appropriate to use for the carrying out of the determination or separation; and
    (e) in the case of separation, whether the separation—
        (i)   would be likely, or
        (ii) if carried out by the only means that are reasonably practicable at that time and place, would be likely,
to prejudice the use of some or all of the separated seizable property for a purpose for which something seized under the power in question is capable of being used.

    [. . .]

[. . .]

Remedies and safeguards

59 APPLICATION TO THE APPROPRIATE JUDICIAL AUTHORITY

(1)   This section applies where anything has been seized in exercise, or purported exercise, of a relevant power of seizure.

(2)   Any person with a relevant interest in the seized property may apply to the appropriate judicial authority, on one or more of the grounds mentioned in subsection (3), for the return of the whole or a part of the seized property.

(3)   Those grounds are—
    (a) that there was no power to make the seizure;
    (b) that the seized property is or contains an item subject to legal privilege that is not comprised in property falling within section 54(2);
    (c) that the seized property is or contains any excluded material or special procedure material which—
        (i)   has been seized under a power to which section 55 applies;
        (ii) is not comprised in property falling within section 55(2) or (3); and
        (iii) is not property the retention of which is authorised by section 56;
    (d) that the seized property is or contains something seized under section 50 or 51 which does not fall within section 53(3);
and subsections (5) and (6) of section 55 shall apply for the purposes of paragraph (c) as they apply for the purposes of that section.

(4)   Subject to subsection (6), the appropriate judicial authority, on an application under subsection (2), shall—
    (a) if satisfied as to any of the matters mentioned in subsection (3), order the return of so much of the seized property as is property in relation to which the authority is so satisfied; and

(b) to the extent that that authority is not so satisfied, dismiss the application.
[. . .]

(9) If a person fails to comply with any order or direction made or given by a judge of the Crown Court in exercise of any jurisdiction under this section—
   (a) the authority may deal with him as if he had committed a contempt of the Crown Court; and
   (b) any enactment relating to contempt of the Crown Court shall have effect in relation to the failure as if it were such a contempt.

(10) The relevant powers of seizure for the purposes of this section are—
   (a) the powers of seizure conferred by sections 50 and 51;
   (b) each of the powers of seizure specified in Parts 1 and 2 of Schedule 1; and
   (c) any power of seizure (not falling within paragraph (a) or (b)) conferred on a constable by or under any enactment, including an enactment passed after this Act.
   [. . .]

[. . .]

As amended by the Identity paragraph 16 of the Schedule to the Documents Act 2010

POLICE REFORM ACT 2002
(c. 30)

An Act to make new provision about the supervision, administration, functions and conduct of police forces, police officers and other persons serving with, or carrying out functions in relation to, the police; to amend police powers and to provide for the exercise of police powers by persons who are not police officers; to amend the law relating to anti-social behaviour orders; to amend the law relating to sex offender orders; and for connected purposes.

[. . .]

Part 2 COMPLAINTS AND MISCONDUCT

The Independent Police Complaints Commission

9 THE INDEPENDENT POLICE COMPLAINTS COMMISSION

(1) There shall be a body corporate to be known as the Independent Police Complaints Commission (in this Part referred to as "the Commission").

(2) The Commission shall consist of—
   (a) a chairman appointed by Her Majesty; and
   (b) not less than ten other members appointed by the Secretary of State.

(3) A person shall not be appointed as the chairman of the Commission, or as another member of the Commission, if—
   (a) he holds or has held office as a constable in any part of the United Kingdom;
   (b) he is or has been under the direction and control of a chief officer or of any person holding an equivalent office in Scotland or Northern Ireland;
   (c) he is a person in relation to whom a designation under section 39 is or has been in force;

(d)   he is a person in relation to whom an accreditation under [section 41 or 41A] is or
      has been in force;

[(da) he is or has been the chairman or a member of, or a member of the staff of, the
      Serious Organised Crime Agency;]

[(db) he is or has been—
      (i)   the chairman or chief executive of, or
      (ii) another member of, or
      (iii) another member of the staff of,
      the National Policing Improvement Agency;

(e)   he [. . .] has been a member of the National Criminal Intelligence Service or the
      National Crime Squad; or

(f)   he is or has at any time been a member of a body of constables which at the time of
      his membership is or was a body of constables in relation to which any procedures
      are or were in force by virtue of an agreement or order under—
      (i)   section 26 of this Act; or
      (ii) section 78 of the 1996 Act or section 96 of the 1984 Act (which made provision
            corresponding to that made by section 26 of this Act).

[. . .]

10 GENERAL FUNCTIONS OF THE COMMISSION

(1)   The functions of the Commission shall be—
      (a)   to secure the maintenance by the Commission itself, and by local policing bodies and
            chief officers, of suitable arrangements with respect to the matters mentioned in
            subsection (2);
      (b)   to keep under review all arrangements maintained with respect to those matters;
      (c)   to secure that arrangements maintained with respect to those matters comply with the
            requirements of the following provisions of this Part, are efficient and effective and
            contain and manifest an appropriate degree of independence;
      (d)   to secure that public confidence is established and maintained in the existence of
            suitable arrangements with respect to those matters and with the operation of the
            arrangements that are in fact maintained with respect to those matters;
      (e)   to make such recommendations, and to give such advice, for the modification of the
            arrangements maintained with respect to those matters, and also of police practice in
            relation to other matters, as appear, from the carrying out by the Commission of its
            other functions, to be necessary or desirable; [. . .]
      (f)   to such extent as it may be required to do so by regulations made by the Secretary of
            State, to carry out functions in relation to [. . .] bodies of constables maintained
            otherwise than by local policing bodies which broadly correspond to those conferred
            on the Commission in relation to police forces by the preceding paragraphs of this
            subsection. [. . .]
      (g)   to carry out functions in relation to the Serious Organised Crime Agency which
            correspond to those conferred on the Commission in relation to police forces by
            paragraph (e) of this subsection.] [; and
      (h)   to carry out functions in relation to the National Policing Improvement Agency which
            correspond to those conferred on the Commission in relation to police forces by
            paragraph (e) of this subsection.

(2)   Those matters are—
      (a)   the handling of complaints made about the conduct of persons serving with the police;
      (b)   the recording of matters from which it appears that there may have been conduct by
            such persons which constitutes or involves the commission of a criminal offence or
            behaviour justifying disciplinary proceedings;

(ba) the recording of matters from which it appears that a person has died or suffered serious injury during, or following, contact with a person serving with the police;.

(c)   the manner in which any such complaints or any such matters as are mentioned in paragraph (b) [or (ba)] are investigated or otherwise handled and dealt with.

[. . .]

11   REPORTS TO THE SECRETARY OF STATE

(1)   As soon as practicable after the end of each of its financial years, the Commission shall make a report to the Secretary of State on the carrying out of its functions during that year.

(2)   The Commission shall also make such reports to the Secretary of State about matters relating generally to the carrying out of its functions as he may, from time to time, require.

[. . .]

Application of Part 2

12   COMPLAINTS, MATTERS AND PERSONS TO WHICH PART 2 APPLIES

(1)   In this Part references to a complaint are references (subject to the following provisions of this section) to any complaint about the conduct of a person serving with the police which is made (whether in writing or otherwise) by—

(a)   a member of the public who claims to be the person in relation to whom the conduct took place;

(b)   a member of the public not falling within paragraph (a) who claims to have been adversely affected by the conduct;

(c)   a member of the public who claims to have witnessed the conduct;

(d)   a person acting on behalf of a person falling within any of paragraphs (a) to (c).

(2)   In this Part "conduct matter" means (subject to the following provisions of this section, paragraph 2(4) of Schedule 3 and any regulations made by virtue of section 23(2)(d)) any matter which is not and has not been the subject of a complaint but in the case of which there is an indication (whether from the circumstances or otherwise) that a person serving with the police may have—

(a)   committed a criminal offence; or

(b)   behaved in a manner which would justify the bringing of disciplinary proceedings.

[(2A) In this Part "death or serious injury matter" (or "DSI matter" for short) means any circumstances (other than those which are or have been the subject of a complaint or which amount to a conduct matter)—

(a)   in or in consequence of which a person has died or has sustained serious injury; and

(b)   in relation to which the requirements of either subsection (2B) or subsection (2C) are satisfied.

(2B) The requirements of this subsection are that at the time of the death or serious injury the person—

(a)   had been arrested by a person serving with the police and had not been released from that arrest; or

(b)   was otherwise detained in the custody of a person serving with the police.

(2C) The requirements of this subsection are that—
  (a) at or before the time of the death or serious injury the person had contact (of whatever kind, and whether direct or indirect) with a person serving with the police who was acting in the execution of his duties; and
  (b) there is an indication that the contact may have caused (whether directly or indirectly) or contributed to the death or serious injury.

(2D) In subsection (2A) the reference to a person includes a person serving with the police, but in relation to such a person "contact" in subsection (2C) does not include contact that he has whilst acting in the execution of his duties.]

(3) The complaints that are complaints for the purposes of this Part by virtue of subsection (1)(b) do not, except in a case falling within subsection (4), include any made by or on behalf of a person who claims to have been adversely affected as a consequence only of having seen or heard the conduct, or any of the alleged effects of the conduct.

(4) A case falls within this subsection if—
  (a) it was only because the person in question was physically present, or sufficiently nearby, when the conduct took place or the effects occurred that he was able to see or hear the conduct or its effects; or
  (b) the adverse effect is attributable to, or was aggravated by, the fact that the person in relation to whom the conduct took place was already known to the person claiming to have suffered the adverse effect.

(5) For the purposes of this section a person shall be taken to have witnessed conduct if, and only if—
  (a) he acquired his knowledge of that conduct in a manner which would make him a competent witness capable of giving admissible evidence of that conduct in criminal proceedings; or
  (b) he has in his possession or under his control anything which would in any such proceedings constitute admissible evidence of that conduct.

(6) For the purposes of this Part a person falling within subsection 1(a) to (c) to shall not be taken to have authorised another person to act on his behalf unless—
  (a) that other person is for the time being designated for the purposes of this Part by the Commission as a person through whom complaints may be made, or he is of a description of persons so designated; or
  (b) the other person has been given, and is able to produce, the written consent to his so acting of the person on whose behalf he acts.

(7) For the purposes of this Part, a person is serving with the police if—
  (a) he is a member of a police force;
  (aa) he is a civilian employee of a police force;
  (b) he is an employee of the Common Council of the City of London who is under the direction and control of a chief officer; or
  (c) he is a special constable who is under the direction and control of a chief officer.

Co-operation, assistance and information

15 GENERAL DUTIES OF LOCAL POLICING BODIES, CHIEF OFFICERS AND INSPECTORS

(1) It shall be the duty of—
  (a) every local policing body maintaining a police force,
  (b) the chief officer of police of every police force, and

(c) every inspector of constabulary carrying out any of his functions in relation to a police force,
to ensure that it or he is kept informed, in relation to that force, about all matters falling within subsection (2).

[. . .]

(2) Those matters are—
(a) matters with respect to which any provision of this Part has effect;
(b) anything which is done under or for the purposes of any such provision; and
(c) any obligations to act or refrain from acting that have arisen by or under this Part but have not yet been complied with, or have been contravened.

(3) Where—
(a) a local policing body maintaining any police force requires the chief officer of that force or of any other force to provide a member of his force for appointment under paragraph 16, 17 or 18 of Schedule 3,
(b) the chief officer of police of any police force requires the chief officer of police of any other police force to provide a member of that other force for appointment under any of those paragraphs, or
(c) a local policing body or chief officer requires the Director General of the Serious Organised Crime Agency to provide a member of the staff of that Agency for appointment under any of those paragraphs,
it shall be the duty of the chief officer [to whom the requirement is addressed or of the Director General to comply with it.

(4) It shall be the duty of—
(a) every local policing body maintaining a police force,
(b) the chief officer of police of every police force, and
(c) the Serious Organised Crime Agency,
to provide the Commission and every member of the Commission's staff with all such assistance as the Commission or that member of staff may reasonably require for the purposes of, or in connection with, the carrying out of any investigation by the Commission under this Part.

(5) It shall be the duty of—
(a) every local policing body maintaining a police force,
(b) the chief officer of every police force, and
[c) the Serious Organised Crime Agency
to ensure that a person appointed under paragraph 16, 17 or 18 of Schedule 3 to carry out an investigation is given all such assistance and co-operation in the carrying out of that investigation as that person may reasonably require

[. . .]

[. . .]

17 PROVISION OF INFORMATION TO THE COMMISSION

(1) It shall be the duty of—
(a) every local policing body, and
(b) every chief officer,
at such times, in such circumstances and in accordance with such other requirements as may be set out in regulations made by the Secretary of State, to provide the Commission with all such information and documents as may be specified or described in regulations so made.

(2)   It shall also be the duty of every local policing body and of every chief officer—
    (a) to provide the Commission with all such other information and documents specified
        or described in a notification given by the Commission to that body or chief officer,
        and
    (b) to produce or deliver up to the Commission all such evidence and other things so
        specified or described,
    as appear to the Commission to be required by it for the purposes of the carrying out of
    any of its functions.

(3)   Anything falling to be provided, produced or delivered up by any person in pursuance
    of a requirement imposed under subsection (2) must be provided, produced or delivered
    up in such form, in such manner and within such period as may be specified in—
    (a) the notification imposing the requirement; or
    (b) in any subsequent notification given by the Commission to that person for the
        purposes of this subsection.

(4)   Nothing in this section shall require a police authority or chief officer—
    (a) to provide the Commission with any information or document, or to produce or
        deliver up any other thing, before the earliest time at which it is practicable for that
        authority or chief officer to do so; or
    (b) to provide, produce or deliver up anything at all in a case in which it never becomes
        practicable for that authority or chief officer to do so.

(5)   A requirement imposed by any regulations or notification under this section may authorise
    or require information or documents to which it relates to be provided to the Commission
    electronically.

    [. . .]

18 INSPECTIONS OF POLICE PREMISES ON BEHALF OF THE COMMISSION

(1)   Where—
    (a) the Commission requires—
        (i)   a local policing body maintaining any police force, or
        (ii) the chief officer of police of any such force,
        to allow a person nominated for the purpose by the Commission to have access to
        any premises occupied for the purposes of that force and to documents and other
        things on those premises, and
    (b) the requirement is imposed for any of the purposes mentioned in subsection (2),
    it shall be the duty of the body or, as the case may be, of the chief officer to secure that
    the required access is allowed to the nominated person.

(2)   Those purposes are—
    (a) the purposes of any examination by the Commission of the efficiency and
        effectiveness of the arrangements made by the force in question for handling
        complaints or dealing with recordable conduct matters [or DSI matters];
    (b) the purposes of any investigation by the Commission under this Part or of any
        investigation carried out under its supervision or management.

(3)   A requirement imposed under this section for the purposes mentioned in subsection (2)(a)
    must be notified to the body or chief officer at least 48 hours before the time at which
    access is required.

(4)   Where—
    (a) a requirement imposed under this section for the purposes mentioned in subsection (2)(a) requires access to any premises, document or thing to be allowed to any person, but
    (b) there are reasonable grounds for not allowing that person to have the required access at the time at which he seeks to have it,
the obligation to secure that the required access is allowed shall have effect as an obligation to secure that the access is allowed to that person at the earliest practicable time after there cease to be any such grounds as that person may specify.

    [. . .]

19 USE OF INVESTIGATORY POWERS BY OR ON BEHALF OF THE COMMISSION

(1)   The Secretary of State may by order make such provision as he thinks appropriate for the purpose of authorising—
    (a) the use of directed and intrusive surveillance, and
    (b) the conduct and use of covert human intelligence sources,
for the purposes of, or for purposes connected with, the carrying out of the Commission's functions.

(2)   An order under this section may, for the purposes of or in connection with any such provision as is mentioned in subsection (1), provide for—
    (a) Parts 2 and 4 the Regulation of Investigatory Powers Act 2000 (c. 23) (surveillance and covert human intelligence sources and scrutiny of investigatory powers), and
    (b) Part 3 of the 1997 Act (authorisations in respect of property),
to have effect with such modifications as may be specified in the order.

    [. . .]

20 DUTY TO KEEP THE COMPLAINANT INFORMED

(1)   In any case in which there is an investigation of a complaint in accordance with the provisions of Schedule 3—
    (a) by the Commission, or
    (b) under its management,
it shall be the duty of the Commission to provide the complainant with all such information as will keep him properly informed, while the investigation is being carried out and subsequently, of all the matters mentioned in subsection (4).

(2)   In any case in which there is an investigation of a complaint in accordance with the provisions of Schedule 3—
    (a) by the appropriate authority on its own behalf, or
    (b) under the supervision of the Commission,
it shall be the duty of the appropriate authority to provide the complainant with all such information as will keep him properly informed, while the investigation is being carried out and subsequently, of all the matters mentioned in subsection (4).

(3)   Where subsection (2) applies, it shall be the duty of the Commission to give the appropriate authority all such directions as it considers appropriate for securing that that authority complies with its duty under that subsection; and it shall be the duty of the appropriate authority to comply with any direction given to it under this subsection.

(4)   The matters of which the complainant must be kept properly informed are—
    (a)   the progress of the investigation;
    (b)   any provisional findings of the person carrying out the investigation;
    (c)   whether any report has been submitted under paragraph 22 of Schedule 3;
    (d)   the action (if any) that is taken in respect of the matters dealt with in any such report; and
    (e)   the outcome of any such action.

(5)   The duties imposed by this section on the Commission and the appropriate authority in relation to any complaint shall be performed in such manner, and shall have effect subject to such exceptions, as may be provided for by regulations made by the Secretary of State.

(6)   The Secretary of State shall not by regulations provide for any exceptions from the duties imposed by this section except so far as he considers it necessary to do so for the purpose of—
    (a)   preventing the premature or inappropriate disclosure of information that is relevant to, or may be used in, any actual or prospective criminal proceedings;
    (b)   preventing the disclosure of information in any circumstances in which it has been determined in accordance with the regulations that its non-disclosure—
        (i)   is in the interests of national security;
        (ii)   is for the purposes of the prevention or detection of crime, or the apprehension or prosecution of offenders;
        (iii)   is required on proportionality grounds; or
        (iv)   is otherwise necessary in the public interest.

(7)   The non-disclosure of information is required on proportionality grounds if its disclosure would cause, directly or indirectly, an adverse effect which would be disproportionate to the benefits arising from its disclosure.

(8)   Regulations under this section may include provision framed by reference to the opinion of, or a determination by, the Commission or any local policing body or chief officer.

(9)   It shall be the duty of a person appointed to carry out an investigation under this Part to provide the Commission or, as the case may be, the appropriate authority with all such information as the Commission or that authority may reasonably require for the purpose of performing its duty under this section.

[. . .]

Part 4 POLICE POWERS ETC.

[. . .]

Chapter 2 PROVISIONS MODIFYING AND SUPPLEMENTING POLICE POWERS

[. . .] Power to require name and address

50 PERSONS ACTING IN AN ANTI-SOCIAL MANNER

(1)   If a constable in uniform has reason to believe that a person has been acting, or is acting, in an anti-social manner (within the meaning of section 1 of the Crime and Disorder Act 1998 (c. 37) (anti-social behaviour orders)), he may require that person to give his name and address to the constable.

    [. . .]

[. . .]

As amended by Police Reform and Social Responsibility Act 2011, Schedule 16, paragraph 278, 281, 284, 285, 286

ANTI-SOCIAL BEHAVIOUR ACT 2003
(c. 38)

An Act to make provision in connection with anti-social behaviour.

[. . .]

Part 1 PREMISES WHERE DRUGS USED UNLAWFULLY

1 CLOSURE NOTICE

(1)   This section applies to premises if a police officer not below the rank of superintendent (the authorising officer) has reasonable grounds for believing—
    (a)   that at any time during the relevant period the premises have been used in connection with the unlawful use, production or supply of a Class A controlled drug, and
    (b)   that the use of the premises is associated with the occurrence of disorder or serious nuisance to members of the public.

(2)   The authorising officer may authorise the issue of a closure notice in respect of premises to which this section applies if he is satisfied—
    (a)   that the local authority for the area in which the premises are situated has been consulted;
    (b)   that reasonable steps have been taken to establish the identity of any person who lives on the premises or who has control of or responsibility for or an interest in the premises.

(3)   An authorisation under subsection (2) may be given orally or in writing, but if it is given orally the authorising officer must confirm it in writing as soon as it is practicable.

    [. . .]

2 CLOSURE ORDER

(1)   If a closure notice has been issued under section 1 a constable must apply under this section to a magistrates' court for the making of a closure order.

(2)   The application must be heard by the magistrates' court not later than 48 hours after the notice was served in pursuance of section 1(6)(a).

(3)   The magistrates' court may make a closure order if and only if it is satisfied that each of the following paragraphs applies—
    (a)   the premises in respect of which the closure notice was issued have been used in connection with the unlawful use, production or supply of a Class A controlled drug;
    (b)   the use of the premises is associated with the occurrence of disorder or serious nuisance to members of the public;
    (c)   the making of the order is necessary to prevent the occurrence of such disorder or serious nuisance for the period specified in the order.

(4)   A closure order is an order that the premises in respect of which the order is made are closed to all persons for such period (not exceeding three months) as the court decides.

(5)   But the order may include such provision as the court thinks appropriate relating to access to any part of the building or structure of which the premises form part.

[. . .]

[. . .]

Part 4 DISPERSAL OF GROUPS ETC.

30 DISPERSAL OF GROUPS AND REMOVAL OF PERSONS UNDER 16 TO THEIR PLACE OF RESIDENCE

(1)   This section applies where a relevant officer has reasonable grounds for believing—
   (a) that any members of the public have been intimidated, harassed, alarmed or distressed as a result of the presence or behaviour of groups of two or more persons in public places in any locality in his police area (the "relevant locality"), and
   (b) that anti-social behaviour is a significant and persistent problem in the relevant locality.

(2)   The relevant officer may give an authorisation that the powers conferred on a constable in uniform by subsections (3) to (6) are to be exercisable for a period specified in the authorisation which does not exceed 6 months.

(3)   Subsection (4) applies if a constable in uniform has reasonable grounds for believing that the presence or behaviour of a group of two or more persons in any public place in the relevant locality has resulted, or is likely to result, in any members of the public being intimidated, harassed, alarmed or distressed.

(4)   The constable may give one or more of the following directions, namely—
   (a) a direction requiring the persons in the group to disperse (either immediately or by such time as he may specify and in such way as he may specify),
   (b) a direction requiring any of those persons whose place of residence is not within the relevant locality to leave the relevant locality or any part of the relevant locality (either immediately or by such time as he may specify and in such way as he may specify), and
   (c) a direction prohibiting any of those persons whose place of residence is not within the relevant locality from returning to the relevant locality or any part of the relevant locality for such period (not exceeding 24 hours) from the giving of the direction as he may specify;
but this subsection is subject to subsection (5).

(5)   A direction under subsection (4) may not be given in respect of a group of persons—

   [. . .]

   (b) who are taking part in a public procession of the kind mentioned in section 11(1) of the Public Order Act 1986 (c. 64) in respect of which—
      (i)   written notice has been given in accordance with section 11 of that Act, or
      (ii) such notice is not required to be given as provided by subsections (1) and (2) of that section.

(6)   If, between the hours of 9pm and 6am, a constable in uniform finds a person in any public place in the relevant locality who he has reasonable grounds for believing—
   (a) is under the age of 16, and
   (b) is not under the effective control of a parent or a responsible person aged 18 or over,

he may remove the person to the person's place of residence unless he has reasonable grounds for believing that the person would, if removed to that place, be likely to suffer significant harm.

[. . .]

31 AUTHORISATIONS: SUPPLEMENTAL

(1)   An authorisation—
   (a)   must be in writing,
   (b)   must be signed by the relevant officer giving it, and
   (c)   must specify—
      (i)   the relevant locality,
      (ii)   the grounds on which the authorisation is given, and
      (iii)   the period during which the powers conferred by section 30(3) to (6) are exercisable.

(2)   An authorisation may not be given without the consent of the local authority or each local authority whose area includes the whole or part of the relevant locality.

[. . .]

[. . .]

36 INTERPRETATION

In this Part—
   "anti-social behaviour" means behaviour by a person which causes or is likely to cause harassment, alarm or distress to one or more other persons not of the same household as the person,

   "local authority" means—
   (a)   in relation to England, a district council, a county council that is the council for a county in which there are no district councils, a London borough council, the Common Council of the City of London or the Council of the Isles of Scilly,
   (b)   in relation to Wales, a county council or a county borough council,

   "public place" means—
   (a)   any highway, and
   (b)   any place to which at the material time the public or any section of the public has access, on payment or otherwise, as of right or by virtue of express or implied permission,
      [. . .]

[. . .]

CRIMINAL JUSTICE ACT 2003
(c. 44)

An Act to make provision about criminal justice (including the powers and duties of the police) and about dealing with offenders; to amend the law relating to jury service; to amend Chapter 1 of Part 1 of the Crime and Disorder Act 1998 and Part 5 of the Police Act 1997; to make provision about civil proceedings brought by offenders; and for connected purposes.

[. . .]

Part 3 CONDITIONAL CAUTIONS

22 CONDITIONAL CAUTIONS

(1)   An authorised person may give a conditional caution to a person aged 18 or over ("the offender") if each of the five requirements in section 23 is satisfied.

(2)   In this Part "conditional caution" means a caution which is given in respect of an offence committed by the offender and which has conditions attached to it with which the offender must comply.

[(3) The conditions which may be attached to such a caution are those which have one or more of the following objects—
      (a) facilitating the rehabilitation of the offender;
      (b) ensuring that the offender makes reparation for the offence;
      (c) punishing the offender.]
      [. . .]

(4)   In this Part "authorised person" means—
      (a) a constable,
      (b) an investigating officer, or
      (c) a person authorised by a relevant prosecutor for the purposes of this section.

23 THE FIVE REQUIREMENTS

(1)   The first requirement is that the authorised person has evidence that the offender has committed an offence.

(2)   The second requirement is that a relevant prosecutor decides—
      (a) that there is sufficient evidence to charge the offender with the offence, and
      (b) that a conditional caution should be given to the offender in respect of the offence.

(3)   The third requirement is that the offender admits to the authorised person that he committed the offence.

(4)   The fourth requirement is that the authorised person explains the effect of the conditional caution to the offender and warns him that failure to comply with any of the conditions attached to the caution may result in his being prosecuted for the offence.

(5)   The fifth requirement is that the offender signs a document which contains—
      (a) details of the offence,
      (b) an admission by him that he committed the offence,
      (c) his consent to being given the conditional caution, and
      (d) the conditions attached to the caution.

24 FAILURE TO COMPLY WITH CONDITIONS

(1)   If the offender fails, without reasonable excuse, to comply with any of the conditions attached to the conditional caution, criminal proceedings may be instituted against the person for the offence in question.

[. . .]

24A ARREST FOR FAILURE TO COMPLY

(1)   If a constable has reasonable grounds for believing that the offender has failed, without reasonable excuse, to comply with any of the conditions attached to the conditional caution, he may arrest him without warrant.

(2)   A person arrested under this section must be—
    (a)   charged with the offence in question,
    (b)   released without charge and on bail to enable a decision to be made as to whether he should be charged with the offence, or
    (c)   released without charge and without bail (with or without any variation in the conditions attached to the caution).]
    [. . .]

Part 10 RETRIAL FOR SERIOUS OFFENCES

Cases that may be retried

75 CASES THAT MAY BE RETRIED

(1)   This Part applies where a person has been acquitted of a qualifying offence in proceedings—
    (a)   on indictment in England and Wales,
    (b)   on appeal against a conviction, verdict or finding in proceedings on indictment in England and Wales, or
    (c)   on appeal from a decision on such an appeal.
[. . .]

Application for retrial

76 APPLICATION TO COURT OF APPEAL

(1)   A prosecutor may apply to the Court of Appeal for an order—
    (a)   quashing a person's acquittal in proceedings within section 75(1), and
    (b)   ordering him to be retried for the qualifying offence.
[. . .]

77 DETERMINATION BY COURT OF APPEAL

(1)   On an application under section 76(1), the Court of Appeal—
    (a)   if satisfied that the requirements of sections 78 and 79 are met, must make the order applied for;
    (b)   otherwise, must dismiss the application.
[. . .]

78 NEW AND COMPELLING EVIDENCE

(1)   The requirements of this section are met if there is new and compelling evidence against the acquitted person in relation to the qualifying offence.

(2)   Evidence is new if it was not adduced in the proceedings in which the person was acquitted (nor, if those were appeal proceedings, in earlier proceedings to which the appeal related).

(3)   Evidence is compelling if—
    (a)   it is reliable,
    (b)   it is substantial, and
    (c)   in the context of the outstanding issues, it appears highly probative of the case against the acquitted person.
[. . .]

79 INTERESTS OF JUSTICE

(1)   The requirements of this section are met if in all the circumstances it is in the interests of justice for the court to make the order under section 77.

(2)   That question is to be determined having regard in particular to—
       (a)   whether existing circumstances make a fair trial unlikely;
       (b)   for the purposes of that question and otherwise, the length of time since the qualifying offence was allegedly committed;
       (c)   whether it is likely that the new evidence would have been adduced in the earlier proceedings against the acquitted person but for a failure by an officer or by a prosecutor to act with due diligence or expedition;
       (d)   whether, since those proceedings or, if later, since the commencement of this Part, any officer or prosecutor has failed to act with due diligence or expedition.

[. . .]

CONSTITUTIONAL REFORM ACT 2005
(c. 4)

An Act to make provision for modifying the office of Lord Chancellor, and to make provision relating to the functions of that office; to establish a Supreme Court of the United Kingdom, and to abolish the appellate jurisdiction of the House of Lords; to make provision about the jurisdiction of the Judicial Committee of the Privy Council and the judicial functions of the President of the Council; to make other provision about the judiciary, their appointment and discipline; and for connected purposes.

[. . .]

Part 1 THE RULE OF LAW

1 THE RULE OF LAW

This Act does not adversely affect—
(a)   the existing constitutional principle of the rule of law, or

(b)   the Lord Chancellor's existing constitutional role in relation to that principle.

Part 2 ARRANGEMENTS TO MODIFY THE OFFICE OF LORD CHANCELLOR

Qualifications for office of Lord Chancellor

2 LORD CHANCELLOR TO BE QUALIFIED BY EXPERIENCE

(1)   A person may not be recommended for appointment as Lord Chancellor unless he appears to the Prime Minister to be qualified by experience.

(2)   The Prime Minister may take into account any of these—
       (a)   experience as a Minister of the Crown;
       (b)   experience as a member of either House of Parliament;
       (c)   experience as a qualifying practitioner;
       (d)   experience as a teacher of law in a university;
       (e)   other experience that the Prime Minister considers relevant.

(3)   In this section "qualifying practitioner" means any of these—
    (a)   a person who has a Senior Courts qualification, within the meaning of section 71 of the Courts and Legal Services Act 1990 (c. 41);
    (b)   an advocate in Scotland or a solicitor entitled to appear in the Court of Session and the High Court of Justiciary;
    (c)   a member of the Bar of Northern Ireland or a solicitor of the Court of Judicature of Northern Ireland.

Continued judicial independence

3   GUARANTEE OF CONTINUED JUDICIAL INDEPENDENCE

(1)   The Lord Chancellor, other Ministers of the Crown and all with responsibility for matters relating to the judiciary or otherwise to the administration of justice must uphold the continued independence of the judiciary.

    [. . .]

(5)   The Lord Chancellor and other Ministers of the Crown must not seek to influence particular judicial decisions through any special access to the judiciary.

(6)   The Lord Chancellor must have regard to—
    (a)   the need to defend that independence;
    (b)   the need for the judiciary to have the support necessary to enable them to exercise their functions;
    (c)   the need for the public interest in regard to matters relating to the judiciary or otherwise to the administration of justice to be properly represented in decisions affecting those matters.

(7)   In this section "the judiciary" includes the judiciary of any of the following—
    (a)   the Supreme Court;
    (b)   any other court established under the law of any part of the United Kingdom;
    (c)   any international court.
    [. . .]

(8)   In subsection (7) "international court" means the International Court of Justice or any other court or tribunal which exercises jurisdiction, or performs functions of a judicial nature, in pursuance of—
    (a)   an agreement to which the United Kingdom or Her Majesty's Government in the United Kingdom is a party, or
    (b)   a resolution of the Security Council or General Assembly of the United Nations.
    [. . .]

Part 3   THE SUPREME COURT

The Supreme Court

23   THE SUPREME COURT

(1)   There is to be a Supreme Court of the United Kingdom.

(2)   The Court consists of 12 judges appointed by Her Majesty by letters patent.

(3)   Her Majesty may from time to time by Order in Council amend subsection (2) so as to increase or further increase the number of judges of the Court.

(4)   No recommendation may be made to Her Majesty in Council to make an Order under subsection (3) unless a draft of the Order has been laid before and approved by resolution of each House of Parliament.

(5)   Her Majesty may by letters patent appoint one of the judges to be President and one to be Deputy President of the Court.

(6)   The judges other than the President and Deputy President are to be styled "Justices of the Supreme Court".

(7)   The Court is to be taken to be duly constituted despite any vacancy among the judges of the Court or in the office of President or Deputy President.

24 FIRST MEMBERS OF THE COURT

On the commencement of section 23—
(a)   the persons who immediately before that commencement are Lords of Appeal in Ordinary become judges of the Supreme Court,

(b)   the person who immediately before that commencement is the senior Lord of Appeal in Ordinary becomes the President of the Court, and

(c)   the person who immediately before that commencement is the second senior Lord of Appeal in Ordinary becomes the Deputy President of the Court.

Appointment of judges

25 QUALIFICATION FOR APPOINTMENT

(1)   A person is not qualified to be appointed a judge of the Supreme Court unless he has (at any time)—
(a) held high judicial office for a period of at least 2 years, [. . .]
[(b) satisfied the judicial-appointment eligibility condition on a 15-year basis, or
(c) been a qualifying practitioner for a period of at least 15 years.]

(2)   A person is a qualifying practitioner for the purposes of this section at any time when—

[. . .]

(b) he is an advocate in Scotland or a solicitor entitled to appear in the Court of Session and the High Court of Justiciary, or
(c) he is a member of the Bar of Northern Ireland or a solicitor of the Court of Judicature of Northern Ireland.

26 SELECTION OF MEMBERS OF THE COURT

(1)   This section applies to a recommendation for an appointment to one of the following offices—
(a) judge of the Supreme Court;
(b) President of the Court;
(c) Deputy President of the Court.

(2)   A recommendation may be made only by the Prime Minister.

(3)   The Prime Minister—
(a) must recommend any person whose name is notified to him under section 29;
(b) may not recommend any other person.

(4)   A person who is not a judge of the Court must be recommended for appointment as a judge if his name is notified to the Prime Minister for an appointment as President or Deputy President.

(5)   If there is a vacancy in one of the offices mentioned in subsection (1), or it appears to him that there will soon be such a vacancy, the Lord Chancellor must convene a selection commission for the selection of a person to be recommended.

[. . .]

(8)   Sections 27 to 31 apply where a selection commission is convened under this section.

27 SELECTION PROCESS

(1)   The commission must—
(a) determine the selection process to be applied,
(b) apply the selection process, and
(c) make a selection accordingly.

(2)   As part of the selection process the commission must consult each of the following—
(a) such of the senior judges as are not members of the commission and are not willing to be considered for selection;
(b) the Lord Chancellor;
(c) the First Minister in Scotland;
(d) [the First Minister for Wales];
(e) the Secretary of State for Northern Ireland.

(3)   If for any part of the United Kingdom no judge of the courts of that part is to be consulted under subsection (2)(a), the commission must consult as part of the selection process the most senior judge of the courts of that part who is not a member of the commission and is not willing to be considered for selection.

(4)   Subsections (5) to (10) apply to any selection under this section or section 31.

(5)   Selection must be on merit.

(6)   A person may be selected only if he meets the requirements of section 25.

(7)   A person may not be selected if he is a member of the commission.

(8)   In making selections for the appointment of judges of the Court the commission must ensure that between them the judges will have knowledge of, and experience of practice in, the law of each part of the United Kingdom.

(9)   The commission must have regard to any guidance given by the Lord Chancellor as to matters to be taken into account (subject to any other provision of this Act) in making a selection.

(10)   Any selection must be of one person only.

28 REPORT

(1)   After complying with section 27 the commission must submit a report to the Lord Chancellor.

(2)   The report must—
(a) state who has been selected;
(b) state the senior judges consulted under section 27(2)(a) and any judge consulted under section 27(3);
(c) contain any other information required by the Lord Chancellor.

(3)   The report must be in a form approved by the Lord Chancellor.

(4)   After submitting the report the commission must provide any further information the Lord Chancellor may require.

(5)   When he receives the report the Lord Chancellor must consult each of the following—
(a)   the senior judges consulted under section 27(2)(a);
(b)   any judge consulted under section 27(3);
(c)   the First Minister in Scotland;
(d)   [the First Minister for Wales];
(e)   the Secretary of State for Northern Ireland.

29 THE LORD CHANCELLOR'S OPTIONS

(1)   This section refers to the following stages—

Stage 1: where a person has been selected under section 27
Stage 2: where a person has been selected following a rejection or reconsideration at stage 1
Stage 3: where a person has been selected following a rejection or reconsideration at stage 2.

(2)   At stage 1 the Lord Chancellor must do one of the following—
(a)   notify the selection;
(b)   reject the selection;
(c)   require the commission to reconsider the selection.

(3)   At stage 2 the Lord Chancellor must do one of the following—
(a)   notify the selection;
(b)   reject the selection, but only if it was made following a reconsideration at stage 1;
(c)   require the commission to reconsider the selection, but only if it was made following a rejection at stage 1.

(4)   At stage 3 the Lord Chancellor must notify the selection, unless subsection (5) applies and he makes a notification under it.

(5)   If a person whose selection the Lord Chancellor required to be reconsidered at stage 1 or 2 was not selected again at the next stage, the Lord Chancellor may at stage 3 notify that person's name to the Prime Minister.

(6)   In this Part references to the Lord Chancellor notifying a selection are references to his notifying to the Prime Minister the name of the person selected.

30 EXERCISE OF POWERS TO REJECT OR REQUIRE RECONSIDERATION

(1)   The power of the Lord Chancellor under section 29 to reject a selection at stage 1 or 2 is exercisable only on the grounds that, in the Lord Chancellor's opinion, the person selected is not suitable for the office concerned.

(2)   The power of the Lord Chancellor under section 29 to require the commission to reconsider a selection at stage 1 or 2 is exercisable only on the grounds that, in the Lord Chancellor's opinion—
(a)   there is not enough evidence that the person is suitable for the office concerned,
(b)   there is evidence that the person is not the best candidate on merit, or

(c) there is not enough evidence that if the person were appointed the judges of the Court would between them have knowledge of, and experience of practice in, the law of each part of the United Kingdom.

(3) The Lord Chancellor must give the commission reasons in writing for rejecting or requiring reconsideration of a selection.

31 SELECTION FOLLOWING REJECTION OR REQUIREMENT TO RECONSIDER

(1) If under section 29 the Lord Chancellor rejects or requires reconsideration of a selection at stage 1 or 2, the commission must select a person in accordance with this section.

(2) If the Lord Chancellor rejects a selection, the commission—
(a) may not select the person rejected, and
(b) where the rejection is following reconsideration of a selection, may not select the person (if different) whose selection it reconsidered.

(3) If the Lord Chancellor requires a selection to be reconsidered, the commission—
(a) may select the same person or a different person, but
(b) where the requirement is following a rejection, may not select the person rejected.

(4) The commission must inform the Lord Chancellor of the person selected following a rejection or requirement to reconsider.

[. . .]

33 TENURE

A judge of the Supreme Court holds that office during good behaviour, but may be removed from it on the address of both Houses of Parliament.

[. . .]

Jurisdiction, relation to other courts etc.

40 JURISDICTION

(1) The Supreme Court is a superior court of record.

(2) An appeal lies to the Court from any order or judgment of the Court of Appeal in England and Wales in civil proceedings.

(3) An appeal lies to the Court from any order or judgment of a court in Scotland if an appeal lay from that court to the House of Lords at or immediately before the commencement of this section.

[. . .]

(5) The Court has power to determine any question necessary to be determined for the purposes of doing justice in an appeal to it under any enactment.

(6) An appeal under subsection (2) lies only with the permission of the Court of Appeal or the Supreme Court; but this is subject to provision under any other enactment restricting such an appeal.

[. . .]

Composition for proceedings

42 COMPOSITION

(1) The Supreme Court is duly constituted in any proceedings only if all of the following conditions are met—
(a) the Court consists of an uneven number of judges;
(b) the Court consists of at least three judges;
(c) more than half of those judges are permanent judges.
[. . .]

43 CHANGES IN COMPOSITION

(1) This section applies if in any proceedings the Court ceases to be duly constituted in accordance with section 42, or in accordance with a direction under this section, because one or more members of the Court are unable to continue.

(2) The presiding judge may direct that the Court is still duly constituted in the proceedings.

(3) The presiding judge may give a direction under this section only if—
(a) the parties agree;
(b) the Court still consists of at least three judges (whether the number of judges is even or uneven);
(c) at least half of those judges are permanent judges.

(4) Subsections (2) and (3) are subject to directions given by the President of the Court.

(5) If in any proceedings the Court is duly constituted under this section with an even number of judges, and those judges are evenly divided, the case is to be re-argued in a Court which is constituted in accordance with section 42.

(6) In this section—
(a) "presiding judge" means the judge who is to preside, or is presiding, over proceedings;
[. . .]

[. . .]

Part 4 JUDICIAL APPOINTMENTS AND DISCIPLINE

Chapter 1 COMMISSION AND OMBUDSMAN

61 THE JUDICIAL APPOINTMENTS COMMISSION

(1) There is to be a body corporate called the Judicial Appointments Commission.

[. . .]

62 JUDICIAL APPOINTMENTS AND CONDUCT OMBUDSMAN

(1) There is to be a Judicial Appointments and Conduct Ombudsman.

[. . .]

Chapter 2 **APPOINTMENTS**

General provisions

63 MERIT AND GOOD CHARACTER

(1)   Subsections (2) and (3) apply to any selection under this Part by the Commission or a selection panel ("the selecting body").

(2)   Selection must be solely on merit.

(3)   A person must not be selected unless the selecting body is satisfied that he is of good character.

64 ENCOURAGEMENT OF DIVERSITY

(1)   The Commission, in performing its functions under this Part, must have regard to the need to encourage diversity in the range of persons available for selection for appointments.

(2)   This section is subject to section 63.

   [. . .]

Chapter 3 **DISCIPLINE**

Disciplinary powers

108 DISCIPLINARY POWERS

(1)   Any power of the Lord Chancellor to remove a person from an office listed in Schedule 14 is exercisable only after the Lord Chancellor has complied with prescribed procedures (as well as any other requirements to which the power is subject).

(2)   The Lord Chief Justice may exercise any of the following powers but only with the agreement of the Lord Chancellor and only after complying with prescribed procedures.

(3)   The Lord Chief Justice may give a judicial office holder formal advice, or a formal warning or reprimand, for disciplinary purposes (but this section does not restrict what he may do informally or for other purposes or where any advice or warning is not addressed to a particular office holder).

(4)   He may suspend a person from a judicial office for any period during which any of the following applies—
   (a) the person is subject to criminal proceedings;
   (b) the person is serving a sentence imposed in criminal proceedings;
   (c) the person has been convicted of an offence and is subject to prescribed procedures in relation to the conduct constituting the offence.

(5)   He may suspend a person from a judicial office for any period if—
   (a) the person has been convicted of a criminal offence,
   (b) it has been determined under prescribed procedures that the person should not be removed from office, and
   (c) it appears to the Lord Chief Justice with the agreement of the Lord Chancellor that the suspension is necessary for maintaining confidence in the judiciary.

(6)   He may suspend a person from office as a senior judge for any period during which the person is subject to proceedings for an Address.

(7)   He may suspend the holder of an office listed in Schedule 14 for any period during which the person—
(a) is under investigation for an offence, or
(b) is subject to prescribed procedures.

(8)   While a person is suspended under this section from any office he may not perform any of the functions of the office (but his other rights as holder of the office are not affected).

[. . .]

SERIOUS ORGANISED CRIME AND POLICE ACT 2005
(c. 15)

An Act to provide for the establishment and functions of the Serious Organised Crime Agency; to make provision about investigations, prosecutions, offenders and witnesses in criminal proceedings and the protection of persons involved in investigations or proceedings; to provide for the implementation of certain international obligations relating to criminal matters; to amend the Proceeds of Crime Act 2002; to make further provision for combatting crime and disorder, including new provision about powers of arrest and search warrants and about parental compensation orders; to make further provision about the police and policing and persons supporting the police; to make provision for protecting certain organisations from interference with their activities; to make provision about criminal records; to provide for the Private Security Industry Act 2001 to extend to Scotland; and for connected purposes.

[. . .]

Part 1 THE SERIOUS ORGANISED CRIME AGENCY

Chapter 1 SOCA: ESTABLISHMENT AND ACTIVITIES

Establishment of SOCA

1 ESTABLISHMENT OF SERIOUS ORGANISED CRIME AGENCY

(1)   There shall be a body corporate to be known as the Serious Organised Crime Agency ("SOCA").

[. . .]

Functions

2 FUNCTIONS OF SOCA AS TO SERIOUS ORGANISED CRIME

(1)   SOCA has the functions of—
(a) preventing and detecting serious organised crime, and
(b) contributing to the reduction of such crime in other ways and to the mitigation of its consequences.
[. . .]

3 FUNCTIONS OF SOCA AS TO INFORMATION RELATING TO CRIME

(1)   SOCA has the function of gathering, storing, analysing and disseminating information relevant to—
(a) the prevention, detection, investigation or prosecution of offences, [. . .]

(b) the reduction of crime in other ways or the mitigation of its consequences [; or

(c) exploitation proceeds investigations (within the meaning of section 341(5) of the Proceeds of Crime Act 2002) or exploitation proceeds orders within the meaning of Part 7 of the Coroners and Justice Act 2009 (or applications for such orders).]

(2) SOCA may disseminate such information to—
   (a) police forces within subsection (3),
   (b) special police forces,
   (c) law enforcement agencies, or
   (d) such other persons as it considers appropriate in connection with any of the matters mentioned in subsection [(1)(a), (b) or (c)].

(3) The police forces within this subsection are—
   (a) police forces in the United Kingdom, and
   (b) the States of Jersey Police Force, the salaried police force of the Island of Guernsey and the Isle of Man Constabulary.
   [. . .]

General powers

5 SOCA'S GENERAL POWERS

(1) SOCA has the general powers conferred by this section.

(2) SOCA may—
   (a) institute criminal proceedings in England and Wales or Northern Ireland;
   (b) at the request of the chief officer of a police force within section 3(3) or of a special police force, act in support of any activities of that force;
   (c) at the request of any law enforcement agency, act in support of any activities of that agency;
   (d) enter into other arrangements for co-operating with bodies or persons (in the United Kingdom or elsewhere) which it considers appropriate in connection with the exercise of any of SOCA's functions under section 2 or 3 [or mentioned in section 2A,] or any activities within subsection (3).

(3) Despite the references to serious organised crime in section 2(1), SOCA may carry on activities in relation to other crime if they are carried on for the purposes of any of the functions conferred on SOCA by section 2 or 3 [or mentioned in section 2A].

[. . .]

Part 2 INVESTIGATIONS, PROSECUTIONS, PROCEEDINGS AND PROCEEDS OF CRIME

Chapter 1 INVESTIGATORY POWERS OF DPP, ETC.

Introductory

60 INVESTIGATORY POWERS OF DPP ETC.

(1) This Chapter confers powers on—
   (a) the Director of Public Prosecutions,
   (b) the Director of Revenue and Customs Prosecutions [. . .]
   (c) the Lord Advocate, [and
   (d) the Director of Public Prosecutions for Northern Ireland,]
   in relation to the giving of disclosure notices in connection with the investigation of offences to which this Chapter applies [or in connection with a terrorist investigation].

   [. . .]

61 OFFENCES TO WHICH THIS CHAPTER APPLIES

(1)   This Chapter applies to the following offences—
    (a)   any offence listed in Schedule 2 to the Proceeds of Crime Act 2002 (c. 29) (lifestyle offences: England and Wales);
    (b)   any offence listed in Schedule 4 to that Act (lifestyle offences: Scotland);
    [(ba)   any offence listed in Schedule 5 to that Act (lifestyle offences: Northern Ireland);]
    (c)   any offence under sections 15 to 18 of the Terrorism Act 2000 (c. 11) (offences relating to fund-raising, money laundering etc.);
    [. . .]

    (e)   any offence under section 17 of the Theft Act 1968 (c. 60) [or section 17 of the Theft Act (Northern Ireland) 1969] (false accounting), or any offence at common law of cheating in relation to the public revenue, which is a qualifying offence;
    (f)   any offence under section 1 of the Criminal Attempts Act 1981 (c. 47) [or Article 3 of the Criminal Attempts and Conspiracy (Northern Ireland) Order 1983], or in Scotland at common law, of attempting to commit any offence in paragraph (c) or any offence in paragraph (d) or (e) which is a qualifying offence;
    (g)   any offence under section 1 of the Criminal Law Act 1977 (c. 45) [or Article 9 of the Criminal Attempts and Conspiracy (Northern Ireland) Order 1983], or in Scotland at common law, of conspiracy to commit any offence in paragraph (c) or any offence in paragraph (d) or (e) which is a qualifying offence.
    [(h)   in England and Wales—
        (i)   any common law offence of bribery;
        (ii)   any offence under section 1 of the Public Bodies Corrupt Practices Act 1889 (c. 69) (corruption in office);
        (iii)   the first two offences under section 1 of the Prevention of Corruption Act 1906 (c. 34) (bribes obtained by or given to agents).]

(2)   For the purposes of subsection (1) an offence in paragraph (d) or (e) of that subsection is a qualifying offence if the Investigating Authority certifies that in his opinion—
    (a)   in the case of an offence in paragraph (d) or an offence of cheating the public revenue, the offence involved or would have involved a loss, or potential loss, to the public revenue of an amount not less than £5,000;
    (b)   in the case of an offence under section 17 of the Theft Act 1968 (c. 60), the offence involved or would have involved a loss or gain, or potential loss or gain, of an amount not less than £5,000.
    [. . .]

Disclosure notices

62 DISCLOSURE NOTICES

(1)   If it appears to the Investigating Authority—
    (a)   that there are reasonable grounds for suspecting that an offence to which this Chapter applies has been committed,
    (b)   that any person has information (whether or not contained in a document) which relates to a matter relevant to the investigation of that offence, and
    (c)   that there are reasonable grounds for believing that information which may be provided by that person in compliance with a disclosure notice is likely to be of substantial value (whether or not by itself) to that investigation,
    he may give, or authorise an appropriate person to give, a disclosure notice to that person.

    [. . .]

(2)   In this Chapter "appropriate person" means—
(a) a constable,
(b) a member of the staff of SOCA who is for the time being designated under section 43, or
(c) an officer of Revenue and Customs.
But in the application of this Chapter to Northern Ireland, this subsection has effect as if paragraph (b) were omitted.

(3)   In this Chapter "disclosure notice" means a notice in writing requiring the person to whom it is given to do all or any of the following things in accordance with the specified requirements, namely—
(a) answer questions with respect to any matter relevant to the investigation;
(b) provide information with respect to any such matter as is specified in the notice;
(c) produce such documents, or documents of such descriptions, relevant to the investigation as are specified in the notice.

(4)   In subsection (3) "the specified requirements" means such requirements specified in the disclosure notice as relate to—
(a) the time at or by which,
(b) the place at which, or
(c) the manner in which,
the person to whom the notice is given is to do any of the things mentioned in paragraphs (a) to (c) of that subsection; and those requirements may include a requirement to do any of those things at once.

[. . .]

64 RESTRICTIONS ON REQUIRING INFORMATION ETC.

(1)   A person may not be required under section 62 or 63—
(a) to answer any privileged question,
(b) to provide any privileged information, or
(c) to produce any privileged document,
except that a lawyer may be required to provide the name and address of a client of his.

[. . .]

(8)   A person may not be required under section 62 or 63 to disclose any information or produce any document in respect of which he owes an obligation of confidence by virtue of carrying on any banking business, unless—
(a) the person to whom the obligation of confidence is owed consents to the disclosure or production, or
(b) the requirement is made by, or in accordance with a specific authorisation given by, the Investigating Authority.

[. . .]

Enforcement

66 POWER TO ENTER AND SEIZE DOCUMENTS

(1)   A justice of the peace may issue a warrant under this section if, on an information on oath laid by the Investigating Authority, he is satisfied—
(a) that any of the conditions mentioned in subsection (2) is met in relation to any documents of a description specified in the information, and
(b) that the documents are on premises so specified.

(2)   The conditions are—
(a)   that a person has been required by a disclosure notice to produce the documents but has not done so;
(b)   that it is not practicable to give a disclosure notice requiring their production;
(c)   that giving such a notice might seriously prejudice the investigation of an offence to which this Chapter applies.

(3)   A warrant under this section is a warrant authorising an appropriate person named in it—
(a)   to enter and search the premises, using such force as is reasonably necessary;
(b)   to take possession of any documents appearing to be documents of a description specified in the information, or to take any other steps which appear to be necessary for preserving, or preventing interference with, any such documents;
(c)   in the case of any such documents consisting of information recorded otherwise than in legible form, to take possession of any computer disk or other electronic storage device which appears to contain the information in question, or to take any other steps which appear to be necessary for preserving, or preventing interference with, that information;
(d)   to take copies of or extracts from any documents or information falling within paragraph (b) or (c);
(e)   to require any person on the premises to provide an explanation of any such documents or information or to state where any such documents or information may be found;
(f)   to require any such person to give the appropriate person such assistance as he may reasonably require for the taking of copies or extracts as mentioned in paragraph (d).
[. . .]

(5)   A warrant under this section must, if so required, be produced for inspection by the owner or occupier of the premises or anyone acting on his behalf.

[. . .]

[. . .]

Part 4 PUBLIC ORDER AND CONDUCT IN PUBLIC PLACES ETC.
[. . .]

Trespass on designated site

128 OFFENCE OF TRESPASSING ON DESIGNATED SITE

(1)   A person commits an offence if he enters, or is on, any [protected] site in England and Wales or Northern Ireland as a trespasser.

(1A)   In this section 'protected site' means—
(a)   a nuclear site; or
(b)   a designated site.

(1B)   In this section 'nuclear site' means—
(a)   so much of any premises in respect of which a nuclear site licence (within the meaning of the Nuclear Installations Act 1965) is for the time being in force as lies within the outer perimeter of the protection provided for those premises; and
(b)   so much of any other premises of which premises falling within paragraph (a) form a part as lies within that outer perimeter.
[. . .]

(2)   A "designated site" means a site—
    (a) specified or described (in any way) in an order made by the Secretary of State, and
    (b) designated for the purposes of this section by the order.
[. . .]

Demonstrations in vicinity of Parliament

Part 5 **MISCELLANEOUS**

Protection of activities of certain organisations

145 INTERFERENCE WITH CONTRACTUAL RELATIONSHIPS SO AS TO HARM ANIMAL RESEARCH ORGANISATION

(1)   A person (A) commits an offence if, with the intention of harming an animal research organisation, he—
    (a) does a relevant act, or
    (b) threatens that he or somebody else will do a relevant act,
       in circumstances in which that act or threat is intended or likely to cause a second person (B) to take any of the steps in subsection (2).

(2)   The steps are—
    (a) not to perform any contractual obligation owed by B to a third person (C) (whether or not such non-performance amounts to a breach of contract);
    (b) to terminate any contract B has with C;
    (c) not to enter into a contract with C.

(3)   For the purposes of this section, a "relevant act" is—
    (a) an act amounting to a criminal offence, or
    (b) a tortious act causing B to suffer loss or damage of any description;
    but paragraph (b) does not include an act which is actionable on the ground only that it induces another person to break a contract with B.

    [. . .]

146 INTIMIDATION OF PERSONS CONNECTED WITH ANIMAL RESEARCH ORGANISATION

(1)   A person (A) commits an offence if, with the intention of causing a second person (B) to abstain from doing something which B is entitled to do (or to do something which B is entitled to abstain from doing)—
    (a) A threatens B that A or somebody else will do a relevant act, and
    (b) A does so wholly or mainly because B is a person falling within subsection (2).

(2)   A person falls within this subsection if he is—
    (a) an employee or officer of an animal research organisation;
    (b) a student at an educational establishment that is an animal research organisation;
    (c) a lessor or licensor of any premises occupied by an animal research organisation;
    (d) a person with a financial interest in, or who provides financial assistance to, an animal research organisation;
    (e) a customer or supplier of an animal research organisation;
    (f) a person who is contemplating becoming someone within paragraph (c), (d) or (e);
    (g) a person who is, or is contemplating becoming, a customer or supplier of someone within paragraph (c), (d), (e) or (f);

(h) an employee or officer of someone within paragraph (c), (d), (e), (f) or (g);

(i) a person with a financial interest in, or who provides financial assistance to, someone within paragraph (c), (d), (e), (f) or (g);

(j) a spouse, civil partner, friend or relative of, or a person who is known personally to, someone within any of paragraphs (a) to (i);

(k) a person who is, or is contemplating becoming, a customer or supplier of someone within paragraph (a), (b), (h), (i) or (j); or

(l) an employer of someone within paragraph (j).

[. . .]

(5) For the purposes of this section, a "relevant act" is—

(a) an act amounting to a criminal offence, or

(b) a tortious act causing B or another person to suffer loss or damage of any description.

[. . .]

As amended by The Police Reform and Social Responsibility Act 2011, s 141

ELECTORAL ADMINISTRATION ACT 2006
(c. 22)

An Act to make provision in relation to the registration of electors and the keeping of electoral registration information; standing for election; the administration and conduct of elections and referendums; and the regulation of political parties.

[. . .]

Part 5 STANDING FOR ELECTION

17 MINIMUM AGE

(1) A person is disqualified for membership of the House of Commons if, on the day on which he is nominated as a candidate, he has not attained the age of 18.

(2) Subject to an order made by the House of Commons under section 6(2) of the House of Commons Disqualification Act 1975 (c. 24) as applied by subsection (3), if a person disqualified by subsection (1) for membership of that House is elected as a member of that House his election is void.

[. . .]

Nomination

21 USE OF CANDIDATES' COMMON NAMES

(1) Schedule 1 to the 1983 Act (parliamentary elections rules) is amended as follows.

[. . .]

(4) In the Appendix of forms, in the Form of nomination paper, for the first table following the words "candidate at the said election" substitute—

"Candidate's surname	Other names in full	Commonly used surname (if any)	Commonly used forenames (if any)	Description (if any)	Home address in full
SULLIVAN	Arthur Seymour	GILBERT	W. S.	Independent	52, Bunthorne Walk, Basingstoke"

[. . .]

Part 6 **CONDUCT OF ELECTIONS ETC.**

Access to election documents
[. . .]

42 ACCESS TO OTHER ELECTION DOCUMENTS

(1)   The relevant officer must—
   (a) make relevant election documents available for inspection by members of the public;
   (b) supply, on request, copies of or extracts from such description of relevant election documents as is prescribed by regulations.

(2)   In the case of an election other than a parliamentary election, a local government election in Scotland or a local election in Northern Ireland, each of the following must, on request, be supplied with a copy of the marked copies of the register, the postal voters list, the list of proxies and the proxy postal voters list—
   (a) a registered party;
   (b) a person who was a candidate at the election in relation to the electoral area for which he was a candidate;
   (c) in the case of an election at which a registered party submits a list of candidates, a person who was appointed as an agent for the candidates on the party's list.

(3)   The Secretary of State may by regulations impose conditions in relation to—
   (a) the inspection of any document in pursuance of subsection (1)(a);
   (b) the supply of any document or part of a document in pursuance of subsection (1)(b);
   (c) the supply of any document or part of a document in pursuance of subsection (2).

(4)   Regulations may also make provision—
   (a) as to the form in which any such document or part is supplied;
   (b) for the payment of a fee in respect of the supply of a document or part.

(5)   Conditions which may be imposed for the purposes of subsection (3)(a) or (b) include conditions as to—
   (a) whether a person may take any copy of a document he is permitted to inspect;
   (b) the manner in which any such copy is to be taken;
   (c) the purposes for which information contained in any document or part of a document which is inspected or supplied in pursuance of subsection (1) may be used.

(6)   Conditions which may be imposed for the purposes of subsection (3)(b) or (c) include conditions as to the extent to which a person to whom a document or part of a document has been supplied may—
   (a) supply that document or part to any other person;
   (b) disclose to any other person any information contained in the document or part;

(c) use any such information for a purpose other than that for which the document or part was supplied to him.

[. . .]

[. . .]

Correction of procedural errors

46 RETURNING OFFICERS: CORRECTION OF PROCEDURAL ERRORS

(1) A returning officer for an election to which this section applies may take such steps as he thinks appropriate to remedy any act or omission on his part, or on the part of a relevant person, which—
(a) arises in connection with any function the returning officer or relevant person has in relation to the election, and
(b) is not in accordance with the rules or any other requirements applicable to the election.

(2) But a returning officer may not under subsection (1) re-count the votes given at an election after the result has been declared.

[. . .]

Part 8 MISCELLANEOUS

[. . .]

Encouraging electoral participation

69 ENCOURAGING ELECTORAL PARTICIPATION

(1) A local electoral officer must take such steps as he thinks appropriate to encourage the participation by electors in the electoral process in the area for which he acts.

(2) A local electoral officer must have regard to any guidance issued by the Electoral Commission for the purposes of this section.

[. . .]

[. . .]

73 ABOLITION OF COMMON LAW INCAPACITY: MENTAL STATE

(1) Any rule of the common law which provides that a person is subject to a legal incapacity to vote by reason of his mental state is abolished.

[. . .]

[. . .]

76 INTERPRETATION

(1) "The 1983 Act" means the Representation of the People Act 1983 (c. 2).

(2) "The 2000 Act" means the Political Parties, Elections and Referendums Act 2000 (c. 41).

[. . .]

EQUALITY ACT 2006
(c. 3)

An Act to make provision for the establishment of the Commission for Equality and Human Rights; to dissolve the Equal Opportunities Commission, the Commission for Racial Equality and the Disability Rights Commission; to make provision about discrimination on grounds of religion or belief; to enable provision to be made about discrimination on grounds of sexual orientation; to impose duties relating to sex discrimination on persons performing public functions; to amend the Disability Discrimination Act 1995; and for connected purposes.

[. . .]

Part 1 THE COMMISSION FOR EQUALITY AND HUMAN RIGHTS

The Commission

1 ESTABLISHMENT

There shall be a body corporate known as the Commission for Equality and Human Rights.

[. . .]

3 GENERAL DUTY

The Commission shall exercise its functions under this Part with a view to encouraging and supporting the development of a society in which—
(a)   people's ability to achieve their potential is not limited by prejudice or discrimination,

(b)   there is respect for and protection of each individual's human rights,

(c)   there is respect for the dignity and worth of each individual,

(d)   each individual has an equal opportunity to participate in society, and

(e)   there is mutual respect between groups based on understanding and valuing of diversity and on shared respect for equality and human rights.

[. . .]

Duties

8 EQUALITY AND DIVERSITY

(1)   The Commission shall, by exercising the powers conferred by this Part—
(a) promote understanding of the importance of equality and diversity,
(b) encourage good practice in relation to equality and diversity,
(c) promote equality of opportunity,
(d) promote awareness and understanding of rights under the Equality Act 2010,
(e) enforce the that Act,
(f) work towards the elimination of unlawful discrimination, and
(g) work towards the elimination of unlawful harassment.
[. . .]

(3)   In promoting equality of opportunity between disabled persons and others, the Commission may, in particular, promote the favourable treatment of disabled persons.

(4)   In this Part "disabled person" means a person who—
    (a)   is a disabled person within the meaning of the Equality Act 2010 (c. 50), or
    (b)   has been a disabled person within that meaning (whether or not at a time when that Act had effect).

9 HUMAN RIGHTS

(1)   The Commission shall, by exercising the powers conferred by this Part—
    (a)   promote understanding of the importance of human rights,
    (b)   encourage good practice in relation to human rights,
    (c)   promote awareness, understanding and protection of human rights, and
    (d)   encourage public authorities to comply with section 6 of the Human Rights Act 1998 (c. 42) (compliance with Convention rights).
    [. . .]

(3)   In determining what action to take in pursuance of this section the Commission shall have particular regard to the importance of exercising the powers conferred by this Part in relation to the Convention rights.

(4)   In fulfilling a duty under section 8 or 10 the Commission shall take account of any relevant human rights.

(5)   A reference in this Part (including this section) to human rights does not exclude any matter by reason only of its being a matter to which section 8 or 10 relates.

10 GROUPS

(1)   The Commission shall, by exercising the powers conferred by this Part—
    (a)   promote understanding of the importance of good relations—
        (i)   between members of different groups, and
        (ii) between members of groups and others,
    (b)   encourage good practice in relation to relations—
        (i)   between members of different groups, and
        (ii) between members of groups and others,
    (c)   work towards the elimination of prejudice against, hatred of and hostility towards members of groups, and
    (d)   work towards enabling members of groups to participate in society.

(2)   In this Part "group" means a group or class of persons who share a common attribute in respect of any of the following matters—
    (a)   age,
    (b)   disability,
    (c)   gender,
    (d)   gender reassignment (within the meaning of section 7 of the Equality Act 2010),
    (e)   race,
    (f)   religion or belief, and
    (g)   sexual orientation.
    [. . .]

11 MONITORING THE LAW

(1)   The Commission shall monitor the effectiveness of the equality and human rights enactments.

    [. . .]

16 INQUIRIES

(1)   The Commission may conduct an inquiry into a matter relating to any of the Commission's duties under sections 8, 9 and 10.

[. . .]

[. . .]

Enforcement powers

20 INVESTIGATIONS

(1)   The Commission may investigate whether or not a person—
    (a) has committed an unlawful act,
    (b) has complied with a requirement imposed by an unlawful act notice under section 21, or
    (c) has complied with an undertaking given under section 23.
    [. . .]

21 UNLAWFUL ACT NOTICE

(1)   The Commission may give a person a notice under this section (an "unlawful act notice") if—
    (a) he is or has been the subject of an investigation under section 20(1)(a), and
    (b) the Commission is satisfied that he has committed an unlawful act.

(2)   A notice must specify—
    (a) the unlawful act, and
    (b) the provision of the Equality Act 2010 by virtue of which the act is unlawful.
    [. . .]

(4)   A notice may—
    (a) require the person to whom the notice is given to prepare an action plan for the purpose of avoiding repetition or continuation of the unlawful act;
    (b) recommend action to be taken by the person for that purpose.
    [. . .]

24 APPLICATIONS TO COURT

(1)   If the Commission thinks that a person is likely to commit an unlawful act, it may apply—
    (a) in England and Wales, to a county court for an injunction restraining the person from committing the act, or
    (b) in Scotland, to the sheriff for an interdict prohibiting the person from committing the act.

(2)   Subsection (3) applies if the Commission thinks that a party to an agreement under section 23 has failed to comply, or is likely not to comply, with an undertaking under the agreement.

(3)   The Commission may apply to a county court (in England and Wales) or to the sheriff (in Scotland) for an order requiring the person—
    (a) to comply with his undertaking, and
    (b) to take such other action as the court or the sheriff may specify.
    [. . .]

[. . .]

30 JUDICIAL REVIEW AND OTHER LEGAL PROCEEDINGS

(1)   The Commission shall have capacity to institute or intervene in legal proceedings, whether for judicial review or otherwise, if it appears to the Commission that the proceedings are relevant to a matter in connection with which the Commission has a function.

(2)   The Commission shall be taken to have title and interest in relation to the subject matter of any legal proceedings in Scotland which it has capacity to institute, or in which it has capacity to intervene, by virtue of subsection (1).

(3)   The Commission may, in the course of legal proceedings for judicial review which it institutes (or in which it intervenes), rely on section 7(1)(b) of the Human Rights Act 1998 (c. 42)(breach of Convention rights); and for that purpose—
   (a)   the Commission need not be a victim or potential victim of the unlawful act to which the proceedings relate,
   (b)   the Commission may act only if there is or would be one or more victims of the unlawful act,
   (c)   section 7(3) and (4) of that Act shall not apply, and
   (d)   no award of damages may be made to the Commission (whether or not the exception in section 8(3) of that Act applies);
   and an expression used in this subsection and in section 7 of the Human Rights Act 1998 has the same meaning in this subsection as in that section.
   [. . .]
[. . .]

As amended by the Equality Act 2010 Schedule 26 paragraph 25 and Schedule 27 Part 1

GOVERNMENT OF WALES ACT 2006
(c. 32)

Note: At the time of editing (1 June 2010), sections 107 and 108 of the Government of Wales Act were not yet in force.

An Act to make provision about the government of Wales.

[. . .]

Part 1 NATIONAL ASSEMBLY FOR WALES

The Assembly

1 THE ASSEMBLY

(1)   There is to be an Assembly for Wales to be known as the National Assembly for Wales or Cynulliad Cenedlaethol Cymru (referred to in this Act as "the Assembly").

(2)   The Assembly is to consist of—
   (a)   one member for each Assembly constituency (referred to in this Act as "Assembly constituency members"), and
   (b)   members for each Assembly electoral region (referred to in this Act as "Assembly regional members").

(3)   Members of the Assembly (referred to in this Act as "Assembly members") are to be returned in accordance with the provision made by and under this Act for—
    (a) the holding of general elections of Assembly members (for the return of the entire Assembly), and
    (b) the filling of vacancies in Assembly seats.

(4)   The validity of any Assembly proceedings is not affected by any vacancy in its membership.

(5)   In this Act "Assembly proceedings" means any proceedings of—
    (a) the Assembly,
    (b) committees of the Assembly, or
    (c) sub-committees of such committees.

2 ASSEMBLY CONSTITUENCIES AND ELECTORAL REGIONS

(1)   The Assembly constituencies are the constituencies specified in the Parliamentary Constituencies and Assembly Electoral Regions (Wales) Order 2006 (S.I. 2006/1041) as amended by—
    (a) the Parliamentary Constituencies and Assembly Electoral Regions (Wales) (Amendment) Order 2008 (S.I. 2008/1791), and
    (b) any Order in Council under the Parliamentary Constituencies Act 1986 giving effect (with or without modifications) to a report falling within section 13(3) or (4) of the Parliamentary Voting System and Constituencies Act 2011.

(2)   There are five Assembly electoral regions.

(3)   The Assembly electoral regions are as specified in the Parliamentary Constituencies and Assembly Electoral Regions (Wales) Order 2006.

(4)   There are four seats for each Assembly electoral region.

Presiding Officer and administration

25 PRESIDING OFFICER ETC.

(1)   The Assembly must, at its first meeting following a general election, elect from among the Assembly members—
    (a) a presiding officer (referred to in this Act as "the Presiding Officer"), and
    (b) a deputy presiding officer (referred to in this Act as "the Deputy Presiding Officer").
    [. . .]

[. . .]

Proceedings etc.
[. . .]

33 CONSULTATION ABOUT UK GOVERNMENT'S LEGISLATIVE PROGRAMME

(1)   As soon as is reasonably practicable after the beginning of each session of Parliament, the Secretary of State for Wales must undertake with the Assembly such consultation about the UK Government's legislative programme for the session as appears to the Secretary of State to be appropriate.

    [. . .]

[. . .]

Part 2 **WELSH ASSEMBLY GOVERNMENT**

Government

45 WELSH ASSEMBLY GOVERNMENT

(1) There is to be a Welsh Assembly Government, or Llywodraeth Cynulliad Cymru, whose members are—
   (a) the First Minister or Prif Weinidog (see sections 46 and 47),
   (b) the Welsh Ministers, or Gweinidogion Cymru, appointed under section 48,
   (c) the Counsel General to the Welsh Assembly Government or Cwnsler Cyffredinol i Lywodraeth Cynulliad Cymru (see section 49) (referred to in this Act as "the Counsel General"), and
   (d) the Deputy Welsh Ministers or Dirprwy Weinidogion Cymru (see section 50).
   [. . .]

Ministers, staff etc.

46 THE FIRST MINISTER

(1) The First Minister is to be appointed by Her Majesty after nomination in accordance with section 47.

(2) The First Minister holds office at Her Majesty's pleasure.

(3) The First Minister may at any time tender resignation to Her Majesty and ceases to hold office as First Minister when it is accepted.

(4) A person ceases to hold office as the First Minister if another person is appointed to that office.

(5) The functions of the First Minister are exercisable by a person designated by the Presiding Officer if—
   (a) the office of the First Minister is vacant,
   (b) the First Minister is for any reason unable to act, or
   (c) the First Minister has ceased to be an Assembly member.

(6) A person may not be designated to exercise the functions of the First Minister unless the person is—
   (a) an Assembly member, or
   (b) if the Assembly has been dissolved, a person who ceased to be an Assembly member by reason of the dissolution.

(7) A person may be designated to exercise the functions of the First Minister only on the recommendation of the Welsh Ministers (unless there is no-one holding office as a Welsh Minister appointed under section 48).

(8) If a person is designated to exercise the functions of the First Minister, the designation continues to have effect even if the Assembly is dissolved.

47 CHOICE OF FIRST MINISTER

(1) If one of the following events occurs, the Assembly must, before the end of the relevant period, nominate an Assembly member for appointment as First Minister.

(2)   The events are—

    (a)   the holding of a poll at a general election,

    (b)   the Assembly resolving that the Welsh Ministers no longer enjoy the confidence of the Assembly,

    (c)   the First Minister tendering resignation to Her Majesty,

    (d)   the First Minister dying or becoming permanently unable to act and to tender resignation, and

    (e)   the First Minister ceasing to be an Assembly member otherwise than by reason of a dissolution.

    [. . .]

48 WELSH MINISTERS

(1)   The First Minister may, with the approval of Her Majesty, appoint Welsh Ministers from among the Assembly members.

    [. . .]

[. . .]

Functions
[. . .]

57 EXERCISE OF FUNCTIONS

(1)   Functions may be conferred or imposed on the Welsh Ministers by that name.

(2)   Functions of the Welsh Ministers, the First Minister and the Counsel General are exercisable on behalf of Her Majesty.

(3)   Functions of the Welsh Ministers are exercisable by the First Minister or any of the Welsh Ministers appointed under section 48.

    [. . .]

[. . .]

60 PROMOTION ETC. OF WELL-BEING

(1)   The Welsh Ministers may do anything which they consider appropriate to achieve any one or more of the following objects—

    (a)   the promotion or improvement of the economic well-being of Wales,

    (b)   the promotion or improvement of the social well-being of Wales, and

    (c)   the promotion or improvement of the environmental well-being of Wales.

    [. . .]

61 SUPPORT OF CULTURE ETC.

The Welsh Ministers may do anything which they consider appropriate to support—

(a)   archaeological remains in Wales,

(b)   ancient monuments in Wales,

(c)   buildings and places of historical or architectural interest in Wales,

(d)   historic wrecks in Wales,

(e)   arts and crafts relating to Wales,

(f)   museums and galleries in Wales,

(g)   libraries in Wales,

(h)   archives and historical records relating to Wales,

(i)   cultural activities and projects relating to Wales,

(j)   sport and recreational activities relating to Wales, and

(k)   the Welsh language.

[. . .]

Part 3 ASSEMBLY MEASURES

Power

93 ASSEMBLY MEASURES

(1)   The Assembly may make laws, to be known as Measures of the National Assembly for Wales or Mesurau Cynulliad Cenedlaethol Cymru (referred to in this Act as "Assembly Measures").

(2)   A proposed Assembly Measure is enacted by being passed by the Assembly and approved by Her Majesty in Council.

[. . .]

94 LEGISLATIVE COMPETENCE

(1)   Subject to the provisions of this Part, an Assembly Measure may make any provision that could be made by an Act of Parliament.

(2)   An Assembly Measure is not law so far as any provision of the Assembly Measure is outside the Assembly's legislative competence.

(3)   A provision of an Assembly Measure is within the Assembly's legislative competence only if it falls within subsection (4) or (5).

(4)   A provision of an Assembly Measure falls within this subsection if—
(a) it relates to one or more of the matters specified in Part 1 of Schedule 5 [and does not fall within any of the exceptions specified in paragraph A1 of Part 2 of that Schedule (whether or not the exception is under a heading corresponding to the field which includes the matter).], and
(b) it neither applies otherwise than in relation to Wales nor confers, imposes, modifies or removes (or gives power to confer, impose, modify or remove) functions exercisable otherwise than in relation to Wales.

(5)   A provision of an Assembly Measure falls within this subsection if—
(a) it provides for the enforcement of a provision (of that or any other Assembly Measure) which falls within subsection (4) or it is otherwise appropriate for making such a provision effective, or
(b) it is otherwise incidental to, or consequential on, such a provision.

(6)   But a provision which falls within subsection (4) or (5) is outside the Assembly's legislative competence if—
    (a)   it breaches any of the restrictions in [paragraphs 1 to 6 of] Part 2 of Schedule 5, having regard to any exception in Part 3 of that Schedule from those restrictions,
    (b)   it extends otherwise than only to England and Wales, or
    (c)   it is incompatible with the Convention rights or with Community law.
    [. . .]

[. . .]

Procedure

97 INTRODUCTION OF PROPOSED ASSEMBLY MEASURES

(1)   A proposed Assembly Measure may, subject to the standing orders, be introduced in the Assembly—
    (a)   by the First Minister, any Welsh Minister appointed under section 48, any Deputy Welsh Minister or the Counsel General, or
    (b)   by any other Assembly member.

(2)   The person in charge of a proposed Assembly Measure must, on or before the introduction of the proposed Assembly Measure, state that, in that person's view, its provisions would be within the Assembly's legislative competence.

(3)   The Presiding Officer must, on or before the introduction of a proposed Assembly Measure in the Assembly—
    (a)   decide whether or not, in the view of the Presiding Officer, the provisions of the proposed Assembly Measure would be within the Assembly's legislative competence, and
    (b)   state that decision.
    [. . .]

[. . .]

Part 4 **ACTS OF THE ASSEMBLY**

Referendum

103 REFERENDUM ABOUT COMMENCEMENT OF ASSEMBLY ACT PROVISIONS

(1)   Her Majesty may by Order in Council cause a referendum to be held throughout Wales about whether the Assembly Act provisions should come into force.

    [. . .]

[. . .]

104 PROPOSAL FOR REFERENDUM BY ASSEMBLY

(1)   This section applies if—
    (a)   the Assembly passes a resolution moved by the First Minister or a Welsh Minister appointed under section 48 that, in its opinion, a recommendation should be made to Her Majesty in Council to make an Order in Council under section 103(1), and
    (b)   the resolution of the Assembly is passed on a vote in which the number of Assembly members voting in favour of it is not less than two-thirds of the total number of Assembly seats.

(2)   The First Minister must, as soon as is reasonably practicable after the resolution is passed, ensure that notice in writing of the resolution is given to the Secretary of State.

(3)   The Secretary of State must, within the period of 120 days beginning immediately after the day on which it is received—
   (a) lay a draft of a statutory instrument containing an Order in Council under section 103(1) before each House of Parliament, or
   (b) give notice in writing to the First Minister of the Secretary of State's refusal to do so and the reasons for that refusal.

(4)   As soon as is reasonably practicable after the First Minister receives notice given under subsection (3)(b)—
   (a) the First Minister must lay a copy of the notice before the Assembly, and
   (b) the Assembly must ensure that the notice is published.
[. . .]

Power

107 ACTS OF THE ASSEMBLY

(1)   The Assembly may make laws, to be known as Acts of the National Assembly for Wales or Deddfau Cynulliad Cenedlaethol Cymru (referred to in this Act as "Acts of the Assembly").

(2)   Proposed Acts of the Assembly are to be known as Bills; and a Bill becomes an Act of the Assembly when it has been passed by the Assembly and has received Royal Assent.

(3)   The validity of an Act of the Assembly is not affected by any invalidity in the Assembly proceedings leading to its enactment.

   [. . .]

108 LEGISLATIVE COMPETENCE

(1)   Subject to the provisions of this Part, an Act of the Assembly may make any provision that could be made by an Act of Parliament.

(2)   An Act of the Assembly is not law so far as any provision of the Act is outside the Assembly's legislative competence.

(3)   A provision of an Act of the Assembly is within the Assembly's legislative competence only if it falls within subsection (4) or (5).

(4)   A provision of an Act of the Assembly falls within this subsection if—
   (a) it relates to one or more of the subjects listed under any of the headings in Part 1 of Schedule 7 and does not fall within any of the exceptions specified in that Part of that Schedule (whether or not under that heading or any of those headings), and
   (b) it neither applies otherwise than in relation to Wales nor confers, imposes, modifies or removes (or gives power to confer, impose, modify or remove) functions exercisable otherwise than in relation to Wales.

(5)   A provision of an Act of the Assembly falls within this subsection if—
   (a) it provides for the enforcement of a provision (of that or any other Act of the Assembly) which falls within subsection (4) or a provision of an Assembly Measure or it is otherwise appropriate for making such a provision effective, or
   (b) it is otherwise incidental to, or consequential on, such a provision.

(6)   But a provision which falls within subsection (4) or (5) is outside the Assembly's legislative competence if—

    (a)   it breaches any of the restrictions in Part 2 of Schedule 7, having regard to any exception in Part 3 of that Schedule from those restrictions,

    (b)   it extends otherwise than only to England and Wales, or

    (c)   it is incompatible with the Convention rights or with Community law.

    [. . .]

[. . .]

SCHEDULE 5 ASSEMBLY MEASURES

Part 1 MATTERS

Field 1: agriculture, fisheries, forestry and rural development

[. . .]

Field 2: ancient monuments and historic buildings

Field 3: culture

Field 4: economic development

Field 5: education and training

[. . .]

Field 6: environment

[. . .]

Field 7: fire and rescue services and promotion of fire safety

Field 8: food

Field 9: health and health services

[. . .]

Field 10: highways and transport

[. . .]

Field 11: housing

Field 12: local government

[. . .]

Field 13: National Assembly for Wales

[. . .]

Field 14: public administration

Field 15: social welfare

[. . .]

Field 16: sport and recreation

[. . .]

Field 17: tourism

Field 18: town and country planning

[. . .]

Field 19: water and flood defence

Field 20: Welsh language

[. . .]

Part 2 [EXCEPTIONS TO MATTERS AND GENERAL RESTRICTIONS]

EXCEPTIONS TO MATTERS

[. . .]

GENERAL RESTRICTIONS

Functions of Ministers of the Crown
1   (1)   A provision of an Assembly Measure cannot remove or modify, or confer power by subordinate legislation to remove or modify, any function of a Minister of the Crown.

    (2)   A provision of an Assembly Measure cannot confer or impose, or confer power by subordinate legislation to confer or impose, any function on a Minister of the Crown.

Criminal offences
2   (1)   A provision of an Assembly Measure cannot create, or confer power by subordinate legislation to create, any criminal offence punishable—
      (a) on summary conviction, with imprisonment for a period exceeding the prescribed term or with a fine exceeding the amount specified as level 5 on the standard scale, or
      (b) on conviction on indictment, with a period of imprisonment exceeding two years.

    (2)   In sub-paragraph (1) "the prescribed term" means—
      (a) where the offence is a summary offence, 51 weeks, and
      (b) where the offence is triable either way, twelve months.

[. . .]

Part 3 [EXCEPTIONS FROM GENERAL RESTRICTIONS IN PART 2]

[INTERPRETATION

6Z   In this Part "general restrictions in Part 2" means paragraphs 1 to 6 of Part 2.]

Functions of Ministers of the Crown
7   (1)   The general restrictions in Part 2 do not prevent a provision of an Assembly Measure removing or modifying, or conferring power by subordinate legislation to remove or modify, any function of a Minister of the Crown if the Secretary of State consents to the provision.

    (2)   Part 2 does not prevent a provision of an Assembly Measure relating to matter 20.1 or 20.2 of Part 1, conferring or imposing, or conferring power by subordinate legislation to confer or impose, any function on a Minister of the Crown if the

Secretary of State consents to the provision, but functions so conferred or imposed may not be made enforceable against Ministers of the Crown by means of criminal offences.

[. . .]

Restatement

9   [The general restrictions in Part 2 do not] prevent a provision of an Assembly Measure—
     (a) restating the law (or restating it with such modifications as are not prevented by that Part), or
     (b) repealing or revoking any spent enactment,
     or conferring power by subordinate legislation to do so.

[. . .]

As amended by The Parliamentary Voting System and Constituencies Act 2011 section 13(1)

As amended by the Parliamentary Voting System and Constituencies Act 2011, s 13(1), (2), Schedule 12

TERRORISM ACT 2006
(c. 11)

An Act to make provision for and about offences relating to conduct carried out, or capable of being carried out, for purposes connected with terrorism; to amend enactments relating to terrorism; to amend the Intelligence Services Act 1994 and the Regulation of Investigatory Powers Act 2000; and for connected purposes.

[. . .]

Part 1 OFFENCES

Encouragement etc. of terrorism

1 ENCOURAGEMENT OF TERRORISM

(1)   This section applies to a statement that is likely to be understood by some or all of the members of the public to whom it is published as a direct or indirect encouragement or other inducement to them to the commission, preparation or instigation of acts of terrorism or Convention offences.

(2)   A person commits an offence if—
      (a) he publishes a statement to which this section applies or causes another to publish such a statement; and
      (b) at the time he publishes it or causes it to be published, he—
           (i)   intends members of the public to be directly or indirectly encouraged or otherwise induced by the statement to commit, prepare or instigate acts of terrorism or Convention offences; or
           (ii) is reckless as to whether members of the public will be directly or indirectly encouraged or otherwise induced by the statement to commit, prepare or instigate such acts or offences.

(3) For the purposes of this section, the statements that are likely to be understood by members of the public as indirectly encouraging the commission or preparation of acts of terrorism or Convention offences include every statement which—

   (a) glorifies the commission or preparation (whether in the past, in the future or generally) of such acts or offences; and

   (b) is a statement from which those members of the public could reasonably be expected to infer that what is being glorified is being glorified as conduct that should be emulated by them in existing circumstances.

(4) For the purposes of this section the questions how a statement is likely to be understood and what members of the public could reasonably be expected to infer from it must be determined having regard both—

   (a) to the contents of the statement as a whole; and

   (b) to the circumstances and manner of its publication.

(5) It is irrelevant for the purposes of subsections (1) to (3)—

   (a) whether anything mentioned in those subsections relates to the commission, preparation or instigation of one or more particular acts of terrorism or Convention offences, of acts of terrorism or Convention offences of a particular description or of acts of terrorism or Convention offences generally; and,

   (b) whether any person is in fact encouraged or induced by the statement to commit, prepare or instigate any such act or offence.

(6) In proceedings for an offence under this section against a person in whose case it is not proved that he intended the statement directly or indirectly to encourage or otherwise induce the commission, preparation or instigation of acts of terrorism or Convention offences, it is a defence for him to show—

   (a) that the statement neither expressed his views nor had his endorsement (whether by virtue of section 3 or otherwise); and

   (b) that it was clear, in all the circumstances of the statement's publication, that it did not express his views and (apart from the possibility of his having been given and failed to comply with a notice under subsection (3) of that section) did not have his endorsement.

   [. . .]

2 DISSEMINATION OF TERRORIST PUBLICATIONS

(1) A person commits an offence if he engages in conduct falling within subsection (2) and, at the time he does so—

   (a) he intends an effect of his conduct to be a direct or indirect encouragement or other inducement to the commission, preparation or instigation of acts of terrorism;

   (b) he intends an effect of his conduct to be the provision of assistance in the commission or preparation of such acts; or

   (c) he is reckless as to whether his conduct has an effect mentioned in paragraph (a) or (b).

(2) For the purposes of this section a person engages in conduct falling within this subsection if he—

   (a) distributes or circulates a terrorist publication;

   (b) gives, sells or lends such a publication;

   (c) offers such a publication for sale or loan;

   (d) provides a service to others that enables them to obtain, read, listen to or look at such a publication, or to acquire it by means of a gift, sale or loan;

   (e) transmits the contents of such a publication electronically; or

(f) has such a publication in his possession with a view to its becoming the subject of conduct falling within any of paragraphs (a) to (e).

(3) For the purposes of this section a publication is a terrorist publication, in relation to conduct falling within subsection (2), if matter contained in it is likely—
(a) to be understood, by some or all of the persons to whom it is or may become available as a consequence of that conduct, as a direct or indirect encouragement or other inducement to them to the commission, preparation or instigation of acts of terrorism; or
(b) to be useful in the commission or preparation of such acts and to be understood, by some or all of those persons, as contained in the publication, or made available to them, wholly or mainly for the purpose of being so useful to them.

(4) For the purposes of this section matter that is likely to be understood by a person as indirectly encouraging the commission or preparation of acts of terrorism includes any matter which—
(a) glorifies the commission or preparation (whether in the past, in the future or generally) of such acts; and
(b) is matter from which that person could reasonably be expected to infer that what is being glorified is being glorified as conduct that should be emulated by him in existing circumstances.

(5) For the purposes of this section the question whether a publication is a terrorist publication in relation to particular conduct must be determined—
(a) as at the time of that conduct; and
(b) having regard both to the contents of the publication as a whole and to the circumstances in which that conduct occurs.

(6) In subsection (1) references to the effect of a person's conduct in relation to a terrorist publication include references to an effect of the publication on one or more persons to whom it is or may become available as a consequence of that conduct.

(7) It is irrelevant for the purposes of this section whether anything mentioned in subsections (1) to (4) is in relation to the commission, preparation or instigation of one or more particular acts of terrorism, of acts of terrorism of a particular description or of acts of terrorism generally.

(8) For the purposes of this section it is also irrelevant, in relation to matter contained in any article whether any person—
(a) is in fact encouraged or induced by that matter to commit, prepare or instigate acts of terrorism; or
(b) in fact makes use of it in the commission or preparation of such acts.

(9) In proceedings for an offence under this section against a person in respect of conduct to which subsection (10) applies, it is a defence for him to show—
(a) that the matter by reference to which the publication in question was a terrorist publication neither expressed his views nor had his endorsement (whether by virtue of section 3 or otherwise); and
(b) that it was clear, in all the circumstances of the conduct, that that matter did not express his views and (apart from the possibility of his having been given and failed to comply with a notice under subsection (3) of that section) did not have his endorsement.

(10) This subsection applies to the conduct of a person to the extent that—
(a) the publication to which his conduct related contained matter by reference to which it was a terrorist publication by virtue of subsection (3)(a); and

(b) that person is not proved to have engaged in that conduct with the intention specified in subsection (1)(a).

[. . .]

3 APPLICATION OF SS. 1 AND 2 TO INTERNET ACTIVITY ETC.

(1)   This section applies for the purposes of sections 1 and 2 in relation to cases where—
  (a) a statement is published or caused to be published in the course of, or in connection with, the provision or use of a service provided electronically; or
  (b) conduct falling within section 2(2) was in the course of, or in connection with, the provision or use of such a service.

(2)   The cases in which the statement, or the article or record to which the conduct relates, is to be regarded as having the endorsement of a person ("the relevant person") at any time include a case in which—
  (a) a constable has given him a notice under subsection (3);
  (b) that time falls more than 2 working days after the day on which the notice was given; and
  (c) the relevant person has failed, without reasonable excuse, to comply with the notice.

(3)   A notice under this subsection is a notice which—
  (a) declares that, in the opinion of the constable giving it, the statement or the article or record is unlawfully terrorism-related;
  (b) requires the relevant person to secure that the statement or the article or record, so far as it is so related, is not available to the public or is modified so as no longer to be so related;
  (c) warns the relevant person that a failure to comply with the notice within 2 working days will result in the statement, or the article or record, being regarded as having his endorsement; and
  (d) explains how, under subsection (4), he may become liable by virtue of the notice if the statement, or the article or record, becomes available to the public after he has complied with the notice.
  [. . .]

(7)   For the purposes of this section a statement or an article or record is unlawfully terrorism-related if it constitutes, or if matter contained in the article or record constitutes—
  (a) something that is likely to be understood, by any one or more of the persons to whom it has or may become available, as a direct or indirect encouragement or other inducement to the commission, preparation or instigation of acts of terrorism or Convention offences; or
  (b) information which—
    (i) is likely to be useful to any one or more of those persons in the commission or preparation of such acts; and
    (ii) is in a form or context in which it is likely to be understood by any one or more of those persons as being wholly or mainly for the purpose of being so useful.

(8)   The reference in subsection (7) to something that is likely to be understood as an indirect encouragement to the commission or preparation of acts of terrorism or Convention offences includes anything which is likely to be understood as—
  (a) the glorification of the commission or preparation (whether in the past, in the future or generally) of such acts or such offences; and
  (b) a suggestion that what is being glorified is being glorified as conduct that should be emulated in existing circumstances.
  [. . .]

[. . .]

Preparation of terrorist acts and terrorist training

5 PREPARATION OF TERRORIST ACTS

(1)   A person commits an offence if, with the intention of—
   (a)   committing acts of terrorism, or
   (b)   assisting another to commit such acts,
   he engages in any conduct in preparation for giving effect to his intention.

   [. . .]

[. . .]

6 TRAINING FOR TERRORISM

(1)   A person commits an offence if—
   (a)   he provides instruction or training in any of the skills mentioned in subsection (3); and
   (b)   at the time he provides the instruction or training, he knows that a person receiving it intends to use the skills in which he is being instructed or trained—
      (i)   for or in connection with the commission or preparation of acts of terrorism or Convention offences; or
      (ii)   for assisting the commission or preparation by others of such acts or offences.

(2)   A person commits an offence if—
   (a)   he receives instruction or training in any of the skills mentioned in subsection (3); and
   (b)   at the time of the instruction or training, he intends to use the skills in which he is being instructed or trained—
      (i)   for or in connection with the commission or preparation of acts of terrorism or Convention offences; or
      (ii)   for assisting the commission or preparation by others of such acts or offences.

(3)   The skills are—
   (a)   the making, handling or use of a noxious substance, or of substances of a description of such substances;
   (b)   the use of any method or technique for doing anything else that is capable of being done for the purposes of terrorism, in connection with the commission or preparation of an act of terrorism or Convention offence or in connection with assisting the commission or preparation by another of such an act or offence; and
   (c)   the design or adaptation for the purposes of terrorism, or in connection with the commission or preparation of an act of terrorism or Convention offence, of any method or technique for doing anything.

   [. . .]

8 ATTENDANCE AT A PLACE USED FOR TERRORIST TRAINING

(1)   A person commits an offence if—
   (a)   he attends at any place, whether in the United Kingdom or elsewhere;
   (b)   while he is at that place, instruction or training of the type mentioned in section 6(1) of this Act or section 54(1) of the Terrorism Act 2000 (c. 11) (weapons training) is provided there;
   (c)   that instruction or training is provided there wholly or partly for purposes connected with the commission or preparation of acts of terrorism or Convention offences; and
   (d)   the requirements of subsection (2) are satisfied in relation to that person.

(2)   The requirements of this subsection are satisfied in relation to a person if—
(a) he knows or believes that instruction or training is being provided there wholly or partly for purposes connected with the commission or preparation of acts of terrorism or Convention offences; or
(b) a person attending at that place throughout the period of that person's attendance could not reasonably have failed to understand that instruction or training was being provided there wholly or partly for such purposes.
[. . .]

Offences involving radioactive devices and materials and nuclear facilities and sites

9 MAKING AND POSSESSION OF DEVICES OR MATERIALS

(1)   A person commits an offence if—
(a) he makes or has in his possession a radioactive device, or
(b) he has in his possession radioactive material,
with the intention of using the device or material in the course of or in connection with the commission or preparation of an act of terrorism or for the purposes of terrorism, or of making it available to be so used.

[. . .]

10 MISUSE OF DEVICES OR MATERIAL AND MISUSE AND DAMAGE OF FACILITIES

(1)   A person commits an offence if he uses—
(a) a radioactive device, or
(b) radioactive material,
in the course of or in connection with the commission of an act of terrorism or for the purposes of terrorism.

[. . .]

Part 3 SUPPLEMENTAL PROVISIONS

36 REVIEW OF TERRORISM LEGISLATION

(1)   The Secretary of State must appoint a person to review the operation of the provisions of the Terrorism Act 2000 and of Part 1 of this Act.

[. . .]

[. . .]

SCHEDULE 1 CONVENTION OFFENCES

Explosives offences
1   (1) Subject to sub-paragraph (3), an offence under any of sections 28 to 30 of the Offences against the Person Act 1861 (c. 100) (causing injury by explosions, causing explosions and handling or placing explosives).

(2) Subject to sub-paragraph (3), an offence under any of the following provisions of the Explosive Substances Act 1883 (c. 3)—
(a) section 2 (causing an explosion likely to endanger life);

(b) section 3 (preparation of explosions);
(c) section 5 (ancillary offences).

[. . .]

Biological weapons

2   An offence under section 1 of the Biological Weapons Act 1974 (c. 6) (development etc. of biological weapons).

[. . .]

Hostage-taking

4   An offence under section 1 of the Taking of Hostages Act 1982 (c. 28) (hostage-taking).

Hijacking and other offences against aircraft

5   Offences under any of the following provisions of the Aviation Security Act 1982 (c. 36)—
(a) section 1 (hijacking);
(b) section 2 (destroying, damaging or endangering safety of aircraft);
(c) section 3 (other acts endangering or likely to endanger safety of aircraft);
(d) section 6(2) (ancillary offences).

OFFENCES INVOLVING NUCLEAR MATERIAL [OR NUCLEAR FACILITIES]

6   (1) An offence mentioned in section 1(1) [(a) to (d)] of the Nuclear Material (Offences) Act 1983 (c. 18) (offences in relation to nuclear material committed outside the United Kingdom) which is committed (whether in the United Kingdom or elsewhere) in relation to or by means of nuclear material.

(2) An offence mentioned in section 1(1)(a) or (b) of that Act where the act making the person guilty of the offence (whether done in the United Kingdom or elsewhere)—
(a) is directed at a nuclear facility or interferes with the operation of such a facility, and
(b) causes death, injury or damage resulting from the emission of ionising radiation or the release of radioactive material.

(3) An offence under any of the following provisions of that Act—
(a) section 1B (offences relating to damage to environment);
(b) section 1C (offences of importing or exporting etc. nuclear material: extended jurisdiction);
(c) section 2 (offences involving preparatory acts and threats).

(4) Expressions used in this paragraph and that Act have the same meanings in this paragraph as in that Act.

[. . .]

Offences involving chemical weapons

8   An offence under section 2 of the Chemical Weapons Act 1996 (c. 6) (use, development etc. of chemical weapons).

[. . .]

Directing terrorist organisations

10   An offence under section 56 of the Terrorism Act 2000 (directing a terrorist organisation).

Offences involving nuclear weapons

11   An offence under section 47 of the Anti-terrorism, Crime and Security Act 2001 (c. 24) (use, development etc. of nuclear weapons).

[. . .]

COUNTER-TERRORISM ACT 2008
(c. 28)

Note: At the time of editing (1 June 2012), sections 1, 3, 4, 5, 6, 7, 8, 22 of the Counter-Terrorism Act were not yet in force.

An Act to confer further powers to gather and share information for counter-terrorism and other purposes; to make further provision about the detention and questioning of terrorist suspects and the prosecution and punishment of terrorist offences; to impose notification requirements on persons convicted of such offences; to confer further powers to act against terrorist financing, money laundering and certain other activities; to provide for review of certain Treasury decisions and about evidence in, and other matters connected with, review proceedings; to amend the law relating to inquiries; to amend the definition of "terrorism"; to amend the enactments relating to terrorist offences, control orders and the forfeiture of terrorist cash; to provide for recovering the costs of policing at certain gas facilities; to amend provisions about the appointment of special advocates in Northern Ireland; and for connected purposes.

[. . .]

Part 1 POWERS TO GATHER AND SHARE INFORMATION

Power to remove documents for examination

1 POWER TO REMOVE DOCUMENTS FOR EXAMINATION

(1)   This section applies to a search under any of the following provisions—
   (a) section 43(1) of the Terrorism Act 2000 (c. 11)(search of suspected terrorist);
   (b) section 43(2) of that Act (search of person arrested under section 41 on suspicion of being a terrorist);
   (c) paragraph 1, 3, 11, 15, 28 or 31 of Schedule 5 to that Act (terrorist investigations);
   (d) section 52(1) or (3)(b) of the Anti-terrorism, Crime and Security Act 2001 (c. 24) (search for evidence of commission of weapons-related offences);
   (f) section 28 of the Terrorism Act 2006 (c. 11) (search for terrorist publications)
   (g) paragraphs 6, 7, 8 or 10 of Schedule 5 to the Terrorism Prevention and Investigation Measures Act 2011.

(2)   A constable who carries out a search to which this section applies may, for the purpose of ascertaining whether a document is one that may be seized, remove the document to another place for examination and retain it there until the examination is completed.

(3)   Where a constable carrying out a search to which this section applies has power to remove a document by virtue of this section, and the document—
   (a) consists of information that is stored in electronic form, and
   (b) is accessible from the premises being searched,
   the constable may require the document to be produced in a form in which it can be taken away, and in which it is visible and legible or from which it can readily be produced in a visible and legible form.

(4) A constable has the same powers of seizure in relation to a document removed under this section as the constable would have if it had not been removed (and if anything discovered on examination after removal had been discovered without it having been removed).

[. . .]

3 ITEMS SUBJECT TO LEGAL PRIVILEGE

(1) Section 1 does not authorise a constable to remove a document if the constable has reasonable cause to believe—
 (a) it is an item subject to legal privilege, or
 (b) it has an item subject to legal privilege comprised in it.
 [. . .]

4 RECORD OF REMOVAL

(1) A constable who removes a document under section 1 must make a written record of the removal.

(2) The record must be made as soon as is reasonably practicable and in any event within the period of 24 hours beginning with the time when the document was removed.

[. . .]

5 RETENTION OF DOCUMENTS

(1) A document may not be retained by virtue of section 1 for more than 48 hours without further authorisation.

(2) A constable of at least the rank of chief inspector may authorise the retention of the document for a further period or periods if satisfied that—
 (a) the examination of the document is being carried out expeditiously, and
 (b) it is necessary to continue the examination for the purpose of ascertaining whether the document is one that may be seized.

(3) This does not permit the retention of a document after the end of the period of 96 hours beginning with the time when it was removed for examination.

6 ACCESS TO DOCUMENTS

(1) Where—
 (a) a document is retained by virtue of section 5, and
 (b) a request for access to the document is made to the officer in charge of the investigation by a person within subsection (3),
 the officer must grant that person access to the document, under the supervision of a constable, subject to subsection (4).

(2) Where—
 (a) a document is retained by virtue of section 5, and
 (b) a request for a copy of the document is made to the officer in charge of the investigation by a person within subsection (3),
 that person must be provided with a copy of the document within a reasonable time from the making of the request, subject to subsection (4).

(3) The persons entitled to make a request under subsection (1) or (2) are—
(a) where the document was found in the course of a search of a person, that person,
(b) where the document was found in the course of a search of any premises—
(i)   the occupier of the premises when it was found, and
(ii) any person who had custody or control of the document when it was found, and
(c) a person acting on behalf of a person within paragraph (a) or (b).

(4) The officer in charge of the investigation may refuse access to the document, or (as the case may be) refuse to provide a copy of it, if the officer has reasonable grounds for believing that to do so—
(a) would prejudice any investigation for the purposes of which—
(i)   the original search was carried out, or
(ii) the document was removed or is being retained,
(b) would prejudice the investigation of any offence,
(c) would prejudice any criminal proceedings that may be brought as the result of an investigation within paragraph (a) or (b), or
(d) would facilitate the commission of an offence.
[. . .]

7 PHOTOGRAPHING AND COPYING OF DOCUMENTS

(1) Where a document is removed under section 1 it must not be photographed or copied, except that—
(a) a document may be copied for the purpose of providing a copy in response to a request under section 6(2), and
(b) a document consisting of information stored in electronic form may be copied for the purpose of producing it in a visible and legible form.

(2) Where the original document is returned, any copy under subsection (1)(b) must—
(a) in the case of a copy in electronic form, be destroyed or made inaccessible as soon as is reasonably practicable, and
(b) in any other case, be returned at the same time as the original document is returned.
[. . .]

8 RETURN OF DOCUMENTS

(1) Where a document removed under section 1 is required to be returned, it must be returned—
(a) where the document was found in the course of a search of a person, to that person;
(b) where the document was found in the course of a search of any premises, to the occupier of the premises when it was found.
[. . .]

[. . .]

Disclosure of information and the intelligence services

19 DISCLOSURE AND THE INTELLIGENCE SERVICES

(1) A person may disclose information to any of the intelligence services for the purposes of the exercise by that service of any of its functions.

(2) Information obtained by any of the intelligence services in connection with the exercise of any of its functions may be used by that service in connection with the exercise of any of its other functions.

(3) Information obtained by the Security Service for the purposes of any of its functions may be disclosed by it—
  (a) for the purpose of the proper discharge of its functions,
  (b) for the purpose of the prevention or detection of serious crime, or
  (c) for the purpose of any criminal proceedings.

(4) Information obtained by the Secret Intelligence Service for the purposes of any of its functions may be disclosed by it—
  (a) for the purpose of the proper discharge of its functions,
  (b) in the interests of national security,
  (c) for the purpose of the prevention or detection of serious crime, or
  (d) for the purpose of any criminal proceedings.

(5) Information obtained by GCHQ for the purposes of any of its functions may be disclosed by it—
  (a) for the purpose of the proper discharge of its functions, or
  (b) for the purpose of any criminal proceedings.
  [. . .]

[. . .]

21 DISCLOSURE AND THE INTELLIGENCE SERVICES: INTERPRETATION

(1) In sections 19 and 20 "the intelligence services" means the Security Service, the Secret Intelligence Service and GCHQ.

  [. . .]

Part 2 POST-CHARGE QUESTIONING OF TERRORIST SUSPECTS

22 POST-CHARGE QUESTIONING: ENGLAND AND WALES

(1) The following provisions apply in England and Wales.

(2) A judge of the Crown Court may authorise the questioning of a person about an offence—
  (a) after the person has been charged with the offence or been officially informed that they may be prosecuted for it, or
  (b) after the person has been sent for trial for the offence,
  if the offence is a terrorism offence or it appears to the judge that the offence has a terrorist connection.

(3) The judge—
  (a) must specify the period during which questioning is authorised, and
  (b) may impose such conditions as appear to be necessary in the interests of justice, which may include conditions as to the place where the questioning is to be carried out.

(4) The period during which questioning is authorised—
  (a) begins when questioning pursuant to the authorisation begins and runs continuously from that time (whether or not questioning continues), and
  (b) must not exceed 48 hours.
  This is without prejudice to any application for a further authorisation under this section.

(5) Where the person is in prison or otherwise lawfully detained, the judge may authorise the person's removal to another place and detention there for the purpose of being questioned.

(6)   A judge must not authorise the questioning of a person under this section unless satisfied—
(a)   that further questioning of the person is necessary in the interests of justice,
(b)   that the investigation for the purposes of which the further questioning is proposed is being conducted diligently and expeditiously, and
(c)   that what is authorised will not interfere unduly with the preparation of the person's defence to the charge in question or any other criminal charge.
[. . .]

[. . .]

Part 8 SUPPLEMENTARY PROVISIONS

General definitions

92 MEANING OF "TERRORISM"

In this Act "terrorism" has the same meaning as in the Terrorism Act 2000 (c. 11) (see section 1 of that Act).
[. . .]

As amended by the Crime and Security Act 2010 section 56(3)

As amended by the Terrorism Prevention and Investigation Measures Act 2011, Schedule 7, paragraph 5

CRIMINAL JUSTICE AND IMMIGRATION ACT 2008
(c. 2)

An Act to make further provision about criminal justice (including provision about the police) and dealing with offenders and defaulters; to make further provision about the management of offenders; to amend the criminal law; to make further provision for combatting crime and disorder; to make provision about the mutual recognition of financial penalties; to amend the Repatriation of Prisoners Act 1984; to make provision for a new immigration status in certain cases involving criminality; to make provision about the automatic deportation of criminals under the UK Borders Act 2007; to amend section 127 of the Criminal Justice and Public Order Act 1994 and to confer power to suspend the operation of that section; and for connected purposes.
[. . .]

Part 5 CRIMINAL LAW

Pornography etc.

63 POSSESSION OF EXTREME PORNOGRAPHIC IMAGES

(1)   It is an offence for a person to be in possession of an extreme pornographic image.

(2)   An "extreme pornographic image" is an image which is both—
(a)   pornographic, and
(b)   an extreme image.

(3)   An image is "pornographic" if it is of such a nature that it must reasonably be assumed to have been produced solely or principally for the purpose of sexual arousal.

[. . .]

(6)   An "extreme image" is an image which—
(a) falls within subsection (7), and
(b) is grossly offensive, disgusting or otherwise of an obscene character.

(7)   An image falls within this subsection if it portrays, in an explicit and realistic way, any of the following—
(a) an act which threatens a person's life,
(b) an act which results, or is likely to result, in serious injury to a person's anus, breasts or genitals,
(c) an act which involves sexual interference with a human corpse, or
(d) a person performing an act of intercourse or oral sex with an animal (whether dead or alive),
and a reasonable person looking at the image would think that any such person or animal was real.

[. . .]

65 DEFENCES: GENERAL

(1)   Where a person is charged with an offence under section 63, it is a defence for the person to prove any of the matters mentioned in subsection (2).

(2)   The matters are—
(a) that the person had a legitimate reason for being in possession of the image concerned;
(b) that the person had not seen the image concerned and did not know, nor had any cause to suspect, it to be an extreme pornographic image;
(c) that the person—
(i)   was sent the image concerned without any prior request having been made by or on behalf of the person, and
(ii) did not keep it for an unreasonable time.

[. . .]

66 DEFENCE: PARTICIPATION IN CONSENSUAL ACTS

(1)   This section applies where—
(a) a person ("D") is charged with an offence under section 63, and
(b) the offence relates to an image that portrays an act or acts within paragraphs (a) to (c) (but none within paragraph (d)) of subsection (7) of that section.

(2)   It is a defence for D to prove—
(a) that D directly participated in the act or any of the acts portrayed, and
(b) that the act or acts did not involve the infliction of any non-consensual harm on any person, and
(c) if the image portrays an act within section 63(7)(c), that what is portrayed as a human corpse was not in fact a corpse.

(3)   For the purposes of this section harm inflicted on a person is "non-consensual" harm if—
(a)   the harm is of such a nature that the person cannot, in law, consent to it being inflicted on himself or herself; or
(b)   where the person can, in law, consent to it being so inflicted, the person does not in fact consent to it being so inflicted.
[. . .]

Self-defence etc.

76 REASONABLE FORCE FOR PURPOSES OF SELF-DEFENCE ETC.

(1)   This section applies where in proceedings for an offence—
(a)   an issue arises as to whether a person charged with the offence ("D") is entitled to rely on a defence within subsection (2), and
(b)   the question arises whether the degree of force used by D against a person ("V") was reasonable in the circumstances.

(2)   The defences are—
(a)   the common law defence of self-defence; and
(b)   the defences provided by section 3(1) of the Criminal Law Act 1967 (c. 58) or section 3(1) of the Criminal Law Act (Northern Ireland) 1967 (c. 18 (N.I.)) (use of force in prevention of crime or making arrest).

(3)   The question whether the degree of force used by D was reasonable in the circumstances is to be decided by reference to the circumstances as D believed them to be, and subsections (4) to (8) also apply in connection with deciding that question.

(4)   If D claims to have held a particular belief as regards the existence of any circumstances—
(a)   the reasonableness or otherwise of that belief is relevant to the question whether D genuinely held it; but
(b)   if it is determined that D did genuinely hold it, D is entitled to rely on it for the purposes of subsection (3), whether or not—
(i)   it was mistaken, or
(ii)   (if it was mistaken) the mistake was a reasonable one to have made.

(5)   But subsection (4)(b) does not enable D to rely on any mistaken belief attributable to intoxication that was voluntarily induced.

(6)   The degree of force used by D is not to be regarded as having been reasonable in the circumstances as D believed them to be if it was disproportionate in those circumstances.

(7)   In deciding the question mentioned in subsection (3) the following considerations are to be taken into account (so far as relevant in the circumstances of the case)—
(a)   that a person acting for a legitimate purpose may not be able to weigh to a nicety the exact measure of any necessary action; and
(b)   that evidence of a person's having only done what the person honestly and instinctively thought was necessary for a legitimate purpose constitutes strong evidence that only reasonable action was taken by that person for that purpose.

(8)   Subsection (7) is not to be read as preventing other matters from being taken into account where they are relevant to deciding the question mentioned in subsection (3).

(9)   This section is intended to clarify the operation of the existing defences mentioned in subsection (2).

(10)   In this section—
    (a) "legitimate purpose" means—
        (i)   the purpose of self-defence under the common law, or
        (ii) the prevention of crime or effecting or assisting in the lawful arrest of persons mentioned in the provisions referred to in subsection (2)(b);
    (b) references to self-defence include acting in defence of another person; and
    (c) references to the degree of force used are to the type and amount of force used.
    [. . .]

Blasphemy

79 ABOLITION OF COMMON LAW OFFENCES OF BLASPHEMY AND BLASPHEMOUS LIBEL

(1)   The offences of blasphemy and blasphemous libel under the common law of England and Wales are abolished.

    [. . .]

PARLIAMENTARY STANDARDS ACT 2009
(c. 13)

Note: At the time of editing (1 June 2012), section 3 (3) of the Parliamentary Standards Act was not yet in force.

An Act to make provision establishing a body corporate known as the Independent Parliamentary Standards Authority and an officer known as the Commissioner for Parliamentary Investigations; to make provision relating to salaries and allowances for members of the House of Commons and to their financial interests and conduct; and for connected purposes.
[. . .]

Independent Parliamentary Standards Authority etc.

3 INDEPENDENT PARLIAMENTARY STANDARDS AUTHORITY ETC.

(1)   There is to be a body corporate known as the Independent Parliamentary Standards Authority ("IPSA").

[. . .]

[(3)   There is to be an officer known as the Compliance Officer for the Independent Parliamentary Standards Authority ("the Compliance Officer")]

[. . .]

(5)   There is to be a committee known as the Speaker's Committee for the Independent Parliamentary Standards Authority ("the Committee").

[. . .]

Salaries and allowances for MPs

4 MPS' SALARIES

(1) The IPSA is to pay the salaries of members of the House of Commons in accordance with the relevant resolutions of the House.

[...]

5 MPS' ALLOWANCES SCHEME

(1) The IPSA is to pay allowances to members of the House of Commons in accordance with the MPs' allowances scheme.

[...]

(3) The IPSA must—
  (a) prepare the scheme;
  (b) review the scheme regularly and revise it as appropriate.

(4) In preparing or revising the scheme, the IPSA must consult—
  (a) the Speaker of the House of Commons,
  (b) the Committee on Standards in Public Life,
  (c) the Leader of the House of Commons,
  (d) any committee of the House of Commons nominated by the Speaker,
  (e) members of the House of Commons,
  (f) the Review Body on Senior Salaries,
  (g) Her Majesty's Revenue and Customs,
  (h) the Treasury, and
  (i) any other person the IPSA considers appropriate.

(5) The Speaker must lay the scheme (or revision) before the House of Commons.

[...]

(7) The scheme may, for example—
  (a) provide for allowances to be payable in respect of specified kinds of expenditure or in specified circumstances;
  (b) provide for allowances to be payable only on specified conditions (such as a condition that claims for allowances must be supported by documentary evidence);
  (c) impose limits on the amounts that may be paid.

(8) The scheme may provide for allowances to be payable in connection with a person's ceasing to be a member of the House of Commons; and in relation to any such allowances, references in this Act to a member of the House of Commons include a former member of that House.

(8A) Any duty of the IPSA to pay an allowance to a member is subject to anything done in relation to the member in the exercise of the disciplinary powers of the House of Commons.

[...]

6 DEALING WITH CLAIMS UNDER THE SCHEME

(1) No allowance is to be paid to a member of the House of Commons under the MPs' allowances scheme unless a claim for the allowance has been made to the IPSA.

[. . .]

(3)   On receipt of a claim, the IPSA must—
    (a) determine whether to allow or refuse the claim, and
    (b) if it is allowed, determine how much of the amount claimed is to be allowed and pay it accordingly.

[. . .]

Investigation and enforcement

10 OFFENCE OF PROVIDING FALSE OR MISLEADING INFORMATION FOR ALLOWANCES CLAIMS

(1)   A member of the House of Commons commits an offence if the member—
    (a) makes a claim under the MPs' allowances scheme, and
    (b) provides information for the purposes of the claim that the member knows to be false or misleading in a material respect.

As amended by the Parliamentary Voting System and Constituencies Act 2011 section 30 and Schedule 5 paragraph 3

CONSTITUTIONAL REFORM AND GOVERNANCE ACT 2010
(c. 25)

An Act to make provision relating to the civil service of the State; to make provision in relation to section 3 of the Act of Settlement; to make provision relating to the ratification of treaties; to make provision relating to the counting of votes in parliamentary elections; to amend the Parliamentary Standards Act 2009 and the European Parliament (Pay and Pensions) Act 1979 and to make provision relating to pensions for members of the House of Commons, Ministers and other office holders; to make provision for treating members of the House of Commons and members of the House of Lords as resident, ordinarily resident and domiciled in the United Kingdom for taxation purposes; to amend the Government Resources and Accounts Act 2000 and to make corresponding provision in relation to Wales; to amend the Public Records Act 1958 and the Freedom of Information Act 2000.

[. . .]

Part 1 THE CIVIL SERVICE

Chapter 1 STATUTORY BASIS FOR MANAGEMENT OF THE CIVIL SERVICE

Application

1 APPLICATION OF CHAPTER

(1)   Subject to subsections (2) and (3), this Chapter applies to the civil service of the State.

[. . .]

Civil Service Commission

2 ESTABLISHMENT OF THE CIVIL SERVICE COMMISSION

(1)   There is to be a body corporate called the Civil Service Commission ("the Commission").

[. . .]

Power to manage the civil service

3 MANAGEMENT OF THE CIVIL SERVICE

(1)   The Minister for the Civil Service has the power to manage the civil service (excluding the diplomatic service).

(2)   The Secretary of State has the power to manage the diplomatic service.

[. . .]

Codes of conduct

5 CIVIL SERVICE CODE

(1)   The Minister for the Civil Service must publish a code of conduct for the civil service (excluding the diplomatic service).

(2)   For this purpose, the Minister may publish separate codes of conduct covering civil servants who serve the Scottish Executive or the Welsh Assembly Government.

[. . .]

6 DIPLOMATIC SERVICE CODE

(1)   The Secretary of State must publish a code of conduct for the diplomatic service.

[. . .]

7 MINIMUM REQUIREMENTS FOR CIVIL SERVICE AND DIPLOMATIC SERVICE CODES

(1)   This section sets out the provision that must be included in a civil service code or the diplomatic service code in relation to the civil servants covered by the code. (The code may include other provision as well.)

(2)   The code must require civil servants who serve an administration mentioned in subsection (3) to carry out their duties for the assistance of the administration as it is duly constituted for the time being, whatever its political complexion.

(3)   The administrations are—
(a) Her Majesty's Government in the United Kingdom;
(b) the Scottish Executive;
(c) the Welsh Assembly Government.

(4)   The code must require civil servants to carry out their duties—
(a) with integrity and honesty, and
(b) with objectivity and impartiality.

[. . .]

9 CONDUCT THAT CONFLICTS WITH A CODE OF CONDUCT: COMPLAINTS BY CIVIL SERVANTS

(1)   This section applies in relation to any civil service code and the diplomatic service code; and "code" is to be read accordingly.

(2)   Subsection (3) applies if a civil servant ("P") covered by a code has reason to believe—
   (a)   that P is being, or has been, required to act in a way that conflicts with the code, or
   (b)   that another civil servant covered by the code is acting, or has acted, in a way that conflicts with the code.

(3)   P may complain to the Commission about the matter.

(4)   A code may include provision about the steps that must be taken by a civil servant before making a complaint (and P must take the steps accordingly).

(5)   The Commission—
   (a)   must determine procedures for the making of complaints and for the investigation and consideration of complaints by the Commission;
   (b)   after considering a complaint, may make recommendations about how the matter should be resolved.

(6)   For the purposes of the investigation or consideration of a complaint, the following must provide the Commission with any information it reasonably requires—
   (a)   civil service management authorities;
   (b)   the complainant;
   (c)   any civil servant whose conduct is covered by the complaint.

[. . .]

Appointment

10 SELECTIONS FOR APPOINTMENTS TO THE CIVIL SERVICE

(1)   This section applies to the selection of persons who are not civil servants for appointment to the civil service.

(2)   A person's selection must be on merit on the basis of fair and open competition.

[. . .]

11 RECRUITMENT PRINCIPLES

(1)   The Commission must publish a set of principles to be applied for the purposes of the requirement in section 10(2).

(2)   Before publishing the set of principles (or any revision of it), the Commission must consult the Minister for the Civil Service.

[. . .]

(4)   Civil service management authorities must comply with the recruitment principles.

[. . .]

Part 2 **RATIFICATION OF TREATIES**

20 TREATIES TO BE LAID BEFORE PARLIAMENT BEFORE RATIFICATION

(1) Subject to what follows, a treaty is not to be ratified unless—
(a) a Minister of the Crown has laid before Parliament a copy of the treaty,
(b) the treaty has been published in a way that a Minister of the Crown thinks appropriate, and
(c) period A has expired without either House having resolved, within period A, that the treaty should not be ratified.

(2) Period A is the period of 21 sitting days beginning with the first sitting day after the date on which the requirement in subsection (1)(a) is met.

(3) Subsections (4) to (6) apply if the House of Commons resolved as mentioned in subsection (1)(c)(whether or not the House of Lords also did so).

(4) The treaty may be ratified if—
(a) a Minister of the Crown has laid before Parliament a statement indicating that the Minister is of the opinion that the treaty should nevertheless be ratified and explaining why, and
(b) period B has expired without the House of Commons having resolved, within period B, that the treaty should not be ratified.

(5) Period B is the period of 21 sitting days beginning with the first sitting day after the date on which the requirement in subsection (4)(a) is met.

(6) A statement may be laid under subsection (4)(a) in relation to the treaty on more than one occasion.

(7) Subsection (8) applies if—
(a) the House of Lords resolved as mentioned in subsection (1)(c), but
(b) the House of Commons did not.

(8) The treaty may be ratified if a Minister of the Crown has laid before Parliament a statement indicating that the Minister is of the opinion that the treaty should nevertheless be ratified and explaining why.

(9) "Sitting day" means a day on which both Houses of Parliament sit.

21 EXTENSION OF 21 SITTING DAY PERIOD

(1) A Minister of the Crown may, in relation to a treaty, extend the period mentioned in section 20(1)(c) by 21 sitting days or less.

(2) The Minister does that by laying before Parliament a statement—
(a) indicating that the period is to be extended, and
(b) setting out the length of the extension.
[. . .]

22 SECTION 20 NOT TO APPLY IN EXCEPTIONAL CASES

(1) Section 20 does not apply to a treaty if a Minister of the Crown is of the opinion that, exceptionally, the treaty should be ratified without the requirements of that section having been met.

(2)   But a treaty may not be ratified by virtue of subsection (1) after either House has resolved, as mentioned in section 20(1)(c), that the treaty should not be ratified.

(3)   If a Minister determines that a treaty is to be ratified by virtue of subsection (1), the Minister must, either before or as soon as practicable after the treaty is ratified—
    (a)   lay before Parliament a copy of the treaty,
    (b)   arrange for the treaty to be published in a way that the Minister thinks appropriate, and
    (c)   lay before Parliament a statement indicating that the Minister is of the opinion mentioned in subsection (1) and explaining why.

23 SECTION 20 NOT TO APPLY TO CERTAIN DESCRIPTIONS OF TREATIES

(1)   Section 20 does not apply to—
    (b)   a treaty covered by section 5 of the European Union (Amendment) Act 2008 (treaty amending Treaty establishing European Atomic Energy Community not to be ratified unless approved by Act of Parliament);
    (c)   a treaty that is subject to a requirement imposed by Part 1 of the European Union Act 2011 (restrictions on treaties and decisions relating to EU).
[. . .]

25 MEANING OF "TREATY" AND "RATIFICATION"

(1)   In this Part "treaty" means a written agreement—
    (a)   between States or between States and international organisations, and
    (b)   binding under international law.

(2)   But "treaty" does not include a regulation, rule, measure, decision or similar instrument made under a treaty (other than one that amends or replaces the treaty (in whole or in part)).

[. . .]

As amended by the European Union Act 2011, s14(2)

EQUALITY ACT 2010

Parts 1 and 2 applicable in England, Scotland and Wales

An Act to make provision to require Ministers of the Crown and others when making strategic decisions about the exercise of their functions to have regard to the desirability of reducing socio-economic inequalities; to reform and harmonise equality law and restate the greater part of the enactments relating to discrimination and harassment related to certain personal characteristics; to enable certain employers to be required to publish information about the differences in pay between male and female employees; to prohibit victimisation in certain circumstances; to require the exercise of certain functions to be with regard to the need to eliminate discrimination and other prohibited conduct; to enable duties to be imposed in relation to the exercise of public procurement functions; to increase equality of opportunity; to amend the law relating to rights and responsibilities in family relationships; and for connected purposes.[8th April 2010]

Be it enacted by the Queen's most Excellent Majesty, by and with the advice and consent of the Lords Spiritual and Temporal, and Commons, in this present Parliament assembled, and by the authority of the same, as follows:—

Part 1 SOCIO-ECONOMIC INEQUALITIES

Part 2 EQUALITY: KEY CONCEPTS

Chapter 1 PROTECTED CHARACTERISTICS

4 THE PROTECTED CHARACTERISTICS

The following characteristics are protected characteristics—
>   age;
>   disability;
>   gender reassignment;
>   marriage and civil partnership;
>   pregnancy and maternity;
>   race;
>   religion or belief;
>   sex;
>   sexual orientation.

5 AGE

(1)   In relation to the protected characteristic of age—
    (a) a reference to a person who has a particular protected characteristic is a reference to a person of a particular age group;
    (b) a reference to persons who share a protected characteristic is a reference to persons of the same age group.

(2)   A reference to an age group is a reference to a group of persons defined by reference to age, whether by reference to a particular age or to a range of ages.

6 DISABILITY

(1)   A person (P) has a disability if—
    (a) P has a physical or mental impairment, and
    (b) the impairment has a substantial and long-term adverse effect on P's ability to carry out normal day-to-day activities.

(2)   A reference to a disabled person is a reference to a person who has a disability.

(3)   In relation to the protected characteristic of disability—
    (a) a reference to a person who has a particular protected characteristic is a reference to a person who has a particular disability;
    (b) a reference to persons who share a protected characteristic is a reference to persons who have the same disability.

(4)   This Act (except Part 12 and section 190) applies in relation to a person who has had a disability as it applies in relation to a person who has the disability; accordingly (except in that Part and that section)—
    (a) a reference (however expressed) to a person who has a disability includes a reference to a person who has had the disability, and

(b) a reference (however expressed) to a person who does not have a disability includes a reference to a person who has not had the disability.

(5) A Minister of the Crown may issue guidance about matters to be taken into account in deciding any question for the purposes of subsection (1).

(6) Schedule 1 (disability: supplementary provision) has effect.

7 GENDER REASSIGNMENT

(1) A person has the protected characteristic of gender reassignment if the person is proposing to undergo, is undergoing or has undergone a process (or part of a process) for the purpose of reassigning the person's sex by changing physiological or other attributes of sex.

(2) A reference to a transsexual person is a reference to a person who has the protected characteristic of gender reassignment.

(3) In relation to the protected characteristic of gender reassignment—
  (a) a reference to a person who has a particular protected characteristic is a reference to a transsexual person;
  (b) a reference to persons who share a protected characteristic is a reference to transsexual persons.

8 MARRIAGE AND CIVIL PARTNERSHIP

(1) A person has the protected characteristic of marriage and civil partnership if the person is married or is a civil partner.

(2) In relation to the protected characteristic of marriage and civil partnership—
  (a) a reference to a person who has a particular protected characteristic is a reference to a person who is married or is a civil partner;
  (b) a reference to persons who share a protected characteristic is a reference to persons who are married or are civil partners.

9 RACE

(1) Race includes—
  (a) colour;
  (b) nationality;
  (c) ethnic or national origins.

(2) In relation to the protected characteristic of race—
  (a) a reference to a person who has a particular protected characteristic is a reference to a person of a particular racial group;
  (b) a reference to persons who share a protected characteristic is a reference to persons of the same racial group.

(3) A racial group is a group of persons defined by reference to race; and a reference to a person's racial group is a reference to a racial group into which the person falls.

(4) The fact that a racial group comprises two or more distinct racial groups does not prevent it from constituting a particular racial group.

(5) A Minister of the Crown may by order—
  (a) amend this section so as to provide for caste to be an aspect of race;

(b) amend this Act so as to provide for an exception to a provision of this Act to apply, or not to apply, to caste or to apply, or not to apply, to caste in specified circumstances.

(6) The power under section 207(4)(b), in its application to subsection (5), includes power to amend this Act.

10 RELIGION OR BELIEF

(1) Religion means any religion and a reference to religion includes a reference to a lack of religion.

(2) Belief means any religious or philosophical belief and a reference to belief includes a reference to a lack of belief.

(3) In relation to the protected characteristic of religion or belief—
   (a) a reference to a person who has a particular protected characteristic is a reference to a person of a particular religion or belief;
   (b) a reference to persons who share a protected characteristic is a reference to persons who are of the same religion or belief.

11 SEX

In relation to the protected characteristic of sex—
(a) a reference to a person who has a particular protected characteristic is a reference to a man or to a woman;

(b) a reference to persons who share a protected characteristic is a reference to persons of the same sex.

12 SEXUAL ORIENTATION

(1) Sexual orientation means a person's sexual orientation towards—
   (a) persons of the same sex,
   (b) persons of the opposite sex, or
   (c) persons of either sex.

(2) In relation to the protected characteristic of sexual orientation—
   (a) a reference to a person who has a particular protected characteristic is a reference to a person who is of a particular sexual orientation;
   (b) a reference to persons who share a protected characteristic is a reference to persons who are of the same sexual orientation.

Chapter 2 **PROHIBITED CONDUCT**

Discrimination

13 DIRECT DISCRIMINATION

(1) A person (A) discriminates against another (B) if, because of a protected characteristic, A treats B less favourably than A treats or would treat others.

(2) If the protected characteristic is age, A does not discriminate against B if A can show A's treatment of B to be a proportionate means of achieving a legitimate aim.

(3)   If the protected characteristic is disability, and B is not a disabled person, A does not discriminate against B only because A treats or would treat disabled persons more favourably than A treats B.

(4)   If the protected characteristic is marriage and civil partnership, this section applies to a contravention of Part 5 (work) only if the treatment is because it is B who is married or a civil partner.

(5)   If the protected characteristic is race, less favourable treatment includes segregating B from others.

(6)   If the protected characteristic is sex—
(a)   less favourable treatment of a woman includes less favourable treatment of her because she is breast-feeding;
(b)   in a case where B is a man, no account is to be taken of special treatment afforded to a woman in connection with pregnancy or childbirth.

(7)   Subsection (6)(a) does not apply for the purposes of Part 5 (work).

(8)   This section is subject to sections 17(6) and 18(7).

Other prohibited conduct

26 HARASSMENT

(1)   A person (A) harasses another (B) if—
(a)   A engages in unwanted conduct related to a relevant protected characteristic, and
(b)   the conduct has the purpose or effect of—
(i)   violating B's dignity, or
(ii)   creating an intimidating, hostile, degrading, humiliating or offensive environment for B.

(2)   A also harasses B if—
(a)   A engages in unwanted conduct of a sexual nature, and
(b)   the conduct has the purpose or effect referred to in subsection (1)(b).

(3)   A also harasses B if—
(a)   A or another person engages in unwanted conduct of a sexual nature or that is related to gender reassignment or sex,
(b)   the conduct has the purpose or effect referred to in subsection (1)(b), and
(c)   because of B's rejection of or submission to the conduct, A treats B less favourably than A would treat B if B had not rejected or submitted to the conduct.

(4)   In deciding whether conduct has the effect referred to in subsection (1)(b), each of the following must be taken into account—
(a)   the perception of B;
(b)   the other circumstances of the case;
(c)   whether it is reasonable for the conduct to have that effect.

(5)   The relevant protected characteristics are—
age;
disability;
gender reassignment;
race;
religion or belief;
sex;
sexual orientation.

27 VICTIMISATION

(1)   A person (A) victimises another person (B) if A subjects B to a detriment because—
    (a)   B does a protected act, or
    (b)   A believes that B has done, or may do, a protected act.

(2)   Each of the following is a protected act—
    (a)   bringing proceedings under this Act;
    (b)   giving evidence or information in connection with proceedings under this Act;
    (c)   doing any other thing for the purposes of or in connection with this Act;
    (d)   making an allegation (whether or not express) that A or another person has contravened this Act.

(3)   Giving false evidence or information, or making a false allegation, is not a protected act if the evidence or information is given, or the allegation is made, in bad faith.

(4)   This section applies only where the person subjected to a detriment is an individual.

(5)   The reference to contravening this Act includes a reference to committing a breach of an equality clause or rule.

EUROPEAN UNION ACT 2011

Act to make provision about treaties relating to the European Union and decisions made under them, including provision implementing the Protocol signed at Brussels on 23 June 2010 amending the Protocol (No. 36) on transitional provisions annexed to the Treaty on European Union, to the Treaty on the Functioning of the European Union and to the Treaty establishing the European Atomic Energy Community; and to make provision about the means by which directly applicable or directly effective European Union law has effect in the United Kingdom.

[19th July 2011]

Be it enacted by the Queen's most Excellent Majesty, by and with the advice and consent of the Lords Spiritual and Temporal, and Commons, in this present Parliament assembled, and by the authority of the same, as follows:—

1 INTERPRETATION OF PART 1

(1)   This section has effect for the interpretation of this Part.

(2)   "TEU" means the Treaty on European Union.

(3)   "TFEU" means the Treaty on the Functioning of the European Union.

(4)   A reference to a treaty which amends TEU or TFEU includes a reference to—
    (a)   a treaty resulting from the application of Article 48(2) to (5) of TEU (ordinary revision procedure);
    (b)   an agreement under Article 49 of TEU (admission of new members).

(5)   An "Article 48(6) decision" means a decision under Article 48(6) of TEU (simplified revision procedure).

(6)   Except in a reference to "the European Council", "the Council" means the Council of the European Union.

(7)   A reference to a Minister of the Crown voting in favour of or otherwise supporting a decision is a reference to a Minister of the Crown—

(a) voting in favour of the decision in the European Council or the Council, or

(b) allowing the decision to be adopted by consensus or unanimity by the European Council or the Council.

2 TREATIES AMENDING OR REPLACING TEU OR TFEU

(1) A treaty which amends or replaces TEU or TFEU is not to be ratified unless—

(a) a statement relating to the treaty was laid before Parliament in accordance with section 5,

(b) the treaty is approved by Act of Parliament, and

(c) the referendum condition or the exemption condition is met.

(2) The referendum condition is that—

(a) the Act providing for the approval of the treaty provides that the provision approving the treaty is not to come into force until a referendum about whether the treaty should be ratified has been held throughout the United Kingdom or, where the treaty also affects Gibraltar, throughout the United Kingdom and Gibraltar,

(b) the referendum has been held, and

(c) the majority of those voting in the referendum are in favour of the ratification of the treaty.

(3) The exemption condition is that the Act providing for the approval of the treaty states that the treaty does not fall within section 4.

3 AMENDMENT OF TFEU UNDER SIMPLIFIED REVISION PROCEDURE

(1) Where the European Council has adopted an Article 48(6) decision subject to its approval by the member States, a Minister of the Crown may not confirm the approval of the decision by the United Kingdom unless—

(a) a statement relating to the decision was laid before Parliament in accordance with section 5,

(b) the decision is approved by Act of Parliament, and

(c) the referendum condition, the exemption condition or the significance condition is met.

(2) The referendum condition is that—

(a) the Act providing for the approval of the decision provides that the provision approving the decision is not to come into force until a referendum about whether the decision should be approved has been held throughout the United Kingdom or, where the decision also affects Gibraltar, throughout the United Kingdom and Gibraltar,

(b) the referendum has been held, and

(c) the majority of those voting in the referendum are in favour of the approval of the decision.

(3) The exemption condition is that the Act providing for the approval of the decision states that the decision does not fall within section 4.

(4) The significance condition is that the Act providing for the approval of the decision states that—

(a) the decision falls within section 4 only because of provision of the kind mentioned in subsection (1)(i) or (j) of that section, and

(b) the effect of that provision in relation to the United Kingdom is not significant.

4 CASES WHERE TREATY OR ARTICLE 48(6) DECISION ATTRACTS A REFERENDUM

(1)   Subject to subsection (4), a treaty or an Article 48(6) decision falls within this section if it involves one or more of the following—

(a) the extension of the objectives of the EU as set out in Article 3 of TEU;

(b) the conferring on the EU of a new exclusive competence;

(c) the extension of an exclusive competence of the EU;

(d) the conferring on the EU of a new competence shared with the member States;

(e) the extension of any competence of the EU that is shared with the member States;

(f) the extension of the competence of the EU in relation to—

(i)   the co-ordination of economic and employment policies, or

(ii) common foreign and security policy;

(g) the conferring on the EU of a new competence to carry out actions to support, co-ordinate or supplement the actions of member States;

(h) the extension of a supporting, co-ordinating or supplementing competence of the EU;

(i)   the conferring on an EU institution or body of power to impose a requirement or obligation on the United Kingdom, or the removal of any limitation on any such power of an EU institution or body;

(j)   the conferring on an EU institution or body of new or extended power to impose sanctions on the United Kingdom;

(k) any amendment of a provision listed in Schedule 1 that removes a requirement that anything should be done unanimously, by consensus or by common accord;

(l)   any amendment of Article 31(2) of TEU (decisions relating to common foreign and security policy to which qualified majority voting applies) that removes or amends the provision enabling a member of the Council to oppose the adoption of a decision to be taken by qualified majority voting;

(m) any amendment of any of the provisions specified in subsection (3) that removes or amends the provision enabling a member of the Council, in relation to a draft legislative act, to ensure the suspension of the ordinary legislative procedure.

(2)   Any reference in subsection (1) to the extension of a competence includes a reference to the removal of a limitation on a competence.

(3)   The provisions referred to in subsection (1)(m) are—

(a) Article 48 of TFEU (social security),

(b) Article 82(3) of TFEU (judicial co-operation in criminal matters), and

(c) Article 83(3) of TFEU (particularly serious crime with a cross-border dimension).

(4)   A treaty or Article 48(6) decision does not fall within this section merely because it involves one or more of the following—

(a) the codification of practice under TEU or TFEU in relation to the previous exercise of an existing competence;

(b) the making of any provision that applies only to member States other than the United Kingdom;

(c) in the case of a treaty, the accession of a new member State.

5 STATEMENT TO BE LAID BEFORE PARLIAMENT

(1)   If a treaty amending TEU or TFEU is agreed in an inter-governmental conference, a Minister of the Crown must lay the required statement before Parliament before the end of the 2 months beginning with the date on which the treaty is agreed.

(2)   If an Article 48(6) decision is adopted by the European Council subject to its approval by the member States, a Minister of the Crown must lay the required statement before Parliament before the end of the 2 months beginning with the date on which the decision is adopted.

(3)   The required statement is a statement as to whether, in the Minister's opinion, the treaty or Article 48(6) decision falls within section 4.

(4)   If the Minister is of the opinion that an Article 48(6) decision falls within section 4 only because of provision of the kind mentioned in subsection (1)(i) or (j) of that section, the statement must indicate whether in the Minister's opinion the effect of that provision in relation to the United Kingdom is significant.

(5)   The statement must give reasons for the Minister's opinion under subsection (3) and, if relevant, subsection (4).

(6)   In relation to an Article 48(6) decision adopted by the European Council before the day on which this section comes into force ("the commencement date"), the condition in section 3(1)(a) is to be taken to be complied with if a statement under this section is laid before Parliament before the end of the 2 months beginning with the commencement date.

6 DECISIONS REQUIRING APPROVAL BY ACT AND BY REFERENDUM

(1)   A Minister of the Crown may not vote in favour of or otherwise support a decision to which this subsection applies unless—
(a)   the draft decision is approved by Act of Parliament, and
(b)   the referendum condition is met.

(2)   Where the European Council has recommended to the member States the adoption of a decision under Article 42(2) of TEU in relation to a common EU defence, a Minister of the Crown may not notify the European Council that the decision is adopted by the United Kingdom unless—
(a)   the decision is approved by Act of Parliament, and
(b)   the referendum condition is met.

(3)   A Minister of the Crown may not give a notification under Article 4 of Protocol (No. 21) on the position of the United Kingdom and Ireland in respect of the area of freedom, security and justice annexed to TEU and TFEU which relates to participation by the United Kingdom in a European Public Prosecutor's Office or an extension of the powers of that Office unless—
(a)   the notification has been approved by Act of Parliament, and
(b)   the referendum condition is met.

(4)   The referendum condition is that set out in section 3(2), with references to a decision being read for the purposes of subsection (1) as references to a draft decision and for the purposes of subsection (3) as references to a notification.

(5)   The decisions to which subsection (1) applies are—
(a)   a decision under the provision of Article 31(3) of TEU that permits the adoption of qualified majority voting;
(b)   a decision under Article 48(7) of TEU which in relation to any provision listed in Schedule 1—
(i)   adopts qualified majority voting, or
(ii) applies the ordinary legislative procedure in place of a special legislative procedure requiring the Council to act unanimously;

(c) a decision under Article 86(1) of TFEU involving participation by the United Kingdom in a European Public Prosecutor's Office;

(d) where the United Kingdom has become a participant in a European Public Prosecutor's Office, a decision under Article 86(4) of TFEU to extend the powers of that Office;

(e) a decision under Article 140(3) of TFEU which would make the euro the currency of the United Kingdom;

(f) a decision under the provision of Article 153(2) of TFEU (social policy) that permits the application of the ordinary legislative procedure in place of a special legislative procedure;

(g) a decision under the provision of Article 192(2) of TFEU (environment) that permits the application of the ordinary legislative procedure in place of a special legislative procedure;

(h) a decision under the provision of Article 312(2) of TFEU (EU finance) that permits the adoption of qualified majority voting;

(i) a decision under the provision of Article 333(1) of TFEU (enhanced co-operation) that permits the adoption of qualified majority voting, where the decision relates to a provision listed in Schedule 1 and the United Kingdom is a participant in the enhanced co-operation to which the decision relates;

(j) a decision under the provision of Article 333(2) of TFEU (enhanced co-operation) that permits the adoption of the ordinary legislative procedure in place of a special legislative procedure, where—
   (i)   the decision relates to a provision listed in Schedule 1,
   (ii) the special legislative procedure requires the Council to act unanimously, and
   (iii) the United Kingdom is a participant in the enhanced co-operation to which the decision relates;

(k) a decision under Article 4 of the Schengen Protocol that removes any border control of the United Kingdom.

(6) In subsection (5)(k) "the Schengen Protocol" means the Protocol (No. 19) on the Schengen acquis integrated into the framework of the European Union, annexed to TEU and TFEU.

7 DECISIONS REQUIRING APPROVAL BY ACT

(1) A Minister of the Crown may not confirm the approval by the United Kingdom of a decision to which this subsection applies unless the decision is approved by Act of Parliament.

(2) The decisions to which subsection (1) applies are—
   (a) a decision under the provision of Article 25 of TFEU that permits the adoption of provisions to strengthen or add to the rights listed in Article 20(2) of that Treaty (rights of citizens of the European Union);
   (b) a decision under the provision of Article 223(1) of TFEU that permits the laying down of the provisions necessary for the election of the members of the European Parliament in accordance with that Article;
   (c) a decision under the provision of Article 262 of TFEU that permits the conferring of jurisdiction on the Court of Justice of the European Union in disputes relating to the application of acts adopted on the basis of the EU Treaties which create European intellectual property rights;
   (d) a decision under the third paragraph of Article 311 of TFEU to adopt a decision laying down provisions relating to the system of own resources of the European Union.

(3)   A Minister of the Crown may not vote in favour of or otherwise support a decision to which this subsection applies unless the draft decision is approved by Act of Parliament.

(4)   The decisions to which subsection (3) applies are—
   (a)   a decision under the provision of Article 17(5) of TEU that permits the alteration of the number of members of the European Commission;
   (b)   a decision under Article 48(7) of TEU which in relation to any provision not listed in Schedule 1—
      (i)   adopts qualified majority voting, or
      (ii)   applies the ordinary legislative procedure in place of a special legislative procedure requiring the Council to act unanimously;
   (c)   a decision under the provision of Article 64(3) of TFEU that permits the adoption of measures which constitute a step backwards in European Union law as regards the liberalisation of the movement of capital to or from third countries;
   (d)   a decision under the provision of Article 126(14) of TFEU that permits the adoption of provisions to replace the Protocol (No. 12) on the excessive deficit procedure annexed to TEU and TFEU;
   (e)   a decision under the provision of Article 333(1) of TFEU (enhanced co-operation) that permits the adoption of qualified majority voting, where the decision relates to a provision not listed in Schedule 1 and the United Kingdom is a participant in the enhanced co-operation to which the decision relates;
   (f)   a decision under the provision of Article 333(2) of TFEU (enhanced co-operation) that permits the adoption of the ordinary legislative procedure in place of a special legislative procedure, where—
      (i)   the decision relates to a provision not listed in Schedule 1,
      (ii)   the special legislative procedure requires the Council to act unanimously, and
      (iii)   the United Kingdom is a participant in the enhanced co-operation to which the decision relates.

8 DECISIONS UNDER ARTICLE 352 OF TFEU

(1)   A Minister of the Crown may not vote in favour of or otherwise support an Article 352 decision unless one of subsections (3) to (5) is complied with in relation to the draft decision.

(2)   An Article 352 decision is a decision under the provision of Article 352 of TFEU that permits the adoption of measures to attain one of the objectives set out in the EU Treaties (but for which those Treaties have not provided the necessary powers).

(3)   This subsection is complied with if a draft decision is approved by Act of Parliament.

(4)   This subsection is complied with if—
   (a)   in each House of Parliament a Minister of the Crown moves a motion that the House approves Her Majesty's Government's intention to support a specified draft decision and is of the opinion that the measure to which it relates is required as a matter of urgency, and
   (b)   each House agrees to the motion without amendment.

(5)   This subsection is complied with if a Minister of the Crown has laid before Parliament a statement specifying a draft decision and stating that in the opinion of the Minister the decision relates only to one or more exempt purposes.

(6)   The exempt purposes are—
   (a)   to make provision equivalent to that made by a measure previously adopted under Article 352 of TFEU, other than an excepted measure;

(b) to prolong or renew a measure previously adopted under that Article, other than an excepted measure;

(c) to extend a measure previously adopted under that Article to another member State or other country;

(d) to repeal existing measures adopted under that Article;

(e) to consolidate existing measures adopted under that Article without any change of substance.

(7) In subsection (6)(a) and (b), "excepted measure" means a measure adopted after the commencement of this section and resulting from a decision in relation to which a Minister of the Crown had relied on compliance with subsection (4).

9 APPROVAL REQUIRED IN CONNECTION WITH TITLE V OF PART 3 OF TFEU

(1) A Minister of the Crown may not give a notification to which this subsection applies unless Parliamentary approval has been given in accordance with subsection (3).

(2) Subsection (1) applies in relation to a notification under Article 3 of Protocol (No. 21) on the position of the United Kingdom and Ireland in respect of the area of freedom, security and justice annexed to TEU and TFEU (the "AFSJ Protocol") that the United Kingdom wishes to take part in the adoption and application of a measure proposed under any of the following—

(a) the provision of Article 81(3) of TFEU (family law) that permits the application of the ordinary legislative procedure in place of a special legislative procedure;

(b) the provision of Article 82(2)(d) of TFEU (criminal procedure) that permits the identification of further specific aspects of criminal procedure to which directives adopted under the ordinary legislative procedure may relate;

(c) the provision of Article 83(1) of TFEU (particularly serious crime with a cross-border dimension) that permits the identification of further areas of crime to which directives adopted under the ordinary legislative procedure may relate.

(3) Parliamentary approval is given if—

(a) in each House of Parliament a Minister of the Crown moves a motion that the House approves Her Majesty's Government's intention to give a notification in respect of a specified measure, and

(b) each House agrees to the motion without amendment.

(4) Despite any Parliamentary approval given for the purposes of subsection (1), a Minister may not vote in favour of or otherwise support a decision under a provision falling within any of paragraphs (a) to (c) of subsection (2) unless the draft decision is approved by Act of Parliament.

(5) A Minister of the Crown may not give a notification under Article 4 of the AFSJ Protocol that the United Kingdom wishes to accept a measure to which this subsection applies unless the notification in respect of the measure has been approved by Act of Parliament.

(6) The measures to which subsection (5) applies are—

(a) a measure adopted under a provision described in any of paragraphs (a) to (c) of subsection (2), or

(b) a measure established under Article 81(3), 82(2)(d) or 83(1) of TFEU by virtue of a previous decision adopted, without the participation of the United Kingdom, under a provision falling within any of those paragraphs.

10 PARLIAMENTARY CONTROL OF CERTAIN DECISIONS NOT REQUIRING APPROVAL BY ACT

(1)   A Minister of the Crown may not vote in favour of or otherwise support a decision under any of the following unless Parliamentary approval has been given in accordance with this section—

    (a)   the provision of Article 56 of TFEU that permits the extension of the provisions of Chapter 3 of Title IV of Part 3 of that Treaty (free movement of services) to nationals of a third country;

    (b)   Article 129(3) of TFEU (amendment of provisions of the Statute of the European System of Central Banks or of the European Central Bank);

    (c)   the provision of Article 252 of TFEU that permits an increase in the number of Advocates-General;

    (d)   the provision of Article 257 of TFEU that permits the establishment of specialised courts attached to the General Court;

    (e)   the provision of Article 281 of TFEU that permits the amendment of the Statute of the Court of Justice of the European Union;

    (f)   the provision of Article 308 of TFEU that permits the amendment of the Statute of the European Investment Bank.

(2)   A Minister of the Crown may not vote in favour of or otherwise support a decision to which this subsection applies unless Parliamentary approval has been given in accordance with this section.

(3)   Subsection (2) applies to a decision under Article 48(7) of TEU which in relation to a provision of TFEU applies the ordinary legislative procedure in place of a special legislative procedure not requiring the Council to act unanimously.

(4)   A Minister of the Crown may not confirm the approval by the United Kingdom of a decision under Article 218(8) of TFEU for the accession of the European Union to the European Convention for the Protection of Human Rights and Fundamental Freedoms in accordance with Article 6(2) of TEU unless Parliamentary approval has been given in accordance with this section.

(5)   Parliamentary approval is given if—

    (a)   in each House of Parliament a Minister of the Crown moves a motion that the House approves Her Majesty's Government's intention to support the adoption of a specified draft decision, and

    (b)   each House agrees to the motion without amendment.

11 PERSONS ENTITLED TO VOTE IN REFERENDUM

(1)   The persons entitled to vote in any referendum held in pursuance of section 2, 3 or 6 are to be as follows—

    (a)   the persons who, on the date of the referendum, would be entitled to vote as an elector at a parliamentary election in a constituency in the United Kingdom;

    (b)   the persons who, on that date, are disqualified by reason of being peers from voting as electors in parliamentary elections but—

        (i)   would be entitled to vote as electors at a local government election in any electoral area in Great Britain,

        (ii)   would be entitled to vote as electors at a local election in any district electoral area in Northern Ireland, or

(iii) would be entitled to vote as electors at a European Parliamentary election in any electoral region by virtue of section 3 of the Representation of the People Act 1985 (peers resident outside the United Kingdom);

[. . .]

[. . .]

12 SEPARATE QUESTIONS

If a referendum is to be held in pursuance of any of sections 2, 3 and 6 in relation to two or more treaties or decisions, or in relation to one or more treaties and one or more decisions, a separate question must be included on the ballot paper in relation to each treaty or decision.

13 ROLE OF ELECTORAL COMMISSION

Where an Act provides for a referendum to be held in pursuance of section 2, 3 or 6, the Electoral Commission—

(a) must take whatever steps they think appropriate to promote public awareness of the referendum and how to vote in it, and

(b) may take whatever steps they think appropriate to promote public awareness of the subject-matter of the referendum.

[. . .]

Part 2 **IMPLEMENTATION OF TRANSITIONAL PROTOCOL ON MEPS**

15 PROTOCOL ON MEPS: APPROVAL, AND ADDITION TO LIST OF TREATIES

(1) The Protocol amending the Protocol (No. 36) on transitional provisions annexed to the Treaty on European Union, to the Treaty on the Functioning of the European Union and to the Treaty establishing the European Atomic Energy Community, signed at Brussels on 23 June 2010, is approved for the purposes of section 5 of the European Union (Amendment) Act 2008 (amendment of founding Treaties: approval by Act of Parliament).

(2) In section 1(2) of the European Communities Act 1972, in the definition of "the Treaties", after paragraph (s) insert— "and

(t) the Protocol amending the Protocol (No. 36) on transitional provisions annexed to the Treaty on European Union, to the Treaty on the Functioning of the European Union and to the Treaty establishing the European Atomic Energy Community, signed at Brussels on 23 June 2010;".

[. . .]

Part 3 **GENERAL STATUS OF EU LAW**

18 STATUS OF EU LAW DEPENDENT ON CONTINUING STATUTORY BASIS

Directly applicable or directly effective EU law (that is, the rights, powers, liabilities, obligations, restrictions, remedies and procedures referred to in section 2(1) of the European Communities Act 1972) falls to be recognised and available in law in the United Kingdom only by virtue of that Act or where it is required to be recognised and available in law by virtue of any other Act.

FINAL PROVISIONS

20 EXTENT

(1)   This Act extends to the whole of the United Kingdom.

[. . .]

FIXED-TERM PARLIAMENTS ACT 2011

An Act to make provision about the dissolution of Parliament and the determination of polling days for parliamentary general elections; and for connected purposes.

[15th September 2011]

Be it enacted by the Queen's most Excellent Majesty, by and with the advice and consent of the Lords Spiritual and Temporal, and Commons, in this present Parliament assembled, and by the authority of the same, as follows:—

1 POLLING DAYS FOR PARLIAMENTARY GENERAL ELECTIONS

(1)   This section applies for the purposes of the Timetable in rule 1 in Schedule 1 to the Representation of the People Act 1983 and is subject to section 2.

(2)   The polling day for the next parliamentary general election after the passing of this Act is to be 7 May 2015.

(3)   The polling day for each subsequent parliamentary general election is to be the first Thursday in May in the fifth calendar year following that in which the polling day for the previous parliamentary general election fell.

(4)   But, if the polling day for the previous parliamentary general election—
(a) was appointed under section 2(7), and
(b) in the calendar year in which it fell, fell before the first Thursday in May,
subsection (3) has effect as if for "fifth" there were substituted " fourth ".

(5)   The Prime Minister may by order made by statutory instrument provide that the polling day for a parliamentary general election in a specified calendar year is to be later than the day determined under subsection (2) or (3), but not more than two months later.

[. . .]

2 EARLY PARLIAMENTARY GENERAL ELECTIONS

(1)   An early parliamentary general election is to take place if—
(a) the House of Commons passes a motion in the form set out in subsection (2), and
(b) if the motion is passed on a division, the number of members who vote in favour of the motion is a number equal to or greater than two thirds of the number of seats in the House (including vacant seats).

(2)   The form of motion for the purposes of subsection (1)(a) is—

"That there shall be an early parliamentary general election."

(3)   An early parliamentary general election is also to take place if—
    (a) the House of Commons passes a motion in the form set out in subsection (4), and
    (b) the period of 14 days after the day on which that motion is passed ends without the House passing a motion in the form set out in subsection (5).

(4)   The form of motion for the purposes of subsection (3)(a) is—

"That this House has no confidence in Her Majesty's Government."

(5)   The form of motion for the purposes of subsection (3)(b) is—

"That this House has confidence in Her Majesty's Government."

[. . .]

3 DISSOLUTION OF PARLIAMENT

(1)   The Parliament then in existence dissolves at the beginning of the 17th working day before the polling day for the next parliamentary general election as determined under section 1 or appointed under section 2(7).

(2)   Parliament cannot otherwise be dissolved.

[. . .]

TERRORISM PREVENTION AND INVESTIGATION MEASURES ACT 2011

An Act to abolish control orders and make provision for the imposition of terrorism prevention and investigation measures.

[14th December 2011]

Be it enacted by the Queen's most Excellent Majesty, by and with the advice and consent of the Lords Spiritual and Temporal, and Commons, in this present Parliament assembled, and by the authority of the same, as follows:—

NEW REGIME TO PROTECT THE PUBLIC FROM TERRORISM

1 ABOLITION OF CONTROL ORDERS

The Prevention of Terrorism Act 2005 (which gives powers to impose control orders) is repealed.

2 IMPOSITION OF TERRORISM PREVENTION AND INVESTIGATION MEASURES

(1)   The Secretary of State may by notice (a "TPIM notice") impose specified terrorism prevention and investigation measures on an individual if conditions A to E in section 3 are met.

(2)   In this Act "terrorism prevention and investigation measures" means requirements, restrictions and other provision which may be made in relation to an individual by virtue of Schedule 1 (terrorism prevention and investigation measures).

(3)   In this section and Part 1 of Schedule 1 "specified" means specified in the TPIM notice.

3 CONDITIONS A TO E

(1)   Condition A is that the Secretary of State reasonably believes that the individual is, or has been, involved in terrorism-related activity (the "relevant activity").

(2)   Condition B is that some or all of the relevant activity is new terrorism-related activity.

(3)   Condition C is that the Secretary of State reasonably considers that it is necessary, for purposes connected with protecting members of the public from a risk of terrorism, for terrorism prevention and investigation measures to be imposed on the individual.

(4)   Condition D is that the Secretary of State reasonably considers that it is necessary, for purposes connected with preventing or restricting the individual's involvement in terrorism-related activity, for the specified terrorism prevention and investigation measures to be imposed on the individual.

(5)   Condition E is that—
   (a) the court gives the Secretary of State permission under section 6, or
   (b) the Secretary of State reasonably considers that the urgency of the case requires terrorism prevention and investigation measures to be imposed without obtaining such permission.

(6)   In this section "new terrorism-related activity" means—
   (a) if no TPIM notice relating to the individual has ever been in force, terrorism-related activity occurring at any time (whether before or after the coming into force of this Act);
   (b) if only one TPIM notice relating to the individual has ever been in force, terrorism-related activity occurring after that notice came into force; or
   (c) if two or more TPIM notices relating to the individual have been in force, terrorism-related activity occurring after such a notice came into force most recently.

4 INVOLVEMENT IN TERRORISM-RELATED ACTIVITY

(1)   For the purposes of this Act, involvement in terrorism-related activity is any one or more of the following—
   (a) the commission, preparation or instigation of acts of terrorism;
   (b) conduct which facilitates the commission, preparation or instigation of such acts, or which is intended to do so;
   (c) conduct which gives encouragement to the commission, preparation or instigation of such acts, or which is intended to do so;
   (d) conduct which gives support or assistance to individuals who are known or believed by the individual concerned to be involved in conduct falling within paragraphs (a) to (c); and for the purposes of this Act it is immaterial whether the acts of terrorism in question are specific acts of terrorism or acts of terrorism in general.

(2)   For the purposes of this Act, it is immaterial whether an individual's involvement in terrorism-related activity occurs before or after the coming into force of this Act.

TWO YEAR LIMIT ON IMPOSITION OF MEASURES WITHOUT NEW TERRORISM-RELATED

5 TWO YEAR LIMIT FOR TPIM NOTICES

(1)   A TPIM notice—
   (a) comes into force when the notice is served on the individual or, if later, at the time specified for this purpose in the notice; and
   (b) is in force for the period of one year.

(2)   The Secretary of State may by notice extend a TPIM notice for a period of one year beginning when the TPIM notice would otherwise expire.

(3)   A TPIM notice—
(a)   may be extended under subsection (2) only if conditions A, C and D are met; and
(b)   may be so extended on only one occasion.

(4)   This section is subject, in particular, to sections 13 (revocation and revival of TPIM notices) and 14 (replacement of TPIM notice that is quashed etc).

COURT SCRUTINY OF IMPOSITION OF MEASURES

6 PRIOR PERMISSION OF THE COURT

(1)   This section applies if the Secretary of State—
(a)   makes the relevant decisions in relation to an individual, and
(b)   makes an application to the court for permission to impose measures on the individual.

(2)   The application must set out a draft of the proposed TPIM notice.

(3)   The function of the court on the application is—
(a)   to determine whether the relevant decisions of the Secretary of State are obviously flawed, and
[. . .]

(4)   The court may consider the application—
(a)   in the absence of the individual;
(b)   without the individual having been notified of the application; and
(c)   without the individual having been given an opportunity (if the individual was aware of the application) of making any representations to the court.

[. . .]

(6)   In determining the application, the court must apply the principles applicable on an application for judicial review.

(7)   In a case where the court determines that a decision of the Secretary of State that condition A, condition B, or condition C is met is obviously flawed, the court may not give permission under this section.

(8)   In any other case, the court may give permission under this section.

(9)   If the court determines that the Secretary of State's decision that condition D is met is obviously flawed, the court may (in addition to giving permission under subsection (8)) give directions to the Secretary of State in relation to the measures to be imposed on the individual.

(10)   In this section "relevant decisions" means the decisions that the following conditions are met—
(a)   condition A;
(b)   condition B;
(c)   condition C; and
(d)   condition D.

[. . .]

20 REVIEWS OF OPERATION OF ACT

(1)   The Secretary of State must appoint a person to review the operation of this Act ("the independent reviewer").

(2)   The independent reviewer must carry out a review of the operation of this Act in respect of each calendar year, starting with the first complete calendar year beginning after the passing of this Act.

(3)   Each review must be completed as soon as reasonably practicable after the end of the calendar year to which the review relates.

(4)   The independent reviewer must send to the Secretary of State a report on the outcome of each review carried out under subsection (2) as soon as reasonably practicable after completion of the review.

(5)   On receiving a report under subsection (4), the Secretary of State must lay a copy of it before Parliament.

[. . .]

LOCALISM ACT 2011

An Act to make provision about the functions and procedures of local and certain other authorities; to make provision about the functions of the Commission for Local Administration in England; to enable the recovery of financial sanctions imposed by the Court of Justice of the European Union on the United Kingdom from local and public authorities; to make provision about local government finance; to make provision about town and country planning, the Community Infrastructure Levy and the authorisation of nationally significant infrastructure projects; to make provision about social and other housing; to make provision about regeneration in London; and for connected purposes.

[15th November 2011]

Be it enacted by the Queen's most Excellent Majesty, by and with the advice and consent of the Lords Spiritual and Temporal, and Commons, in this present Parliament assembled, and by the authority of the same, as follows:—

1 LOCAL AUTHORITY'S GENERAL POWER OF COMPETENCE

(1)   A local authority has power to do anything that individuals generally may do.

(2)   Subsection (1) applies to things that an individual may do even though they are in nature, extent or otherwise—
    (a) unlike anything the authority may do apart from subsection (1), or
    (b) unlike anything that other public bodies may do.

(3)   In this section "individual" means an individual with full capacity.

(4)   Where subsection (1) confers power on the authority to do something, it confers power (subject to sections 2 to 4) to do it in any way whatever, including—
    (a) power to do it anywhere in the United Kingdom or elsewhere,
    (b) power to do it for a commercial purpose or otherwise for a charge, or without charge, and
    (c) power to do it for, or otherwise than for, the benefit of the authority, its area or persons resident or present in its area.

(5)   The generality of the power conferred by subsection (1) ("the general power") is not limited by the existence of any other power of the authority which (to any extent) overlaps the general power.

(6)   Any such other power is not limited by the existence of the general power (but see section 5(2)).

[. . .]

8 INTERPRETATION OF CHAPTER

(1)   In this Chapter—

"the general power" means the power conferred by section 1(1);

"local authority" means—

(a) a county council in England,
(b) a district council,
(c) a London borough council,
(d) the Common Council of the City of London in its capacity as a local authority,
[ ], or
(f)   an eligible parish council;
[. . .]

[. . .]

15 POWER TO TRANSFER LOCAL PUBLIC FUNCTIONS TO PERMITTED AUTHORITIES

(1)   The Secretary of State may by order make provision—
(a) transferring a local public function from the public authority whose function it is to a permitted authority;
(b) about the discharge of local public functions that are transferred to permitted authorities under this section (including provision enabling the discharge of those functions to be delegated).

(2)   An order under this section may modify any enactment (whenever passed or made) for the purpose of making the provision mentioned in subsection (1).

[. . .]

(4)   An order under this section may disapply, or modify the application of, Chapter 4 of Part 1A of the Local Government Act 2000 (changing local authority governance arrangements) in relation to a county council or district council to which the order transfers a local public function.

(5)   The Secretary of State may not make an order under this section unless the Secretary of State considers that it is likely that making the order would—
(a) promote economic development or wealth creation, or
(b) increase local accountability in relation to each local public function transferred by the order.

(6)   For the purposes of subsection (5)(b), in relation to a local public function, local accountability is increased if the exercise of the function becomes more accountable to persons living or working in the area of the permitted authority to which it is transferred.

[. . .]

(8)   The Secretary of State may not make an order under this section transferring a local public function to a permitted authority unless the authority has consented to the transfer.

(9)   Before making an order under this section, the Secretary of State must consult such persons as the Secretary of State considers appropriate:

20 INTERPRETATION OF CHAPTER

In this Chapter—

"enactment" includes an enactment contained in a local Act or comprised in subordinate legislation (within the meaning of the Interpretation Act 1978);

"Minister of the Crown" has the same meaning as in the Ministers of the Crown Act 1975;

"local public function", in relation to a permitted authority, means a public function in so far as it relates to—
(a) the permitted authority's area, or
(b) persons living, working or carrying on activities in that area;
"permitted authority" means—

(a) a county council in England,
(b) a district council,
(c) an economic prosperity board established under section 88 of the Local Democracy, Economic Development and Construction Act 2009, or
(d) a combined authority established under section 103 of that Act;

"public authority" includes a Minister of the Crown or a government department;

"public function" means a function of a public authority that does not consist of a power to make regulations or other instruments of a legislative character.

PROTECTION OF FREEDOMS ACT 2012

An Act to provide for the destruction, retention, use and other regulation of certain evidential material; to impose consent and other requirements in relation to certain processing of biometric information relating to children; to provide for a code of practice about surveillance camera systems and for the appointment and role of the Surveillance Camera Commissioner; to provide for judicial approval in relation to certain authorisations and notices under the Regulation of Investigatory Powers Act 2000; to provide for the repeal or rewriting of powers of entry and associated powers and for codes of practice and other safeguards in relation to such powers; to make provision about vehicles left on land; to amend the maximum detention period for terrorist suspects; to replace certain stop and search powers and to provide for a related code of practice; to make provision about the safeguarding of vulnerable groups and about criminal records including provision for the establishment of the Disclosure and Barring Service and the dissolution of the Independent Safeguarding Authority; to disregard convictions and cautions for certain abolished offences; to make provision about the release and publication of datasets held by public authorities and to make other provision about freedom of information and the Information Commissioner; to make provision about the trafficking of people for exploitation and about stalking; to repeal certain enactments; and for connected purposes.

[1st May 2012]

Be it enacted by the Queen's most Excellent Majesty, by and with the advice and consent of the Lords Spiritual and Temporal, and Commons, in this present Parliament assembled, and by the authority of the same, as follows:—

[. . .]

39 REPEALING ETC. UNNECESSARY OR INAPPROPRIATE POWERS OF ENTRY

(1) The appropriate national authority may by order repeal any power of entry or associated power which the appropriate national authority considers to be unnecessary or inappropriate.

[. . .]

40 ADDING SAFEGUARDS TO POWERS OF ENTRY

(1) The appropriate national authority may by order provide for safeguards in relation to any power of entry or associated power.

(2) Such safeguards may, in particular, include—
    (a) restrictions as to the premises over which the power may be exercised,
    (b) restrictions as to the times at which the power may be exercised,
    (c) restrictions as to the number or description of persons who may exercise the power,
    (d) a requirement for a judicial or other authorisation before the power may be exercised,
    (e) a requirement to give notice within a particular period before the power may be exercised,
    (f) other conditions which must be met before the power may be exercised,
    (g) modifications of existing conditions which must be met before the power may be exercised,
    (h) other restrictions on the circumstances in which the power may be exercised,
    (i) new obligations on the person exercising the power which must be met before, during or after its exercise,
    (j) modifications of existing obligations which must be met by the person exercising the power before, during or after its exercise,
    (k) restrictions on any power to use force, or any other power, which may be exercised in connection with the power of entry or associated power.

[. . .]

These provisions came into force 1st July 2012

International and Regional Instruments

UNIVERSAL DECLARATION OF HUMAN RIGHTS 1948

PREAMBLE

Whereas recognition of the inherent dignity and of the equal and inalienable rights of all members of the human family is the foundation of freedom, justice and peace in the world,

Whereas disregard and contempt for human rights have resulted in barbarous acts which have outraged the conscience of mankind, and the advent of a world in which human beings shall enjoy freedom of speech and belief and freedom from fear and want has been proclaimed as the highest aspiration of the common people,

Whereas it is essential, if man is not to be compelled to have recourse, as a last resort, to rebellion against tyranny and oppression, that human rights should be protected by the rule of law,

Whereas it is essential to promote the development of friendly relations between nations,

Whereas the peoples of the United Nations have in the Charter reaffirmed their faith in fundamental human rights, in the dignity and worth of the human person and in the equal rights of men and women and have determined to promote social progress and better standards of life in larger freedom,

Whereas Member States have pledged themselves to achieve, in co-operation with the United Nations, the promotion of universal respect for and observance of human rights and fundamental freedoms,

Whereas a common understanding of these rights and freedoms is of the greatest importance for the full realization of this pledge,

Now, Therefore THE GENERAL ASSEMBLY proclaims THIS UNIVERSAL DECLARATION OF HUMAN RIGHTS as a common standard of achievement for all peoples and all nations, to the end that every individual and every organ of society, keeping this Declaration constantly in mind, shall strive by teaching and education to promote respect for these rights and freedoms and by progressive measures, national and international, to secure their universal and effective recognition and observance, both among the peoples of Member States themselves and among the peoples of territories under their jurisdiction.

Article 1

All human beings are born free and equal in dignity and rights. They are endowed with reason and conscience and should act towards one another in a spirit of brotherhood.

Article 2
Everyone is entitled to all the rights and freedoms set forth in this Declaration, without distinction of any kind, such as race, colour, sex, language, religion, political or other opinion, national or social origin, property, birth or other status. Furthermore, no distinction shall be made on the basis of the political, jurisdictional or international status of the country or territory to which a person belongs, whether it be independent, trust, non-self-governing or under any other limitation of sovereignty.

Article 3
Everyone has the right to life, liberty and security of person.

Article 4
No one shall be held in slavery or servitude; slavery and the slave trade shall be prohibited in all their forms.

Article 5
No one shall be subjected to torture or to cruel, inhuman or degrading treatment or punishment.

Article 6
Everyone has the right to recognition everywhere as a person before the law.

Article 7
All are equal before the law and are entitled without any discrimination to equal protection of the law. All are entitled to equal protection against any discrimination in violation of this Declaration and against any incitement to such discrimination.

Article 8
Everyone has the right to an effective remedy by the competent national tribunals for acts violating the fundamental rights granted him by the constitution or by law.

Article 9
No one shall be subjected to arbitrary arrest, detention or exile.

Article 10
Everyone is entitled in full equality to a fair and public hearing by an independent and impartial tribunal, in the determination of his rights and obligations and of any criminal charge against him.

Article 11
(1)   Everyone charged with a penal offence has the right to be presumed innocent until proved guilty according to law in a public trial at which he has had all the guarantees necessary for his defence.

(2)   No one shall be held guilty of any penal offence on account of any act or omission which did not constitute a penal offence, under national or international law, at the time when it was committed. Nor shall a heavier penalty be imposed than the one that was applicable at the time the penal offence was committed.

Article 12
No one shall be subjected to arbitrary interference with his privacy, family, home or correspondence, nor to attacks upon his honour and reputation. Everyone has the right to the protection of the law against such interference or attacks.

Article 13

(1)   Everyone has the right to freedom of movement and residence within the borders of each state.

(2)   Everyone has the right to leave any country, including his own, and to return to his country.

Article 14

(1)   Everyone has the right to seek and to enjoy in other countries asylum from persecution.

(2)   This right may not be invoked in the case of prosecutions genuinely arising from non-political crimes or from acts contrary to the purposes and principles of the United Nations.

Article 15

(1)   Everyone has the right to a nationality.

(2)   No one shall be arbitrarily deprived of his nationality nor denied the right to change his nationality.

Article 16

(1)   Men and women of full age, without any limitation due to race, nationality or religion, have the right to marry and to found a family. They are entitled to equal rights as to marriage, during marriage and at its dissolution.

(2)   Marriage shall be entered into only with the free and full consent of the intending spouses.

(3)   The family is the natural and fundamental group unit of society and is entitled to protection by society and the State.

Article 17

(1)   Everyone has the right to own property alone as well as in association with others.

(2)   No one shall be arbitrarily deprived of his property.

Article 18

Everyone has the right to freedom of thought, conscience and religion; this right includes freedom to change his religion or belief, and freedom, either alone or in community with others and in public or private, to manifest his religion or belief in teaching, practice, worship and observance.

Article 19

Everyone has the right to freedom of opinion and expression; this right includes freedom to hold opinions without interference and to seek, receive and impart information and ideas through any media and regardless of frontiers.

Article 20

(1)   Everyone has the right to freedom of peaceful assembly and association.

(2)   No one may be compelled to belong to an association.

Article 21

(1)   Everyone has the right to take part in the government of his country, directly or through freely chosen representatives.

(2)   Everyone has the right of equal access to public service in his country.

(3)   The will of the people shall be the basis of the authority of government; this will shall be expressed in periodic and genuine elections which shall be by universal and equal suffrage and shall be held by secret vote or by equivalent free voting procedures.

Article 22

Everyone, as a member of society, has the right to social security and is entitled to realization, through national effort and international co-operation and in accordance with the organization and resources of each State, of the economic, social and cultural rights indispensable for his dignity and the free development of his personality.

Article 23

(1)   Everyone has the right to work, to free choice of employment, to just and favourable conditions of work and to protection against unemployment.

(2)   Everyone, without any discrimination, has the right to equal pay for equal work.

(3)   Everyone who works has the right to just and favourable remuneration ensuring for himself and his family an existence worthy of human dignity, and supplemented, if necessary, by other means of social protection.

(4)   Everyone has the right to form and to join trade unions for the protection of his interests.

Article 24

Everyone has the right to rest and leisure, including reasonable limitation of working hours and periodic holidays with pay.

Article 25

(1)   Everyone has the right to a standard of living adequate for the health and well-being of himself and of his family, including food, clothing, housing and medical care and necessary social services, and the right to security in the event of unemployment, sickness, disability, widowhood, old age or other lack of livelihood in circumstances beyond his control.

(2)   Motherhood and childhood are entitled to special care and assistance. All children, whether born in or out of wedlock, shall enjoy the same social protection.

Article 26

(1)   Everyone has the right to education. Education shall be free, at least in the elementary and fundamental stages. Elementary education shall be compulsory. Technical and professional education shall be made generally available and higher education shall be equally accessible to all on the basis of merit.

(2)   Education shall be directed to the full development of the human personality and to the strengthening of respect for human rights and fundamental freedoms. It shall promote understanding, tolerance and friendship among all nations, racial or religious groups, and shall further the activities of the United Nations for the maintenance of peace.

(3)   Parents have a prior right to choose the kind of education that shall be given to their children.

Article 27

(1)   Everyone has the right freely to participate in the cultural life of the community, to enjoy the arts and to share in scientific advancement and its benefits.

(2)   Everyone has the right to the protection of the moral and material interests resulting from any scientific, literary or artistic production of which he is the author.

Article 28
Everyone is entitled to a social and international order in which the rights and freedoms set forth in this Declaration can be fully realized.

Article 29
(1)   Everyone has duties to the community in which alone the free and full development of his personality is possible.

(2)   In the exercise of his rights and freedoms, everyone shall be subject only to such limitations as are determined by law solely for the purpose of securing due recognition and respect for the rights and freedoms of others and of meeting the just requirements of morality, public order and the general welfare in a democratic society.

(3)   These rights and freedoms may in no case be exercised contrary to the purposes and principles of the United Nations.

Article 30
Nothing in this Declaration may be interpreted as implying for any State, group or person any right to engage in any activity or to perform any act aimed at the destruction of any of the rights and freedoms set forth herein.

EUROPEAN CONVENTION FOR THE PROTECTION OF HUMAN RIGHTS AND FUNDAMENTAL FREEDOMS 1950

The governments signatory hereto, being members of the Council of Europe,

Considering the Universal Declaration of Human Rights proclaimed by the General Assembly of the United Nations on 10th December 1948;

Considering that this Declaration aims at securing the universal and effective recognition and observance of the Rights therein declared;

Considering that the aim of the Council of Europe is the achievement of greater unity between its members and that one of the methods by which that aim is to be pursued is the maintenance and further realisation of human rights and fundamental freedoms;

Reaffirming their profound belief in those fundamental freedoms which are the foundation of justice and peace in the world and are best maintained on the one hand by an effective political democracy and on the other by a common understanding and observance of the human rights upon which they depend;

Being resolved, as the governments of European countries which are like-minded and have a common heritage of political traditions, ideals, freedom and the rule of law, to take the first steps for the collective enforcement of certain of the rights stated in the Universal Declaration,

Have agreed as follows:

Article 1 OBLIGATION TO RESPECT HUMAN RIGHTS

The High Contracting Parties shall secure to everyone within their jurisdiction the rights and freedoms defined in Section I of this Convention.

Section I RIGHTS AND FREEDOMS

Article 2 RIGHT TO LIFE

1   Everyone's right to life shall be protected by law. No one shall be deprived of his life intentionally save in the execution of a sentence of a court following his conviction of a crime for which this penalty is provided by law.

2   Deprivation of life shall not be regarded as inflicted in contravention of this article when it results from the use of force which is no more than absolutely necessary:
   a   in defence of any person from unlawful violence;
   b   in order to effect a lawful arrest or to prevent the escape of a person lawfully detained;
   c   in action lawfully taken for the purpose of quelling a riot or insurrection.

Article 3 PROHIBITION OF TORTURE

No one shall be subjected to torture or to inhuman or degrading treatment or punishment.

Article 4 PROHIBITION OF SLAVERY AND FORCED LABOUR

1   No one shall be held in slavery or servitude.

2   No one shall be required to perform forced or compulsory labour.

3   For the purpose of this article the term "forced or compulsory labour" shall not include:
   a   any work required to be done in the ordinary course of detention imposed according to the provisions of Article 5 of this Convention or during conditional release from such detention;
   b   any service of a military character or, in case of conscientious objectors in countries where they are recognised, service exacted instead of compulsory military service;
   c   any service exacted in case of an emergency or calamity threatening the life or well-being of the community;
   d   any work or service which forms part of normal civic obligations.

Article 5 RIGHT TO LIBERTY AND SECURITY

1   Everyone has the right to liberty and security of person. No one shall be deprived of his liberty save in the following cases and in accordance with a procedure prescribed by law:
   a   the lawful detention of a person after conviction by a competent court;
   b   the lawful arrest or detention of a person for non- compliance with the lawful order of a court or in order to secure the fulfilment of any obligation prescribed by law;
   c   the lawful arrest or detention of a person effected for the purpose of bringing him before the competent legal authority on reasonable suspicion of having committed an offence or when it is reasonably considered necessary to prevent his committing an offence or fleeing after having done so;
   d   the detention of a minor by lawful order for the purpose of educational supervision or his lawful detention for the purpose of bringing him before the competent legal authority;
   e   the lawful detention of persons for the prevention of the spreading of infectious diseases, of persons of unsound mind, alcoholics or drug addicts or vagrants;
   f   the lawful arrest or detention of a person to prevent his effecting an unauthorised entry into the country or of a person against whom action is being taken with a view to deportation or extradition.

2   Everyone who is arrested shall be informed promptly, in a language which he understands, of the reasons for his arrest and of any charge against him.

3   Everyone arrested or detained in accordance with the provisions of paragraph 1.c of this article shall be brought promptly before a judge or other officer authorised by law to exercise judicial power and shall be entitled to trial within a reasonable time or to release pending trial. Release may be conditioned by guarantees to appear for trial.

4   Everyone who is deprived of his liberty by arrest or detention shall be entitled to take proceedings by which the lawfulness of his detention shall be decided speedily by a court and his release ordered if the detention is not lawful.

5   Everyone who has been the victim of arrest or detention in contravention of the provisions of this article shall have an enforceable right to compensation.

Article 6 RIGHT TO A FAIR TRIAL

1   In the determination of his civil rights and obligations or of any criminal charge against him, everyone is entitled to a fair and public hearing within a reasonable time by an independent and impartial tribunal established by law. Judgment shall be pronounced publicly but the press and public may be excluded from all or part of the trial in the interests of morals, public order or national security in a democratic society, where the interests of juveniles or the protection of the private life of the parties so require, or to the extent strictly necessary in the opinion of the court in special circumstances where publicity would prejudice the interests of justice.

2   Everyone charged with a criminal offence shall be presumed innocent until proved guilty according to law.

3   Everyone charged with a criminal offence has the following minimum rights:
   a   to be informed promptly, in a language which he understands and in detail, of the nature and cause of the accusation against him;
   b   to have adequate time and facilities for the preparation of his defence;
   c   to defend himself in person or through legal assistance of his own choosing or, if he has not sufficient means to pay for legal assistance, to be given it free when the interests of justice so require;
   d   to examine or have examined witnesses against him and to obtain the attendance and examination of witnesses on his behalf under the same conditions as witnesses against him;
   e   to have the free assistance of an interpreter if he cannot understand or speak the language used in court.

Article 7 NO PUNISHMENT WITHOUT LAW

1   No one shall be held guilty of any criminal offence on account of any act or omission which did not constitute a criminal offence under national or international law at the time when it was committed. Nor shall a heavier penalty be imposed than the one that was applicable at the time the criminal offence was committed.

2   This article shall not prejudice the trial and punishment of any person for any act or omission which, at the time when it was committed, was criminal according to the general principles of law recognised by civilised nations.

Article 8 RIGHT TO RESPECT FOR PRIVATE AND FAMILY LIFE

1   Everyone has the right to respect for his private and family life, his home and his correspondence.

2   There shall be no interference by a public authority with the exercise of this right except such as is in accordance with the law and is necessary in a democratic society in the interests of national security, public safety or the economic well-being of the country, for the prevention of disorder or crime, for the protection of health or morals, or for the protection of the rights and freedoms of others.

Article 9 FREEDOM OF THOUGHT, CONSCIENCE AND RELIGION

1   Everyone has the right to freedom of thought, conscience and religion; this right includes freedom to change his religion or belief and freedom, either alone or in community with others and in public or private, to manifest his religion or belief, in worship, teaching, practice and observance.

2   Freedom to manifest one's religion or beliefs shall be subject only to such limitations as are prescribed by law and are necessary in a democratic society in the interests of public safety, for the protection of public order, health or morals, or for the protection of the rights and freedoms of others.

Article 10 FREEDOM OF EXPRESSION

1   Everyone has the right to freedom of expression. This right shall include freedom to hold opinions and to receive and impart information and ideas without interference by public authority and regardless of frontiers. This article shall not prevent States from requiring the licensing of broadcasting, television or cinema enterprises.

2   The exercise of these freedoms, since it carries with it duties and responsibilities, may be subject to such formalities, conditions, restrictions or penalties as are prescribed by law and are necessary in a democratic society, in the interests of national security, territorial integrity or public safety, for the prevention of disorder or crime, for the protection of health or morals, for the protection of the reputation or rights of others, for preventing the disclosure of information received in confidence, or for maintaining the authority and impartiality of the judiciary.

Article 11 FREEDOM OF ASSEMBLY AND ASSOCIATION

1   Everyone has the right to freedom of peaceful assembly and to freedom of association with others, including the right to form and to join trade unions for the protection of his interests.

2   No restrictions shall be placed on the exercise of these rights other than such as are prescribed by law and are necessary in a democratic society in the interests of national security or public safety, for the prevention of disorder or crime, for the protection of health or morals or for the protection of the rights and freedoms of others. This article shall not prevent the imposition of lawful restrictions on the exercise of these rights by members of the armed forces, of the police or of the administration of the State.

Article 12 RIGHT TO MARRY

Men and women of marriageable age have the right to marry and to found a family, according to the national laws governing the exercise of this right.

Article 13 RIGHT TO AN EFFECTIVE REMEDY

Everyone whose rights and freedoms as set forth in this Convention are violated shall have an effective remedy before a national authority notwithstanding that the violation has been committed by persons acting in an official capacity.

Article 14 PROHIBITION OF DISCRIMINATION

The enjoyment of the rights and freedoms set forth in this Convention shall be secured without discrimination on any ground such as sex, race, colour, language, religion, political or other opinion, national or social origin, association with a national minority, property, birth or other status.

Article 15 DEROGATION IN TIME OF EMERGENCY

1   In time of war or other public emergency threatening the life of the nation any High Contracting Party may take measures derogating from its obligations under this Convention to the extent strictly required by the exigencies of the situation, provided that such measures are not inconsistent with its other obligations under international law.

2   No derogation from Article 2, except in respect of deaths resulting from lawful acts of war, or from Articles 3, 4 (paragraph 1) and 7 shall be made under this provision.

3   Any High Contracting Party availing itself of this right of derogation shall keep the Secretary General of the Council of Europe fully informed of the measures which it has taken and the reasons therefor. It shall also inform the Secretary General of the Council of Europe when such measures have ceased to operate and the provisions of the Convention are again being fully executed.

Article 16 RESTRICTIONS ON POLITICAL ACTIVITY OF ALIENS

Nothing in Articles 10, 11 and 14 shall be regarded as preventing the High Contracting Parties from imposing restrictions on the political activity of aliens.

Article 17 PROHIBITION OF ABUSE OF RIGHTS

Nothing in this Convention may be interpreted as implying for any State, group or person any right to engage in any activity or perform any act aimed at the destruction of any of the rights and freedoms set forth herein or at their limitation to a greater extent than is provided for in the Convention.

Article 18 LIMITATION ON USE OF RESTRICTIONS ON RIGHTS

The restrictions permitted under this Convention to the said rights and freedoms shall not be applied for any purpose other than those for which they have been prescribed.

[. . .]

PROTOCOL NO. 1 TO THE CONVENTION FOR THE PROTECTION OF HUMAN RIGHTS [1952]

The governments signatory hereto, being members of the Council of Europe,

Being resolved to take steps to ensure the collective enforcement of certain rights and freedoms other than those already included in Section I of the Convention for the Protection of Human Rights and Fundamental Freedoms signed at Rome on 4 November 1950 (hereinafter referred to as "the Convention"),

Have agreed as follows:

Article 1 PROTECTION OF PROPERTY

Every natural or legal person is entitled to the peaceful enjoyment of his possessions. No one shall be deprived of his possessions except in the public interest and subject to the conditions provided for by law and by the general principles of international law.

The preceding provisions shall not, however, in any way impair the right of a State to enforce such laws as it deems necessary to control the use of property in accordance with the general interest or to secure the payment of taxes or other contributions or penalties.

Article 2 RIGHT TO EDUCATION

No person shall be denied the right to education. In the exercise of any functions which it assumes in relation to education and to teaching, the State shall respect the right of parents to ensure such education and teaching in conformity with their own religious and philosophical convictions.

Article 3 RIGHT TO FREE ELECTIONS

The High Contracting Parties undertake to hold free elections at reasonable intervals by secret ballot, under conditions which will ensure the free expression of the opinion of the people in the choice of the legislature.

[. . .]

PROTOCOL NO. 13 TO THE CONVENTION FOR THE PROTECTION OF HUMAN RIGHTS AND FUNDAMENTAL FREEDOMS CONCERNING THE ABOLITION OF THE DEATH PENALTY [2002]

The member States of the Council of Europe signatory hereto,

Convinced that everyone's right to life is a basic value in a democratic society and that the abolition of the death penalty is essential for the protection of this right and for the full recognition of the inherent dignity of all human beings;

Wishing to strengthen the protection of the right to life guaranteed by the Convention for the Protection of Human Rights and Fundamental Freedoms signed at Rome on 4 November 1950 (hereinafter referred to as "the Convention");

Noting that Protocol No. 6 to the Convention, concerning the Abolition of the Death Penalty, signed at Strasbourg on 28 April 1983, does not exclude the death penalty in respect of acts committed in time of war or of imminent threat of war;

Being resolved to take the final step in order to abolish the death penalty in all circumstances,

Have agreed as follows:

Article 1 ABOLITION OF THE DEATH PENALTY

The death penalty shall be abolished. No one shall be condemned to such penalty or executed.

Article 2 PROHIBITION OF DEROGATIONS

No derogation from the provisions of this Protocol shall be made under Article 15 of the Convention.

Article 3 PROHIBITION OF RESERVATIONS

No reservation may be made under Article 57 of the Convention in respect of the provisions of this Protocol.

[. . .]

CHARTER OF FUNDAMENTAL RIGHTS OF THE EUROPEAN UNION [2000]

THE PREAMBLE

The peoples of Europe, in creating an ever closer union among them, are resolved to share a peaceful future based on common values.

Conscious of its spiritual and moral heritage, the Union is founded on the indivisible, universal values of human dignity, freedom, equality and solidarity; it is based on the principles of democracy and the rule of law. It places the individual at the heart of its activities, by establishing the citizenship of the Union and by creating an area of freedom, security and justice.

The Union contributes to the preservation and to the development of these common values while respecting the diversity of the cultures and traditions of the peoples of Europe as well as the national identities of the Member States and the organisation of their public authorities at national, regional and local levels; it seeks to promote balanced and sustainable development and ensures free movement of persons, services, goods and capital, and the freedom of establishment.

To this end, it is necessary to strengthen the protection of fundamental rights in the light of changes in society, social progress and scientific and technological developments by making those rights more visible in a Charter.

This Charter reaffirms, with due regard for the powers and tasks of the Union and the principle of subsidiarity, the rights as they result, in particular, from the constitutional traditions and international obligations common to the Member States, the European Convention for the Protection of Human Rights and Fundamental Freedoms, the Social Charters adopted by the Union and by the Council of Europe and the case-law of the Court of Justice of the European Union and of the European Court of Human Rights. In this context the Charter will be interpreted by the courts of the Union and the Member States with due regard to the explanations prepared under the authority of the Praesidium of the Convention which drafted the Charter and updated under the responsibility of the Praesidium of the European Convention.

Enjoyment of these rights entails responsibilities and duties with regard to other persons, to the human community and to future generations.

The Union therefore recognises the rights, freedoms and principles set out hereafter.

DIGNITY

Article 1. **HUMAN DIGNITY**
Human Dignity is inviolable. It must be respected and protected.

Article 2. **RIGHT TO LIFE**
1.   Everyone has the right to life.

2.   No one shall be condemned to the death penalty, or executed.

Article 3. **RIGHT TO THE INTEGRITY OF THE PERSON**
1.   Everyone has the right to respect for his or her physical and mental integrity.

2.   In the fields of medicine and biology, the following must be respected in particular:

- the free and informed consent of the person concerned, according to the procedures laid down by law,
- the prohibition of eugenic practices, in particular those aiming at the selection of persons,
- the prohibition on making the human body and its parts as such a source of financial gain,
- the prohibition of the reproductive cloning of human beings.

Article 4. PROHIBITION OF TORTURE AND INHUMAN OR DEGRADING TREATMENT

No one shall be subjected to torture or to inhuman or degrading treatment or punishment.

Article 5. PROHIBITION OF SLAVERY

No one shall be held in slavery or servitude. No one shall be required to perform forced or compulsory labour. Trafficking in human beings is prohibited.

FREEDOMS

Article 6. RIGHT TO LIBERTY AND SECURITY

Everyone has the right to liberty and security of person.

Article 7. RESPECT FOR PRIVATE AND FAMILY LIFE

Everyone has the right to respect for his or her private and family life, home and communications.

Article 8. PROTECTION OF PERSONAL DATA

- Everyone has the right to the protection of personal data concerning him or her.
- Such data must be processed fairly for specified purposes and on the basis of the consent of the person concerned or some other legitimate basis laid down by law. Everyone has the right of access to data which has been collected concerning him or her, and the right to have it rectified.
- Compliance with these rules shall be subject to control by an independent authority.

Article 9. RIGHT TO MARRY AND RIGHT TO FOUND A FAMILY

The right to marry and the right to found a family shall be guaranteed in accordance with the national laws governing the exercise of these rights.

Art 10. FREEDOM OF THOUGHT, CONSCIENCE AND RELIGION

Everyone has the right to freedom of thought, conscience and religion. This right includes the freedom to change religion or belief and freedom, either alone or in community with others and in public or in private, to manifest religion or belief, in worship, teaching, practice and observance. The right to conscientious objection is recognised, in accordance with the national laws governing the exercise of this right.

Article 11. FREEDOM OF EXPRESSION AND INFORMATION

Everyone has the right to freedom of expression. This right shall include freedom to hold opinions and to receive and impart information and ideas without interference by public authority and regardless of frontiers. The freedom and pluralism of the media shall be respected.

Article 12. FREEDOM OF ASSEMBLY AND OF ASSOCIATION

1. Everyone has the right to freedom of peaceful assembly and to freedom of association at all levels, in particular in political, trade union and civic matters, which implies the right of everyone to form and to join trade unions for the protection of his or her interests.

2. Political parties at Union level contribute to expressing the political will of the citizens of the Union.

Article 13. FREEDOM OF THE ARTS AND SCIENCES

The arts and sciences research shall be free of constraint. Academic freedom shall be respected.

Article 14. RIGHT TO EDUCATION

1. Everyone has the right to education and to have access to vocational and continuing training.

2. This right includes the possibility to receive free compulsory education.

3. The freedom to found educational establishments with due respect for democratic principles and the right of parents to ensure the education and teaching of their children in conformity with their religious, philosophical and pedagogical convictions shall be respected, in accordance with the national laws governing the exercise of such freedom and right.

Article 15. FREEDOM TO CHOOSE AN OCCUPATION AND RIGHT TO ENGAGE IN WORK

1. Everyone has the right to engage in work and to pursue a freely chosen or accepted occupation.

2. Every citizen of the Union has the freedom to seek employment, to work, to exercise the right of establishment and to provide services in any Member State.

3. Nationals of third countries who are authorised to work in the territories of the Member States are entitled to working conditions equivalent to those of citizens of the Union.

Article 16. FREEDOM TO CONDUCT A BUSINESS

The Freedom to conduct a business in accordance with Community law and national laws and practices is recognised.

Article 17. RIGHT TO PROPERTY

1. Everyone has the right to own, use, dispose of and bequeath his or her lawfully acquired possessions. No one may be deprived of his or her possessions, except in the public interest and in the cases and under the conditions provided for by law, subject to fair compensation being paid in good time for their loss. The use of property may be regulated by law insofar as is necessary for the general interest.

2. Intellectual property shall be protected.

Article 18. RIGHT TO ASYLUM

The right to asylum shall be guaranteed with due respect for the rules of the Geneva Convention of 28 July 1951 and the Protocol of 31 January 1967 relating to the status of refugees and in accordance with the Treaty establishing the European Community.

[ ]

EQUALITY

Article 20. EQUALITY BEFORE THE LAW
Everyone is equal before the law

Article 21. NON-DISCRIMINATION
1.   Any discrimination based on any ground such as sex, race, colour, ethnic or social origin, genetic features, language, religion or belief, political or any other opinion, membership of a national minority, property, birth, disability, age or sexual orientation shall be prohibited.

2.   Within the scope of application of the Treaty establishing the European Community and of the Treaty on European Union, and without prejudice to the special provisions of those Treaties, any discrimination on grounds of nationality shall be prohibited.

[. . .]

SOLIDARITY
[. . .]

CITIZENS' RIGHTS
[. . .]

JUSTICE

Article 47. RIGHT TO AN EFFECTIVE REMEDY AND TO A FAIR TRIAL
Everyone whose rights and freedoms guaranteed by the law of the Union are violated has the right to an effective remedy before a tribunal in compliance with the conditions laid down in this Article.

Everyone is entitled to a fair and public hearing within a reasonable time by an independent and impartial tribunal previously established by law. Everyone shall have the possibility of being advised, defended and represented.

Legal aid shall be made available to those who lack sufficient resources insofar as such aid is necessary to ensure effective access to justice.

Article 48. PRESUMPTION OF INNOCENCE AND RIGHT OF DEFENCE
1.   Everyone who has been charged shall be presumed innocent until proved guilty according to law.

2.   Respect for the rights of the defence of anyone who has been charged shall be guaranteed.

[. . .]

GENERAL PROVISIONS

INTERNATIONAL COVENANT ON CIVIL AND POLITICAL RIGHTS 1966

PREAMBLE

The States Parties to the present Covenant,

Considering that, in accordance with the principles proclaimed in the Charter of the United Nations, recognition of the inherent dignity and of the equal and inalienable rights of all members of the human family is the foundation of freedom, justice and peace in the world,

Recognizing that these rights derive from the inherent dignity of the human person,

Recognizing that, in accordance with the Universal Declaration of Human Rights, the ideal of free human beings enjoying civil and political freedom and freedom from fear and want can only be achieved if conditions are created whereby everyone may enjoy his civil and political rights, as well as his economic, social and cultural rights,

Considering the obligation of States under the Charter of the United Nations to promote universal respect for, and observance of, human rights and freedoms,

Realizing that the individual, having duties to other individuals and to the community to which he belongs, is under a responsibility to strive for the promotion and observance of the rights recognized in the present Covenant,

Agree upon the following articles:

Part I

Article 1

1.   All peoples have the right of self-determination. By virtue of that right they freely determine their political status and freely pursue their economic, social and cultural development.

2.   All peoples may, for their own ends, freely dispose of their natural wealth and resources without prejudice to any obligations arising out of international economic co-operation, based upon the principle of mutual benefit, and international law. In no case may a people be deprived of its own means of subsistence.

3.   The States Parties to the present Covenant, including those having responsibility for the administration of Non-Self-Governing and Trust Territories, shall promote the realization of the right of self-determination, and shall respect that right, in conformity with the provisions of the Charter of the United Nations.

Part II

Article 2

1.   Each State Party to the present Covenant undertakes to respect and to ensure to all individuals within its territory and subject to its jurisdiction the rights recognized in the present Covenant, without distinction of any kind, such as race, colour, sex, language, religion, political or other opinion, national or social origin, property, birth or other status.

2. Where not already provided for by existing legislative or other measures, each State Party to the present Covenant undertakes to take the necessary steps, in accordance with its constitutional processes and with the provisions of the present Covenant, to adopt such laws or other measures as may be necessary to give effect to the rights recognized in the present Covenant.

3. Each State Party to the present Covenant undertakes:
    (a) To ensure that any person whose rights or freedoms as herein recognized are violated shall have an effective remedy, notwithstanding that the violation has been committed by persons acting in an official capacity;
    (b) To ensure that any person claiming such a remedy shall have his right thereto determined by competent judicial, administrative or legislative authorities, or by any other competent authority provided for by the legal system of the State, and to develop the possibilities of judicial remedy;
    (c) To ensure that the competent authorities shall enforce such remedies when granted.

Article 3
The States Parties to the present Covenant undertake to ensure the equal right of men and women to the enjoyment of all civil and political rights set forth in the present Covenant.

Article 4
1. In time of public emergency which threatens the life of the nation and the existence of which is officially proclaimed, the States Parties to the present Covenant may take measures derogating from their obligations under the present Covenant to the extent strictly required by the exigencies of the situation, provided that such measures are not inconsistent with their other obligations under international law and do not involve discrimination solely on the ground of race, colour, sex, language, religion or social origin.

2. No derogation from articles 6, 7, 8 (paragraphs 1 and 2), 11, 15, 16 and 18 may be made under this provision.

3. Any State Party to the present Covenant availing itself of the right of derogation shall immediately inform the other States Parties to the present Covenant, through the intermediary of the Secretary-General of the United Nations, of the provisions from which it has derogated and of the reasons by which it was actuated. A further communication shall be made, through the same intermediary, on the date on which it terminates such derogation.

Article 5
1. Nothing in the present Covenant may be interpreted as implying for any State, group or person any right to engage in any activity or perform any act aimed at the destruction of any of the rights and freedoms recognized herein or at their limitation to a greater extent than is provided for in the present Covenant.

2. There shall be no restriction upon or derogation from any of the fundamental human rights recognized or existing in any State Party to the present Covenant pursuant to law, conventions, regulations or custom on the pretext that the present Covenant does not recognize such rights or that it recognizes them to a lesser extent.

Part III

Article 6
1. Every human being has the inherent right to life. This right shall be protected by law. No one shall be arbitrarily deprived of his life.

2.   In countries which have not abolished the death penalty, sentence of death may be imposed only for the most serious crimes in accordance with the law in force at the time of the commission of the crime and not contrary to the provisions of the present Covenant and to the Convention on the Prevention and Punishment of the Crime of Genocide. This penalty can only be carried out pursuant to a final judgment rendered by a competent court.

3.   When deprivation of life constitutes the crime of genocide, it is understood that nothing in this article shall authorize any State Party to the present Covenant to derogate in any way from any obligation assumed under the provisions of the Convention on the Prevention and Punishment of the Crime of Genocide.

4.   Anyone sentenced to death shall have the right to seek pardon or commutation of the sentence. Amnesty, pardon or commutation of the sentence of death may be granted in all cases.

5.   Sentence of death shall not be imposed for crimes committed by persons below eighteen years of age and shall not be carried out on pregnant women.

6.   Nothing in this article shall be invoked to delay or to prevent the abolition of capital punishment by any State Party to the present Covenant.

Article 7
No one shall be subjected to torture or to cruel, inhuman or degrading treatment or punishment. In particular, no one shall be subjected without his free consent to medical or scientific experimentation.

Article 8
1.   No one shall be held in slavery; slavery and the slave-trade in all their forms shall be prohibited.

2.   No one shall be held in servitude.

3.   (a) No one shall be required to perform forced or compulsory labour;
     (b) Paragraph 3(a) shall not be held to preclude, in countries where imprisonment with hard labour may be imposed as a punishment for a crime, the performance of hard labour in pursuance of a sentence to such punishment by a competent court;
     (c) For the purpose of this paragraph the term "forced or compulsory labour" shall not include:
          (i)   Any work or service, not referred to in subparagraph (b), normally required of a person who is under detention in consequence of a lawful order of a court, or of a person during conditional release from such detention;
          (ii) Any service of a military character and, in countries where conscientious objection is recognized, any national service required by law of conscientious objectors;
          (iii) Any service exacted in cases of emergency or calamity threatening the life or well-being of the community;
          (iv) Any work or service which forms part of normal civil obligations.

Article 9
1.   Everyone has the right to liberty and security of person. No one shall be subjected to arbitrary arrest or detention. No one shall be deprived of his liberty except on such grounds and in accordance with such procedure as are established by law.

2.   Anyone who is arrested shall be informed, at the time of arrest, of the reasons for his arrest and shall be promptly informed of any charges against him.

3.   Anyone arrested or detained on a criminal charge shall be brought promptly before a judge or other officer authorized by law to exercise judicial power and shall be entitled to trial within a reasonable time or to release. It shall not be the general rule that persons awaiting trial shall be detained in custody, but release may be subject to guarantees to appear for trial, at any other stage of the judicial proceedings, and, should occasion arise, for execution of the judgment.

4.   Anyone who is deprived of his liberty by arrest or detention shall be entitled to take proceedings before a court, in order that that court may decide without delay on the lawfulness of his detention and order his release if the detention is not lawful.

5.   Anyone who has been the victim of unlawful arrest or detention shall have an enforceable right to compensation.

Article 10
1.   All persons deprived of their liberty shall be treated with humanity and with respect for the inherent dignity of the human person.

2.   (a) Accused persons shall, save in exceptional circumstances, be segregated from convicted persons and shall be subject to separate treatment appropriate to their status as unconvicted persons;
      (b) Accused juvenile persons shall be separated from adults and brought as speedily as possible for adjudication.

3.   The penitentiary system shall comprise treatment of prisoners the essential aim of which shall be their reformation and social rehabilitation. Juvenile offenders shall be segregated from adults and be accorded treatment appropriate to their age and legal status.

Article 11
No one shall be imprisoned merely on the ground of inability to fulfil a contractual obligation.

Article 12
1.   Everyone lawfully within the territory of a State shall, within that territory, have the right to liberty of movement and freedom to choose his residence.

2.   Everyone shall be free to leave any country, including his own.

3.   The above-mentioned rights shall not be subject to any restrictions except those which are provided by law, are necessary to protect national security, public order (ordre public), public health or morals or the rights and freedoms of others, and are consistent with the other rights recognized in the present Covenant.

4.   No one shall be arbitrarily deprived of the right to enter his own country.

Article 13
An alien lawfully in the territory of a State Party to the present Covenant may be expelled therefrom only in pursuance of a decision reached in accordance with law and shall, except where compelling reasons of national security otherwise require, be allowed to submit the reasons against his expulsion and to have his case reviewed by, and be represented for the purpose before, the competent authority or a person or persons especially designated by the competent authority.

Article 14
1.   All persons shall be equal before the courts and tribunals. In the determination of any criminal charge against him, or of his rights and obligations in a suit at law, everyone shall

be entitled to a fair and public hearing by a competent, independent and impartial tribunal established by law. The press and the public may be excluded from all or part of a trial for reasons of morals, public order (ordre public) or national security in a democratic society, or when the interest of the private lives of the parties so requires, or to the extent strictly necessary in the opinion of the court in special circumstances where publicity would prejudice the interests of justice; but any judgment rendered in a criminal case or in a suit at law shall be made public except where the interest of juvenile persons otherwise requires or the proceedings concern matrimonial disputes or the guardianship of children.

2.   Everyone charged with a criminal offence shall have the right to be presumed innocent until proved guilty according to law.

3.   In the determination of any criminal charge against him, everyone shall be entitled to the following minimum guarantees, in full equality:
   (a) To be informed promptly and in detail in a language which he understands of the nature and cause of the charge against him;
   (b) To have adequate time and facilities for the preparation of his defence and to communicate with counsel of his own choosing;
   (c) To be tried without undue delay;
   (d) To be tried in his presence, and to defend himself in person or through legal assistance of his own choosing; to be informed, if he does not have legal assistance, of this right; and to have legal assistance assigned to him, in any case where the interests of justice so require, and without payment by him in any such case if he does not have sufficient means to pay for it;
   (e) To examine, or have examined, the witnesses against him and to obtain the attendance and examination of witnesses on his behalf under the same conditions as witnesses against him;
   (f) To have the free assistance of an interpreter if he cannot understand or speak the language used in court;
   (g) Not to be compelled to testify against himself or to confess guilt.

4.   In the case of juvenile persons, the procedure shall be such as will take account of their age and the desirability of promoting their rehabilitation.

5.   Everyone convicted of a crime shall have the right to his conviction and sentence being reviewed by a higher tribunal according to law.

6.   When a person has by a final decision been convicted of a criminal offence and when subsequently his conviction has been reversed or he has been pardoned on the ground that a new or newly discovered fact shows conclusively that there has been a miscarriage of justice, the person who has suffered punishment as a result of such conviction shall be compensated according to law, unless it is proved that the non-disclosure of the unknown fact in time is wholly or partly attributable to him.

7.   No one shall be liable to be tried or punished again for an offence for which he has already been finally convicted or acquitted in accordance with the law and penal procedure of each country.

Article 15
1.   No one shall be held guilty of any criminal offence on account of any act or omission which did not constitute a criminal offence, under national or international law, at the time when it was committed. Nor shall a heavier penalty be imposed than the one that was applicable at the time when the criminal offence was committed. If, subsequent to the commission of the offence, provision is made by law for the imposition of the lighter penalty, the offender shall benefit thereby.

2.   Nothing in this article shall prejudice the trial and punishment of any person for any act or omission which, at the time when it was committed, was criminal according to the general principles of law recognized by the community of nations.

Article 16
Everyone shall have the right to recognition everywhere as a person before the law.

Article 17
1.   No one shall be subjected to arbitrary or unlawful interference with his privacy, family, home or correspondence, nor to unlawful attacks on his honour and reputation.

2.   Everyone has the right to the protection of the law against such interference or attacks.

Article 18
1.   Everyone shall have the right to freedom of thought, conscience and religion. This right shall include freedom to have or to adopt a religion or belief of his choice, and freedom, either individually or in community with others and in public or private, to manifest his religion or belief in worship, observance, practice and teaching.

2.   No one shall be subject to coercion which would impair his freedom to have or to adopt a religion or belief of his choice.

3.   Freedom to manifest one's religion or beliefs may be subject only to such limitations as are prescribed by law and are necessary to protect public safety, order, health, or morals or the fundamental rights and freedoms of others.

4.   The States Parties to the present Covenant undertake to have respect for the liberty of parents and, when applicable, legal guardians to ensure the religious and moral education of their children in conformity with their own convictions.

Article 19
1.   Everyone shall have the right to hold opinions without interference.

2.   Everyone shall have the right to freedom of expression; this right shall include freedom to seek, receive and impart information and ideas of all kinds, regardless of frontiers, either orally, in writing or in print, in the form of art, or through any other media of his choice.

3.   The exercise of the rights provided for in paragraph 2 of this article carries with it special duties and responsibilities. It may therefore be subject to certain restrictions, but these shall only be such as are provided by law and are necessary:
      (a) For respect of the rights or reputations of others;
      (b) For the protection of national security or of public order (ordre public), or of public health or morals.

Article 20
1.   Any propaganda for war shall be prohibited by law.

2.   Any advocacy of national, racial or religious hatred that constitutes incitement to discrimination, hostility or violence shall be prohibited by law.

Article 21
The right of peaceful assembly shall be recognized. No restrictions may be placed on the exercise of this right other than those imposed in conformity with the law and which are necessary in a democratic society in the interests of national security or public safety, public order (ordre public), the protection of public health or morals or the protection of the rights and freedoms of others.

Article 22

1. Everyone shall have the right to freedom of association with others, including the right to form and join trade unions for the protection of his interests.

2. No restrictions may be placed on the exercise of this right other than those which are prescribed by law and which are necessary in a democratic society in the interests of national security or public safety, public order (ordre public), the protection of public health or morals or the protection of the rights and freedoms of others. This article shall not prevent the imposition of lawful restrictions on members of the armed forces and of the police in their exercise of this right.

3. Nothing in this article shall authorize States Parties to the International Labour Organisation Convention of 1948 concerning Freedom of Association and Protection of the Right to Organize to take legislative measures which would prejudice, or to apply the law in such a manner as to prejudice, the guarantees provided for in that Convention.

Article 23

1. The family is the natural and fundamental group unit of society and is entitled to protection by society and the State.

2. The right of men and women of marriageable age to marry and to found a family shall be recognized.

3. No marriage shall be entered into without the free and full consent of the intending spouses.

4. States Parties to the present Covenant shall take appropriate steps to ensure equality of rights and responsibilities of spouses as to marriage, during marriage and at its dissolution. In the case of dissolution, provision shall be made for the necessary protection of any children.

Article 24

1. Every child shall have, without any discrimination as to race, colour, sex, language, religion, national or social origin, property or birth, the right to such measures of protection as are required by his status as a minor, on the part of his family, society and the State.

2. Every child shall be registered immediately after birth and shall have a name.

3. Every child has the right to acquire a nationality.

Article 25

Every citizen shall have the right and the opportunity, without any of the distinctions mentioned in article 2 and without unreasonable restrictions:

(a) To take part in the conduct of public affairs, directly or through freely chosen representatives;

(b) To vote and to be elected at genuine periodic elections which shall be by universal and equal suffrage and shall be held by secret ballot, guaranteeing the free expression of the will of the electors;

(c) To have access, on general terms of equality, to public service in his country.

Article 26

All persons are equal before the law and are entitled without any discrimination to the equal protection of the law. In this respect, the law shall prohibit any discrimination and guarantee to all persons equal and effective protection against discrimination on any ground such as race, colour, sex, language, religion, political or other opinion, national or social origin, property, birth or other status.

Article 27
In those States in which ethnic, religious or linguistic minorities exist, persons belonging to such minorities shall not be denied the right, in community with the other members of their group, to enjoy their own culture, to profess and practise their own religion, or to use their own language.

THE CONSTITUTION OF THE UNITED STATES OF AMERICA [1787]

THE PREAMBLE

We the People of the United States, in Order to form a more perfect Union, establish Justice, insure domestic Tranquility, provide for the common defence, promote the general Welfare, and secure the Blessings of Liberty to ourselves and our Posterity, do ordain and establish this Constitution for the United States of America.

Article. I.

Section 1.
All legislative Powers herein granted shall be vested in a Congress of the United States, which shall consist of a Senate and House of Representatives.
[. . .]

Article. II.

Section. 1.
Clause 1: The executive Power shall be vested in a President of the United States of America. He shall hold his Office during the Term of four Years, and, together with the Vice President, chosen for the same Term, be elected, as follows
[. . .]

Article. III.

Section. 1.
The judicial Power of the United States, shall be vested in one supreme Court, and in such inferior Courts as the Congress may from time to time ordain and establish. The Judges, both of the supreme and inferior Courts, shall hold their Offices during good Behaviour, and shall, at stated Times, receive for their Services, a Compensation, which shall not be diminished during their Continuance in Office.
[. . .]

CONSTITUTION OF THE REPUBLIC OF SOUTH AFRICA 1996, CHAPTER 2 BILL OF RIGHTS

7. RIGHTS

1.   This Bill of Rights is a cornerstone of democracy in South Africa. It enshrines the rights of all people in our country and affirms the democratic values of human dignity, equality and freedom.

2. The state must respect, protect, promote and fulfil the rights in the Bill of Rights.

3. The rights in the Bill of Rights are subject to the limitations contained or referred to in section 36, or elsewhere in the Bill.

8. APPLICATION

1. The Bill of Rights applies to all law, and binds the legislature, the executive, the judiciary and all organs of state.

2. A provision of the Bill of Rights binds a natural or a juristic person if, and to the extent that, it is applicable, taking into account the nature of the right and the nature of any duty imposed by the right.

3. When applying a provision of the Bill of Rights to a natural or juristic person in terms of subsection (2), a court
    a. in order to give effect to a right in the Bill, must apply, or if necessary develop, the common law to the extent that legislation does not give effect to that right; and
    b. may develop rules of the common law to limit the right, provided that the limitation is in accordance with section 36(1).
    A juristic person is entitled to the rights in the Bill of Rights to the extent required by the nature of the rights and the nature of that juristic person.

9. EQUALITY

1. Everyone is equal before the law and has the right to equal protection and benefit of the law.

2. Equality includes the full and equal enjoyment of all rights and freedoms. To promote the achievement of equality, legislative and other measures designed to protect or advance persons, or categories of persons, disadvantaged by unfair discrimination may be taken.

3. The state may not unfairly discriminate directly or indirectly against anyone on one or more grounds, including race, gender, sex, pregnancy, marital status, ethnic or social origin, colour, sexual orientation, age, disability, religion, conscience, belief, culture, language and birth.

4. No person may unfairly discriminate directly or indirectly against anyone on one or more grounds in terms of subsection (3). National legislation must be enacted to prevent or prohibit unfair discrimination.

5. Discrimination on one or more of the grounds listed in subsection (3) is unfair unless it is established that the discrimination is fair.

10. HUMAN DIGNITY

Everyone has inherent dignity and the right to have their dignity respected and protected.

11. LIFE

Everyone has the right to life.

12. FREEDOM AND SECURITY OF THE PERSON

1. Everyone has the right to freedom and security of the person, which includes the right
    a. not to be deprived of freedom arbitrarily or without just cause;
    b. not to be detained without trial;

    c.   to be free from all forms of violence from either public or private sources;
    d.   not to be tortured in any way; and
    e.   not to be treated or punished in a cruel, inhuman or degrading way.

2.   Everyone has the right to bodily and psychological integrity, which includes the right
    a.   to make decisions concerning reproduction;
    b.   to security in and control over their body; and
    c.   not to be subjected to medical or scientific experiments without their informed consent.

13. SLAVERY, SERVITUDE AND FORCED LABOUR

No one may be subjected to slavery, servitude or forced labour.

14. PRIVACY

Everyone has the right to privacy, which includes the right not to have
a.   their person or home searched;

b.   their property searched;

c.   their possessions seized; or

d.   the privacy of their communications infringed.

15. FREEDOM OF RELIGION, BELIEF AND OPINION

1.   Everyone has the right to freedom of conscience, religion, thought, belief and opinion.

2.   Religious observances may be conducted at state or state-aided institutions, provided that
    a.   those observances follow rules made by the appropriate public authorities;
    b.   they are conducted on an equitable basis; and
    c.   attendance at them is free and voluntary.

3.   a. This section does not prevent legislation recognising
        i.   marriages concluded under any tradition, or a system of religious, personal or family law; or
        ii. systems of personal and family law under any tradition, or adhered to by persons professing a particular religion.
    b. Recognition in terms of paragraph (a) must be consistent with this section and the other provisions of the Constitution.

16. FREEDOM OF EXPRESSION

1.   Everyone has the right to freedom of expression, which includes
    a.   freedom of the press and other media;
    b.   freedom to receive or impart information or ideas;
    c.   freedom of artistic creativity; and
    d.   academic freedom and freedom of scientific research.

2.   The right in subsection (1) does not extend to
    a.   propaganda for war;
    b.   incitement of imminent violence; or
    c.   advocacy of hatred that is based on race, ethnicity, gender or religion, and that constitutes incitement to cause harm.

17. ASSEMBLY, DEMONSTRATION, PICKET AND PETITION

Everyone has the right, peacefully and unarmed, to assemble, to demonstrate, to picket and to present petitions.

18. FREEDOM OF ASSOCIATION

Everyone has the right to freedom of association.

19. POLITICAL RIGHTS

1. Every citizen is free to make political choices, which includes the right
    a. to form a political party;
    b. to participate in the activities of, or recruit members for, a political party; and
    c. to campaign for a political party or cause.

2. Every citizen has the right to free, fair and regular elections for any legislative body established in terms of the Constitution.

3. Every adult citizen has the right
    a. to vote in elections for any legislative body established in terms of the Constitution, and to do so in secret; and
    b. to stand for public office and, if elected, to hold office.

20. CITIZENSHIP

No citizen may be deprived of citizenship.

21. FREEDOM OF MOVEMENT AND RESIDENCE

1. Everyone has the right to freedom of movement.

2. Everyone has the right to leave the Republic.

3. Every citizen has the right to enter, to remain in and to reside anywhere in, the Republic.

4. Every citizen has the right to a passport.

22. FREEDOM OF TRADE, OCCUPATION AND PROFESSION

Every citizen has the right to choose their trade, occupation or profession freely. The practice of a trade, occupation or profession may be regulated by law.

23. LABOUR RELATIONS

1. Everyone has the right to fair labour practices.

2. Every worker has the right
    a. to form and join a trade union;
    b. to participate in the activities and programmes of a trade union; and
    c. to strike.

3. Every employer has the right
    a. to form and join an employers' organisation; and
    b. to participate in the activities and programmes of an employers' organisation.

4.   Every trade union and every employers' organisation has the right
     a.   to determine its own administration, programmes and activities;
     b.   to organise; and
     c.   to form and join a federation.

5.   Every trade union, employers' organisation and employer has the right to engage in
     collective bargaining. National legislation may be enacted to regulate collective
     bargaining. To the extent that the legislation may limit a right in this Chapter, the
     limitation must comply with section 36(1).

6.   National legislation may recognise union security arrangements contained in collective
     agreements. To the extent that the legislation may limit a right in this Chapter, the
     limitation must comply with section 36(1).

24. ENVIRONMENT

Everyone has the right
a.   to an environment that is not harmful to their health or well-being; and

b.   to have the environment protected, for the benefit of present and future generations,
     through reasonable legislative and other measures that
     i.   prevent pollution and ecological degradation;
     ii.   promote conservation; and
     iii. secure ecologically sustainable development and use of natural resources while
           promoting justifiable economic and social development.

25. PROPERTY

1.   No one may be deprived of property except in terms of law of general application, and no
     law may permit arbitrary deprivation of property.

2.   Property may be expropriated only in terms of law of general application
     a.   for a public purpose or in the public interest; and
     b.   subject to compensation, the amount of which and the time and manner of payment
          of which have either been agreed to by those affected or decided or approved by a
          court.

3.   The amount of the compensation and the time and manner of payment must be just and
     equitable, reflecting an equitable balance between the public interest and the interests of
     those affected, having regard to all relevant circumstances, including
     a.   the current use of the property;
     b.   the history of the acquisition and use of the property;
     c.   the market value of the property;
     d.   the extent of direct state investment and subsidy in the acquisition and beneficial
          capital improvement of the property; and
     e.   the purpose of the expropriation.

4.   For the purposes of this section
     a.   the public interest includes the nation's commitment to land reform, and to reforms to
          bring about equitable access to all South Africa's natural resources; and
     b.   property is not limited to land.

5.   The state must take reasonable legislative and other measures, within its available
     resources, to foster conditions which enable citizens to gain access to land on an equitable
     basis.

6.   A person or community whose tenure of land is legally insecure as a result of past racially discriminatory laws or practices is entitled, to the extent provided by an Act of Parliament, either to tenure which is legally secure or to comparable redress.

7.   A person or community dispossessed of property after 19 June 1913 as a result of past racially discriminatory laws or practices is entitled, to the extent provided by an Act of Parliament, either to restitution of that property or to equitable redress.

8.   No provision of this section may impede the state from taking legislative and other measures to achieve land, water and related reform, in order to redress the results of past racial discrimination, provided that any departure from the provisions of this section is in accordance with the provisions of section 36(1).

9.   Parliament must enact the legislation referred to in subsection (6).

26. HOUSING

1.   Everyone has the right to have access to adequate housing.

2.   The state must take reasonable legislative and other measures, within its available resources, to achieve the progressive realisation of this right.

3.   No one may be evicted from their home, or have their home demolished, without an order of court made after considering all the relevant circumstances. No legislation may permit arbitrary evictions.

27. HEALTH CARE, FOOD, WATER AND SOCIAL SECURITY

1.   Everyone has the right to have access to
     a.   health care services, including reproductive health care;
     b.   sufficient food and water; and
     c.   social security, including, if they are unable to support themselves and their dependants, appropriate social assistance.

2.   The state must take reasonable legislative and other measures, within its available resources, to achieve the progressive realisation of each of these rights.

3.   No one may be refused emergency medical treatment.

28. CHILDREN

1.   Every child has the right
     a.   to a name and a nationality from birth;
     b.   to family care or parental care, or to appropriate alternative care when removed from the family environment;
     c.   to basic nutrition, shelter, basic health care services and social services;
     d.   to be protected from maltreatment, neglect, abuse or degradation;
     e.   to be protected from exploitative labour practices;
     f.   not to be required or permitted to perform work or provide services that
          i.   are inappropriate for a person of that child's age; or
          ii.   place at risk the child's well-being, education, physical or mental health or spiritual, moral or social development;
     g.   not to be detained except as a measure of last resort, in which case, in addition to the rights a child enjoys under sections 12 and 35, the child may be detained only for the shortest appropriate period of time, and has the right to be

       i.   kept separately from detained persons over the age of 18 years; and

      ii.   treated in a manner, and kept in conditions, that take account of the child's age;

  h.   to have a legal practitioner assigned to the child by the state, and at state expense, in civil proceedings affecting the child, if substantial injustice would otherwise result; and

  i.   not to be used directly in armed conflict, and to be protected in times of armed conflict.

2.   A child's best interests are of paramount importance in every matter concerning the child.

3.   In this section "child" means a person under the age of 18 years.

29. EDUCATION

1.   Everyone has the right
  a.   to a basic education, including adult basic education; and
  b.   to further education, which the state, through reasonable measures, must make progressively available and accessible.

2.   Everyone has the right to receive education in the official language or languages of their choice in public educational institutions where that education is reasonably practicable. In order to ensure the effective access to, and implementation of, this right, the state must consider all reasonable educational alternatives, including single medium institutions, taking into account
  a.   equity;
  b.   practicability; and
  c.   the need to redress the results of past racially discriminatory laws and practices.

3.   Everyone has the right to establish and maintain, at their own expense, independent educational institutions that
  a.   do not discriminate on the basis of race;
  b.   are registered with the state; and
  c.   maintain standards that are not inferior to standards at comparable public educational institutions.

4.   Subsection (3) does not preclude state subsidies for independent educational institutions.

30. LANGUAGE AND CULTURE

Everyone has the right to use the language and to participate in the cultural life of their choice, but no one exercising these rights may do so in a manner inconsistent with any provision of the Bill of Rights.

31. CULTURAL, RELIGIOUS AND LINGUISTIC COMMUNITIES

1.   Persons belonging to a cultural, religious or linguistic community may not be denied the right, with other members of that community
  a.   to enjoy their culture, practise their religion and use their language; and
  b.   to form, join and maintain cultural, religious and linguistic associations and other organs of civil society.

2.   The rights in subsection (1) may not be exercised in a manner inconsistent with any provision of the Bill of Rights.

32. ACCESS TO INFORMATION

1. Everyone has the right of access to
    a. any information held by the state; and
    b. any information that is held by another person and that is required for the exercise or protection of any rights.

2. National legislation must be enacted to give effect to this right, and may provide for reasonable measures to alleviate the administrative and financial burden on the state.

33. JUST ADMINISTRATIVE ACTION

1. Everyone has the right to administrative action that is lawful, reasonable and procedurally fair.

2. Everyone whose rights have been adversely affected by administrative action has the right to be given written reasons.

3. National legislation must be enacted to give effect to these rights, and must
    a. provide for the review of administrative action by a court or, where appropriate, an independent and impartial tribunal;
    b. impose a duty on the state to give effect to the rights in subsections (1) and (2); and
    c. promote an efficient administration.

34. ACCESS TO COURTS

Everyone has the right to have any dispute that can be resolved by the application of law decided in a fair public hearing before a court or, where appropriate, another independent and impartial tribunal or forum.

35. ARRESTED, DETAINED AND ACCUSED PERSONS

1. Everyone who is arrested for allegedly committing an offence has the right
    a. to remain silent;
    b. to be informed promptly
        i.   of the right to remain silent; and
        ii. of the consequences of not remaining silent;
    c. not to be compelled to make any confession or admission that could be used in evidence against that person;
    d. to be brought before a court as soon as reasonably possible, but not later than
        i.   48 hours after the arrest; or
        ii. the end of the first court day after the expiry of the 48 hours, if the 48 hours expire outside ordinary court hours or on a day which is not an ordinary court day;
    e. at the first court appearance after being arrested, to be charged or to be informed of the reason for the detention to continue, or to be released; and
    f. to be released from detention if the interests of justice permit, subject to reasonable conditions.

2. Everyone who is detained, including every sentenced prisoner, has the right
    a. to be informed promptly of the reason for being detained;
    b. to choose, and to consult with, a legal practitioner, and to be informed of this right promptly;

c. to have a legal practitioner assigned to the detained person by the state and at state expense, if substantial injustice would otherwise result, and to be informed of this right promptly;

d. to challenge the lawfulness of the detention in person before a court and, if the detention is unlawful, to be released;

e. to conditions of detention that are consistent with human dignity, including at least exercise and the provision, at state expense, of adequate accommodation, nutrition, reading material and medical treatment; and

f. to communicate with, and be visited by, that person's

    i. spouse or partner;

    ii. next of kin;

    iii. chosen religious counsellor; and

    iv. chosen medical practitioner.

3.   Every accused person has a right to a fair trial, which includes the right

a. to be informed of the charge with sufficient detail to answer it;

b. to have adequate time and facilities to prepare a defence;

c. to a public trial before an ordinary court;

d. to have their trial begin and conclude without unreasonable delay;

e. to be present when being tried;

f. to choose, and be represented by, a legal practitioner, and to be informed of this right promptly;

g. to have a legal practitioner assigned to the accused person by the state and at state expense, if substantial injustice would otherwise result, and to be informed of this right promptly;

h. to be presumed innocent, to remain silent, and not to testify during the proceedings;

i. to adduce and challenge evidence;

j. not to be compelled to give self-incriminating evidence;

k. to be tried in a language that the accused person understands or, if that is not practicable, to have the proceedings interpreted in that language;

l. not to be convicted for an act or omission that was not an offence under either national or international law at the time it was committed or omitted;

m. not to be tried for an offence in respect of an act or omission for which that person has previously been either acquitted or convicted;

n. to the benefit of the least severe of the prescribed punishments if the prescribed punishment for the offence has been changed between the time that the offence was committed and the time of sentencing; and

o. of appeal to, or review by, a higher court.

4.   Whenever this section requires information to be given to a person, that information must be given in a language that the person understands.

5.   Evidence obtained in a manner that violates any right in the Bill of Rights must be excluded if the admission of that evidence would render the trial unfair or otherwise be detrimental to the administration of justice.

36. LIMITATION OF RIGHTS

1.   The rights in the Bill of Rights may be limited only in terms of law of general application to the extent that the limitation is reasonable and justifiable in an open and democratic society based on human dignity, equality and freedom, taking into account all relevant factors, including

a. the nature of the right;

b. the importance of the purpose of the limitation;

    c.   the nature and extent of the limitation;

    d.   the relation between the limitation and its purpose; and

    e.   less restrictive means to achieve the purpose.

2.   Except as provided in subsection (1) or in any other provision of the Constitution, no law may limit any right entrenched in the Bill of Rights.

    [. . .]

38. ENFORCEMENT OF RIGHTS

Anyone listed in this section has the right to approach a competent court, alleging that a right in the Bill of Rights has been infringed or threatened, and the court may grant appropriate relief, including a declaration of rights. The persons who may approach a court are –

a.   anyone acting in their own interest;

b.   anyone acting on behalf of another person who cannot act in their own name;

c.   anyone acting as a member of, or in the interest of, a group or class of persons;

d.   anyone acting in the public interest; and

e.   an association acting in the interest of its members.

39. INTERPRETATION OF BILL OF RIGHTS

1.   When interpreting the Bill of Rights, a court, tribunal or forum
    a.   must promote the values that underlie an open and democratic society based on human dignity, equality and freedom;
    b.   must consider international law; and
    c.   may consider foreign law.

2.   When interpreting any legislation, and when developing the common law or customary law, every court, tribunal or forum must promote the spirit, purport and objects of the Bill of Rights.

3.   The Bill of Rights does not deny the existence of any other rights or freedoms that are recognised or conferred by common law, customary law or legislation, to the extent that they are consistent with the Bill.

TREATY ON THE FUNCTIONING OF THE EUROPEAN UNION (TREATY OF ROME) [CONSOLIDATED VERSION] 1957

HIS MAJESTY THE KING OF THE BELGIANS, THE PRESIDENT OF THE FEDERAL REPUBLIC OF GERMANY, THE PRESIDENT OF THE FRENCH REPUBLIC, THE PRESIDENT OF THE ITALIAN REPUBLIC, HER ROYAL HIGHNESS THE GRAND DUCHESS OF LUXEMBOURG, HER MAJESTY THE QUEEN OF THE NETHERLANDS, [. . .]

DETERMINED to lay the foundations of an ever closer union among the peoples of Europe,

RESOLVED to ensure the economic and social progress of their States by common action to eliminate the barriers which divide Europe,

AFFIRMING as the essential objective of their efforts the constant improvements of the living and working conditions of their peoples,

RECOGNISING that the removal of existing obstacles calls for concerted action in order to guarantee steady expansion, balanced trade and fair competition,

ANXIOUS to strengthen the unity of their economies and to ensure their harmonious development by reducing the differences existing between the various regions and the backwardness of the less favoured regions,

DESIRING to contribute, by means of a common commercial policy, to the progressive abolition of restrictions on international trade,

INTENDING to confirm the solidarity which binds Europe and the overseas countries and desiring to ensure the development of their prosperity, in accordance with the principles of the Charter of the United Nations,

RESOLVED by thus pooling their resources to preserve and strengthen peace and liberty, and calling upon the other peoples of Europe who share their ideal to join in their efforts,

DETERMINED to promote the development of the highest possible level of knowledge for their peoples through a wide access to education and through its continuous updating,

[. . .] and to this end have designated as their Plenipotentiaries:

[. . .]

WHO, having exchanged their full powers, found in good and due form, have agreed as follows.

Part One PRINCIPLES

Article 1
1. This Treaty organises the functioning of the Union and determines the areas of, delimitation of, and arrangements for exercising its competences.

2. This Treaty and the Treaty on European Union constitute the Treaties on which the Union is founded. These two Treaties, which have the same legal value, shall be referred to as 'the Treaties'.

Article 2
1. When the Treaties confer on the Union exclusive competence in a specific area, only the Union may legislate and adopt legally binding acts, the Member States being able to do so themselves only if so empowered by the Union or for the implementation of Union acts.

2. When the Treaties confer on the Union a competence shared with the Member States in a specific area, the Union and the Member States may legislate and adopt legally binding acts in that area. The Member States shall exercise their competence to the extent that the Union has not exercised its competence. The Member States shall again exercise their competence to the extent that the Union has decided to cease exercising its competence.

    [. . .]

4. The Union shall have competence, in accordance with the provisions of the Treaty on European Union, to define and implement a common foreign and security policy, including the progressive framing of a common defence policy.

Article 3
1.   The Union shall have exclusive competence in the following areas:
      (a) customs union;
      (b) the establishing of the competition rules necessary for the functioning of the internal
           market;
      (c) monetary policy for the Member States whose currency is the euro;
      (d) the conservation of marine biological resources under the common fisheries policy;
      (e) common commercial policy.

2.   The Union shall also have exclusive competence for the conclusion of an international
      agreement when its conclusion is provided for in a legislative act of the Union or is
      necessary to enable the Union to exercise its internal competence, or in so far as its
      conclusion may affect common rules or alter their scope.

Article 4
1.   The Union shall share competence with the Member States where the Treaties confer on it
      a competence which does not relate to the areas referred to in Articles 3 and 6.

2.   Shared competence between the Union and the Member States applies in the following
      principal areas:
      (a) internal market;
      (b) social policy, for the aspects defined in this Treaty;
      (c) economic, social and territorial cohesion;
      (d) agriculture and fisheries, excluding the conservation of marine biological resources;
      (e) environment;
      (f) consumer protection;
      (g) transport;
      (h) trans-European networks;
      (i) energy;
      (j) area of freedom, security and justice;
      (k) common safety concerns in public health matters, for the aspects defined in this Treaty.

3.   In the areas of research, technological development and space, the Union shall have
      competence to carry out activities, in particular to define and implement programmes;
      however, the exercise of that competence shall not result in Member States being
      prevented from exercising theirs.

4.   In the areas of development cooperation and humanitarian aid, the Union shall have
      competence to carry out activities and conduct a common policy; however, the exercise of
      that competence shall not result in Member States being prevented from exercising theirs.

TITLE II – PROVISIONS HAVING GENERAL APPLICATION

Article 7
The Union shall ensure consistency between its policies and activities, taking all of its objectives
into account and in accordance with the principle of conferral of powers.

Article 8
In all its activities, the Union shall aim to eliminate inequalities, and to promote equality,
between men and women.

Article 9
In defining and implementing its policies and activities, the Union shall take into account
requirements linked to the promotion of a high level of employment, the guarantee of adequate

social protection, the fight against social exclusion, and a high level of education, training and protection of human health.

Article 10

In defining and implementing its policies and activities, the Union shall aim to combat discrimination based on sex, racial or ethnic origin, religion or belief, disability, age or sexual orientation.

Article 11

Environmental protection requirements must be integrated into the definition and implementation of the Union's policies and activities, in particular with a view to promoting sustainable development.

[. . .]

Article 15

1.   In order to promote good governance and ensure the participation of civil society, the Union's institutions, bodies, offices and agencies shall conduct their work as openly as possible.

2.   The European Parliament shall meet in public, as shall the Council when considering and voting on a draft legislative act.

3.   [. . .]

Each institution, body, office or agency shall ensure that its proceedings are transparent and shall elaborate in its own Rules of Procedure specific provisions regarding access to its documents, in accordance with the regulations referred to in the second subparagraph.

The Court of Justice of the European Union, the European Central Bank and the European Investment Bank shall be subject to this paragraph only when exercising their administrative tasks.

[. . .]

Article 17

1.   The Union respects and does not prejudice the status under national law of churches and religious associations or communities in the Member States.

2.   The Union equally respects the status under national law of philosophical and non-confessional organisations.

[. . .]

Part Two NON-DISCRIMINATION AND CITIZENSHIP OF THE UNION

Article 18

Within the scope of application of the Treaties, and without prejudice to any special provisions contained therein, any discrimination on grounds of nationality shall be prohibited.

The European Parliament and the Council, acting in accordance with the ordinary legislative procedure, may adopt rules designed to prohibit such discrimination.

Article 19

1.   Without prejudice to the other provisions of the Treaties and within the limits of the powers conferred by them upon the Union, the Council, acting unanimously in accordance with a special legislative procedure and after obtaining the consent of the

European Parliament, may take appropriate action to combat discrimination based on sex, racial or ethnic origin, religion or belief, disability, age or sexual orientation.

[...]

Article 20

1. Citizenship of the Union is hereby established. Every person holding the nationality of a Member State shall be a citizen of the Union. Citizenship of the Union shall be additional to and not replace national citizenship.

2. Citizens of the Union shall enjoy the rights and be subject to the duties provided for in the Treaties. They shall have, inter alia:
    (a) the right to move and reside freely within the territory of the Member States;
    (b) the right to vote and to stand as candidates in elections to the European Parliament and in municipal elections in their Member State of residence, under the same conditions as nationals of that State;
    (c) the right to enjoy, in the territory of a third country in which the Member State of which they are nationals is not represented, the protection of the diplomatic and consular authorities of any Member State on the same conditions as the nationals of that State;
    (d) the right to petition the European Parliament, to apply to the European Ombudsman, and to address the institutions and advisory bodies of the Union in any of the Treaty languages and to obtain a reply in the same language.

These rights shall be exercised in accordance with the conditions and limits defined by the Treaties and by the measures adopted thereunder.

Article 21

1. Every citizen of the Union shall have the right to move and reside freely within the territory of the Member States, subject to the limitations and conditions laid down in the Treaties and by the measures adopted to give them effect.

[...]

Article 22

1. Every citizen of the Union residing in a Member State of which he is not a national shall have the right to vote and to stand as a candidate at municipal elections in the Member State in which he resides, under the same conditions as nationals of that State. This right shall be exercised subject to detailed arrangements adopted by the Council, acting unanimously in accordance with a special legislative procedure and after consulting the European Parliament; these arrangements may provide for derogations where warranted by problems specific to a Member State.

2. Without prejudice to Article 223(1) and to the provisions adopted for its implementation, every citizen of the Union residing in a Member State of which he is not a national shall have the right to vote and to stand as a candidate in elections to the European Parliament in the Member State in which he resides, under the same conditions as nationals of that State. This right shall be exercised subject to detailed arrangements adopted by the Council, acting unanimously in accordance with a special legislative procedure and after consulting the European Parliament; these arrangements may provide for derogations where warranted by problems specific to a Member State.

Article 23

Every citizen of the Union shall, in the territory of a third country in which the Member State of which he is a national is not represented, be entitled to protection by the diplomatic or consular authorities of any Member State, on the same conditions as the nationals of that State. Member

States shall adopt the necessary provisions and start the international negotiations required to secure this protection.

The Council, acting in accordance with a special legislative procedure and after consulting the European Parliament, may adopt directives establishing the coordination and cooperation measures necessary to facilitate such protection.

[. . .]

Part Three   UNION POLICIES AND INTERNAL ACTIONS

TITLE I – THE INTERNAL MARKET

Article 26
1.   The Union shall adopt measures with the aim of establishing or ensuring the functioning of the internal market, in accordance with the relevant provisions of the Treaties.

2.   The internal market shall comprise an area without internal frontiers in which the free movement of goods, persons, services and capital is ensured in accordance with the provisions of the Treaties.

3.   The Council, on a proposal from the Commission, shall determine the guidelines and conditions necessary to ensure balanced progress in all the sectors concerned.

[. . .]

TITLE II – FREE MOVEMENT OF GOODS

Article 28
1.   The Union shall comprise a customs union which shall cover all trade in goods and which shall involve the prohibition between Member States of customs duties on imports and exports and of all charges having equivalent effect, and the adoption of a common customs tariff in their relations with third countries.

[. . .]

Chapter 1 THE CUSTOMS UNION

Article 30
Customs duties on imports and exports and charges having equivalent effect shall be prohibited between Member States. This prohibition shall also apply to customs duties of a fiscal nature.

[. . .]

Chapter 3 PROHIBITION OF QUANTITATIVE RESTRICTIONS BETWEEN MEMBER STATES

Article 34
Quantitative restrictions on imports and all measures having equivalent effect shall be prohibited between Member States.

Article 35
Quantitative restrictions on exports, and all measures having equivalent effect, shall be prohibited between Member States.

[. . .]

TITLE IV – FREE MOVEMENT OF PERSONS, SERVICES AND CAPITAL

Chapter 1 WORKERS

Article 45

1.   Freedom of movement for workers shall be secured within the Union.

2.   Such freedom of movement shall entail the abolition of any discrimination based on nationality between workers of the Member States as regards employment, remuneration and other conditions of work and employment.

3.   It shall entail the right, subject to limitations justified on grounds of public policy, public security or public health:
   (a) to accept offers of employment actually made;
   (b) to move freely within the territory of Member States for this purpose;
   (c) to stay in a Member State for the purpose of employment in accordance with the provisions governing the employment of nationals of that State laid down by law, regulation or administrative action;
   (d) to remain in the territory of a Member State after having been employed in that State, subject to conditions which shall be embodied in regulations to be drawn up by the Commission.

[. . .]

Chapter 2 RIGHT OF ESTABLISHMENT

Article 49

Within the framework of the provisions set out below, restrictions on the freedom of establishment of nationals of a Member State in the territory of another Member State shall be prohibited. Such prohibition shall also apply to restrictions on the setting-up of agencies, branches or subsidiaries by nationals of any Member State established in the territory of any Member State.

Freedom of establishment shall include the right to take up and pursue activities as self-employed persons and to set up and manage undertakings, in particular companies or firms within the meaning of the second paragraph of Article 54, under the conditions laid down for its own nationals by the law of the country where such establishment is effected, subject to the provisions of the Chapter relating to capital.

[. . .]

Chapter 3 SERVICES

Article 56

Within the framework of the provisions set out below, restrictions on freedom to provide services within the Union shall be prohibited in respect of nationals of Member States who are established in a Member State other than that of the person for whom the services are intended.

The European Parliament and the Council, acting in accordance with the ordinary legislative procedure, may extend the provisions of the Chapter to nationals of a third country who provide services and who are established within the Union.

[. . .]

Chapter 4 CAPITAL AND PAYMENTS

Article 63

1.   Within the framework of the provisions set out in this Chapter, all restrictions on the movement of capital between Member States and between Member States and third countries shall be prohibited.

2.   Within the framework of the provisions set out in this Chapter, all restrictions on payments between Member States and between Member States and third countries shall be prohibited.

[. . .]

TITLE V – AREA OF FREEDOM, SECURITY AND JUSTICE

Chapter 1 GENERAL PROVISIONS

Article 67

1.   The Union shall constitute an area of freedom, security and justice with respect for fundamental rights and the different legal systems and traditions of the Member States.

2.   It shall ensure the absence of internal border controls for persons and shall frame a common policy on asylum, immigration and external border control, based on solidarity between Member States, which is fair towards third-country nationals. For the purpose of this Title, stateless persons shall be treated as third-country nationals.

3.   The Union shall endeavour to ensure a high level of security through measures to prevent and combat crime, racism and xenophobia, and through measures for coordination and cooperation between police and judicial authorities and other competent authorities, as well as through the mutual recognition of judgments in criminal matters and, if necessary, through the approximation of criminal laws.

4.   The Union shall facilitate access to justice, in particular through the principle of mutual recognition of judicial and extrajudicial decisions in civil matters.

TITLE VIII – ECONOMIC AND MONETARY POLICY

Article 119

1.   For the purposes set out in Article 3 of the Treaty on European Union, the activities of the Member States and the Union shall include, as provided in the Treaties, the adoption of an economic policy which is based on the close coordination of Member States' economic policies, on the internal market and on the definition of common objectives, and conducted in accordance with the principle of an open market economy with free competition.

2.   Concurrently with the foregoing, and as provided in the Treaties and in accordance with the procedures set out therein, these activities shall include a single currency, the euro, and the definition and conduct of a single monetary policy and exchange-rate policy the primary objective of both of which shall be to maintain price stability and, without prejudice to this objective, to support the general economic policies in the Union, in accordance with the principle of an open market economy with free competition.

3.   These activities of the Member States and the Union shall entail compliance with the following guiding principles: stable prices, sound public finances and monetary conditions and a sustainable balance of payments.

[. . .]

Part Five **THE UNION'S EXTERNAL ACTION**
[. . .]

TITLE V – INTERNATIONAL AGREEMENTS

Article 216
1.   The Union may conclude an agreement with one or more third countries or international organisations where the Treaties so provide or where the conclusion of an agreement is necessary in order to achieve, within the framework of the Union's policies, one of the objectives referred to in the Treaties, or is provided for in a legally binding Union act or is likely to affect common rules or alter their scope.

2.   Agreements concluded by the Union are binding upon the institutions of the Union and on its Member States.

[. . .]

Part Six **INSTITUTIONAL AND FINANCIAL PROVISIONS**

TITLE I – INSTITUTIONAL PROVISIONS

Chapter 1 **THE INSTITUTIONS**
[. . .]

Section 5 **THE COURT OF JUSTICE OF THE EUROPEAN UNION**

Article 251
The Court of Justice shall sit in chambers or in a Grand Chamber, in accordance with the rules laid down for that purpose in the Statute of the Court of Justice of the European Union.

When provided for in the Statute, the Court of Justice may also sit as a full Court.

[. . .]

Article 263
The Court of Justice of the European Union shall review the legality of legislative acts, of acts of the Council, of the Commission and of the European Central Bank, other than recommendations and opinions, and of acts of the European Parliament and of the European Council intended to produce legal effects *vis-à-vis* third parties. It shall also review the legality of acts of bodies, offices or agencies of the Union intended to produce legal effects *vis-à-vis* third parties.

It shall for this purpose have jurisdiction in actions brought by a Member State, the European Parliament, the Council or the Commission on grounds of lack of competence, infringement of an essential procedural requirement, infringement of the Treaties or of any rule of law relating to their application, or misuse of powers.

The Court shall have jurisdiction under the same conditions in actions brought by the Court of Auditors, by the European Central Bank and by the Committee of the Regions for the purpose of protecting their prerogatives.

Any natural or legal person may, under the conditions laid down in the first and second paragraphs, institute proceedings against an act addressed to that person or which is of direct and individual concern to them, and against a regulatory act which is of direct concern to them and does not entail implementing measures.

[. . .]

Article 264

If the action is well founded, the Court of Justice of the European Union shall declare the act concerned to be void.

However, the Court shall, if it considers this necessary, state which of the effects of the act which it has declared void shall be considered as definitive.

[. . .]

Article 267

The Court of Justice of the European Union shall have jurisdiction to give preliminary rulings concerning:

(a)   the interpretation of the Treaties;

(b)   the validity and interpretation of acts of the institutions, bodies, offices or agencies of the Union;

Where such a question is raised before any court or tribunal of a Member State, that court or tribunal may, if it considers that a decision on the question is necessary to enable it to give judgment, request the Court to give a ruling thereon.

Where any such question is raised in a case pending before a court or tribunal of a Member State against whose decisions there is no judicial remedy under national law, that court or tribunal shall bring the matter before the Court.

If such a question is raised in a case pending before a court or tribunal of a Member State with regard to a person in custody, the Court of Justice of the European Union shall act with the minimum of delay.

Chapter 2 LEGAL ACTS OF THE UNION, ADOPTION PROCEDURES AND OTHER PROVISIONS

SECTION 1 THE LEGAL ACTS OF THE UNION

Article 288

To exercise the Union's competences, the institutions shall adopt regulations, directives, decisions, recommendations and opinions.

A regulation shall have general application. It shall be binding in its entirety and directly applicable in all Member States.

A directive shall be binding, as to the result to be achieved, upon each Member State to which it is addressed, but shall leave to the national authorities the choice of form and methods.

A decision shall be binding in its entirety. A decision which specifies those to whom it is addressed shall be binding only on them.

Recommendations and opinions shall have no binding force.

Article 289

1.   The ordinary legislative procedure shall consist in the joint adoption by the European Parliament and the Council of a regulation, directive or decision on a proposal from the Commission. This procedure is defined in Article 294.

2.   In the specific cases provided for by the Treaties, the adoption of a regulation, directive or decision by the European Parliament with the participation of the Council, or by the latter with the participation of the European Parliament, shall constitute a special legislative procedure.

3.   Legal acts adopted by legislative procedure shall constitute legislative acts.

[. . .]

Article 291

1.   Member States shall adopt all measures of national law necessary to implement legally binding Union acts.

[. . .]

SECTION 2 PROCEDURES FOR THE ADOPTION OF ACTS AND OTHER PROVISIONS

Article 294

1.   Where reference is made in the Treaties to the ordinary legislative procedure for the adoption of an act, the following procedure shall apply.

2.   The Commission shall submit a proposal to the European Parliament and the Council.

First reading

3.   The European Parliament shall adopt its position at first reading and communicate it to the Council.

4.   If the Council approves the European Parliament's position, the act concerned shall be adopted in the wording which corresponds to the position of the European Parliament.

5.   If the Council does not approve the European Parliament's position, it shall adopt its position at first reading and communicate it to the European Parliament.

6.   The Council shall inform the European Parliament fully of the reasons which led it to adopt its position at first reading. The Commission shall inform the European Parliament fully of its position.

Second reading

7.   If, within three months of such communication, the European Parliament:
   (a) approves the Council's position at first reading or has not taken a decision, the act concerned shall be deemed to have been adopted in the wording which corresponds to the position of the Council;
   (b) rejects, by a majority of its component members, the Council's position at first reading, the proposed act shall be deemed not to have been adopted;
   (c) proposes, by a majority of its component members, amendments to the Council's position at first reading, the text thus amended shall be forwarded to the Council and to the Commission, which shall deliver an opinion on those amendments.

8.   If, within three months of receiving the European Parliament's amendments, the Council, acting by a qualified majority:
   (a) approves all those amendments, the act in question shall be deemed to have been adopted;
   (b) does not approve all the amendments, the President of the Council, in agreement with the President of the European Parliament, shall within six weeks convene a meeting of the Conciliation Committee.

9.   The Council shall act unanimously on the amendments on which the Commission has delivered a negative opinion.

Conciliation

10. The Conciliation Committee, which shall be composed of the members of the Council or their representatives and an equal number of members representing the European Parliament, shall have the task of reaching agreement on a joint text, by a qualified majority of the members of the Council or their representatives and by a majority of the members representing the European Parliament within six weeks of its being convened, on the basis of the positions of the European Parliament and the Council at second reading.

11. The Commission shall take part in the Conciliation Committee's proceedings and shall take all necessary initiatives with a view to reconciling the positions of the European Parliament and the Council.

12. If, within six weeks of its being convened, the Conciliation Committee does not approve the joint text, the proposed act shall be deemed not to have been adopted.

Third reading

13. If, within that period, the Conciliation Committee approves a joint text, the European Parliament, acting by a majority of the votes cast, and the Council, acting by a qualified majority, shall each have a period of six weeks from that approval in which to adopt the act in question in accordance with the joint text. If they fail to do so, the proposed act shall be deemed not to have been adopted.

14. The periods of three months and six weeks referred to in this Article shall be extended by a maximum of one month and two weeks respectively at the initiative of the European Parliament or the Council.

[. . .]

Part Seven GENERAL AND FINAL PROVISIONS

Article 335
In each of the Member States, the Union shall enjoy the most extensive legal capacity accorded to legal persons under their laws; it may, in particular, acquire or dispose of movable and immovable property and may be a party to legal proceedings. To this end, the Union shall be represented by the Commission. However, the Union shall be represented by each of the institutions, by virtue of their administrative autonomy, in matters relating to their respective operation.

[. . .]

Article 356
This Treaty is concluded for an unlimited period.

TREATY ON EUROPEAN UNION (MAASTRICHT TREATY) [CONSOLIDATED VERSION] 1992

HIS MAJESTY THE KING OF THE BELGIANS, HER MAJESTY THE QUEEN OF DENMARK, THE PRESIDENT OF THE FEDERAL REPUBLIC OF GERMANY, THE PRESIDENT OF THE HELLENIC REPUBLIC, HIS MAJESTY THE KING OF SPAIN, THE PRESIDENT OF THE FRENCH REPUBLIC, THE PRESIDENT OF IRELAND, THE PRESIDENT OF THE ITALIAN REPUBLIC, HIS ROYAL HIGHNESS THE GRAND DUKE OF LUXEMBOURG, HER MAJESTY THE QUEEN OF THE NETHERLANDS, THE PRESIDENT OF THE PORTUGUESE REPUBLIC, HER MAJESTY THE QUEEN OF THE UNITED KINGDOM OF GREAT BRITAIN AND NORTHERN IRELAND,

RESOLVED to mark a new stage in the process of European integration undertaken with the establishment of the European Communities,

DRAWING INSPIRATION from the cultural, religious and humanist inheritance of Europe, from which have developed the universal values of the inviolable and inalienable rights of the human person, freedom, democracy, equality and the rule of law,

RECALLING the historic importance of the ending of the division of the European continent and the need to create firm bases for the construction of the future Europe,

CONFIRMING their attachment to the principles of liberty, democracy and respect for human rights and fundamental freedoms and of the rule of law,

CONFIRMING their attachment to fundamental social rights as defined in the European Social Charter signed at Turin on 18 October 1961 and in the 1989 Community Charter of the Fundamental Social Rights of Workers,

DESIRING to deepen the solidarity between their peoples while respecting their history, their culture and their traditions,

DESIRING to enhance further the democratic and efficient functioning of the institutions so as to enable them better to carry out, within a single institutional framework, the tasks entrusted to them,

RESOLVED to achieve the strengthening and the convergence of their economies and to establish an economic and monetary union including, in accordance with the provisions of this Treaty and of the Treaty on the Functioning of the European Union, a single and stable currency,

DETERMINED to promote economic and social progress for their peoples, taking into account the principle of sustainable development and within the context of the accomplishment of the internal market and of reinforced cohesion and environmental protection, and to implement policies ensuring that advances in economic integration are accompanied by parallel progress in other fields,

RESOLVED to establish a citizenship common to nationals of their countries,

RESOLVED to implement a common foreign and security policy including the progressive framing of a common defence policy, which might lead to a common defence in accordance with the provisions of Article 17, thereby reinforcing the European identity and its independence in order to promote peace, security and progress in Europe and in the world,

RESOLVED to facilitate the free movement of persons, while ensuring the safety and security of their peoples, by establishing an area of freedom, security and justice, in accordance with the provisions of this Treaty and of the Treaty on the Functioning of the European Union,

RESOLVED to continue the process of creating an ever closer union among the peoples of Europe, in which decisions are taken as closely as possible to the citizen in accordance with the principle of subsidiarity,

IN VIEW of further steps to be taken in order to advance European integration,

HAVE DECIDED to establish a European Union and to this end have designated as their Plenipotentiaries:

[. . .]

WHO, having exchanged their full powers, found in good and due form, have agreed as follows.

TITLE I – COMMON PROVISIONS

Article 1

By this Treaty, the HIGH CONTRACTING PARTIES establish among themselves a EUROPEAN UNION, hereinafter called 'the Union', on which the Member States confer competences to attain objectives they have in common.

This Treaty marks a new stage in the process of creating an ever closer union among the peoples of Europe, in which decisions are taken as openly as possible and as closely as possible to the citizen.

The Union shall be founded on the present Treaty and on the Treaty on the Functioning of the European Union (hereinafter referred to as 'the Treaties'). Those two Treaties shall have the same legal value. The Union shall replace and succeed the European Community.

Article 2

The Union is founded on the values of respect for human dignity, freedom, democracy, equality, the rule of law and respect for human rights, including the rights of persons belonging to minorities. These values are common to the Member States in a society in which pluralism, non-discrimination, tolerance, justice, solidarity and equality between women and men prevail.

Article 3

1.   The Union's aim is to promote peace, its values and the well-being of its peoples.

2.   The Union shall offer its citizens an area of freedom, security and justice without internal frontiers, in which the free movement of persons is ensured in conjunction with appropriate measures with respect to external border controls, asylum, immigration and the prevention and combating of crime.

3.   The Union shall establish an internal market. It shall work for the sustainable development of Europe based on balanced economic growth and price stability, a highly competitive social market economy, aiming at full employment and social progress, and a high level of protection and improvement of the quality of the environment. It shall promote scientific and technological advance.

      It shall combat social exclusion and discrimination, and shall promote social justice and protection, equality between women and men, solidarity between generations and protection of the rights of the child.

      It shall promote economic, social and territorial cohesion, and solidarity among Member States.

      It shall respect its rich cultural and linguistic diversity, and shall ensure that Europe's cultural heritage is safeguarded and enhanced.

4.   The Union shall establish an economic and monetary union whose currency is the euro.

5.   In its relations with the wider world, the Union shall uphold and promote its values and interests and contribute to the protection of its citizens. It shall contribute to peace, security, the sustainable development of the Earth, solidarity and mutual respect among peoples, free and fair trade, eradication of poverty and the protection of human rights, in particular the rights of the child, as well as to the strict observance and the development of international law, including respect for the principles of the United Nations Charter.

6.   The Union shall pursue its objectives by appropriate means commensurate with the competences which are conferred upon it in the Treaties.

Article 4

1. In accordance with Article 5, competences not conferred upon the Union in the Treaties remain with the Member States.

2. The Union shall respect the equality of Member States before the Treaties as well as their national identities, inherent in their fundamental structures, political and constitutional, inclusive of regional and local self-government. It shall respect their essential State functions, including ensuring the territorial integrity of the State, maintaining law and order and safeguarding national security. In particular, national security remains the sole responsibility of each Member State.

[. . .]

Article 5

1. The limits of Union competences are governed by the principle of conferral. The use of Union competences is governed by the principles of subsidiarity and proportionality.

2. Under the principle of conferral, the Union shall act only within the limits of the competences conferred upon it by the Member States in the Treaties to attain the objectives set out therein. Competences not conferred upon the Union in the Treaties remain with the Member States.

3. Under the principle of subsidiarity, in areas which do not fall within its exclusive competence, the Union shall act only if and in so far as the objectives of the proposed action cannot be sufficiently achieved by the Member States, either at central level or at regional and local level, but can rather, by reason of the scale or effects of the proposed action, be better achieved at Union level.

[. . .]

4. Under the principle of proportionality, the content and form of Union action shall not exceed what is necessary to achieve the objectives of the Treaties.

[. . .]

Article 6

1. The Union recognises the rights, freedoms and principles set out in the Charter of Fundamental Rights of the European Union of 7 December 2000, as adapted at Strasbourg, on 12 December 2007, which shall have the same legal value as the Treaties.

[. . .]

2. The Union shall accede to the European Convention for the Protection of Human Rights and Fundamental Freedoms. Such accession shall not affect the Union's competences as defined in the Treaties.

3. Fundamental rights, as guaranteed by the European Convention for the Protection of Human Rights and Fundamental Freedoms and as they result from the constitutional traditions common to the Member States, shall constitute general principles of the Union's law.

[. . .]

TITLE II – PROVISIONS ON DEMOCRATIC PRINCIPLES

Article 9
In all its activities, the Union shall observe the principle of the equality of its citizens, who shall receive equal attention from its institutions, bodies, offices and agencies. Every national of a Member State shall be a citizen of the Union. Citizenship of the Union shall be additional to and not replace national citizenship.

Article 10
1.   The functioning of the Union shall be founded on representative democracy.

2.   Citizens are directly represented at Union level in the European Parliament.

      Member States are represented in the European Council by their Heads of State or Government and in the Council by their governments, themselves democratically accountable either to their national Parliaments, or to their citizens.

3.   Every citizen shall have the right to participate in the democratic life of the Union. Decisions shall be taken as openly and as closely as possible to the citizen.

4.   Political parties at European level contribute to forming European political awareness and to expressing the will of citizens of the Union.

[. . .]

TITLE III – PROVISIONS ON THE INSTITUTIONS

Article 13
1.   The Union shall have an institutional framework which shall aim to promote its values, advance its objectives, serve its interests, those of its citizens and those of the Member States, and ensure the consistency, effectiveness and continuity of its policies and actions.

      The Union's institutions shall be:

      — the European Parliament,
      — the European Council,
      — the Council,
      — the European Commission (hereinafter referred to as 'the Commission'),
      — the Court of Justice of the European Union,
      — the European Central Bank,
      — the Court of Auditors.
      [. . .]

Article 14
1.   The European Parliament shall, jointly with the Council, exercise legislative and budgetary functions. It shall exercise functions of political control and consultation as laid down in the Treaties. It shall elect the President of the Commission.

2.   The European Parliament shall be composed of representatives of the Union's citizens. They shall not exceed seven hundred and fifty in number, plus the President. Representation of citizens shall be degressively proportional, with a minimum threshold of six members per Member State. No Member State shall be allocated more than ninety-six seats.

      The European Council shall adopt by unanimity, on the initiative of the European Parliament and with its consent, a decision establishing the composition of the European Parliament, respecting the principles referred to in the first subparagraph.

3.   The members of the European Parliament shall be elected for a term of five years by direct universal suffrage in a free and secret ballot.

[. . .]

Article 15

1.   The European Council shall provide the Union with the necessary impetus for its development and shall define the general political directions and priorities thereof. It shall not exercise legislative functions.

2.   The European Council shall consist of the Heads of State or Government of the Member States, together with its President and the President of the Commission. The High Representative of the Union for Foreign Affairs and Security Policy shall take part in its work.

3.   The European Council shall meet twice every six months, convened by its President. When the agenda so requires, the members of the European Council may decide each to be assisted by a minister and, in the case of the President of the Commission, by a member of the Commission. When the situation so requires, the President shall convene a special meeting of the European Council.

4.   Except where the Treaties provide otherwise, decisions of the European Council shall be taken by consensus.

5.   The European Council shall elect its President, by a qualified majority, for a term of two and a half years, renewable once. In the event of an impediment or serious misconduct, the European Council can end the President's term of office in accordance with the same procedure.

6.   The President of the European Council:
      (a) shall chair it and drive forward its work;
      (b) shall ensure the preparation and continuity of the work of the European Council in cooperation with the President of the Commission, and on the basis of the work of the General Affairs Council;
      (c) shall endeavour to facilitate cohesion and consensus within the European Council;
      (d) shall present a report to the European Parliament after each of the meetings of the European Council.
      The President of the European Council shall, at his level and in that capacity, ensure the external representation of the Union on issues concerning its common foreign and security policy, without prejudice to the powers of the High Representative of the Union for Foreign Affairs and Security Policy.

      The President of the European Council shall not hold a national office.

Article 16

1.   The Council shall, jointly with the European Parliament, exercise legislative and budgetary functions. It shall carry out policy-making and coordinating functions as laid down in the Treaties.

2.   The Council shall consist of a representative of each Member State at ministerial level, who may commit the government of the Member State in question and cast its vote.

[. . .]

Article 17

1.   The Commission shall promote the general interest of the Union and take appropriate initiatives to that end. It shall ensure the application of the Treaties, and of measures adopted by the institutions pursuant to them. It shall oversee the application of Union law under the control of the Court of Justice of the European Union. It shall execute the budget and manage programmes. It shall exercise coordinating, executive and management functions, as laid down in the Treaties. With the exception of the common foreign and security policy, and other cases provided for in the Treaties, it shall ensure the Union's external representation. It shall initiate the Union's annual and multiannual programming with a view to achieving interinstitutional agreements.

2.   Union legislative acts may only be adopted on the basis of a Commission proposal, except where the Treaties provide otherwise. Other acts shall be adopted on the basis of a Commission proposal where the Treaties so provide.

3.   The Commission's term of office shall be five years.

The members of the Commission shall be chosen on the ground of their general competence and European commitment from persons whose independence is beyond doubt.

In carrying out its responsibilities, the Commission shall be completely independent. Without prejudice to Article 18(2), the members of the Commission shall neither seek nor take instructions from any Government or other institution, body, office or entity. They shall refrain from any action incompatible with their duties or the performance of their tasks.

[. . .]

Article 18

1.   The European Council, acting by a qualified majority, with the agreement of the President of the Commission, shall appoint the High Representative of the Union for Foreign Affairs and Security Policy. The European Council may end his term of office by the same procedure.

2.   The High Representative shall conduct the Union's common foreign and security policy. He shall contribute by his proposals to the development of that policy, which he shall carry out as mandated by the Council. The same shall apply to the common security and defence policy.

3.   The High Representative shall preside over the Foreign Affairs Council.

[. . .]

Article 19

1.   The Court of Justice of the European Union shall include the Court of Justice, the General Court and specialised courts. It shall ensure that in the interpretation and application of the Treaties the law is observed.

Member States shall provide remedies sufficient to ensure effective legal protection in the fields covered by Union law.

2.   The Court of Justice shall consist of one judge from each Member State. It shall be assisted by Advocates-General.

The General Court shall include at least one judge per Member State.

The Judges and the Advocates-General of the Court of Justice and the Judges of the General Court shall be chosen from persons whose independence is beyond doubt and who satisfy the conditions set out in Articles 253 and 254 of the Treaty on the Functioning of the European Union. They shall be appointed by common accord of the governments of the Member States for six years. Retiring Judges and Advocates-General may be reappointed.

3.   The Court of Justice of the European Union shall, in accordance with the Treaties:
    (a)   rule on actions brought by a Member State, an institution or a natural or legal person;
    (b)   give preliminary rulings, at the request of courts or tribunals of the Member States, on the interpretation of Union law or the validity of acts adopted by the institutions;
    (c)   rule in other cases provided for in the Treaties.

[. . .]

[. . .]

TITLE VI – FINAL PROVISIONS

Article 47
The Union shall have legal personality.

[. . .]

Article 53
This Treaty is concluded for an unlimited period.

TREATY OF LISBON AMENDING THE TREATY ON EUROPEAN UNION AND THE TREATY ESTABLISHING THE EUROPEAN COMMUNITY 2007

PREAMBLE

HIS MAJESTY THE KING OF THE BELGIANS, THE PRESIDENT OF THE REPUBLIC OF BULGARIA, THE PRESIDENT OF THE CZECH REPUBLIC, HER MAJESTY THE QUEEN OF DENMARK, THE PRESIDENT OF THE FEDERAL REPUBLIC OF GERMANY, THE PRESIDENT OF THE REPUBLIC OF ESTONIA, THE PRESIDENT OF IRELAND,

THE PRESIDENT OF THE HELLENIC REPUBLIC, HIS MAJESTY THE KING OF SPAIN,

THE PRESIDENT OF THE FRENCH REPUBLIC, THE PRESIDENT OF THE ITALIAN REPUBLIC, THE PRESIDENT OF THE REPUBLIC OF CYPRUS, THE PRESIDENT OF THE REPUBLIC OF LATVIA, THE PRESIDENT OF THE REPUBLIC OF LITHUANIA, HIS ROYAL HIGHNESS THE GRAND DUKE OF LUXEMBOURG, THE PRESIDENT OF THE REPUBLIC OF HUNGARY, THE PRESIDENT OF MALTA, HER MAJESTY THE QUEEN OF THE NETHERLANDS, THE FEDERAL PRESIDENT OF THE REPUBLIC OF AUSTRIA,

THE PRESIDENT OF THE REPUBLIC OF POLAND, THE PRESIDENT OF THE PORTUGUESE REPUBLIC, THE PRESIDENT OF ROMANIA, THE PRESIDENT OF THE REPUBLIC OF SLOVENIA, THE PRESIDENT OF THE SLOVAK REPUBLIC,

THE PRESIDENT OF THE REPUBLIC OF FINLAND, THE GOVERNMENT OF THE KINGDOM OF SWEDEN, HER MAJESTY THE QUEEN OF THE UNITED KINGDOM OF GREAT BRITAIN AND NORTHERN IRELAND,

DESIRING to complete the process started by the Treaty of Amsterdam and by the Treaty of Nice with a view to enhancing the efficiency and democratic legitimacy of the Union and to improving the coherence of its action,

HAVE RESOLVED to amend the Treaty on European Union, the Treaty establishing the European Community and the Treaty establishing the European Atomic Energy Community, and to this end have designated as their Plenipotentiaries:

[. . .]

WHO, having exchanged their full powers, found in good and due form,

HAVE AGREED AS FOLLOWS:

AMENDMENTS TO THE TREATY ON EUROPEAN UNION AND TO THE TREATY

ESTABLISHING THE EUROPEAN COMMUNITY

Article 1
The Treaty on European Union shall be amended in accordance with the provisions of this Article[1].
[. . .]

Article 2
The Treaty establishing the European Community shall be amended in accordance with the provisions of this Article[2].
[. . .]

FINAL PROVISIONS

Article 3
This Treaty is concluded for an unlimited period.

[. . .]

Article 6
1.   This Treaty shall be ratified by the High Contracting Parties in accordance with their respective constitutional requirements. The instruments of ratification shall be deposited with the Government of the Italian Republic.

2.   This Treaty shall enter into force on 1 January 2009, provided that all the instruments of ratification have been deposited, or, failing that, on the first day of the month following the deposit of the instrument of ratification by the last signatory State to take this step.

Article 7
This Treaty, referred to as the Treaty of Lisbon, drawn up in a single original in the Bulgarian, Czech, Danish, Dutch, English, Estonian, Finnish, French, German, Greek, Hungarian, Irish, Italian, Latvian, Lithuanian, Maltese, Polish, Portuguese, Romanian, Slovak, Slovenian, Spanish

---

[1]   The amendments introduced through this article have been incorporated in the relevant amended instruments.
[2]   The amendments introduced through this article have been incorporated in the relevant amended instruments.

and Swedish languages, the texts in each of these languages being equally authentic, shall be deposited in the archives of the Government of the Italian Republic, which will transmit a certified copy to each of the governments of the other signatory States.

IN WITNESS WHEREOF the undersigned Plenipotentiaries have signed this Treaty.

The Constitution of the United States

Article I

Section 1
All legislative Powers herein granted shall be vested in a Congress of the United States, which shall consist of a Senate and House of Representatives.

Article II

Section 1
Clause 1: The executive Power shall be vested in a President of the United States of America. He shall hold his Office during the Term of four Years, and, together with the Vice President, chosen for the same Term, be elected, as follows

Article III

Section 1
The judicial Power of the United States, shall be vested in one supreme Court, and in such inferior Courts as the Congress may from time to time ordain and establish. The Judges, both of the supreme and inferior Courts, shall hold their Offices during good Behaviour, and shall, at stated Times, receive for their Services, a Compensation, which shall not be diminished during their Continuance in Office.

Codes of Practice to the Police and Criminal Evidence Act 1984

CODE A: CODE OF PRACTICE FOR THE EXERCISE BY: POLICE OFFICERS OF STATUTORY POWERS OF STOP AND SEARCH; POLICE OFFICERS AND POLICE STAFF OF REQUIREMENTS TO RECORD PUBLIC ENCOUNTERS

Commencement – Transitional Arrangements

This code applies to any search by a police officer and the recording of public encounters taking place after midnight on 06 March 2011.

GENERAL

This code of practice must be readily available at all police stations for consultation by police officers, police staff, detained persons and members of the public.

The notes for guidance included are not provisions of this code, but are guidance to police officers and others about its application and interpretation. Provisions in the annexes to the code are provisions of this code.

This code governs the exercise by police officers of statutory powers to search a person or a vehicle without first making an arrest. The main stop and search powers to which this code applies are set out in Annex A, but that list should not be regarded as definitive. [See Note 1] In addition, it covers requirements on police officers and police staff to record encounters not governed by statutory powers. This code does not apply to:

(a) the powers of stop and search under;
 (i) Aviation Security Act 1982, section 27(2);
 (ii) Police and Criminal Evidence Act 1984, section 6(1) (which relates specifically to powers of constables employed by statutory undertakers on the premises of the statutory undertakers).

(b) searches carried out for the purposes of examination under Schedule 7 to the Terrorism Act 2000 and to which the Code of Practice issued under paragraph 6 of Schedule 14 to the Terrorism Act 2000 applies.

1 PRINCIPLES GOVERNING STOP AND SEARCH

1.1   Powers to stop and search must be used fairly, responsibly, with respect for people being searched and without unlawful discrimination. The Equality Act 2010 makes it unlawful for police officers to discriminate against, harass or victimise any person on the grounds of the 'protected characteristics' of age, disability, gender reassignment, race, religion or belief, sex and sexual orientation, marriage and civil partnership, pregnancy and maternity when using their powers. When police forces are carrying out their functions they also have a duty to have regard to the need to eliminate unlawful discrimination, harassment and victimisation and to take steps to foster good relations.

1.2   The intrusion on the liberty of the person stopped or searched must be brief and detention for the purposes of a search must take place at or near the location of the stop.

1.3   If these fundamental principles are not observed the use of powers to stop and search may be drawn into question. Failure to use the powers in the proper manner reduces their effectiveness. Stop and search can play an important role in the detection and prevention of crime, and using the powers fairly makes them more effective.

1.4   The primary purpose of stop and search powers is to enable officers to allay or confirm suspicions about individuals without exercising their power of arrest. Officers may be required to justify the use or authorisation of such powers, in relation both to individual searches and the overall pattern of their activity in this regard, to their supervisory officers or in court. Any misuse of the powers is likely to be harmful to policing and lead to mistrust of the police. Officers must also be able to explain their actions to the member of the public searched. The misuse of these powers can lead to disciplinary action.

1.5   An officer must not search a person, even with his or her consent, where no power to search is applicable. Even where a person is prepared to submit to a search voluntarily, the person must not be searched unless the necessary legal power exists, and the search must be in accordance with the relevant power and the provisions of this Code. The only exception, where an officer does not require a specific power, applies to searches of persons entering sports grounds or other premises carried out with their consent given as a condition of entry.

2 EXPLANATION OF POWERS TO STOP AND SEARCH

2.1   This code applies to powers of stop and search as follows:
   (a) powers which require reasonable grounds for suspicion, before they may be exercised; that articles unlawfully obtained or possessed are being carried, or under Section 43 of the Terrorism Act 2000 that a person is a terrorist;
   (b) authorised under section 60 of the Criminal Justice and Public Order Act 1994, based upon a reasonable belief that incidents involving serious violence may take place or that people are carrying dangerous instruments or offensive weapons within any locality in the police area or that it is expedient to use the powers to find such instruments or weapons that have been used in incidents of serious violence;
   (c) authorised under section 44(1) of the Terrorism Act 2000 based upon a consideration that the exercise of the power is necessary for the prevention of acts of terrorism (see paragraph 2.18A), and
   (d) powers to search a person who has not been arrested in the exercise of a power to search premises (see Code B paragraph 2.4).

Searches requiring reasonable grounds for suspicion
2.2   Reasonable grounds for suspicion depend on the circumstances in each case. There must be an objective basis for that suspicion based on facts, information, and/or intelligence

which are relevant to the likelihood of finding an article of a certain kind or, in the case of searches under section 43 of the Terrorism Act 2000, to the likelihood that the person is a terrorist. Reasonable suspicion can never be supported on the basis of personal factors. It must rely on intelligence or information about, or some specific behaviour by, the person concerned. For example, unless the police have a description of a suspect, a person's physical appearance (including any of the 'protected characteristics' set out in the Equality Act 2010 (see paragraph 1.1), or the fact that the person is known to have a previous conviction, cannot be used alone or in combination with each other, or in combination with any other factor, as the reason for searching that person. Reasonable suspicion cannot be based on generalisations or stereotypical images of certain groups or categories of people as more likely to be involved in criminal activity.

2.3   Reasonable suspicion may also exist without specific information or intelligence and on the basis of the behaviour of a person. For example, if an officer encounters someone on the street at night who is obviously trying to hide something, the officer may (depending on the other surrounding circumstances) base such suspicion on the fact that this kind of behaviour is often linked to stolen or prohibited articles being carried. Similarly, for the purposes of section 43 of the Terrorism Act 2000, suspicion that a person is a terrorist may arise from the person's behaviour at or near a location which has been identified as a potential target for terrorists.

2.4   However, reasonable suspicion should normally be linked to accurate and current intelligence or information, such as information describing an article being carried, a suspected offender, or a person who has been seen carrying a type of article known to have been stolen recently from premises in the area. Searches based on accurate and current intelligence or information are more likely to be effective. Targeting searches in a particular area at specified crime problems increases their effectiveness and minimises inconvenience to law-abiding members of the public. It also helps in justifying the use of searches both to those who are searched and to the public. This does not however prevent stop and search powers being exercised in other locations where such powers may be exercised and reasonable suspicion exists.

2.5   Searches are more likely to be effective, legitimate, and secure public confidence when reasonable suspicion is based on a range of factors. The overall use of these powers is more likely to be effective when up to date and accurate intelligence or information is communicated to officers and they are well-informed about local crime patterns.

2.6   Where there is reliable information or intelligence that members of a group or gang habitually carry knives unlawfully or weapons or controlled drugs, and wear a distinctive item of clothing or other means of identification to indicate their membership of the group or gang, that distinctive item of clothing or other means of identification may provide reasonable grounds to stop and search a person. [See Note 9]

2.7   A police officer may have reasonable grounds to suspect that a person is in innocent possession of a stolen or prohibited article or other item for which he or she is empowered to search. In that case the officer may stop and search the person even though there would be no power of arrest.

2.8   Under section 43(1) of the Terrorism Act 2000 a constable may stop and search a person whom the officer reasonably suspects to be a terrorist to discover whether the person is in possession of anything which may constitute evidence that the person is a terrorist. These searches may only be carried out by an officer of the same sex as the person searched (see Annex F). An authorisation under section 44(1) of the Terrorism Act 2000 allows vehicles to be stopped and searched by a constable in uniform who reasonably suspects that articles which could be used in connection with terrorism will be found in the vehicle or in anything in or on that vehicle. See paragraph 2.18A below.

2.9   An officer who has reasonable grounds for suspicion may detain the person concerned in order to carry out a search. Before carrying out a search the officer may ask questions about the person's behaviour or presence in circumstances which gave rise to the suspicion. As a result of questioning the detained person, the reasonable grounds for suspicion necessary to detain that person may be confirmed or, because of a satisfactory explanation, be eliminated. [See Notes 2 and 3] Questioning may also reveal reasonable grounds to suspect the possession of a different kind of unlawful article from that originally suspected. Reasonable grounds for suspicion however cannot be provided retrospectively by such questioning during a person's detention or by refusal to answer any questions put.

2.10   If, as a result of questioning before a search, or other circumstances which come to the attention of the officer, there cease to be reasonable grounds for suspecting that an article is being carried of a kind for which there is a power to stop and search, no search may take place. [See Note 3] In the absence of any other lawful power to detain, the person is free to leave at will and must be so informed.

2.11   There is no power to stop or detain a person in order to find grounds for a search. Police officers have many encounters with members of the public which do not involve detaining people against their will. If reasonable grounds for suspicion emerge during such an encounter, the officer may search the person, even though no grounds existed when the encounter began. If an officer is detaining someone for the purpose of a search, he or she should inform the person as soon as detention begins.

Searches authorised under section 60 of the Criminal Justice and Public Order Act 1994

2.12   Authority for a constable in uniform to stop and search under section 60 of the Criminal Justice and Public Order Act 1994 may be given if the authorising officer reasonably believes:
(a)   that incidents involving serious violence may take place in any locality in the officer's police area, and it is expedient to use these powers to prevent their occurrence;
(b)   that persons are carrying dangerous instruments or offensive weapons without good reason in any locality in the officer's police area or
(c)   that an incident involving serious violence has taken place in the officer's police area, a dangerous instrument or offensive weapon used in the incident is being carried by a person in any locality in that police area, and it is expedient to use these powers to find that instrument or weapon.

2.13   An authorisation under section 60 may only be given by an officer of the rank of inspector or above and in writing, or orally if paragraph 2.12(c) applies and it is not practicable to give the authorisation in writing. The authorisation (whether written or oral) must specify the grounds on which it was given, the locality in which the powers may be exercised and the period of time for which they are in force. The period authorised shall be no longer than appears reasonably necessary to prevent, or seek to prevent incidents of serious violence, or to deal with the problem of carrying dangerous instruments or offensive weapons or to find a dangerous instrument or offensive weapon that has been used. It may not exceed 24 hours. An oral authorisation given where paragraph 2.12(c) applies must be recorded in writing as soon as practicable. [See Notes 10–13]

2.14   An inspector who gives an authorisation must, as soon as practicable, inform an officer of or above the rank of superintendent. This officer may direct that the authorisation shall be extended for a further 24 hours, if violence or the carrying of dangerous instruments or offensive weapons has occurred, or is suspected to have occurred, and the continued use of the powers is considered necessary to prevent or deal with further such activity or to find a dangerous instrument or offensive weapon used that has been used. That direction must be given in writing unless it is not practicable to do so, in which case it must be recorded in writing as soon as practicable afterwards. [See Note 12]

2.14A The selection of persons and vehicles under section 60 to be stopped and, if appropriate, searched should reflect an objective assessment of the nature of the incident or weapon in question and the individuals and vehicles thought likely to be associated with that incident or those weapons (see Notes 10 and 11). The powers must not be used to stop and search persons and vehicles for reasons unconnected with the purpose of the authorisation. When selecting persons and vehicles to be stopped in response to a specific threat or incident, officers must take care not to discriminate unlawfully against anyone on the grounds of any of the protected characteristics set out in the Equality Act 2010 (see paragraph 1.1).

2.14B The driver of a vehicle which is stopped under section 60 and any person who is searched under section 60 are entitled to a written statement to that effect if they apply within twelve months from the day the vehicle was stopped or the person was searched. This statement is a record which states that the vehicle was stopped or (as the case may be) that the person was searched under section 60 and it may form part of the search record or be supplied as a separate record.

Powers to require removal of face coverings

2.15 Section 60AA of the Criminal Justice and Public Order Act 1994 also provides a power to demand the removal of disguises. The officer exercising the power must reasonably believe that someone is wearing an item wholly or mainly for the purpose of concealing identity. There is also a power to seize such items where the officer believes that a person intends to wear them for this purpose. There is no power to stop and search for disguises. An officer may seize any such item which is discovered when exercising a power of search for something else, or which is being carried, and which the officer reasonably believes is intended to be used for concealing anyone's identity. This power can only be used if an authorisation given under section 60 or under section 60AA, is in force. [See Note 4]

2.16 Authority under section 60AA for a constable in uniform to require the removal of disguises and to seize them may be given if the authorising officer reasonably believes that activities may take place in any locality in the officer's police area that are likely to involve the commission of offences and it is expedient to use these powers to prevent or control these activities.

2.17 An authorisation under section 60AA may only be given by an officer of the rank of inspector or above, in writing, specifying the grounds on which it was given, the locality in which the powers may be exercised and the period of time for which they are in force. The period authorised shall be no longer than appears reasonably necessary to prevent, or seek to prevent the commission of offences. It may not exceed 24 hours. [See Notes 10–13]

2.18 An inspector who gives an authorisation must, as soon as practicable, inform an officer of or above the rank of superintendent. This officer may direct that the authorisation shall be extended for a further 24 hours, if crimes have been committed, or are suspected to have been committed, and the continued use of the powers is considered necessary to prevent or deal with further such activity. This direction must also be given in writing at the time or as soon as practicable afterwards. [See Note 12]

Searches authorised under section 44 of the Terrorism Act 2000

2.18A The European Court of Human Rights has ruled that the stop and search powers under sections 44 to 47 of the Terrorism Act 2000 are not compatible with the right to a private life under Article 8 of the European Convention on Human Rights. Neither the European Court ruling nor the provisions of this Code can amend these statutory provisions. However, in an oral statement made by the Home Secretary in the House of Commons on 8 July 2010, interim guidelines were announced pending a review (with a view to legislative amendment) of these provisions to ensure that police do not exercise any powers under section 44 in a way which would be incompatible with Convention rights. Under these guidelines:

(i) Authorisations under section 44(1) should be given, and may be confirmed by the Secretary of State, only:
   • in relation to searches of vehicles and anything in or on vehicles, but not searches of drivers or passengers or anything being carried by a driver or passenger; and
   • if such searches are considered necessary for the prevention of acts of terrorism. Note: Section 44(3) provides that an authorising officer may give an authorisation when they consider it is 'expedient' for the prevention of acts of terrorism, but the test now to be applied is that of necessity – taking account of all of the circumstances.

(ii) A search of a vehicle or of anything in or on a vehicle under section 44(1) should only be carried out if it is reasonably suspected that articles which could be used in connection with terrorism will be found in the vehicle or in anything in or on that vehicle.
   Note: This now applies despite the provision in section 45(1)(b) which allows the power to be exercised whether or not the constable has grounds for suspecting the presence of such articles.

(iii) Authorisations to search pedestrians, drivers of vehicles and passengers in vehicles and anything carried by a driver or passenger, are not to be given under section 44(1) or (2) and if given, will not be confirmed. For these searches police must rely on the power under section 43 which requires the person who may be searched to be reasonably suspected of being a terrorist, but does not authorise the removal of headgear or footwear in public.

The provisions of paragraphs 2.1, 2.8, 2.19 to 2.26, 3.5, Annex A paragraphs 15 and 16 and Annex C paragraph 1 are amended by this Code to reflect these guidelines:

2.19 An officer of the rank of assistant chief constable (or equivalent) or above, may give authority under section 44(1) of the Terrorism Act 2000 for a constable in uniform to exercise the power to stop and search any vehicle and anything in or on any vehicle, in the whole or any part or parts of the authorising officer's police area. An authorisation may only be given if the officer considers it is necessary for the prevention of acts of terrorism.

2.20 If an authorisation is given orally at first, it must be confirmed in writing by the officer who gave it as soon as reasonably practicable.

2.21 When giving an authorisation, the officer must specify the geographical area in which the power may be used, and the time and date that the authorisation ends (up to a maximum of 28 days from the time the authorisation was given). [See Notes 12 and 13]

2.22 The officer giving an authorisation under section 44(1) must cause the Secretary of State to be informed, as soon as reasonably practicable, that such an authorisation has been given. An authorisation which is not confirmed by the Secretary of State within 48 hours of its having been given, shall have effect up until the end of that 48 hour period or the end of the period specified in the authorisation (whichever is the earlier). [See Note 14]

2.23 Following notification of the authorisation, the Secretary of State may:
   (i) cancel the authorisation with immediate effect or with effect from such other time as he or she may direct;

(ii) confirm it but for a shorter period than that specified in the authorisation;

(iii) or confirm the authorisation as given.

2.24 When an authorisation under section 44(1) is given, a constable in uniform may exercise the power:

(a) only for the purpose of stopping and searching a vehicle and anything in or on a vehicle for articles of a kind which could be used in connection with terrorism (see paragraph 2.25); and

(b) only if there are reasonable grounds for suspecting the presence of such articles. See paragraphs 2.2 to 2.11, "Searches requiring reasonable grounds for suspicion"

2.24A When a Community Support Officer on duty and in uniform has been conferred powers under Section 44(1) of the Terrorism Act 2000 by a Chief Officer of their force, the exercise of this power must comply with the requirements of this Code of Practice, including the recording requirements.

2.25 Paragraphs 2.2 to 2.11 above ("Searches requiring reasonable grounds for suspicion") are to be applied to the stopping and searching of vehicles when an authorisation under section 44(1) is given.

2.26 The powers under sections 43 and 44(1) of the Terrorism Act 2000 allow a constable to search only for articles which could be used for terrorist purposes. However, this would not prevent a search being carried out under other powers if, in the course of exercising these powers, the officer formed reasonable grounds for suspicion.

Powers to search in the exercise of a power to search premises

2.27 The following powers to search premises also authorise the search of a person, not under arrest, who is found on the premises during the course of the search:

(a) section 139B of the Criminal Justice Act 1988 under which a constable may enter school premises and search the premises and any person on those premises for any bladed or pointed article or offensive weapon;

(b) under a warrant issued under section 23(3) of the Misuse of Drugs Act 1971 to search premises for drugs or documents but only if the warrant specifically authorises the search of persons found on the premises; and

(c) under a search warrant or order issued under paragraph 1, 3 or 11 of Schedule 5 to the Terrorism Act 2000 to search premises and any person found there for material likely to be of substantial value to a terrorist investigation.

2.28 Before the power under section 139B of the Criminal Justice Act 1988 may be exercised, the constable must have reasonable grounds to believe that an offence under section 139A of the Criminal Justice Act 1988 (having a bladed or pointed article or offensive weapon on school premises) has been or is being committed. A warrant to search premises and persons found therein may be issued under section 23(3) of the Misuse of Drugs Act 1971 if there are reasonable grounds to suspect that controlled drugs or certain documents are in the possession of a person on the premises.

2.29 The powers in paragraph 2.27 do not require prior specific grounds to suspect that the person to be searched is in possession of an item for which there is an existing power to search. However, it is still necessary to ensure that the selection and treatment of those searched under these powers is based upon objective factors connected with the search of the premises, and not upon personal prejudice.

3 CONDUCT OF SEARCHES

3.1 All stops and searches must be carried out with courtesy, consideration and respect for the person concerned. This has a significant impact on public confidence in the police. Every reasonable effort must be made to minimise the embarrassment that a person being searched may experience. [See Note 4]

3.2 The co-operation of the person to be searched must be sought in every case, even if the person initially objects to the search. A forcible search may be made only if it has been established that the person is unwilling to co-operate or resists. Reasonable force may be used as a last resort if necessary to conduct a search or to detain a person or vehicle for the purposes of a search.

3.3 The length of time for which a person or vehicle may be detained must be reasonable and kept to a minimum. Where the exercise of the power requires reasonable suspicion, the thoroughness and extent of a search must depend on what is suspected of being carried, and by whom. If the suspicion relates to a particular article which is seen to be slipped into a person's pocket, then, in the absence of other grounds for suspicion or an opportunity for the article to be moved elsewhere, the search must be confined to that pocket. In the case of a small article which can readily be concealed, such as a drug, and which might be concealed anywhere on the person, a more extensive search may be necessary. In the case of searches mentioned in paragraph 2.1(b), (c), and (d), which do not require reasonable grounds for suspicion, officers may make any reasonable search to look for items for which they are empowered to search. [See Note 5]

3.4 The search must be carried out at or near the place where the person or vehicle was first detained. [See Note 6]

3.5 There is no power to require a person to remove any clothing in public other than an outer coat, jacket or gloves, except under section 60AA of the Criminal Justice and Public Order Act 1994 (which empowers a constable to require a person to remove any item worn to conceal identity). [See Notes 4 and 6] A search in public of a person's clothing which has not been removed must be restricted to superficial examination of outer garments. This does not, however, prevent an officer from placing his or her hand inside the pockets of the outer clothing, or feeling round the inside of collars, socks and shoes if this is reasonably necessary in the circumstances to look for the object of the search or to remove and examine any item reasonably suspected to be the object of the search. For the same reasons, subject to the restrictions on the removal of headgear, a person's hair may also be searched in public (see paragraphs 3.1 and 3.3).

3.6 Where on reasonable grounds it is considered necessary to conduct a more thorough search (e.g. by requiring a person to take off a T-shirt), this must be done out of public view, for example, in a police van unless paragraph 3.7 applies, or police station if there is one nearby. [See Note 6] Any search involving the removal of more than an outer coat, jacket, gloves, headgear or footwear, or any other item concealing identity, may only be made by an officer of the same sex as the person searched and may not be made in the presence of anyone of the opposite sex unless the person being searched specifically requests it. [See Annex F and Notes 4, 7 and 8]

3.7 Searches involving exposure of intimate parts of the body must not be conducted as a routine extension of a less thorough search, simply because nothing is found in the course of the initial search. Searches involving exposure of intimate parts of the body may be carried out only at a nearby police station or other nearby location which is out of public view (but not a police vehicle). These searches must be conducted in accordance with paragraph 11 of Annex A to Code C except that an intimate search mentioned in paragraph 11(f) of Annex A to Code C may not be authorised or carried out under any stop and search powers. The other provisions of Code C do not apply to the conduct and recording of searches of persons detained at police stations in the exercise of stop and search powers. [See Note 7]

Steps to be taken prior to a search

3.8 Before any search of a detained person or attended vehicle takes place the officer must take reasonable steps, if not in uniform (see paragraph 3.9), to show their warrant card to the person to be searched or in charge of the vehicle to be searched and whether or not in uniform, to give that person the following information:

(a) that they are being detained for the purposes of a search

(b) the officer's name (except in the case of enquiries linked to the investigation of terrorism, or otherwise where the officer reasonably believes that giving his or her name might put him or her in danger, in which case a warrant or other identification number shall be given) and the name of the police station to which the officer is attached;

(c) the legal search power which is being exercised; and

(d) a clear explanation of:

   (i) the object of the search in terms of the article or articles for which there is a power to search; and

   (ii) in the case of:

- the power under section 60 of the Criminal Justice and Public Order Act 1994 (see paragraph 2.1(b)), the nature of the power, the authorisation and the fact that it has been given;

- the power under section 44 of the Terrorism Act 2000, the nature of the power, the authorisation and the fact that it has been given and the grounds for suspicion; (see paragraph 2.1(c) and 2.18A.

- all other powers requiring reasonable suspicion (see paragraph 2.1(a)), the grounds for that suspicion.

(e) that they are entitled to a copy of the record of the search if one is made (see section 4 below) if they ask within 3 months from the date of the search and:

   (i) if they are not arrested and taken to a police station as a result of the search and it is practicable to make the record on the spot, that immediately after the search is completed they will be given, if they request, either:

- a copy of the record, or

- a receipt which explains how they can obtain a copy of the full record or access to an electronic copy of the record, or

   (ii) if they are arrested and taken to a police station as a result of the search, that the record will be made at the station as part of their custody record and they will be given, if they request, a copy of their custody record which includes a record of the search as soon as practicable whilst they are at the station. [See Note 16]

3.9 Stops and searches under the powers mentioned in paragraphs 2.1(b), and (c) may be undertaken only by a constable in uniform.

3.10 The person should also be given information about police powers to stop and search and the individual's rights in these circumstances.

3.11 If the person to be searched, or in charge of a vehicle to be searched, does not appear to understand what is being said, or there is any doubt about the person's ability to understand English, the officer must take reasonable steps to bring information regarding the person's rights and any relevant provisions of this Code to his or her attention. If the person is deaf or cannot understand English and is accompanied by someone, then the officer must try to establish whether that person can interpret or otherwise help the officer to give the required information.

4 RECORDING REQUIREMENTS

(a) Searches which do not result in an arrest

4.1   When an officer carries out a search in the exercise of any power to which this Code applies and the search does not result in the person searched or person in charge of the vehicle searched being arrested and taken to a police station, a record must be made of it, electronically or on paper, unless there are exceptional circumstances which make this wholly impracticable (e.g. in situations involving public disorder or when the recording officer's presence is urgently required elsewhere). If a record is to be made, the officer carrying out the search must make the record on the spot unless this is not practicable, in which case, the officer must make the record as soon as practicable after the search is completed. [See Note 16.]

4.2   If the record is made at the time, the person who has been searched or who is in charge of the vehicle that has been searched must be asked if they want a copy and if they do, they must be given immediately, either:
- a copy of the record, or
- a receipt which explains how they can obtain a copy of the full record or access to an electronic copy of the record

4.2A   An officer is not required to provide a copy of the full record or a receipt at the time if they are called to an incident of higher priority. [See Note 21]

(b) Searches which result in an arrest

4.2B   If a search in the exercise of any power to which this Code applies results in a person being arrested and taken to a police station, the officer carrying out the search is responsible for ensuring that a record of the search is made as part of their custody record. The custody officer must then ensure that the person is asked if they want a copy of the record and if they do, that they are given a copy as soon as practicable. [See Note 16].

(c) Record of search

4.3   The record of a search must always include the following information:
   (a) A note of the self defined ethnicity, and if different, the ethnicity as perceived by the officer making the search, of the person searched or of the person in charge of the vehicle searched (as the case may be); [See Note 18]
   (b) The date, time and place the person or vehicle was searched [See Note 6];
   (c) The object of the search in terms of the article or articles for which there is a power to search;
   (d) In the case of:
   - the power under section 60 of the Criminal Justice and Public Order Act 1994 (see paragraph 2.1(b)), the nature of the power, the authorisation and the fact that it has been given; [See Note 17]
   - the power under section 44 of the Terrorism Act 2000, the nature of the power, the authorisation and the fact that it has been given and the grounds for suspicion; [see paragraphs 2.1(c) and 2.18A and Note 17].
   - all other powers requiring reasonable suspicion (see paragraph 2.1(a)), the grounds for that suspicion.
   (e) subject to paragraph 3.8(b), the identity of the officer carrying out the search. [See Note 15]

4.3A   For the purposes of completing the search record, there is no requirement to record the name, address and date of birth of the person searched or the person in charge of a vehicle which is searched and the person is under no obligation to provide this information.

4.4   Nothing in paragraph 4.3 requires the names of police officers to be shown on the search record or any other record required to be made under this code in the case of enquiries linked to the investigation of terrorism or otherwise where an officer reasonably believes that recording names might endanger the officers. In such cases the record must show the officers' warrant or other identification number and duty station.

4.5   A record is required for each person and each vehicle searched. However, if a person is in a vehicle and both are searched, and the object and grounds of the search are the same, only one record need be completed. If more than one person in a vehicle is searched, separate records for each search of a person must be made. If only a vehicle is searched, the self-defined ethnic background of the person in charge of the vehicle must be recorded, unless the vehicle is unattended.

4.6   The record of the grounds for making a search must, briefly but informatively, explain the reason for suspecting the person concerned, by reference to the person's behaviour and/or other circumstances.

4.7   Where officers detain an individual with a view to performing a search, but the need to search is eliminated as a result of questioning the person detained, a search should not be carried out and a record is not required. [See paragraph 2.10, Notes 3 and 22A]

4.8   After searching an unattended vehicle, or anything in or on it, an officer must leave a notice in it (or on it, if things on it have been searched without opening it) recording the fact that it has been searched.

4.9   The notice must include the name of the police station to which the officer concerned is attached and state where a copy of the record of the search may be obtained and how (if applicable) an electronic copy may be accessed and where any application for compensation should be directed.

4.10   The vehicle must if practicable be left secure.

[. . .]

Recording of encounters not governed by statutory powers

[. . .]

4.12   There is no national requirement for an officer who requests a person in a public place to account for themselves, i.e. their actions, behaviour, presence in an area or possession of anything, to make any record of the encounter or to give the person a receipt. [See Notes 22A and 22B]

[. . .]

5   MONITORING AND SUPERVISING THE USE OF STOP AND SEARCH POWERS

5.1   Supervising officers must monitor the use of stop and search powers and should consider in particular whether there is any evidence that they are being exercised on the basis of stereotyped images or inappropriate generalisations. Supervising officers should satisfy themselves that the practice of officers under their supervision in stopping, searching and recording is fully in accordance with this Code. Supervisors must also examine whether the records reveal any trends or patterns which give cause for concern, and if so take appropriate action to address this.

5.2   Senior officers with area or force-wide responsibilities must also monitor the broader use of stop and search powers and, where necessary, take action at the relevant level.

5.3   Supervision and monitoring must be supported by the compilation of comprehensive statistical records of stops and searches at force, area and local level. Any apparently disproportionate use of the powers by particular officers or groups of officers or in relation to specific sections of the community should be identified and investigated.

5.4   In order to promote public confidence in the use of the powers, forces in consultation with police authorities must make arrangements for the records to be scrutinised by representatives of the community, and to explain the use of the powers at a local level. [See Note 19].

Notes for Guidance

Officers exercising stop and search powers

1   This code does not affect the ability of an officer to speak to or question a person in the ordinary course of the officer's duties without detaining the person or exercising any element of compulsion. It is not the purpose of the code to prohibit such encounters between the police and the community with the co-operation of the person concerned and neither does it affect the principle that all citizens have a duty to help police officers to prevent crime and discover offenders. This is a civic rather than a legal duty; but when a police officer is trying to discover whether, or by whom, an offence has been committed he or she may question any person from whom useful information might be obtained, subject to the restrictions imposed by Code C. A person's unwillingness to reply does not alter this entitlement, but in the absence of a power to arrest, or to detain in order to search, the person is free to leave at will and cannot be compelled to remain with the officer.

2   In some circumstances preparatory questioning may be unnecessary, but in general a brief conversation or exchange will be desirable not only as a means of avoiding unsuccessful searches, but to explain the grounds for the stop/search, to gain co-operation and reduce any tension there might be surrounding the stop/search.

3   Where a person is lawfully detained for the purpose of a search, but no search in the event takes place, the detention will not thereby have been rendered unlawful.

4   Many people customarily cover their heads or faces for religious reasons – for example, Muslim women, Sikh men, Sikh or Hindu women, or Rastafarian men or women. A police officer cannot order the removal of a head or face covering except where there is reason to believe that the item is being worn by the individual wholly or mainly for the purpose of disguising identity, not simply because it disguises identity. Where there may be religious sensitivities about ordering the removal of such an item, the officer should permit the item to be removed out of public view. Where practicable, the item should be removed in the presence of an officer of the same sex as the person and out of sight of anyone of the opposite sex [see Annex F].

5   A search of a person in public should be completed as soon as possible.

6   A person may be detained under a stop and search power at a place other than where the person was first detained, only if that place, be it a police station or elsewhere, is nearby. Such a place should be located within a reasonable travelling distance using whatever mode of travel (on foot or by car) is appropriate. This applies to all searches under stop and search powers, whether or not they involve the removal of clothing or Codes of practice – Code A Exercise by police officers of statutory powers of stop and search exposure of intimate parts of the body (see paragraphs 3.6 and 3.7) or take place in or out of public view. It means, for example, that a search under the stop and search power in section 23 of the Misuse of Drugs Act 1971 which involves the compulsory removal of more than a person's outer coat, jacket or gloves cannot be carried out unless a place

which is both nearby the place they were first detained and out of public view, is available. If a search involves exposure of intimate parts of the body and a police station is not nearby, particular care must be taken to ensure that the location is suitable in that it enables the search to be conducted in accordance with the requirements of paragraph 11 of Annex A to Code C.

7   A search in the street itself should be regarded as being in public for the purposes of paragraphs 3.6 and 3.7 above, even though it may be empty at the time a search begins. Although there is no power to require a person to do so, there is nothing to prevent an officer from asking a person voluntarily to remove more than an outer coat, jacket or gloves in public.

8   Not used

9   Other means of identification might include jewellery, insignias, tattoos or other features which are known to identify members of the particular gang or group.

Authorising officers

10   The powers under section 60 are separate from and additional to the normal stop and search powers which require reasonable grounds to suspect an individual of carrying an offensive weapon (or other article). Their overall purpose is to prevent serious violence and the widespread carrying of weapons which might lead to persons being seriously injured by disarming potential offenders or finding weapons that have been used in circumstances where other powers would not be sufficient. They should not therefore be used to replace or circumvent the normal powers for dealing with routine crime problems. A particular example might be an authorisation to prevent serious violence or the carrying of offensive weapons at a sports event by rival team supporters when the expected general appearance and age range of those likely to be responsible, alone, would not be sufficiently distinctive to support reasonable suspicion (see paragraph 2.6). The purpose of the powers under section 60AA is to prevent those involved in intimidatory or violent protests using face coverings to disguise identity.

11   Authorisations under section 60 require a reasonable belief on the part of the authorising officer. This must have an objective basis, for example: intelligence or relevant information such as a history of antagonism and violence between particular groups; previous incidents of violence at, or connected with, particular events or locations; a significant increase in knife-point robberies in a limited area; reports that individuals are regularly carrying weapons in a particular locality; information following an incident in which weapons were used about where the weapons might be found or in the case of section 60AA previous incidents of crimes being committed while wearing face coverings to conceal identity.

12   It is for the authorising officer to determine the period of time during which the powers mentioned in paragraph 2.1(b) and (c) may be exercised. The officer should set the minimum period he or she considers necessary to deal with the risk of violence, the carrying of knives or offensive weapons, or terrorism or to find dangerous instruments or weapons that have been used. A direction to extend the period authorised under the powers mentioned in paragraph 2.1(b) may be given only once. Thereafter further use of the powers requires a new authorisation. There is no provision to extend an authorisation of the powers mentioned in paragraph 2.1(c); further use of the powers requires a new authorisation.

13   It is for the authorising officer to determine the geographical area in which the use of the powers is to be authorised. In doing so the officer may wish to take into account factors such as the nature and venue of the anticipated incident or the incident which has taken

place, the number of people who may be in the immediate area of that incident, their access to surrounding areas and the anticipated or actual level of violence. The officer should not set a geographical area which is wider than that he or she believes necessary for the purpose of preventing anticipated violence, the carrying of knives or offensive weapons, acts of terrorism, finding a dangerous instrument or weapon that has been used or, in the case of section 60AA, the prevention of commission of offences. It is particularly important to ensure that constables exercising such powers are fully aware of where they may be used. If the area specified is smaller than the whole force area, the officer giving the authorisation should specify either the streets which form the boundary of the area or a divisional boundary within the force area. If the power is to be used in response to a threat or incident that straddles police force areas, an officer from each of the forces concerned will need to give an authorisation.

14   An officer who has authorised the use of powers under section 44(1) of the Terrorism Act 2000 must take immediate steps to send a copy of the authorisation to the National Joint Unit, Metropolitan Police Special Branch, who will forward it to the Secretary of State. The Secretary of State should be informed of the reasons for the authorisation. The National Joint Unit will inform the force concerned, within 48 hours of the authorisation being made, whether the Secretary of State has confirmed or cancelled or altered the authorisation. See paragraph 2.18A.

Recording

15   Where a stop and search is conducted by more than one officer the identity of all the officers engaged in the search must be recorded on the record. Nothing prevents an officer who is present but not directly involved in searching from completing the record during the course of the encounter.

16   When the search results in the person searched or in charge of a vehicle which is searched being arrested, the requirement to make the record of the search as part of the person's custody record does not apply if the person is granted "street bail" after arrest (see section 30A of PACE) to attend a police station and is not taken in custody to the police station An arrested person's entitlement to a copy of the search record which is made as part of their custody record does not affect their entitlement to a copy of their custody record or any other provisions of PACE Code C section 2 (Custody records).

17   It is important for monitoring purposes to specify whether the authority for exercising a stop and search power was given under section 60 of the Criminal Justice and Public Order Act 1994, or under section 44(1) of the Terrorism Act 2000.

18   Officers should record the self-defined ethnicity of every person stopped according to the categories used in the 2001 census question listed in Annex B. The person should be asked to select one of the five main categories representing broad ethnic groups and then a more specific cultural background from within this group. The ethnic classification should be coded for recording purposes using the coding system in Annex B. An additional "Not stated" box is available but should not be offered to respondents explicitly. Officers should be aware and explain to members of the public, especially where concerns are raised, that this information is required to obtain a true picture of stop and search activity and to help improve ethnic monitoring, tackle discriminatory practice, and promote effective use of the powers. If the person gives what appears to the officer to be an "incorrect" answer (e.g. a person who appears to be white states that they are black), the officer should record the response that has been given and then record their own perception of the person's ethnic background by using the PNC classification system. If the "Not stated" category is used the reason for this must be recorded on the form.

19   Arrangements for public scrutiny of records should take account of the right to confidentiality of those stopped and searched. Anonymised forms and/or statistics generated from records should be the focus of the examinations by members of the public.

20   Not used

21   In situations where it is not practicable to provide a written copy of the record or immediate access to an electronic copy of the record or a receipt of the search at the time (see paragraph 4.2A above), the officer should consider giving the person details of the station which they may attend for a copy of the record. A receipt may take the form of a simple business card which includes sufficient information to locate the record should the person ask for copy, for example, the date and place of the search, a reference number or the name of the officer who carried out the search (unless paragraph 4.4 applies).

22   Not used

22A   Where there are concerns which make it necessary to monitor any local disproportionality, forces have discretion to direct officers to record the self-defined ethnicity of persons they request to account for themselves in a public place or who they detain with a view to searching but do not search. Guidance should be provided locally and efforts made to minimise the bureaucracy involved. Records should be closely monitored and supervised in line with paragraphs 5.1 to 5.4 and forces can suspend or re-instate recording of these encounters as appropriate.

22B   A person who is asked to account for themselves should, if they request, be given information about how they can report their dissatisfaction about how they have been treated.

Definition of Offensive Weapon

23   'Offensive weapon' is defined as any article made or adapted for use for causing injury to the person, or intended by the person having it with him for such use or by someone else. There are three categories of offensive weapons: those made for causing injury to the person; those adapted for such a purpose; and those not so made or adapted, but carried with the intention of causing injury to the person. A firearm, as defined by section 57 of the Firearms Act 1968, would fall within the definition of offensive weapon if any of the criteria above apply.

24   Not used

25   Not used

[. . .]

CODE B: CODE OF PRACTICE FOR SEARCHES OF PREMISES BY POLICE OFFICERS AND THE SEIZURE OF PROPERTY FOUND BY POLICE OFFICERS ON PERSONS OR PREMISES

Presented to Parliament under section 67(7B) of the Police and Criminal Evidence Act 1984 (PACE)

Commencement – Transitional Arrangements
This code applies to applications for warrants made after midnight on 06 March 2011 and to searches and seizures taking place after midnight on 06 March 2011.

1 INTRODUCTION

1.1   This Code of Practice deals with police powers to:
- search premises
- seize and retain property found on premises and persons

1.1A   These powers may be used to find:
- property and material relating to a crime
- wanted persons
- children who abscond from local authority accommodation where they have been remanded or committed by a court

1.2   A justice of the peace may issue a search warrant granting powers of entry, search and seizure, e.g. warrants to search for stolen property, drugs, firearms and evidence of serious offences. Police also have powers without a search warrant. The main ones provided by the Police and Criminal Evidence Act 1984 (PACE) include powers to search premises:
- to make an arrest
- after an arrest

1.3   The right to privacy and respect for personal property are key principles of the Human Rights Act 1998. Powers of entry, search and seizure should be fully and clearly justified before use because they may significantly interfere with the occupier's privacy. Officers should consider if the necessary objectives can be met by less intrusive means.

1.3A   Powers to search and seize must be used fairly, responsibly, with respect for people who occupy premises being searched or are in charge of property being seized and without unlawful discrimination. The Equality Act 2010 makes it unlawful for police officers to discriminate against, harass or victimise any person on the grounds of the 'protected characteristics' of age, disability, gender reassignment, race, religion or belief, sex and sexual orientation, marriage and civil partnership, pregnancy and maternity when using their powers. When police forces are carrying out their functions they also have a duty to have regard to the need to eliminate unlawful discrimination, harassment and victimisation and to take steps to foster good relations.

1.4   In all cases, police should therefore:
- exercise their powers courteously and with respect for persons and property
- only use reasonable force when this is considered necessary and proportionate to the circumstances

1.5   If the provisions of PACE and this Code are not observed, evidence obtained from a search may be open to question.

2 GENERAL

2.1   This Code must be readily available at all police stations for consultation by:
- police officers
- police staff
- detained persons
- members of the public

2.2   The Notes for Guidance included are not provisions of this Code.

2.3   This Code applies to searches of premises:
(a) by police for the purposes of an investigation into an alleged offence, with the occupier's consent, other than:

- routine scene of crime searches;
- calls to a fire or burglary made by or on behalf of an occupier or searches following the activation of fire or burglar alarms or discovery of insecure premises;
- searches when paragraph 5.4 applies;
- bomb threat calls;

(b) under powers conferred on police officers by PACE, sections 17, 18 and 32;

(c) undertaken in pursuance of search warrants issued to and executed by constables in accordance with PACE, sections 15 and 16. See Note 2A;

(d) subject to paragraph 2.6, under any other power given to police to enter premises with or without a search warrant for any purpose connected with the investigation into an alleged or suspected offence. See Note 2B.

For the purposes of this Code, 'premises' as defined in PACE, section 23, includes any place, vehicle, vessel, aircraft, hovercraft, tent or movable structure and any offshore installation as defined in the Mineral Workings (Offshore Installations) Act 1971, section 1. See Note 2D

2.4   A person who has not been arrested but is searched during a search of premises should be searched in accordance with Code A. See Note 2C

2.5   This Code does not apply to the exercise of a statutory power to enter premises or to inspect goods, equipment or procedures if the exercise of that power is not dependent on the existence of grounds for suspecting that an offence may have been committed and the person exercising the power has no reasonable grounds for such suspicion.

2.6   This Code does not affect any directions or requirements of a search warrant, order or other power to search and seize lawfully exercised in England or Wales that any item or evidence seized under that warrant, order or power be handed over to a police force, court, tribunal, or other authority outside England or Wales. For example, warrants and orders issued in Scotland or Northern Ireland, see Note 2B(f) and search warrants and powers provided for in sections 14 to 17 of the Crime (International Co-operation) Act 2003.

2.7   When this Code requires the prior authority or agreement of an officer of at least inspector or superintendent rank, that authority may be given by a sergeant or chief inspector authorised to perform the functions of the higher rank under PACE, section 107.

2.8   Written records required under this Code not made in the search record shall, unless otherwise specified, be made:
- in the recording officer's pocket book ('pocket book' includes any official report book issued to police officers) or
- on forms provided for the purpose

2.9   Nothing in this Code requires the identity of officers, or anyone accompanying them during a search of premises, to be recorded or disclosed:

(a) in the case of enquiries linked to the investigation of terrorism; or

(b) if officers reasonably believe recording or disclosing their names might put them in danger.

In these cases officers should use warrant or other identification numbers and the name of their police station. Police staff should use any identification number provided to them by the police force. See Note 2E

2.10   The 'officer in charge of the search' means the officer assigned specific duties and responsibilities under this Code. Whenever there is a search of premises to which this Code applies one officer must act as the officer in charge of the search. See Note 2F

2.11 In this Code:
(a) 'designated person' means a person other than a police officer, designated under the Police Reform Act 2002, Part 4 who has specified powers and duties of police officers conferred or imposed on them. See Note 2G.
(b) any reference to a police officer includes a designated person acting in the exercise or performance of the powers and duties conferred or imposed on them by their designation.
(c) a person authorised to accompany police officers or designated persons in the execution of a warrant has the same powers as a constable in the execution of the warrant and the search and seizure of anything related to the warrant. These powers must be exercised in the company and under the supervision of a police officer. See Note 3C.

2.12 If a power conferred on a designated person:
(a) allows reasonable force to be used when exercised by a police officer, a designated person exercising that power has the same entitlement to use force;
(b) includes power to use force to enter any premises, that power is not exercisable by that designated person except:
(i)   in the company and under the supervision of a police officer; or
(ii) for the purpose of:
• saving life or limb; or
• preventing serious damage to property.

2.13 Designated persons must have regard to any relevant provisions of the Codes of Practice.

Notes for guidance
2A   PACE sections 15 and 16 apply to all search warrants issued to and executed by constables under any enactment, e.g. search warrants issued by a:
(a) justice of the peace under the:
• Theft Act 1968, section 26 – stolen property;
• Misuse of Drugs Act 1971, section 23 – controlled drugs;
• PACE, section 8 – evidence of an indictable offence;
• Terrorism Act 2000, Schedule 5, paragraph 1;
• Prevention of Terrorism Act 2005, section 7C – monitoring compliance with control order (see paragraph 10.1).
(b) Circuit judge under:
• PACE, Schedule 1;
• Terrorism Act 2000, Schedule 5, paragraph 11.

2B   Examples of the other powers in paragraph 2.3(d) include:
(a) Road Traffic Act 1988, section 6E(1) giving police power to enter premises under section 6E(1) to:
• require a person to provide a specimen of breath; or
• arrest a person following:
~ a positive breath test;
~ failure to provide a specimen of breath;
(b) Transport and Works Act 1992, section 30(4) giving police powers to enter premises mirroring the powers in (a) in relation to specified persons working on transport systems to which the Act applies;
(c) Criminal Justice Act 1988, section 139B giving police power to enter and search school premises for offensive weapons, bladed or pointed articles;
(d) Terrorism Act 2000, Schedule 5, paragraphs 3 and 15 empowering a superintendent in urgent cases to give written authority for police to enter and search premises for the purposes of a terrorist investigation;

(e) Explosives Act 1875, section 73(b) empowering a superintendent to give written authority for police to enter premises, examine and search them for explosives;

(f) search warrants and production orders or the equivalent issued in Scotland or Northern Ireland endorsed under the Summary Jurisdiction (Process) Act 1881 or the Petty Sessions (Ireland) Act 1851 respectively for execution in England and Wales.

(g) Sections 7A and 7B of the Prevention of Terrorism Act 2005, searches connected with the enforcement of control orders (see paragraph 10.1).

2C   The Criminal Justice Act 1988, section 139B provides that a constable who has reasonable grounds to believe an offence under the Criminal Justice Act 1988, section 139A has or is being committed may enter school premises and search the premises and any persons on the premises for any bladed or pointed article or offensive weapon. Persons may be searched under a warrant issued under the Misuse of Drugs Act 1971, section 23(3) to search premises for drugs or documents only if the warrant specifically authorises the search of persons on the premises. Powers to search premises under certain terrorism provisions also authorise the search of persons on the premises, for example, under paragraphs 1, 2, 11 and 15 of Schedule 5 to the Terrorism Act 2000 and section 52 of the Anti-terrorism, Crime and Security Act 2001.

2D   The Immigration Act 1971, Part III and Schedule 2 gives immigration officers powers to enter and search premises, seize and retain property, with and without a search warrant. These are similar to the powers available to police under search warrants issued by a justice of the peace and without a warrant under PACE, sections 17, 18, 19 and 32 except they only apply to specified offences under the Immigration Act 1971 and immigration control powers. For certain types of investigations and enquiries these powers avoid the need for the Immigration Service to rely on police officers becoming directly involved. When exercising these powers, immigration officers are required by the Immigration and Asylum Act 1999, section 145 to have regard to this Code's corresponding provisions. When immigration officers are dealing with persons or property at police stations, police officers should give appropriate assistance to help them discharge their specific duties and responsibilities.

2E   The purpose of paragraph 2.9(b) is to protect those involved in serious organised crime investigations or arrests of particularly violent suspects when there is reliable information that those arrested or their associates may threaten or cause harm to the officers or anyone accompanying them during a search of premises. In cases of doubt, an officer of inspector rank or above should be consulted.

2F   For the purposes of paragraph 2.10, the officer in charge of the search should normally be the most senior officer present. Some exceptions are:

(a) a supervising officer who attends or assists at the scene of a premises search may appoint an officer of lower rank as officer in charge of the search if that officer is:
   • more conversant with the facts;
   • a more appropriate officer to be in charge of the search;

(b) when all officers in a premises search are the same rank. The supervising officer if available must make sure one of them is appointed officer in charge of the search, otherwise the officers themselves must nominate one of their number as the officer in charge;

(c) a senior officer assisting in a specialist role. This officer need not be regarded as having a general supervisory role over the conduct of the search or be appointed or expected to act as the officer in charge of the search.

Except in (c), nothing in this Note diminishes the role and responsibilities of a supervisory officer who is present at the search or knows of a search taking place.

2G   An officer of the rank of inspector or above may direct a designated investigating officer not to wear a uniform for the purposes of a specific operation.

3 SEARCH WARRANTS AND PRODUCTION ORDERS

(a) Before making an application

3.1 When information appears to justify an application, the officer must take reasonable steps to check the information is accurate, recent and not provided maliciously or irresponsibly. An application may not be made on the basis of information from an anonymous source if corroboration has not been sought. See Note 3A

3.2 The officer shall ascertain as specifically as possible the nature of the articles concerned and their location.

3.3 The officer shall make reasonable enquiries to:
   (i) establish if:
       • anything is known about the likely occupier of the premises and the nature of the premises themselves;
       • the premises have been searched previously and how recently;
   (ii) obtain any other relevant information.

3.4 An application:
   (a) to a justice of the peace for a search warrant or to a Circuit judge for a search warrant or production order under PACE, Schedule 1 must be supported by a signed written authority from an officer of inspector rank or above:
       Note: If the case is an urgent application to a justice of the peace and an inspector or above is not readily available, the next most senior officer on duty can give the written authority.
   (b) to a circuit judge under the Terrorism Act 2000, Schedule 5 for
       • a production order;
       • search warrant; or
       • an order requiring an explanation of material seized or produced under such a warrant or production order
       • must be supported by a signed written authority from an officer of superintendent rank or above.

3.5 Except in a case of urgency, if there is reason to believe a search might have an adverse effect on relations between the police and the community, the officer in charge shall consult the local police/community liaison officer:
       • before the search; or
       • in urgent cases, as soon as practicable after the search

(b) Making an application

3.6 A search warrant application must be supported in writing, specifying:
   (a) the enactment under which the application is made, see Note 2A;
   (b) (i) whether the warrant is to authorise entry and search of:
           • one set of premises; or
           • if the application is under PACE section 8, or Schedule 1, paragraph 12, more than one set of specified premises or all premises occupied or controlled by a specified person, and
       (ii) the premises to be searched;
   (c) the object of the search, see Note 3B;
   (d) the grounds for the application, including, when the purpose of the proposed search is to find evidence of an alleged offence, an indication of how the evidence relates to the investigation;
   (da) Where the application is under PACE section 8, or Schedule 1, paragraph 12 for a single warrant to enter and search:

    (i)   more than one set of specified premises, the officer must specify each set of premises which it is desired to enter and search

    (ii) all premises occupied or controlled by a specified person, the officer must specify;
- as many sets of premises which it is desired to enter and search as it is reasonably practicable to specify
- the person who is in occupation or control of those premises and any others which it is desired to search
- why it is necessary to search more premises than those which can be specified
- why it is not reasonably practicable to specify all the premises which it is desired to enter and search

(db) Whether an application under PACE section 8 is for a warrant authorising entry and search on more than one occasion, and if so, the officer must state the grounds for this and whether the desired number of entries authorised is unlimited or a specified maximum.

(e)   there are no reasonable grounds to believe the material to be sought, when making application to a:

    (i)   justice of the peace or a Circuit judge consists of or includes items subject to legal privilege;

    (ii) justice of the peace, consists of or includes excluded material or special procedure material;

         Note: this does not affect the additional powers of seizure in the Criminal Justice and Police Act 2001, Part 2 covered in paragraph 7.7, see Note 3B;

(f)   if applicable, a request for the warrant to authorise a person or persons to accompany the officer who executes the warrant, see Note 3C.

3.7   A search warrant application under PACE, Schedule 1, paragraph 12(a), shall if appropriate indicate why it is believed service of notice of an application for a production order may seriously prejudice the investigation. Applications for search warrants under the Terrorism Act 2000, Schedule 5, paragraph 11 must indicate why a production order would not be appropriate.

3.8   If a search warrant application is refused, a further application may not be made for those premises unless supported by additional grounds.

Notes for guidance

3A   The identity of an informant need not be disclosed when making an application, but the officer should be prepared to answer any questions the magistrate or judge may have about:
- the accuracy of previous information from that source
- any other related matters

3B   The information supporting a search warrant application should be as specific as possible, particularly in relation to the articles or persons being sought and where in the premises it is suspected they may be found. The meaning of 'items subject to legal privilege', 'excluded material' and 'special procedure material' are defined by PACE, sections 10, 11 and 14 respectively.

3C   Under PACE, section 16(2), a search warrant may authorise persons other than police officers to accompany the constable who executes the warrant. This includes, e.g. any suitably qualified or skilled person or an expert in a particular field whose presence is needed to help accurately identify the material sought or to advise where certain evidence is most likely to be found and how it should be dealt with. It does not give them any right to force entry, but it gives them the right to be on the premises during the search and to search for or seize property without the occupier's permission.

4 ENTRY WITHOUT WARRANT – PARTICULAR POWERS

(a) Making an arrest etc

4.1   The conditions under which an officer may enter and search premises without a warrant are set out in PACE, section 17. It should be noted that this section does not create or confer any powers of arrest. See other powers in Note 2B(a).

(b) Search of premises where arrest takes place or the arrested person was immediately before arrest

4.2   When a person has been arrested for an indictable offence, a police officer has power under PACE, section 32 to search the premises where the person was arrested or where the person was immediately before being arrested.

(c) Search of premises occupied or controlled by the arrested person

4.3   The specific powers to search premises which are occupied or controlled by a person arrested for an indictable offence are set out in PACE, section 18. They may not be exercised, except if section 18(5) applies, unless an officer of inspector rank or above has given written authority. That authority should only be given when the authorising officer is satisfied that the premises are occupied or controlled by the arrested person and that the necessary grounds exist. If possible the authorising officer should record the authority on the Notice of Powers and Rights and, subject to paragraph 2.9, sign the Notice. The record of the grounds for the search and the nature of the evidence sought as required by section 18(7) of the Act should be made in:
- the custody record if there is one, otherwise
- the officer's pocket book, or
- the search record

5 SEARCH WITH CONSENT

5.1   Subject to paragraph 5.4, if it is proposed to search premises with the consent of a person entitled to grant entry the consent must, if practicable, be given in writing on the Notice of Powers and Rights before the search. The officer must make any necessary enquiries to be satisfied the person is in a position to give such consent. See Notes 5A and 5B

5.2   Before seeking consent the officer in charge of the search shall state the purpose of the proposed search and its extent. This information must be as specific as possible, particularly regarding the articles or persons being sought and the parts of the premises to be searched. The person concerned must be clearly informed they are not obliged to consent, that any consent given can be withdrawn at any time, including before the search starts or while it is underway and anything seized may be produced in evidence. If at the time the person is not suspected of an offence, the officer shall say this when stating the purpose of the search.

5.3   An officer cannot enter and search or continue to search premises under paragraph 5.1 if consent is given under duress or withdrawn before the search is completed.

5.4   It is unnecessary to seek consent under paragraphs 5.1 and 5.2 if this would cause disproportionate inconvenience to the person concerned. See Note 5C

Notes for guidance

5A   In a lodging house, hostel or similar accommodation, every reasonable effort should be made to obtain the consent of the tenant, lodger or occupier. A search should not be made solely on the basis of the landlord's consent.

5B   If the intention is to search premises under the authority of a warrant or a power of entry and search without warrant, and the occupier of the premises co-operates in accordance with paragraph 6.4, there is no need to obtain written consent.

5C   Paragraph 5.4 is intended to apply when it is reasonable to assume innocent occupiers would agree to, and expect, police to take the proposed action, e.g. if:
- a suspect has fled the scene of a crime or to evade arrest and it is necessary quickly to check surrounding gardens and readily accessible places to see if the suspect is hiding
- police have arrested someone in the night after a pursuit and it is necessary to make a brief check of gardens along the pursuit route to see if stolen or incriminating articles have been discarded

6 SEARCHING PREMISES – GENERAL CONSIDERATIONS

(a) Time of searches

6.1   Searches made under warrant must be made within three calendar months of the date of the warrant's issue.

6.2   Searches must be made at a reasonable hour unless this might frustrate the purpose of the search.

6.3   When the extent or complexity of a search mean it is likely to take a long time, the officer in charge of the search may consider using the seize and sift powers referred to in section 7.

6.3A   A warrant under PACE, section 8 may authorise entry to and search of premises on more than one occasion if, on the application, the justice of the peace is satisfied that it is necessary to authorise multiple entries in order to achieve the purpose for which the warrant is issued. No premises may be entered or searched on any subsequent occasions without the prior written authority of an officer of the rank of inspector who is not involved in the investigation. All other warrants authorise entry on one occasion only.

6.3B   Where a warrant under PACE section 8, or Schedule 1, paragraph 12 authorises entry to and search of all premises occupied or controlled by a specified person, no premises which are not specified in the warrant may be entered and searched without the prior written authority of an officer of the rank of inspector who is not involved in the investigation.

(b) Entry other than with consent

6.4   The officer in charge of the search shall first try to communicate with the occupier, or any other person entitled to grant access to the premises, explain the authority under which entry is sought and ask the occupier to allow entry, unless:
(i)   the search premises are unoccupied;
(ii)   the occupier and any other person entitled to grant access are absent;
(iii) there are reasonable grounds for believing that alerting the occupier or any other person entitled to grant access would frustrate the object of the search or endanger officers or other people.

6.5   Unless sub-paragraph 6.4(iii) applies, if the premises are occupied the officer, subject to paragraph 2.9, shall, before the search begins:
(i)   identify him or herself, show their warrant card (if not in uniform) and state the purpose of and grounds for the search;
(ii)   identify and introduce any person accompanying the officer on the search (such persons should carry identification for production on request) and briefly describe that person's role in the process.

6.6   Reasonable and proportionate force may be used if necessary to enter premises if the officer in charge of the search is satisfied the premises are those specified in any warrant, or in exercise of the powers described in paragraphs 4.1 to 4.3, and if:
   (i)   the occupier or any other person entitled to grant access has refused entry;
   (ii) it is impossible to communicate with the occupier or any other person entitled to grant access; or
   (iii) any of the provisions of paragraph 6.4 apply.

(c) Notice of Powers and Rights
6.7   If an officer conducts a search to which this Code applies the officer shall, unless it is impracticable to do so, provide the occupier with a copy of a Notice in a standard format:
   (i)   specifying if the search is made under warrant, with consent, or in the exercise of the powers described in paragraphs 4.1 to 4.3. Note: the notice format shall provide for authority or consent to be indicated, see paragraphs 4.3 and 5.1;
   (ii) summarising the extent of the powers of search and seizure conferred by PACE and other relevant legislation as appropriate;
   (iii) explaining the rights of the occupier, and the owner of the property seized;
   (iv) explaining compensation may be payable in appropriate cases for damages caused entering and searching premises, and giving the address to send a compensation application, see Note 6A;
   (v)   stating this Code is available at any police station.

6.8   If the occupier is:
   •   present, copies of the Notice and warrant shall, if practicable, be given to them before the search begins, unless the officer in charge of the search reasonably believes this would frustrate the object of the search or endanger officers or other people
   •   not present, copies of the Notice and warrant shall be left in a prominent place on the premises or appropriate part of the premises and endorsed, subject to paragraph 2.9 with the name of the officer in charge of the search, the date and time of the search
   The warrant shall be endorsed to show this has been done.

(d) Conduct of searches
6.9   Premises may be searched only to the extent necessary to achieve the purpose of the search, having regard to the size and nature of whatever is sought.

6.9A   A search may not continue under:
   •   a warrant's authority once all the things specified in that warrant have been found;
   •   any other power once the object of that search has been achieved.

6.9B   No search may continue once the officer in charge of the search is satisfied whatever is being sought is not on the premises. See Note 6B. This does not prevent a further search of the same premises if additional grounds come to light supporting a further application for a search warrant or exercise or further exercise of another power. For example, when, as a result of new information, it is believed articles previously not found or additional articles are on the premises.

6.10   Searches must be conducted with due consideration for the property and privacy of the occupier and with no more disturbance than necessary. Reasonable force may be used only when necessary and proportionate because the co-operation of the occupier cannot be obtained or is insufficient for the purpose. See Note 6C

6.11   A friend, neighbour or other person must be allowed to witness the search if the occupier wishes unless the officer in charge of the search has reasonable grounds for believing the presence of the person asked for would seriously hinder the investigation or endanger officers or other people. A search need not be unreasonably delayed for this purpose. A record of the action taken should be made on the premises search record including the grounds for refusing the occupier's request.

6.12   A person is not required to be cautioned prior to being asked questions that are solely necessary for the purpose of furthering the proper and effective conduct of a search, see Code C, paragraph 10.1(c). For example, questions to discover the occupier of specified premises, to find a key to open a locked drawer or cupboard or to otherwise seek co-operation during the search or to determine if a particular item is liable to be seized.

6.12A If questioning goes beyond what is necessary for the purpose of the exemption in Code C, the exchange is likely to constitute an interview as defined by Code C, paragraph 11.1A and would require the associated safeguards included in Code C, section 10.

(e) Leaving premises

6.13   If premises have been entered by force, before leaving the officer in charge of the search must make sure they are secure by:
- arranging for the occupier or their agent to be present
- any other appropriate means

(f) Searches under PACE Schedule 1 or the Terrorism Act 2000, Schedule 5

6.14   An officer shall be appointed as the officer in charge of the search, see paragraph 2.10, in respect of any search made under a warrant issued under PACE Act 1984, Schedule 1 or the Terrorism Act 2000, Schedule 5. They are responsible for making sure the search is conducted with discretion and in a manner that causes the least possible disruption to any business or other activities carried out on the premises.

[. . .]

6B   It is important that, when possible, all those involved in a search are fully briefed about any powers to be exercised and the extent and limits within which it should be conducted.

6C   In all cases the number of officers and other persons involved in executing the warrant should be determined by what is reasonable and necessary according to the particular circumstances.

7 SEIZURE AND RETENTION OF PROPERTY

(a) Seizure

7.1   Subject to paragraph 7.2, an officer who is searching any person or premises under any statutory power or with the consent of the occupier may seize anything:
(a) covered by a warrant
(b) the officer has reasonable grounds for believing is evidence of an offence or has been obtained in consequence of the commission of an offence but only if seizure is necessary to prevent the items being concealed, lost, disposed of, altered, damaged, destroyed or tampered with
(c) covered by the powers in the Criminal Justice and Police Act 2001, Part 2 allowing an officer to seize property from persons or premises and retain it for sifting or examination elsewhere

See Note 7B

7.2   No item may be seized which an officer has reasonable grounds for believing to be subject to legal privilege, as defined in PACE, section 10, other than under the Criminal Justice and Police Act 2001, Part 2.

7.3   Officers must be aware of the provisions in the Criminal Justice and Police Act 2001, section 59, allowing for applications to a judicial authority for the return of property seized and the subsequent duty to secure in section 60, see paragraph 7.12(iii).

7.4   An officer may decide it is not appropriate to seize property because of an explanation from the person holding it but may nevertheless have reasonable grounds for believing it was obtained in consequence of an offence by some person. In these circumstances, the officer should identify the property to the holder, inform the holder of their suspicions and explain the holder may be liable to civil or criminal proceedings if they dispose of, alter or destroy the property.

7.5   An officer may arrange to photograph, image or copy, any document or other article they have the power to seize in accordance with paragraph 7.1. This is subject to specific restrictions on the examination, imaging or copying of certain property seized under the Criminal Justice and Police Act 2001, Part 2. An officer must have regard to their statutory obligation to retain an original document or other article only when a photograph or copy is not sufficient.

7.6   If an officer considers information stored in any electronic form and accessible from the premises could be used in evidence, they may require the information to be produced in a form:
  •   which can be taken away and in which it is visible and legible; or
  •   from which it can readily be produced in a visible and legible form

(b) Criminal Justice and Police Act 2001: Specific procedures for seize and sift powers
7.7   The Criminal Justice and Police Act 2001, Part 2 gives officers limited powers to seize property from premises or persons so they can sift or examine it elsewhere. Officers must be careful they only exercise these powers when it is essential and they do not remove any more material than necessary. The removal of large volumes of material, much of which may not ultimately be retainable, may have serious implications for the owners, particularly when they are involved in business or activities such as journalism or the provision of medical services. Officers must carefully consider if removing copies or images of relevant material or data would be a satisfactory alternative to removing originals. When originals are taken, officers must be prepared to facilitate the provision of copies or images for the owners when reasonably practicable. See Note 7C

7.8   Property seized under the Criminal Justice and Police Act 2001, sections 50 or 51 must be kept securely and separately from any material seized under other powers. An examination under section 53 to determine which elements may be retained must be carried out at the earliest practicable time, having due regard to the desirability of allowing the person from whom the property was seized, or a person with an interest in the property, an opportunity of being present or represented at the examination.

7.8A All reasonable steps should be taken to accommodate an interested person's request to be present, provided the request is reasonable and subject to the need to prevent harm to, interference with, or unreasonable delay to the investigatory process. If an examination proceeds in the absence of an interested person who asked to attend or their representative, the officer who exercised the relevant seizure power must give that person a written notice of why the examination was carried out in those circumstances. If it is necessary for security reasons or to maintain confidentiality officers may exclude interested persons from decryption or other processes which facilitate the examination but do not form part of it. See Note 7D

7.9   It is the responsibility of the officer in charge of the investigation to make sure property is returned in accordance with sections 53 to 55. Material which there is no power to retain must be:

- separated from the rest of the seized property
- returned as soon as reasonably practicable after examination of all the seized property

7.9A Delay is only warranted if very clear and compelling reasons exist, e.g. the:
- unavailability of the person to whom the material is to be returned
- need to agree a convenient time to return a large volume of material

7.9B Legally privileged, excluded or special procedure material which cannot be retained must be returned:
- as soon as reasonably practicable
- without waiting for the whole examination

7.9C As set out in section 58, material must be returned to the person from whom it was seized, except when it is clear some other person has a better right to it. See Note 7E

7.10 When an officer involved in the investigation has reasonable grounds to believe a person with a relevant interest in property seized under section 50 or 51 intends to make an application under section 59 for the return of any legally privileged, special procedure or excluded material, the officer in charge of the investigation should be informed as soon as practicable and the material seized should be kept secure in accordance with section 61. See Note 7C

7.11 The officer in charge of the investigation is responsible for making sure property is properly secured. Securing involves making sure the property is not examined, copied, imaged or put to any other use except at the request, or with the consent, of the applicant or in accordance with the directions of the appropriate judicial authority. Any request, consent or directions must be recorded in writing and signed by both the initiator and the officer in charge of the investigation. See Notes 7F and 7G

7.12 When an officer exercises a power of seizure conferred by sections 50 or 51 they shall provide the occupier of the premises or the person from whom the property is being seized with a written notice:
(i) specifying what has been seized under the powers conferred by that section;
(ii) specifying the grounds for those powers;
(iii) setting out the effect of sections 59 to 61 covering the grounds for a person with a relevant interest in seized property to apply to a judicial authority for its return and the duty of officers to secure property in certain circumstances when an application is made;
(iv) specifying the name and address of the person to whom:
- notice of an application to the appropriate judicial authority in respect of any of the seized property must be given;
- an application may be made to allow attendance at the initial examination of the property.

7.13 If the occupier is not present but there is someone in charge of the premises, the notice shall be given to them. If no suitable person is available, so the notice will easily be found it should either be:
- left in a prominent place on the premises
- attached to the exterior of the premises

(c) Retention

7.14 Subject to paragraph 7.15, anything seized in accordance with the above provisions may be retained only for as long as is necessary. It may be retained, among other purposes:
(i) for use as evidence at a trial for an offence;
(ii) to facilitate the use in any investigation or proceedings of anything to which it is inextricably linked, see Note 7H;

      (iii) for forensic examination or other investigation in connection with an offence;

      (iv) in order to establish its lawful owner when there are reasonable grounds for believing it has been stolen or obtained by the commission of an offence.

7.15 Property shall not be retained under paragraph 7.14(i), (ii) or (iii) if a copy or image would be sufficient.

(d) Rights of owners etc

7.16 If property is retained, the person who had custody or control of it immediately before seizure must, on request, be provided with a list or description of the property within a reasonable time.

7.17 That person or their representative must be allowed supervised access to the property to examine it or have it photographed or copied, or must be provided with a photograph or copy, in either case within a reasonable time of any request and at their own expense, unless the officer in charge of an investigation has reasonable grounds for believing this would:

    (i)   prejudice the investigation of any offence or criminal proceedings; or

    (ii) lead to the commission of an offence by providing access to unlawful material such as pornography;

    A record of the grounds shall be made when access is denied.

Notes for guidance

7A   Any person claiming property seized by the police may apply to a magistrates' court under the Police (Property) Act 1897 for its possession and should, if appropriate, be advised of this procedure.

7B   The powers of seizure conferred by PACE, sections 18(2) and 19(3) extend to the seizure of the whole premises when it is physically possible to seize and retain the premises in their totality and practical considerations make seizure desirable. For example, police may remove premises such as tents, vehicles or caravans to a police station for the purpose of preserving evidence.

7C   Officers should consider reaching agreement with owners and/or other interested parties on the procedures for examining a specific set of property, rather than awaiting the judicial authority's determination. Agreement can sometimes give a quicker and more satisfactory route for all concerned and minimise costs and legal complexities.

7D   What constitutes a relevant interest in specific material may depend on the nature of that material and the circumstances in which it is seized. Anyone with a reasonable claim to ownership of the material and anyone entrusted with its safe keeping by the owner should be considered.

7E   Requirements to secure and return property apply equally to all copies, images or other material created because of seizure of the original property.

7F   The mechanics of securing property vary according to the circumstances; "bagging up", i.e. placing material in sealed bags or containers and strict subsequent control of access is the appropriate procedure in many cases.

7G   When material is seized under the powers of seizure conferred by PACE, the duty to retain it under the Code of Practice issued under the Criminal Procedure and Investigations Act 1996 is subject to the provisions on retention of seized material in PACE, section 22.

7H   Paragraph 7.14 (ii) applies if inextricably linked material is seized under the Criminal Justice and Police Act 2001, sections 50 or 51. Inextricably linked material is material it is not reasonably practicable to separate from other linked material without prejudicing the use of that other material in any investigation or proceedings. For example, it may not be possible to separate items of data held on computer disk without damaging their evidential integrity. Inextricably linked material must not be examined, imaged, copied or used for any purpose other than for proving the source and/or integrity of the linked material.

8 ACTION AFTER SEARCHES

8.1   If premises are searched in circumstances where this Code applies, unless the exceptions in paragraph 2.3(a) apply, on arrival at a police station the officer in charge of the search shall make or have made a record of the search, to include:
(i)   the address of the searched premises;
(ii)   the date, time and duration of the search;
(iii)   the authority used for the search:
  • if the search was made in exercise of a statutory power to search premises without warrant, the power which was used for the search:
  • if the search was made under a warrant or with written consent;
    – a copy of the warrant and the written authority to apply for it, see paragraph 3.4; or
    – the written consent;
    shall be appended to the record or the record shall show the location of the copy warrant or consent.
(iv)   subject to paragraph 2.9, the names of:
  • the officer(s) in charge of the search;
  • all other officers and authorised persons who conducted the search;
(v)   the names of any people on the premises if they are known;
(vi)   any grounds for refusing the occupier's request to have someone present during the search, see paragraph 6.11;
(vii)   a list of any articles seized or the location of a list and, if not covered by a warrant, the grounds for their seizure;
(viii) whether force was used, and the reason;
(ix)   details of any damage caused during the search, and the circumstances;
(x)   if applicable, the reason it was not practicable:
    (a) to give the occupier a copy of the Notice of Powers and Rights, see paragraph 6.7;
    (b) before the search to give the occupier a copy of the Notice, see paragraph 6.8;
(xi)   when the occupier was not present, the place where copies of the Notice of Powers and Rights and search warrant were left on the premises, see paragraph 6.8.

8.2   On each occasion when premises are searched under warrant, the warrant authorising the search on that occasion shall be endorsed to show:
(i)   if any articles specified in the warrant were found and the address where found;
(ii)   if any other articles were seized;
(iii) the date and time it was executed and if present, the name of the occupier or if the occupier is not present the name of the person in charge of the premises;
(iv)   subject to paragraph 2.9, the names of the officers who executed it and any authorised persons who accompanied them;
(v)   if a copy, together with a copy of the Notice of Powers and Rights was:
  • handed to the occupier; or
  • endorsed as required by paragraph 6.8; and left on the premises and where.

8.3   Any warrant shall be returned within three calendar months of its issue or sooner on completion of the search(es) authorised by that warrant, if it was issued by a:

- justice of the peace, to the designated officer for the local justice area in which the justice was acting when issuing the warrant; or
- judge, to the appropriate officer of the court concerned,

9 SEARCH REGISTERS

9.1   A search register will be maintained at each sub-divisional or equivalent police station. All search records required under paragraph 8.1 shall be made, copied, or referred to in the register. See Note 9A

CODE C: CODE OF PRACTICE FOR THE DETENTION, TREATMENT AND QUESTIONING OF PERSONS BY POLICE OFFICERS

1 GENERAL

1.1   All persons in custody must be dealt with expeditiously, and released as soon as the need for detention no longer applies.

1.1A   A custody officer must perform the functions in this Code as soon as practicable. A custody officer will not be in breach of this Code if delay is justifiable and reasonable steps are taken to prevent unnecessary delay. The custody record shall show when a delay has occurred and the reason. See Note 1H.

1.2   This Code of Practice must be readily available at all police stations for consultation by:
- police officers
- police staff
- detained persons
- members of the public.

1.3   The provisions of this Code:
- include the Annexes
- do not include the Notes for Guidance.

1.4   If an officer has any suspicion, or is told in good faith, that a person of any age may be mentally disordered or otherwise mentally vulnerable, in the absence of clear evidence to dispel that suspicion, the person shall be treated as such for the purposes of this Code. See Note 1G.

1.5   If anyone appears to be under 17, they shall be treated as a juvenile for the purposes of this Code in the absence of clear evidence that they are older.

1.6   If a person appears to be blind, seriously visually impaired, deaf, unable to read or speak or has difficulty orally because of a speech impediment, they shall be treated as such for the purposes of this Code in the absence of clear evidence to the contrary.

1.7   "The appropriate adult" means, in the case of a:
(a) juvenile:
    (i) the parent, guardian or, if the juvenile is in local authority or voluntary organisation care, or is otherwise being looked after under the Children Act 1989, a person representing that authority or organisation;
    (ii) a social worker of a local authority;

       (iii) failing these, some other responsible adult aged 18 or over who is not a police officer or employed by the police;

   (b) person who is mentally disordered or mentally vulnerable: See Note 1D

       (iv) a relative, guardian or other person responsible for their care or custody;

       (v) someone experienced in dealing with mentally disordered or mentally vulnerable people but who is not a police officer or employed by the police;

       (vi) failing these, some other responsible adult aged 18 or over who is not a police officer or employed by the police.

1.8 If this Code requires a person be given certain information, they do not have to be given it if at the time they are incapable of understanding what is said, are violent or may become violent or in urgent need of medical attention, but they must be given it as soon as practicable.

[. . .]

2 CUSTODY RECORDS

2.1A When a person is brought to a police station:
- under arrest
- is arrested at the police station having attended there voluntarily or
- attends a police station to answer bail

they should be brought before the custody officer as soon as practicable after their arrival at the station or, if appropriate, following arrest after attending the police station voluntarily. This applies to designated and non-designated police stations. A person is deemed to be "at a police station" for these purposes if they are within the boundary of any building or enclosed yard which forms part of that police station.

2.1 A separate custody record must be opened as soon as practicable for each person brought to a police station under arrest or arrested at the station having gone there voluntarily or attending a police station in answer to street bail. All information recorded under this Code must be recorded as soon as practicable in the custody record unless otherwise specified. Any audio or video recording made in the custody area is not part of the custody record.

2.2 If any action requires the authority of an officer of a specified rank, subject to paragraph 2.6A, their name and rank must be noted in the custody record.

2.3 The custody officer is responsible for the custody record's accuracy and completeness and for making sure the record or copy of the record accompanies a detainee if they are transferred to another police station. The record shall show the:
- time and reason for transfer;
- time a person is released from detention.

2.4 A solicitor or appropriate adult must be permitted to consult a detainee's custody record as soon as practicable after their arrival at the station and at any other time whilst the person is detained. Arrangements for this access must be agreed with the custody officer and may not unreasonably interfere with the custody officer's duties.

2.4A When a detainee leaves police detention or is taken before a court they, their legal representative or appropriate adult shall be given, on request, a copy of the custody record as soon as practicable. This entitlement lasts for 12 months after release.

2.5 The detainee, appropriate adult or legal representative shall be permitted to inspect the original custody record after the detainee has left police detention provided they give reasonable notice of their request. Any such inspection shall be noted in the custody record.

[. . .]

3 INITIAL ACTION

(a) Detained persons – normal procedure

3.1   When a person is brought to a police station under arrest or arrested at the station having gone there voluntarily, the custody officer must make sure the person is told clearly about the following continuing rights which may be exercised at any stage during the period in custody:
   (i)   the right to have someone informed of their arrest as in section 5;
   (ii) the right to consult privately with a solicitor and that free independent legal advice is available;
   (iii) the right to consult these Codes of Practice. See Note 3D.

3.2   The detainee must also be given:
   •   a written notice setting out:
       —   the above three rights;
       —   the arrangements for obtaining legal advice;
       —   the right to a copy of the custody record as in paragraph 2.4A;
       —   the caution in the terms prescribed in section 10.
   •   an additional written notice briefly setting out their entitlements while in custody, see Notes 3A and 3B.
   Note: The detainee shall be asked to sign the custody record to acknowledge receipt of these notices. Any refusal must be recorded on the custody record.

3.3   A citizen of an independent Commonwealth country or a national of a foreign country, including the Republic of Ireland, must be informed as soon as practicable about their rights of communication with their High Commission, Embassy or Consulate. See section 7.

3.4   The custody officer shall:
   •   record the offence(s) that the detainee has been arrested for and the reason(s) for the arrest on the custody record. See paragraph 10.3 and Code G paragraphs 2.2 and 4.3;
   •   note on the custody record any comment the detainee makes in relation to the arresting officer's account but shall not invite comment. If the arresting officer is not physically present when the detainee is brought to a police station, the arresting officer's account must be made available to the custody officer remotely or by a third party on the arresting officer's behalf. If the custody officer authorises a person's detention the detainee must be informed of the grounds as soon as practicable and before they are questioned about any offence;
   •   note any comment the detainee makes in respect of the decision to detain them but shall not invite comment;
   •   not put specific questions to the detainee regarding their involvement in any offence, nor in respect of any comments they may make in response to the arresting officer's account or the decision to place them in detention. Such an exchange is likely to constitute an interview as in paragraph 11.1A and require the associated safeguards in section 11.
   See paragraph 11.13 in respect of unsolicited comments.

3.5   The custody officer shall:
   (a)   ask the detainee, whether at this time, they:
         (i)   would like legal advice, see paragraph 6.5;
         (ii)   want someone informed of their detention, see section 5;
   (b)   ask the detainee to sign the custody record to confirm their decisions in respect of (a);
   (c)   determine whether the detainee:
         (iii) is, or might be, in need of medical treatment or attention, see section 9;
         (iv)   requires:
               •   an appropriate adult;
               •   help to check documentation;
               •   an interpreter;
   (d)   record the decision in respect of (c).
[. . .]

3.11 If video cameras are installed in the custody area, notices shall be prominently displayed showing cameras are in use. Any request to have video cameras switched off shall be refused.

[. . .]

(c) Persons attending a police station voluntarily
3.21 Anybody attending a police station voluntarily to assist with an investigation may leave at will unless arrested. See Note 1K. If it is decided they shall not be allowed to leave, they must be informed at once that they are under arrest and brought before the custody officer, who is responsible for making sure they are notified of their rights in the same way as other detainees. If they are not arrested but are cautioned as in section 10, the person who gives the caution must, at the same time, inform them they are not under arrest, they are not obliged to remain at the station but if they remain at the station they may obtain free and independent legal advice if they want. They shall be told the right to legal advice includes the right to speak with a solicitor on the telephone and be asked if they want to do so.

3.22 If a person attending the police station voluntarily asks about their entitlement to legal advice, they shall be given a copy of the notice explaining the arrangements for obtaining legal advice. See paragraph 3.2.

[. . .]

4 DETAINEE'S PROPERTY

(a) Action
4.1   The custody officer is responsible for:
   (a)   ascertaining what property a detainee:
         (i)   has with them when they come to the police station, whether on:
               •   arrest or re-detention on answering to bail;
               •   commitment to prison custody on the order or sentence of a court;
               •   lodgement at the police station with a view to their production in court from prison custody;
               •   transfer from detention at another station or hospital;
               •   detention under the Mental Health Act 1983, section 135 or 136;
               •   remand into police custody on the authority of a court;
         (ii)   might have acquired for an unlawful or harmful purpose while in custody;
   (b)   the safekeeping of any property taken from a detainee which remains at the police station.

The custody officer may search the detainee or authorise their being searched to the extent they consider necessary, provided a search of intimate parts of the body or involving the removal of more than outer clothing is only made as in Annex A. A search may only be carried out by an officer of the same sex as the detainee. See Note 4A.

[. . .]

5 RIGHT NOT TO BE HELD INCOMMUNICADO

(a) Action

5.1   Any person arrested and held in custody at a police station or other premises may, on request, have one person known to them or likely to take an interest in their welfare informed at public expense of their whereabouts as soon as practicable. If the person cannot be contacted the detainee may choose up to two alternatives. If they cannot be contacted, the person in charge of detention or the investigation has discretion to allow further attempts until the information has been conveyed. See Notes 5C and 5D.

5.2   The exercise of the above right in respect of each person nominated may be delayed only in accordance with Annex B.

5.3   The above right may be exercised each time a detainee is taken to another police station.

5.4   The detainee may receive visits at the custody officer's discretion. See Note 5B.

5.5   If a friend, relative or person with an interest in the detainee's welfare enquires about their whereabouts, this information shall be given if the suspect agrees and Annex B does not apply. See Note 5D.

5.6   The detainee shall be given writing materials, on request, and allowed to telephone one person for a reasonable time, see Notes 5A and 5E. Either or both these privileges may be denied or delayed if an officer of inspector rank or above considers sending a letter or making a telephone call may result in any of the consequences in:
(a)   Annex B paragraphs 1 and 2 and the person is detained in connection with an indictable offence;
(b)   Not used.
Nothing in this paragraph permits the restriction or denial of the rights in paragraphs 5.1 and 6.1.

5.7   Before any letter or message is sent, or telephone call made, the detainee shall be informed that what they say in any letter, call or message (other than in a communication to a solicitor) may be read or listened to and may be given in evidence. A telephone call may be terminated if it is being abused. The costs can be at public expense at the custody officer's discretion.

5.7A Any delay or denial of the rights in this section should be proportionate and should last no longer than necessary.

[. . .]

6 RIGHT TO LEGAL ADVICE

(a) Action

6.1   Unless Annex B applies, all detainees must be informed that they may at any time consult and communicate privately with a solicitor, whether in person, in writing or by telephone, and that free independent legal advice is available. See paragraph 3.1, Note 6B, 6B1, 6B2 and Note 6J.

6.2   Not used.

6.3   A poster advertising the right to legal advice must be prominently displayed in the charging area of every police station. See Note 6H.

6.4   No police officer should, at any time, do or say anything with the intention of dissuading a detainee from obtaining legal advice.

6.5   The exercise of the right of access to legal advice may be delayed only as in Annex B. Whenever legal advice is requested, and unless Annex B applies, the custody officer must act without delay to secure the provision of such advice. If, on being informed or reminded of this right, the detainee declines to speak to a solicitor in person, the officer should point out that the right includes the right to speak with a solicitor on the telephone. If the detainee continues to waive this right the officer should ask them why and any reasons should be recorded on the custody record or the interview record as appropriate. Reminders of the right to legal advice must be given as in paragraphs 3.5, 11.2, 15.4, 16.4, 2B of Annex A, 3 of Annex K and 16.5 and Code D, paragraphs 3.17(ii) and 6.3. Once it is clear a detainee does not want to speak to a solicitor in person or by telephone they should cease to be asked their reasons. See Note 6K.

6.5A In the case of a juvenile, an appropriate adult should consider whether legal advice from a solicitor is required. If the juvenile indicates that they do not want legal advice, the appropriate adult has the right to ask for a solicitor to attend if this would be in the best interests of the person. However, the detained person cannot be forced to see the solicitor if he is adamant that he does not wish to do so.

6.6   A detainee who wants legal advice may not be interviewed or continue to be interviewed until they have received such advice unless:
       (a) Annex B applies, when the restriction on drawing adverse inferences from silence in Annex C will apply because the detainee is not allowed an opportunity to consult a solicitor; or
       (b) an officer of superintendent rank or above has reasonable grounds for believing that:
            (i)   the consequent delay might:
                  • lead to interference with, or harm to, evidence connected with an offence;
                  • lead to interference with, or physical harm to, other people;
                  • lead to serious loss of, or damage to, property;
                  • lead to alerting other people suspected of having committed an offence but not yet arrested for it;
                  • hinder the recovery of property obtained in consequence of the commission of an offence.
            (ii) when a solicitor, including a duty solicitor, has been contacted and has agreed to attend, awaiting their arrival would cause unreasonable delay to the process of investigation.
            Note: In these cases the restriction on drawing adverse inferences from silence in Annex C will apply because the detainee is not allowed an opportunity to consult a solicitor;
       (c) the solicitor the detainee has nominated or selected from a list:
            (i)   cannot be contacted;
            (ii) has previously indicated they do not wish to be contacted; or
            (iii) having been contacted, has declined to attend; and the detainee has been advised of the Duty Solicitor Scheme but has declined to ask for the duty solicitor. In these circumstances the interview may be started or continued without further delay provided an officer of inspector rank or above has agreed to the interview proceeding.

Note: The restriction on drawing adverse inferences from silence in Annex C will not apply because the detainee is allowed an opportunity to consult the duty solicitor;

(d) the detainee changes their mind, about wanting legal advice.

In these circumstances the interview may be started or continued without delay provided that:

(i)   the detainee agrees to do so, in writing or on the interview record made in accordance with Code E or F; and

(ii) an officer of inspector rank or above has inquired about the detainee's reasons for their change of mind and gives authority for the interview to proceed.

Confirmation of the detainee's agreement, their change of mind, the reasons for it if given and, subject to paragraph 2.6A, the name of the authorising officer shall be recorded in the written interview record or the interview record made in accordance with Code E or F. See Note 6I. Note: In these circumstances the restriction on drawing adverse inferences from silence in Annex C will not apply because the detainee is allowed an opportunity to consult a solicitor if they wish.

6.7   If paragraph 6.6(b)(i) applies, once sufficient information has been obtained to avert the risk, questioning must cease until the detainee has received legal advice unless paragraph 6.6(a), (b)(ii), (c) or (d) applies.

6.8   A detainee who has been permitted to consult a solicitor shall be entitled on request to have the solicitor present when they are interviewed unless one of the exceptions in paragraph 6.6 applies.

6.9   The solicitor may only be required to leave the interview if their conduct is such that the interviewer is unable properly to put questions to the suspect. See Notes 6D and 6E.

6.10 If the interviewer considers a solicitor is acting in such a way, they will stop the interview and consult an officer not below superintendent rank, if one is readily available, and otherwise an officer not below inspector rank not connected with the investigation. After speaking to the solicitor, the officer consulted will decide if the interview should continue in the presence of that solicitor. If they decide it should not, the suspect will be given the opportunity to consult another solicitor before the interview continues and that solicitor given an opportunity to be present at the interview. See Note 6E.

6.11 The removal of a solicitor from an interview is a serious step and, if it occurs, the officer of superintendent rank or above who took the decision will consider if the incident should be reported to the Law Society. If the decision to remove the solicitor has been taken by an officer below superintendent rank, the facts must be reported to an officer of superintendent rank or above who will similarly consider whether a report to the Law Society would be appropriate. When the solicitor concerned is a duty solicitor, the report should be both to the Law Society and to the Legal Services Commission.

[...]

8 CONDITIONS OF DETENTION

(a) Action

8.1   So far as it is practicable, not more than one detainee should be detained in each cell.

8.2   Cells in use must be adequately heated, cleaned and ventilated. They must be adequately lit, subject to such dimming as is compatible with safety and security to allow people detained overnight to sleep. No additional restraints shall be used within a locked cell unless absolutely necessary and then only restraint equipment, approved for use in that force by the Chief Officer, which is reasonable and necessary in the circumstances having regard to the detainee's demeanour and with a view to ensuring their safety and the safety of others. If a detainee is deaf, mentally disordered or otherwise mentally vulnerable, particular care must be taken when deciding whether to use any form of approved restraints.

8.3   Blankets, mattresses, pillows and other bedding supplied shall be of a reasonable standard and in a clean and sanitary condition. See Note 8A.

8.4   Access to toilet and washing facilities must be provided.

8.5   If it is necessary to remove a detainee's clothes for the purposes of investigation, for hygiene, health reasons or cleaning, replacement clothing of a reasonable standard of comfort and cleanliness shall be provided. A detainee may not be interviewed unless adequate clothing has been offered.

8.6   At least two light meals and one main meal should be offered in any 24 hour period. See Note 8B. Drinks should be provided at meal times and upon reasonable request between meals. Whenever necessary, advice shall be sought from the appropriate health care professional, see Note 9A, on medical and dietary matters. As far as practicable, meals provided shall offer a varied diet and meet any specific dietary needs or religious beliefs the detainee may have. The detainee may, at the custody officer's discretion, have meals supplied by their family or friends at their expense. See Note 8A.

8.7   Brief outdoor exercise shall be offered daily if practicable.

8.8   A juvenile shall not be placed in a police cell unless no other secure accommodation is available and the custody officer considers it is not practicable to supervise them if they are not placed in a cell or that a cell provides more comfortable accommodation than other secure accommodation in the station. A juvenile may not be placed in a cell with a detained adult.

[. . .]

9 CARE AND TREATMENT OF DETAINED PERSONS

(a) General
9.1   Nothing in this section prevents the police from calling the police surgeon or, if appropriate, some other health care professional, to examine a detainee for the purposes of obtaining evidence relating to any offence in which the detainee is suspected of being involved. See Note 9A.

9.2   If a complaint is made by, or on behalf of, a detainee about their treatment since their arrest, or it comes to notice that a detainee may have been treated improperly, a report must be made as soon as practicable to an officer of inspector rank or above not connected with the investigation. If the matter concerns a possible assault or the possibility of the unnecessary or unreasonable use of force, an appropriate health care professional must also be called as soon as practicable.

[. . .]

(b) Clinical treatment and attention
9.5   The custody officer must make sure a detainee receives appropriate clinical attention as soon as reasonably practicable if the person:

(a) appears to be suffering from physical illness; or
(b) is injured; or
(c) appears to be suffering from a mental disorder; or
(d) appears to need clinical attention.

9.5A This applies even if the detainee makes no request for clinical attention and whether or not they have already received clinical attention elsewhere. If the need for attention appears urgent, e.g. when indicated as in Annex H, the nearest available health care professional or an ambulance must be called immediately.

[. . .]

10 CAUTIONS

(a) When a caution must be given

10.1 A person whom there are grounds to suspect of an offence, see Note 10A, must be cautioned before any questions about an offence, or further questions if the answers provide the grounds for suspicion, are put to them if either the suspect's answers or silence, (i.e. failure or refusal to answer or answer satisfactorily) may be given in evidence to a court in a prosecution. A person need not be cautioned if questions are for other necessary purposes, e.g.:
(a) solely to establish their identity or ownership of any vehicle;
(b) to obtain information in accordance with any relevant statutory requirement, see paragraph 10.9;
(c) in furtherance of the proper and effective conduct of a search, e.g. to determine the need to search in the exercise of powers of stop and search or to seek cooperation while carrying out a search;
(d) to seek verification of a written record as in paragraph 11.13;
(e) Not used.

10.2 Whenever a person not under arrest is initially cautioned, or reminded they are under caution, that person must at the same time be told they are not under arrest and are free to leave if they want to. See Note 10C.

10.3 A person who is arrested, or further arrested, must be informed at the time, or as soon as practicable thereafter, that they are under arrest and the grounds for their arrest, see paragraph 3.4, Note 10B and Code G, paragraphs 2.2 and 4.3.

10.4 As per Code G, section 3, a person who is arrested, or further arrested, must also be cautioned unless:
(a) it is impracticable to do so by reason of their condition or behaviour at the time;
(b) they have already been cautioned immediately prior to arrest as in paragraph 10.1.

(b) Terms of the cautions

10.5 The caution which must be given on:
(a) arrest;
(b) all other occasions before a person is charged or informed they may be prosecuted, see section 16,
should, unless the restriction on drawing adverse inferences from silence applies, see Annex C, be in the following terms:

> "You do not have to say anything. But it may harm your defence if you do not mention when questioned something which you later rely on in Court. Anything you do say may be given in evidence."

Where the use of the Welsh Language is appropriate, a constable may provide the caution directly in Welsh in the following terms:

"Does dim rhaid i chi ddweud dim byd. Ond gall niweidio eich amddiffyniad os na fyddwch chi'n sôn, wrth gael eich holi, am rywbeth y byddwch chi'n dibynnu arno nes ymlaen yn y Llys. Gall unrhyw beth yr ydych yn ei ddweud gael ei roi fel tystiolaeth."

See Note 10G.

10.6   Annex C, paragraph 2 sets out the alternative terms of the caution to be used when the restriction on drawing adverse inferences from silence applies.

10.7   Minor deviations from the words of any caution given in accordance with this Code do not constitute a breach of this Code, provided the sense of the relevant caution is preserved. See Note 10D.

10.8   After any break in questioning under caution, the person being questioned must be made aware they remain under caution. If there is any doubt the relevant caution should be given again in full when the interview resumes. See Note 10E.

10.9   When, despite being cautioned, a person fails to co-operate or to answer particular questions which may affect their immediate treatment, the person should be informed of any relevant consequences and that those consequences are not affected by the caution. Examples are when a person's refusal to provide:
    • their name and address when charged may make them liable to detention;
    • particulars and information in accordance with a statutory requirement, e.g. under the Road Traffic Act 1988, may amount to an offence or may make the person liable to a further arrest.

[. . .]

(d) Juveniles and persons who are mentally disordered or otherwise mentally vulnerable
10.12 If a juvenile or a person who is mentally disordered or otherwise mentally vulnerable is cautioned in the absence of the appropriate adult, the caution must be repeated in the adult's presence.

(e) Documentation
10.13 A record shall be made when a caution is given under this section, either in the interviewer's pocket book or in the interview record.

[. . .]

11 INTERVIEWS – GENERAL

(a) Action
11.1A An interview is the questioning of a person regarding their involvement or suspected involvement in a criminal offence or offences which, under paragraph 10.1, must be carried out under caution. Whenever a person is interviewed they must be informed of the nature of the offence, or further offence. Procedures under the Road Traffic Act 1988, section 7 or the Transport and Works Act 1992, section 31 do not constitute interviewing for the purpose of this Code.

11.1   Following a decision to arrest a suspect, they must not be interviewed about the relevant offence except at a police station or other authorised place of detention, unless the consequent delay would be likely to:

(a) lead to:
- interference with, or harm to, evidence connected with an offence;
- interference with, or physical harm to, other people; or
- serious loss of, or damage to, property;

(b) lead to alerting other people suspected of committing an offence but not yet arrested for it; or

(c) hinder the recovery of property obtained in consequence of the commission of an offence.

Interviewing in any of these circumstances shall cease once the relevant risk has been averted or the necessary questions have been put in order to attempt to avert that risk.

11.2   Immediately prior to the commencement or re-commencement of any interview at a police station or other authorised place of detention, the interviewer should remind the suspect of their entitlement to free legal advice and that the interview can be delayed for legal advice to be obtained, unless one of the exceptions in paragraph 6.6 applies. It is the interviewer's responsibility to make sure all reminders are recorded in the interview record.

11.3   Not used.

11.4   At the beginning of an interview the interviewer, after cautioning the suspect, see section 10, shall put to them any significant statement or silence which occurred in the presence and hearing of a police officer or other police staff before the start of the interview and which have not been put to the suspect in the course of a previous interview. See Note 11A. The interviewer shall ask the suspect whether they confirm or deny that earlier statement or silence and if they want to add anything.

11.4A   A significant statement is one which appears capable of being used in evidence against the suspect, in particular a direct admission of guilt. A significant silence is a failure or refusal to answer a question or answer satisfactorily when under caution, which might, allowing for the restriction on drawing adverse inferences from silence, see Annex C, give rise to an inference under the Criminal Justice and Public Order Act 1994, Part III.

11.5   No interviewer may try to obtain answers or elicit a statement by the use of oppression. Except as in paragraph 10.9, no interviewer shall indicate, except to answer a direct question, what action will be taken by the police if the person being questioned answers questions, makes a statement or refuses to do either. If the person asks directly what action will be taken if they answer questions, make a statement or refuse to do either, the interviewer may inform them what action the police propose to take provided that action is itself proper and warranted.

11.6   The interview or further interview of a person about an offence with which that person has not been charged or for which they have not been informed they may be prosecuted, must cease when:

(a) the officer in charge of the investigation is satisfied all the questions they consider relevant to obtaining accurate and reliable information about the offence have been put to the suspect, this includes allowing the suspect an opportunity to give an innocent explanation and asking questions to test if the explanation is accurate and reliable, e.g. to clear up ambiguities or clarify what the suspect said;

(b) the officer in charge of the investigation has taken account of any other available evidence; and

(c) the officer in charge of the investigation, or in the case of a detained suspect, the custody officer, see paragraph 16.1, reasonably believes there is sufficient evidence to provide a realistic prospect of conviction for that offence. See Note 11B.

This paragraph does not prevent officers in revenue cases or acting under the confiscation provisions of the Criminal Justice Act 1988 or the Drug Trafficking Act

1994 from inviting suspects to complete a formal question and answer record after the interview is concluded.

(b) Interview records

11.7 (a) An accurate record must be made of each interview, whether or not the interview takes place at a police station

(b) The record must state the place of interview, the time it begins and ends, any interview breaks and, subject to paragraph 2.6A, the names of all those present; and must be made on the forms provided for this purpose or in the interviewer's pocket book or in accordance with the Codes of Practice E or F;

(c) Any written record must be made and completed during the interview, unless this would not be practicable or would interfere with the conduct of the interview, and must constitute either a verbatim record of what has been said or, failing this, an account of the interview which adequately and accurately summarises it.

[. . .]

(c) Juveniles and mentally disordered or otherwise mentally vulnerable people

11.15 A juvenile or person who is mentally disordered or otherwise mentally vulnerable must not be interviewed regarding their involvement or suspected involvement in a criminal offence or offences, or asked to provide or sign a written statement under caution or record of interview, in the absence of the appropriate adult unless paragraphs 11.1, 11.18 to 11.20 apply. See Note 11C.

11.16 Juveniles may only be interviewed at their place of education in exceptional circumstances and only when the principal or their nominee agrees. Every effort should be made to notify the parent(s) or other person responsible for the juvenile's welfare and the appropriate adult, if this is a different person, that the police want to interview the juvenile and reasonable time should be allowed to enable the appropriate adult to be present at the interview. If awaiting the appropriate adult would cause unreasonable delay, and unless the juvenile is suspected of an offence against the educational establishment, the principal or their nominee can act as the appropriate adult for the purposes of the interview.

11.17 If an appropriate adult is present at an interview, they shall be informed:
- they are not expected to act simply as an observer; and
- the purpose of their presence is to:
  — advise the person being interviewed;
  — observe whether the interview is being conducted properly and fairly;
  — facilitate communication with the person being interviewed.

[. . .]

11.19 These interviews may not continue once sufficient information has been obtained to avert the consequences in paragraph 11.1(a) to (c).

11.20 A record shall be made of the grounds for any decision to interview a person under paragraph 11.18.

12 INTERVIEWS IN POLICE STATIONS

(a) Action

12.1 If a police officer wants to interview or conduct enquiries which require the presence of a detainee, the custody officer is responsible for deciding whether to deliver the detainee into the officer's custody.

12.2 Except as below, in any period of 24 hours a detainee must be allowed a continuous period of at least 8 hours for rest, free from questioning, travel or any interruption in connection with the investigation concerned. This period should normally be at night or other appropriate time which takes account of when the detainee last slept or rested. If a detainee is arrested at a police station after going there voluntarily, the period of 24 hours runs from the time of their arrest and not the time of arrival at the police station. The period may not be interrupted or delayed, except:

(a) when there are reasonable grounds for believing not delaying or interrupting the period would:
   (i)   involve a risk of harm to people or serious loss of, or damage to, property;
   (ii) delay unnecessarily the person's release from custody;
   (iii) otherwise prejudice the outcome of the investigation;
(b) at the request of the detainee, their appropriate adult or legal representative;
(c) when a delay or interruption is necessary in order to:
   (i)   comply with the legal obligations and duties arising under section 15;
   (ii) to take action required under section 9 or in accordance with medical advice.

If the period is interrupted in accordance with (a), a fresh period must be allowed. Interruptions under (b) and (c), do not require a fresh period to be allowed.

[. . .]

12.4 As far as practicable interviews shall take place in interview rooms which are adequately heated, lit and ventilated.

12.5 A suspect whose detention without charge has been authorised under PACE, because the detention is necessary for an interview to obtain evidence of the offence for which they have been arrested, may choose not to answer questions but police do not require the suspect's consent or agreement to interview them for this purpose. If a suspect takes steps to prevent themselves being questioned or further questioned, e.g. by refusing to leave their cell to go to a suitable interview room or by trying to leave the interview room, they shall be advised their consent or agreement to interview is not required. The suspect shall be cautioned as in section 10, and informed if they fail or refuse to co-operate, the interview may take place in the cell and that their failure or refusal to cooperate may be given in evidence. The suspect shall then be invited to co-operate and go into the interview room.

12.6 People being questioned or making statements shall not be required to stand.

12.7 Before the interview commences each interviewer shall, subject to paragraph 2.6A, identify themselves and any other persons present to the interviewee.

12.8 Breaks from interviewing should be made at recognised meal times or at other times that take account of when an interviewee last had a meal. Short refreshment breaks shall be provided at approximately two hour intervals, subject to the interviewer's discretion to delay a break if there are reasonable grounds for believing it would:
(i)   involve a:
   • risk of harm to people;
   • serious loss of, or damage to, property;
(ii) unnecessarily delay the detainee's release;
(iii) otherwise prejudice the outcome of the investigation.
See Note 12B.

12.9 If during the interview a complaint is made by or on behalf of the interviewee concerning the provisions of this Code, the interviewer should:
(i)   record it in the interview record;
(ii) inform the custody officer, who is then responsible for dealing with it as in section 9.

[. . .]

16 CHARGING DETAINED PERSONS

(a) Action

16.1   When the officer in charge of the investigation reasonably believes there is sufficient evidence to provide a realistic prospect of conviction for the offence (see paragraph 11.6), they shall without delay, and subject to the following qualification, inform the custody officer who will be responsible for considering whether the detainee should be charged. See Notes 11B and 16A. When a person is detained in respect of more than one offence it is permissible to delay informing the custody officer until the above conditions are satisfied in respect of all the offences, but see paragraph 11.6. If the detainee is a juvenile, mentally disordered or otherwise mentally vulnerable, any resulting action shall be taken in the presence of the appropriate adult if they are present at the time. See Notes 16B and 16C.

16.1A   Where guidance issued by the Director of Public Prosecutions under section 37A is in force the custody officer must comply with that Guidance in deciding how to act in dealing with the detainee. See Notes 16AA and 16AB.

16.1B   Where in compliance with the DPP's Guidance the custody officer decides that the case should be immediately referred to the CPS to make the charging decision, consultation should take place with a Crown Prosecutor as soon as is reasonably practicable. Where the Crown Prosecutor is unable to make the charging decision on the information available at that time, the detainee may be released without charge and on bail (with conditions if necessary) under section 37(7)(a). In such circumstances, the detainee should be informed that they are being released to enable the Director of Public Prosecutions to make a decision under section 37B.

16.2   When a detainee is charged with or informed they may be prosecuted for an offence, see Note 16B, they shall, unless the restriction on drawing adverse inferences from silence applies, see Annex C, be cautioned as follows:

> "You do not have to say anything. But it may harm your defence if you do not mention now something which you later rely on in court. Anything you do say may be given in evidence."

Where the use of the Welsh Language is appropriate, a constable may provide the caution directly in Welsh in the following terms:

> "Does dim rhaid i chi ddweud dim byd. Ond gall niweidio eich amddiffyniad os na fyddwch chi'n sôn, yn awr, am rywbeth y byddwch chi'n dibynnu arno nes ymlaen yn y llys. Gall unrhyw beth yr ydych yn ei ddweud gael ei roi fel tystiolaeth."

Annex C, paragraph 2 sets out the alternative terms of the caution to be used when the restriction on drawing adverse inferences from silence applies.

16.3   When a detainee is charged they shall be given a written notice showing particulars of the offence and, subject to paragraph 2.6A, the officer's name and the case reference number. As far as possible the particulars of the charge shall be stated in simple terms, but they shall also show the precise offence in law with which the detainee is charged.

The notice shall begin:

"You are charged with the offence(s) shown below." Followed by the caution.

If the detainee is a juvenile, mentally disordered or otherwise mentally vulnerable, the notice should be given to the appropriate adult.

16.4   If, after a detainee has been charged with or informed they may be prosecuted for an offence, an officer wants to tell them about any written statement or interview with another person relating to such an offence, the detainee shall either be handed a true copy of the written statement or the content of the interview record brought to their attention. Nothing shall be done to invite any reply or comment except to:
(a) caution the detainee, "You do not have to say anything, but anything you do say may be given in evidence.";

Where the use of the Welsh Language is appropriate, caution the detainee in the following terms:

> "Does dim rhaid i chi ddweud dim byd, ond gall unrhyw beth yr ydych yn ei ddweud gael ei roi fel tystiolaeth."

and
(b) remind the detainee about their right to legal advice.

16.4A If the detainee:
- cannot read, the document may be read to them
- is a juvenile, mentally disordered or otherwise mentally vulnerable, the appropriate adult shall also be given a copy, or the interview record shall be brought to their attention

16.5   A detainee may not be interviewed about an offence after they have been charged with, or informed they may be prosecuted for it, unless the interview is necessary:
- to prevent or minimise harm or loss to some other person, or the public
- to clear up an ambiguity in a previous answer or statement
- in the interests of justice for the detainee to have put to them, and have an opportunity to comment on, information concerning the offence which has come to light since they were charged or informed they might be prosecuted

Before any such interview, the interviewer shall:
(a) caution the detainee, "You do not have to say anything, but anything you do say may be given in evidence."
Where the use of the Welsh Language is appropriate, the interviewer shall caution the detainee, "Does dim rhaid i chi ddweud dim byd, ond gall unrhyw beth yr ydych yn ei ddweud gael ei roi fel tystiolaeth."
(b) remind the detainee about their right to legal advice.
See Note 16B.

[. . .]

CODE G: CODE OF PRACTICE ON STATUTORY POWER OF ARREST BY POLICE OFFICERS

1 INTRODUCTION

1.1   This Code of Practice deals with statutory power of police to arrest persons suspected of involvement in a criminal offence.

1.2   The right to liberty is a key principle of the Human Rights Act 1998. The exercise of the power of arrest represents an obvious and significant interference with that right.

1.3   The use of the power must be fully justified and officers exercising the power should consider if the necessary objectives can be met by other, less intrusive means. Arrest must never be used simply because it can be used. Absence of justification for exercising the powers of arrest may lead to challenges should the case proceed to court. When the power of arrest is exercised it is essential that it is exercised in a nondiscriminatory and proportionate manner.

1.4   Section 24 of the Police and Criminal Evidence Act 1984 (as substituted by section 110 of the Serious Organised Crime and Police Act 2005) provides the statutory power of arrest. If the provisions of the Act and this Code are not observed, both the arrest and the conduct of any subsequent investigation may be open to question.

1.5   This code of practice must be readily available at all police stations for consultation by police officers and police staff, detained persons and members of the public.

1.6   The notes for guidance are not provisions of this code.

2 ELEMENTS OF ARREST UNDER SECTION 24 PACE

2.1   A lawful arrest requires two elements:

A person's involvement or suspected involvement or attempted involvement in the commission of a criminal offence;

AND

Reasonable grounds for believing that the person's arrest is necessary.

2.2   Arresting officers are required to inform the person arrested that they have been arrested, even if this fact is obvious, and of the relevant circumstances of the arrest in relation to both elements and to inform the custody officer of these on arrival at the police station. See Code C paragraph 3.4.

INVOLVEMENT IN THE COMMISSION OF AN OFFENCE'

2.3   A constable may arrest without warrant in relation to any offence, except for the single exception listed in Note for Guidance 1. A constable may arrest anyone:
- who is about to commit an offence or is in the act of committing an offence
- whom the officer has reasonable grounds for suspecting is about to commit an offence or to be committing an offence
- whom the officer has reasonable grounds to suspect of being guilty of an offence which he or she has reasonable grounds for suspecting has been committed
- anyone who is guilty of an offence which has been committed or anyone whom the officer has reasonable grounds for suspecting to be guilty of that offence.

NECESSITY CRITERIA

2.4   The power of arrest is only exercisable if the constable has reasonable grounds for believing that it is necessary to arrest the person. The criteria for what may constitute necessity are set out in paragraph 2.9. It remains an operational decision at the discretion of the arresting officer as to:
- what action he or she may take at the point of contact with the individual;
- the necessity criterion or criteria (if any) which applies to the individual; and
- whether to arrest, report for summons, grant street bail, issue a fixed penalty notice or take any other action that is open to the officer.

2.5   In applying the criteria, the arresting officer has to be satisfied that at least one of the reasons supporting the need for arrest is satisfied.

2.6   Extending the power of arrest to all offences provides a constable with the ability to use that power to deal with any situation. However applying the necessity criteria requires the constable to examine and justify the reason or reasons why a person needs to be taken to a police station for the custody officer to decide whether the person should be placed in police detention.

2.7   The criteria below are set out in section 24 of PACE as substituted by section 110 of the Serious Organised Crime and Police Act 2005. The criteria are exhaustive. However, the circumstances that may satisfy those criteria remain a matter for the operational discretion of individual officers. Some examples are given below of what those circumstances may be.

2.8   In considering the individual circumstances, the constable must take into account the situation of the victim, the nature of the offence, the circumstances of the suspect and the needs of the investigative process.

2.9   The criteria are that the arrest is necessary:
(a)   to enable the name of the person in question to be ascertained (in the case where the constable does not know, and cannot readily ascertain, the person's name, or has reasonable grounds for doubting whether a name given by the person as his name is his real name)
(b)   correspondingly as regards the person's address an address is a satisfactory address for service of summons if the person will be at it for a sufficiently long period for it to be possible to serve him or her with a summons; or, that some other person at that address specified by the person will accept service of the summons on their behalf.
(c)   to prevent the person in question –
(i)   causing physical injury to himself or any other person;
(ii)   suffering physical injury;
(iii)   causing loss or damage to property;
(iv)   committing an offence against public decency (only applies where members of the public going about their normal business cannot reasonably be expected to avoid the person in question); or
(v)   causing an unlawful obstruction of the highway;
(d)   to protect a child or other vulnerable person from the person in question
(e)   to allow the prompt and effective investigation of the offence or of the conduct of the person in question.
This may include cases such as:
(i)   Where there are reasonable grounds to believe that the person:
• has made false statements;
• has made statements which cannot be readily verified;
• has presented false evidence;
• may steal or destroy evidence;
• may make contact with co-suspects or conspirators;
• may intimidate or threaten or make contact with witnesses;
• where it is necessary to obtain evidence by questioning; or
(ii)   when considering arrest in connection with an indictable offence, there is a need to:
• enter and search any premises occupied or controlled by a person
• search the person
• prevent contact with others
• take fingerprints, footwear impressions, samples or photographs of the suspect
(iii)   ensuring compliance with statutory drug testing requirements.

(f) to prevent any prosecution for the offence from being hindered by the disappearance of the person in question.
This may arise if there are reasonable grounds for believing that
- if the person is not arrested he or she will fail to attend court;
- street bail after arrest would be insufficient to deter the suspect from trying to evade prosecution.

3 INFORMATION TO BE GIVEN ON ARREST

(a) Cautions – when a caution must be given (taken from Code C section 10)
[. . .]

4 RECORDS OF ARREST

(a) General
4.1 The arresting officer is required to record in his pocket book or by other methods used for recording information:
- the nature and circumstances of the offence leading to the arrest
- the reason or reasons why arrest was necessary
- the giving of the caution
- anything said by the person at the time of arrest.

4.2 Such a record should be made at the time of the arrest unless impracticable to do. If not made at that time, the record should then be completed as soon as possible thereafter.

[. . .]

Thematic Index